Horatio King

Turning on the Light

A Dispassionate Survey of President Buchanan's Administration, from 1860 to its

Close

Horatio King

Turning on the Light
A Dispassionate Survey of President Buchanan's Administration, from 1860 to its Close

ISBN/EAN: 9783337248857

Printed in Europe, USA, Canada, Australia, Japan

Cover: Foto ©ninafisch / pixelio.de

More available books at **www.hansebooks.com**

Turning on the Light.

A DISPASSIONATE SURVEY OF
PRESIDENT BUCHANAN'S ADMINISTRATION,
FROM 1860 TO ITS CLOSE.

INCLUDING

A BIOGRAPHICAL SKETCH OF THE AUTHOR, EIGHT LETTERS
FROM MR. BUCHANAN NEVER BEFORE PUBLISHED, AND
NUMEROUS MISCELLANEOUS ARTICLES.

BY

HORATIO KING,

EX-POSTMASTER-GENERAL OF THE UNITED STATES.

PHILADELPHIA:
J. B. LIPPINCOTT COMPANY.
1895.

CONTENTS.

PART II.

PART III.

6   CONTENTS.

BIOGRAPHICAL SKETCH

OF

HORATIO KING.

FOR one who has loved, admired, and revered the subject of this sketch from earliest recollection, to write a brief biography without prejudice is not an easy matter. His life for more than fourscore years has been without spot or blemish in my sight, and, to avoid the appearance of undue partiality, I shall rely mainly upon the comments of those who knew him well and intimately, although not connected with him by ties of consanguinity.

Horatio King was the son of Samuel and Sally (Hall) King, and was born in Paris, Maine, June 21, 1811. His father was a farmer and emigrated from Massachusetts. His grandfather was George King, of Raynham, in the State last named, who, with his three brothers, served in the war for independence. George was orderly-sergeant and clerk of the Raynham Company, and one of his brothers fell in the war. Like most of the old and patriotic stock of the Revolution and their immediate descendants, these ancestral relatives of his were stanchly Democratic, which may, so far as early impressions go, account for Mr. King's political orthodoxy. Like most of the country-reared young men of that period, he was brought up on the farm and had a personal knowledge of what life upon the farm is, or rather what it was at that time, for it is somewhat different now. His poem herein, entitled "Employment Necessary to Happiness," may be taken as descriptive in no slight degree of his farm life.

In the ordinary acceptance of that term, Mr. King was

not liberally educated, though he supplemented by careful study and voluminous reading and research the education which the common schools afforded. To a strongly practical training he added by his own exertions unusual literary culture, acquiring among other accomplishments a good knowledge of the French language, which aided him greatly in his subsequent official career.

The whole course of his education, meaning by that word the training of mind and body to the full development of their powers and usefulness, has been eminently practical. For the elementary knowledge essential or highly useful to every pursuit in life, such as reading, spelling, writing, grammar, arithmetic, and geography, there were no better schools in the world than the common schools of New England; and of these, in childhood and early youth, he enjoyed the full benefits; and for the useful concerns of life, a knowledge of human nature, of human character, and the varied transactions of human life and of our political and social conditions and institutions,—never to be learned or understood in college,—perhaps no one pursuit is so truly and widely useful as that of the printer and newspaper editor.

At an early age, in the spring of 1829, Mr. King went into the office of the *Jeffersonian*, a thorough Jackson Democratic paper, then published in his native town, for the purpose of acquiring an expert knowledge of the printing business and to befit himself to conduct the paper, in case he should like the business well enough to purchase the establishment. After being in the office about a year he became connected with the paper as one of its proprietors, and six months after became sole proprietor, being then about nineteen years of age, employing a village lawyer, at a salary of twelve York shillings a week, to assist him in editing the sheet. In 1832 he cast his first vote for General Jackson, and shortly afterwards assumed the entire editorial management of his paper. Its files show him to have been consistent and earnest in his denunciation of South Carolina nullification, and throughout General Jackson's administration the *Jeffersonian* firmly, consistently, and energetically supported the Old Hero; and when Mr. Van Buren was, by the refusal of the Senate to confirm his nomination, recalled from England, where, during the recess, the President had sent him as minister, the *Jeffersonian* was among the first papers in the country to run up his name for the Presidency.

In 1833 the unfortunate division of the Democracy of Maine took place, and Mr. King was induced to remove his press to Portland in May of that year. The consequence was a sharp family quarrel on State and local matters, which lasted two or three years, when many of his principal competitors, with their journalists at their head, went over bodily to the enemy. From first to last Mr. King has combated with like zeal every scheme which looked towards disunion.

He continued to edit the *Jeffersonian* until 1838, when he sold the paper to the *Standard,* which was soon after merged in the *Eastern Argus,* and may be said to "still live" in the columns of that stanch advocate of Democratic principles. This terminated his professional connection with the public press.

But if anything more were wanting to complete Mr. King's practical education and his knowledge of business and of human nature, what better school could have been found than that which he enjoyed in his twenty-two years' connection with all the various concerns and operations of the Post-Office Department? There, if anywhere, the whole lesson was presented, and by a careful, diligent, and intelligent observer could be thoroughly learned. And in that school, as was proved by his successive promotions, and especially by his eminent fitness for and usefulness in the responsible and important positions which he occupied, he was neither an indifferent nor an unsuccessful student. Gifted with a clear head, a quick perception, and indomitable industry, coupled with a firm resolution to know thoroughly whatever his actual business or pursuit rendered

it neeessary or desirable for him to know, and brought eon-
tinually into business contact with shrewd, active minds,
his business education was most complete and effectual.

In the fall of 1838, Mr. King went to Washington to look
for a newspaper opening, and, not finding one to his mind,
he, in March, 1839, accepted a clerkship at $1000 per annum
in the Post-Office Department, tendered him by the then
Postmaster-General, Amos Kendall. Thus, at the foot of
the ladder, he commenced that connection which proved
alike beneficial to the country and honorable to himself,
and whence he climbed, every step marked by his ability and
energy, to the chief position. For a series of years he was
corresponding clerk for New England in the Contract Office,
a position of considerable responsibility and requiring for
the proper discharge of its duties the closest application and
a large amount of labor.

Towards the close of 1850 commenced his connection
with the foreign mail service, he being at that time transferred to a corresponding desk having that matter in charge.
In this connection his services were of the most beneficial
character, and have fully entitled him to the lasting gratitude of his countrymen, from the success which, under his
management, attended the effort to extend and improve our
postal arrangements with foreign nations. In these days,
when lines of steamships map the ocean as lines of railroads
do the land, when almost every important commercial city
of Europe, the islands, and South America have their corresponding connection with some city of our Union, whoever really and essentially has improved this branch of the
service has conferred a benefit upon nations which not only
the present but future generations will fully appreciate.

Up to 1851 no postal conventions had been entered into
with any European governments except Great Britain and
Bremen; and thus, as has been well said by another, "an
entirely new field was left to be explored, and one which,
in view of the various lines of Atlantic steamers, just then

projected and becoming more and more objects of interest and attention, opened not only an untried field, but one of vast complications and perplexities. It was to this wide and interesting field of endeavor that he was invited, and the results which have followed were eminently his work. To his comprehensive genius and that characteristic energy which he possesses in an eminent degree, the nation is primarily indebted for those splendid results which have extended our postal arrangements to every part of the commercial world, and gone hand in hand with the rapidly advancing strides which steam and lightning have taken in every direction. Here Mr. King found scope for every latent energy of his mind. He was obliged to familiarize himself with statistics and with a vast range of inquiries not heretofore made in this country. He found the postal arrangements already made with Great Britain and Bremen imperfect and unsatisfactory. They were revised and improved. With regard to Bremen, he and Hon. Rudolph Schleiden, the Bremen Minister, prepared articles of agreement, approved by their respective governments, by which the half-ounce letter-rate was reduced from twenty cents (then, 1853, the lowest rate to Europe) to ten cents, which was the beginning of low postage across the Atlantic. Besides this, postal arrangements were soon in rapid succession effected with the West Indies, with several of the South American states, and with Prussia, France, Hamburg, and Belgium.

The giving of credit for these things to the subject of this sketch does not at all detract from nor depreciate the merits or services of his official superiors. They are justly entitled to the general credit of these important arrangements, in the same degree that the President enjoys the credit of a successful administration of the affairs of the government. In both cases the laborious details are planned, arranged, and perfected by assistants and advisers; yet as the responsibility mainly attaches to the head, so the general credit should follow. But this detracts no whit from the merits or the just appreciation of the laborious and intelligent subordinate, who ascertains facts, systematizes and arranges details, and in reality gets up the entire matter, which the superior has only to examine and sanction. In this respect Mr. King, in the work of these postal arrangements, is entitled to the very highest credit, as no one could have performed the duties of his position with more correctness and ability.

In the spring of 1854, on the death of Major Hobbie, Mr. King, without solicitation on his part, was appointed by President Pierce to the office of First Assistant Postmaster-General. To his subordinates he was considerate, kind, and obliging; requiring of them, as he should, to have all the business entrusted to them speedily and properly done and their work kept up, but never acting captiously nor finding fault needlessly. One secret of his official success was his exactitude in keeping all his business in hand, his desk at the close of each day being always clear of papers, and his positive requirement of his clerks that everything sent to their desks should be promptly attended to. It may be mentioned here, also, that he never allowed his office door to be locked, never cared for cards, but was always ready to receive official callers whose business he was there to perform without any hinderance or embarrassment of personal introduction.

His success in dealing with so many men of all parties and all positions in life without making enemies is remarkable. It may, perhaps, be accounted for in two ways: that he had no personal interest to subserve in what was done, and manifestly cared only to know and to do what was right; and that when obliged to refuse a request, he remembered and put in practice the old saying, that " to refuse kindly what is asked of you is itself a boon."

As a public officer Mr. King was indefatigable, and devoted his whole time and all the energies of his mind and body to the duties of his position. His constant endeavor was to have the work of the people, so far as he was concerned, well and faithfully executed. His efforts to protect the Department against fraud and loss of revenue were persistent. He especially labored to defeat all attempts to use the mails without paying for the privilege in contravention of the law and to the detriment of an already overburdened Department. As one of the many evidences of his zeal in this matter, I recall the fact of his sitting up all night and laboring in the House of Representatives to secure the passage of the law requiring prepayment of postage on letters, which was actually passed at five o'clock on a Sunday morning. The law exacting prepayment by stamps on transient printed matter was also drafted by him; and no one having any acquaintance with our postal affairs will need to be told that this law effects a large saving to the Department, both in respect to the weight of the mails and the extra amount of postage received.

Few men ever had the hardihood to approach Mr. King with a dishonorable proposition of any kind. The reputation for stern integrity, and the possession of it, in a place like that filled by him, are of the very highest importance; and in both respects he was entirely suited to the place. His memory, too, of what occurred in the Department during his connection with it was remarkable, and showed that, unlike many officials, he was not satisfied with the simple performance of the routine duties of his office, but had an intelligent eye to the whole operations of each Bureau, and a vivid and long-enduring recollection of whatever took place under his own particular supervision.

Nor, while constantly immersed in business since the early age of nineteen, had Mr. King neglected the pursuits of literature or of science, but was proficient in both. Every leisure hour has always been sedulously devoted to the acquirement of knowledge.

As a writer, his style is terse, simple, vigorous, and

manly. His points are clear, his arguments pertinent and forcible, and his language choice and chaste.

As a politician Mr. King has been always a firm, consistent, unflinching Democrat, though not ultra. He has lent a willing and hearty support to every Democratic administration since he has been old enough to exercise the privileges of a citizen.

He held the position of First Assistant Postmaster-General until the 1st of January, 1861, when he became Acting Postmaster-General, and on the 1st of February he was nominated by President Buchanan and on the 12th confirmed by the Senate as Postmaster-General, serving in that capacity until the inauguration of President Lincoln and the appointment of his successor, March 7, 1861. He filled all these important places with fidelity and distinguished ability. He was Postmaster-General when treason stalked with a bold front through the streets of the national capital.

As a life-long Democrat, Mr. King was loyal to the core, and remained so during the entire struggle. Though exempted by the law from the performance of military duty, he furnished a representative recruit, who was duly mustered in and served in the Union Army. This exhibition of patriotism and public spirit received official acknowledgment from the Government.

After retiring from the Post-Office Department, he was appointed, in April, 1862, one of a Board of Commissioners to carry out the provisions of the Emancipation Proclamation in the District of Columbia. This position was tendered him by President Lincoln unsolicited, and doubtless on account of his conspicuous services near the close of the previous administration.

His associate commissioners were Daniel R. Goodloe and Dr. John M. Brodhead, with Wm. R. Woodward as clerk and B. M. Campbell as expert. Of this important work, Mr. Goodloe wrote:

"The whole number of claims presented within the time limited by law was nine hundred and sixty-six, and the number of slaves embraced by them was three thousand one hundred. Of these claims, thirty-six in whole and twenty-one in part were rejected as the result of our investigations, for reasons of disloyalty or for defects in the titles. These rejected claims embraced one hundred and eleven slaves, for whom compensation was withheld, and, as above stated, two thousand nine hundred and eighty-nine were paid for under the Act of April 16, 1862.

"In addition to these cases, thirteen other applications were made after the expiration of three months, that being the time within which petitions were required by the act to be presented. Under the circumstances of absence and ignorance of the existence of the law, it was decided to value the slaves, twenty-eight in number, embraced in these thirteen cases, and recommend them to the favorable consideration of Congress. The claims were all paid by special appropriations. The total number of slaves paid for, therefore, was three thousand and seventeen. The twenty-eight above referred to fell below the average, the award for them being only $9912.50. The commissioners recommended also two or three other cases to Congress,—cases in which the right of the slaves to freedom under the act was contested on the ground that they were here as runaways. In such instances the commissioners leaned to the side of freedom, but at the same time were not unwilling for the parties to have the benefits of the law as loyal claimants."

The duty having been expeditiously and satisfactorily completed, the commission waited upon President Lincoln. "He received us," says Mr. Goodloe, " as he did every one, with the frankness and cordiality of the honest and true-hearted man he was. When we informed him that we had finished our work, he replied that he was glad to know that somebody had finished something, and that he wished his work was done. After some pleasant conversation our commission retired, and adjourned *sine die.*"

The service of the commission was limited to nine months, and, on finally leaving office, Mr. King went into a quiet business as an attorney before the executive departments and international commissions, which he followed until about twenty years ago, when he retired as far as practicable from active work. Mr. King has twice made the tour of Europe, first in 1867 and again in 1875-76. The latter tour was somewhat more extended than the first, and on his return he published a book, entitled "Sketches of Travel, or Twelve Months in Europe." He has written much and upon a great variety of topics, and has also lectured on various occasions. He delivered an oration before the Union Literary Society of Washington in 1841, which was published. He also originated a series of Saturday evening literary entertainments at his private residence, which became very popular. February 2, 1884, the hundredth meeting was held, and the proceedings were printed in a neat pamphlet of forty-eight pages. He has for many years been a contributor to newspapers and magazines on historical, political, and literary subjects, some of the articles being translations from the French.

He has retained in a remarkable degree both his mental and physical powers. Never idle, each day finds some new and congenial work for his ready hands. During the comparatively long period of freedom from professional labors, he has had abundant time to cultivate the social amenities prominent in his disposition. Among his numerous associations he has enjoyed especially the close friendship of the venerable Justin S. Morrill, Senator from Vermont, and Robert C. Winthrop, of Massachusetts, recently deceased. Of late years, at every recurring birthday anniversary of these honored gentlemen, he has been accustomed to address to each some appropriate greeting in rhyme, literary waifs, so to speak, of which the following are examples:

"WASHINGTON, May 12, 1886.

"HON. ROBERT C. WINTHROP,
"Boston, Mass.

"MY DEAR SIR,—We read that Horace Walpole said, 'A careless song with a little nonsense in it, now and then, does not misbecome a monarch;' and some rhymer, like the present, has popularized the sentiment by the trite couplet,—

'A little nonsense now and then
Is relished by the wisest men.'

"I venture, therefore, to inflict on you another birthday effusion. But I honestly think Lord Tennyson and I had better quit rhyming, if *we* expect to go down to posterity with colors untarnished!—*he* because he is evidently getting past his time, and *I* because I do not seem to have arrived at mine!

"With profound respect,
"Very sincerely yours,
"HORATIO KING."

"WASHINGTON, May 12, 1886.

"DEAR MR. WINTHROP,—

"Is there any fine,
Or other penalty, for writing rhyme?
As time rolls round and brings the genial spring,
All Nature smiles and birds their carols sing.
Then why not I, 'a bird of passage,' too,
Send, greeting, some poetic notes to you?
Sure I will try, in spite of sprites and gnomes,
If you will make it right with Lowell and Holmes!
Far be it from remotest thought of mine
Their well-earned reputation to outshine!
But, without verse, how could I well convey
Congratulations on your Natal Day—
The seventy-seventh, now the 12th of May—
The real purpose of this humble lay?
Long life and happiness to THEE and THINE!
Receive the wish sincere of ME and MINE,
Who come warm greetings from our hearts to bring,
Dear Friend,
Most truly yours,
HORATIO KING.

"HON'BLE ROBT. C. WINTHROP,
"Boston, Mass."

And the following, addressed to his elder brother, Alonzo, now deceased, on his eighty-first birthday:

"DEAR BROTHER: We are growing old,
Your hair is thin and gray;
I've passed my 'threescore years and ten,'—
You're eighty-one to-day.

2

" But, though we count our years by scores,
    We reckon not by time;
  Our spirits, fresh and full of life,
    Are still but in their prime.

" Methinks I see us boys again,
    At work upon the farm,
  Or, task well done, in healthful play,
    With naught to dread or harm.

" O blessed days of youth at home,
    Where all looked bright and fair,
  And under the paternal roof
    We felt no weight of care !

" Mind you when we were twelve at home,
    With parents, sisters three,
  And brothers seven, in union sweet ?—
    A pleasant sight to see !

" Oh, happy, happy days were those
    When life with us was new,
  And no dark cloud had crossed our path
    To shadow hope's bright view.

" But in this world of ceaseless change,
    How strong soe'er the tie
  Of kindred, friends, of all mankind,
    The word is, ' once to die.'

" Thus, in the course of fleeting years,
    We find our little band
  Reduced one-half—half here, and half
    Gone to the spirit-land.

" Thrice happy they who wait for us
    On that celestial shore;
  They've entered into heavenly rest,
    To grieve and weep no more.

" And as we near that happy land,
    It is a joy to know
  Dear friends stand waiting for us there,
    Who loved us here below.

"Then let us cheerful bide our time,
　　Nor yield to doubt or gloom:
　The 'silver lining' on the cloud
　　Appears beyond the tomb.

　　　　　　　　　　　" Affectionately,
　　　　　　　　　　　　" HORATIO KING.
" WASHINGTON, D. C., February 3, 1882."

I venture also to insert still another, addressed to Senator Justin S. Morrill, on his eighty-second birthday, April 14, 1892.

　"DEAR MR. MORRILL:
　　"Once more, by promise bound, I come to greet
　　　You warmly on your natal day,—the eighth
　　　Since, self-appointed, I became, in sooth,
　　　The Poet-Laureate, in MORRILL sense
　　　Par excellence, if not to King or Queen,
　　　At least to one of high estate and true,
　　　Whose laurel wreath, entwined around his brow,
　　　Is mark conclusive of his noble rank.

　　"FOURSCORE AND TWO!　This, surely, is a theme
　　　On which to *moralize* in sober thought,
　　　In view of life's remotest bounds, and when
　　　So near must seem, to all who reach that goal,
　　　The portals of the bright celestial spheres.

　　" Although, three years ago, in playful mood,
　　　I greeted you, ' As Youth to Age,' the truth
　　　Demands admission frank that I have come
　　　So close upon your steps, I now behold
　　　Your fresh-made footprints near the hither shore.

　　" What matters it, though eighty years, or more,
　　　Crowd close upon us, if in mind and strength
　　　We hold our place intact in active life?
　　　And then, what matters, when our work is done,
　　　If summons sudden come to call us home?
　　　It is not death, though bearing that dread name,
　　　But birth, since real life begins, not ends,
　　　When darkness shrouds the silent tomb.

"Doubt not!
But trust implicit in a Love Divine.

"Peace, health, and joy attend you evermore.
"Very sincerely,
"HORATIO KING."

For sixteen years he took great pleasure in his duties as a member, and most of the time as secretary, of the Washington National Monument Society, and had the great satisfaction of witnessing the completion and dedication of the beautiful marble obelisk,—a magnificent tribute to the memory of the Father of his Country. Congress, having put the monument and everything concerning it under the charge of the War Department, and the work allotted to the Society having been accomplished, he, with other of his associates, tendered their resignations.

Mr. King spends his winters in Washington, and since 1882, about four months each season, has resided at his summer home in West Newton, Mass., where with his own hands he has cultivated a garden and raised most of the vegetables required for his own family.

On May 25, 1835, he married Ann Collins, of Portland, Maine, by whom he had seven children,—only three of whom, Mrs. Annie A. Cole, of Washington, D. C.; General Horatio C. King, of Brooklyn, N. Y., and Henry F. King, of West Newton, Mass., survive. The others died young.

His first wife died September 22, 1869, and he married, February 8, 1875, Isabella G. Osborne, of Auburn, N. Y.

Mr. King's somewhat eventful life has been one of great usefulness. In all the positions he has filled he has inaugurated important improvements, including, within the last few years, that of the official "Penalty Envelope," a convenient and economical device; and by his literary efforts he has contributed much to elevate the tone of society at the national capital. He is a notable example to the youth of his country. Born and bred under circumstances which gave him no greater advantages than are enjoyed by a large majority of the young men of our Union, he has attained by his own energy, industry, and perseverance an exalted station, and made for himself a name and a reputation of which any man may well be proud. He has succeeded because he has diligently and untiringly used the means, and the only sure means, to accomplish those ends. Our country has its thousands and tens of thousands as richly gifted by nature, and as much favored by circumstances, as was the subject of this sketch, who, by pursuing the same methods, may attain equally distinguished success.

HORATIO C. KING.

TURNING ON THE LIGHT.

PART I.

CHAPTER I.

ELECTION OF ABRAHAM LINCOLN.

Treasonable Course of the *Constitution* Newspaper—Correspondence of
ex-President Pierce, John A. Dix, Postmaster of New York, Nahum
Capen, Postmaster of Boston, Hon. D. S. Dickinson, and the Author,
with Remarks on the Loyalty of President Buchanan.

I HAVE often regretted that I did not keep a complete
diary of the more important events at Washington during
the fall and winter of 1860–61; but the truth is, I had not
the requisite time and strength to do it, so onerous were
the official duties then devolving upon me. I did, however,
find time to make some brief notes, and these, with some
of my private letters hastily thrown off in connection with
my official correspondence, serve to refresh my recollection
of many of the startling occurrences of that appalling epoch.
Many of these private notes were addressed to General Dix
and Mr. Capen, the postmasters of New York and Boston,
through whose kindness I obtained copies of them, those
from General Dix having been received about a year before
his death. Of others of my letters I fortunately retained
copies, and all, together with the answers to some of them,
have been shown to a few friends, who have earnestly advised me to allow them to be published. To this I have
consented, hesitatingly, with the assurance that any seem-

ing egotism will be pardoned, if not overlooked, since it is apparent that I am not actuated by any selfish motive.

I have put the letters as nearly in their order of date as practicable, introducing only such explanatory remarks as may seem necessary to their correct understanding.

"P. O. DEPARTMENT, WASHINGTON, D. C.,
"October 16, 1860.

"MY DEAR SIR,— . . . Politically the signs look dark. It is painful to hear so many sound and conservative men give it as their decided opinion that there will certainly be resistance to Lincoln's administration of the government. Property holders in this district are greatly concerned.

"Very respectfully and truly yours,
"HORATIO KING.

"HON. JOHN A. DIX, P. M., New York."

"P. O. DEPARTMENT, November 7, 1860.

"MY DEAR SIR,— . . . I write this (on the business of the department) early in the morning, before seeing hardly any one. The bright sun is shining into my office window, and everything is quiet, but a weight presses on my heart which I never felt so sensibly before—all foreboding 'breakers ahead.'

"Very respectfully and truly,
"HORATIO KING.

"HON. JOHN A. DIX, New York."

"P. O. DEPARTMENT, APPT. OFFICE,
"November 7, 1860.

"MY DEAR SIR,—As indicating how I feel to-day, I take the liberty of enclosing a copy of a letter I sent to the President this forenoon.

"The article in the '*Constitution*' referred to will do infinite mischief, and I am not certain that the writer of it ought not to be stretched up as a traitor. I presume, however, it is the result only of bad judgment.

"Very truly,
"HORATIO KING.

"HON. JOHN A. DIX, New York."

"WASHINGTON, November 7, 1860.

"MY DEAR SIR,—The die is cast, and Lincoln is elected.

"Shall we now fan the flame of disunion, or shall we exert our influence toward calming the already excited sentiment of the South?

"What course should we, here in the District of Columbia, pursue? Should we join hands with the disunionists and help on the storm, or should we not rather pour oil on the troubled waters? . . .

"My own will illustrate the condition of thousands in this district. With us everything depends on the Union being preserved.

"What, then, was my indignation on learning that men holding office here under your administration were parading the streets here this morning with disunion cockades on their hats! and the leading article of the 'Constitution' to-day can have no other effect than to encourage and fan the flame of disunion, both here and at the South.

"You will bear me witness that I have never intruded myself upon your counsels. But may I not, in the most respectful yet in the most earnest manner, now appeal to you—for if you are silent your enemies will, I am sure, attempt to hold you responsible for these things—to use your power in at once checking this dread spirit of disunion here in our midst?

"With great respect,
"Very sincerely your friend,
"HORATIO KING.

"HIS EXCELLENCY, JAMES BUCHANAN."

The editorial article of the *Constitution* referred to in the preceding letter concludes as follows:

"We can understand the effect that will be produced in every Southern mind when he reads the news that he is now called on to decide for himself, his children, and his children's children, whether he will submit tamely to the rule of one elected on account of his hostility to him and his, or whether he will make a struggle to defend his rights, his inheritance, and his honor."

"CONCORD, N. H., November 7, 1860.

"MY DEAR SIR,—Your note of the 5th inst. has just been received, and I must thank you for your prompt attention to my little request, in which I, of course, had no personal interest.

"So far as returns of the election have reached us, I can discern but one green spot, and that the Fifth Massachusetts District. Mr. Appleton's election is important in several aspects, but under the circumstances it could have been predicted with no confidence.

"Indeed, it is singular, considering the sweep of this foul current, that the only signal defeat should have met a man who has floated so long and securely upon its surface as Mr. Burlingame. As the overthrow of a party merely, the result [of the presidential election] is comparatively of little moment. As a distinct and unequivocal denial of the co-equal rights of these States I cannot help regarding it as fearful.

"My apprehensions, I confess, are stronger than my hopes, but I will trust in that good Providence which has hitherto held together these confederated States. Will you present my very kindest regards to Mr. Holt? I shall never cease to prize his friendship.

"Yours truly,

"FRANKLIN PIERCE.

"HON. HORATIO KING, 1st Assist. P. M. General, Washington, D. C."

"(PRIVATE.)

"NEW YORK, November 22, 1860.

"MY DEAR SIR,— . . . We have divers reports of disagreements in the Cabinet in regard to the disunion movements in the South. I hear nothing from Cobb in reply to my letter.

"There is a great fallacy at the basis of all the secession movements. It is this, that the violation of a compact by one of the parties releases all, assuming our federal system to be identical with a contract between individuals for certain purposes. It is totally different, and is not subject to the same reasoning and conclusions. The States have organized a central government and ceded to it a part of their sovereignty. The violation of the compact, to warrant a release of the parties, must be on the part of the central government, and not of one of the associates. Mr. Cushing, in his late letter, loses sight of this distinction—a vital one, as I think, in all our reasonings concerning the present disunion movements. In haste, I am,

"Truly yours,

"JOHN A. DIX.

"HON. HORATIO KING."

"(CONFIDENTIAL.)

"P. O. DEPARTMENT, APPT. OFFICE, November 23, 1860.

"MY DEAR SIR,—Your private note of yesterday is received. I have shown it to the Postmaster-General. I am told both the President and Mr. Cobb are under a good deal of excitement. I have no doubt the friends of the President are determined to know whether there is secession in the Cabinet, and whether the President is responsible for the infamous course of the *Constitution*. And all you can do to this end will be a public benefit. . . .

"Things are looking a little better in Georgia to-day.

"Very respectfully and truly yours,

"HORATIO KING.

"HON. JOHN A. DIX, New York."

"WASHINGTON, November 25, 1860.

"MY DEAR SIR,—I would call and report to you what I know of the feelings of your friends whom I met recently in a flying visit to my native State, but that I know you are much occupied. May I not, therefore, be allowed to say to you briefly, in writing, that their most anxious desire is that the President will cast the whole weight of his influence against the secession movements at the South and in support of the Union? Among those whom I met was General Dix, who, of course, is greatly concerned with reference to the present excitement. He had written both to Mr. Cobb and Mr. Breckinridge, pressing them to come out boldly against secession. The inclosed note from him may be interesting to you. You need not trouble yourself to return it.

"I hope I shall not be deemed obtrusive. My great desire is that the Union may be preserved, and that in your noble efforts to that end you may know that all your *true friends* will stand by you to the last.

"I have the honor to be,

"Very sincerely your friend,

"HORATIO KING.

"HIS EXCELLENCY, JAMES BUCHANAN."

"(CONFIDENTIAL.)

"P. O. DEPT., November 25, 1860.

"MY DEAR SIR,—I have good reason to believe that the President is beset by secessionists, who are almost exclusively occupying his attention; and it is important that the *true friends* of the Union should do all in their power to strengthen his hands. Why will you not either write or come and see him, and get all the strong men of your city to do the same? I cannot call names, but rest assured what I tell you is true. The course of the '*Constitution*' is infamous, but the President, I presume, has no means of controlling it. Pray let him hear from you all in a most decided manner on this subject. Let him know how much the paper and suspicions of disunion influences near him are injuring him.

"Stephens's speech is admirable; but observe that you do not see it, or anything like it, in the '*Constitution.*' Get the papers to come out and denounce the '*Constitution.*' You may rely upon it, all its secession articles are directly against the feelings of the President.

"As the existence of the Department depends on the stability of the Union, I shall treat this as 'on official business.'

"Yours truly,

"HORATIO KING.

"HON. JOHN A. DIX, New York."

"(UNOFFICIAL.)

"P. O., NEW YORK, November 27, 1860.

"MY DEAR SIR,—It is impossible for me to leave here at this moment, and I have an insuperable repugnance to a visit to Washington. On receipt of your letter I sat down to write to the President, but constant interruptions prevented me from finishing it. Besides I have some doubt whether it would do good. I have made some inquiry in regard to the editor of the '*Constitution*,' and incline to the belief that he cannot be influenced from this quarter. At all events, those who might influence him think as he does. I am, in a quiet way, doing all I can to promote a better feeling at the South. I am sorry to say that nothing I have yet done has met with a response from any of our Southern friends. I believe we shall have to rely entirely on the efforts of our conservative friends there. They seem at present to be overborne by the general excitement. I cannot think this will last. There must, at least, be an effort to prevent a dissolution. I trust events here may aid the conservative movement there. Vermont is moving to repeal her personal liberty bills, with what success remains to be seen. Massachusetts will follow her lead, and, I think, will repeal.

"I shall send my letter to the President this evening or to-morrow.

"With sincere regards, yours,

"JOHN A. DIX.

"HON. HORATIO KING."

"P. O. DEPT., APPT. OFFICE, November 27, 1860.

"MY DEAR SIR,—Our chief clerk, Mr. Clements, and myself had an hour with the President last evening, and our interview was most satisfactory. Mr. C. has just returned from Tennessee, and brings good news from that State to the effect that nearly everybody there is opposed to the hasty action of South Carolina, and is in favor of one more effort to preserve their rights in the Union. The President appeared to be much gratified to be reassured of this. He is, as I supposed, a firm Union man. I told him about your writing to and not receiving any answer from Mr. Cobb, and he remarked that it would not do the slightest good to write to him. I expressed myself freely to him about the course of the *Constitution* newspaper, and told him how much it had injured him, etc., etc. I have no doubt he will take strong ground in his message against secession, as well as the right of secession; but were I allowed to guess, I would say that he will not be in favor of using force unless the property of the United States is interfered with, such as the taking of the forts, etc., when he would be obliged to act.

"Very truly,

"HORATIO KING.

"HON. JOHN A. DIX, P. M., New York."

"(CONFIDENTIAL.)

"P. O. DEPT., APPT. OFFICE, November 25, 1860.

" MY DEAR SIR,—I am well assured that the President is beset by men who are for breaking up the Union,—secessionists, who strongly advocate the right of secession,—while the true friends of the Union seem, to a great extent, to keep aloof. Why they keep away I cannot comprehend, unless they think the *Constitution* newspaper speaks the sentiments of the President, which is certainly not the fact. Rest assured, the President will stand firmly for the Union ; and what I think is now important is that his hands should be strengthened from every quarter. You can do much to this end by writing him briefly and pointedly on this subject, and you can get other strong men in Boston to do the same. You will know best whom to call on ; but let this be strictly confidential so far as my name is concerned.

" Don't hesitate to denounce the disunion course of the *Constitution*, and speak of the reports of secession feelings in the Cabinet as most unfortunate for the country and highly injurious to the President's reputation.

" Act immediately. Things look worse and worse every day.

" Very truly yours,

" HORATIO KING.

"NAHUM CAPEN, P. M., Boston, Mass."

" BOSTON, November 28, 1860.

" MY DEAR SIR,—I have read your note to several gentlemen of note, and all agree as to the importance of your views and agree with you, but they have a delicacy about writing to the President unasked. I inclose a note which I received last evening from Mr. Everett, and though I do not exactly agree with him, yet I can understand how he and others may entertain such opinions and have such feelings.

"Of course, I did not mention your name, because you requested me not to do so. I simply stated that the letter was from a distinguished person—one who was fully advised of what was going forward.

" The feeling here is decidedly that the New England States will repeal their nullification enactments. Vermont has the subject up, and I am told to-day that Connecticut will do it by a large majority. The same is expected of Massachusetts.

" Very sincerely,

" NAHUM CAPEN.

"HON. HORATIO KING, Washington."

A word further of explanation here. I saw how the President was beset by the leading secessionists, and I was most anxious to have earnest Union men come to his relief. I felt sure, too, that the latter were kept away on account of the very fact that the former were known to occupy a large part of his time and attention. It was unquestionably owing in a great degree to the persistency of these determined disunionists in this regard, that the President's health and strength were so nearly exhausted toward the last that it was only with great and painful effort that he was enabled to perform the fearful duties devolving upon him. Some days, I remember, the Cabinet sessions were held in the library, because he was too unwell to come into his office. No sooner were the members of his Cabinet dismissed than one or more of the leaders stood ready to be ushered into his presence, and one after another, often several together, they came, keeping him up until late in the night. No one can tell what torture he must have been thus subjected to by them in their efforts to attain their ends. Never before, I imagine, was a president more rejoiced to be relieved from the responsibilities of office than James Buchanan, on the 4th of March, 1861.

"LOWELL, MASS., Nov. 26, 1860.

"MY DEAR SIR,—Your letter was received at Concord on Saturday, and I should have answered it while there if I could have found a little interval of leisure. I am here to-day on business, and can therefore do scarcely more than to thank you; but let so much, at least, be said. The apprehensions which you so forcibly express did not increase mine. You know how sincerely and earnestly I have for years deprecated the causes which, if not removed, I foresaw must produce the fearful crisis which is now upon us; and I know how ineffectual, in this section, have been all warnings of patriotism and ordinary forecast. Now, for the first time, men are compelled to open their eyes, as if aroused from some strange delusion, upon a full view of the nearness and magnitude of impending calamities. It is worse than idle—it is foolhardy—to discuss the question of probable relative suffering and loss in different sections of the Union. In case of disruption we shall all be involved in common financial embarrassment and ruin, and, I fear, in common destruction so much more appalling than any attendant upon mere sacrifice of property, that one involuntarily turns from its contemplation. To my mind one thing is clear: no wise man can, under existing circumstances, dream of coercion. The first blow struck in that direction will be a blow fatal even to hope.

" You have observed, of course, how seriously commercial confidence, and consequently the price of stocks, etc., have already been shaken at the North, and yet there is in the public mind a very imperfect apprehension of the danger. Still, there are indications of a disposition to repeal laws directed against the constitutional rights of the Southern States,— such as personal liberty bills, etc.—and if we could gain a little time, there would seem to be ground of hope that these just causes of distrust and dissatisfaction may be removed. I trust the South will make a large draft on their devotion to the Union, and be guided by the wise moderation which the exigency so urgently calls for. Can it be that this flag, with all the stars in their places, is no longer to float, at home, abroad, and always, as an emblem of our *united* power, common freedom, and unchallenged security? Can it be that it is to go down in darkness, if not in blood, before we have completed a single century of our independent national existence? I agree with you that madness has ruled the hour in pushing forward a line of aggressions upon the South, but I will not despair of returning reason and of a re-awakened sense of constitutional right and duty. I will still look with earnest hope for the full and speedy vindication of the co-equal rights and co-equal obligations of these States, and for restored fraternity under the present Constitution— fraternity secured by following the example of the fathers of the republic—fraternity based upon admission and cheerful maintenance of all the provisions and requirements of the sacred instrument under which they and their children have been so signally blessed. When that hope shall perish, if perish it must, life itself, my friend, will lose its value for you and me. It is apparent that much will depend upon the views expressed and the tone and temper manifested during the early days of the session of Congress now near at hand. May the God of our fathers guide the counsels of those who in the different departments of government are invested in this critical epoch with responsibilities unknown since the sitting of the convention which framed the Constitution.

" Your friend,

" FRANKLIN PIERCE."

"CONCORD, N. H., Dec. 6, 1860.

" MY DEAR SIR,—Your letter of November 30 I found here on my return from Hillsboro yesterday, and also several northern papers containing my letter to Secretary Thompson.

"Since the action of the Vermont Legislature upon the report of the Judiciary Committee of the House of Representatives, declaring the ' personal liberty bill' of that State to be clearly unconstitutional, I am in despair with regard to any amendment of errors at the North, so far as the question of slavery is concerned. Reason has surrendered its throne, all sense of patriotism, justice, and right seems to have departed forever from the black Republican portion of the country. If the legislature of this State were convened to-day, I do not believe that they would repeal their unconstitutional laws. When I say this you will understand that I think the Union has already reached its termination.

"It seems to me that few men in this crisis suffer so keenly as I do. With regard to pecuniary loss, it is nothing. I do not take it into the account. It is not worth considering. We can all have bread, if we will work for it, but we shall never have again the glorious ensign of our country, which has been the object of our just admiration, the type of our power, and the shield of our protection the world over.

"Your friend,
"Franklin Pierce.

"Hon. Horatio King, Washington, D. C."

"P. O. Dept., Appt. Office, Dec. 10, 1860.

"My Dear Sir,— . . . Madness still rules the hour. Would it not be well to call public meetings at the North to give expression to the conservative sentiment and show the true men of the South the importance of standing by their Northern friends *in the Union?*

"Very truly,
"Horatio King.

"Nahum Capen, Esq., P. M., Boston, Mass."

"Washington, D. C., Dec. 10, 1860.

"My Dear Sir,— . . . Things look at present very dark; but some of the mad and drunken spirits from the South are acting so outrageously that the better-disposed Southern men are becoming disgusted. I was credibly informed that yesterday, or day before, not less than six Southern Representatives, who are open disunionists, were so drunk that they were wholly unfit for any business,—indeed, disgracefully drunk! and these are the kind of men into whose hands the destinies of our country seem at this moment to have been placed!

"Cobb has resigned.   "Very truly,

"Gen. Dix, New York."   "Horatio King.

"New York, Dec. 11, 1860.

"Dear Sir,— . . . Alas for the Union! I fear its safety is hopeless if it depends on such as your note describes. But I will not cease to hope.

"Very sincerely,

"Hon. Horatio King."   "John A. Dix.

" (PRIVATE.)

"P. O. DEPT., APPT. OFFICE, Dec. 12, 1860.

"MY DEAR SIR,—Your note of yesterday is received.

"It is becoming every day more and more apparent that there is quite a large party at the South who, traitors at heart, are resolved on effecting a dissolution of the Union, even though the North were to yield to the utmost of their former demands, and these men are now in the lead. One of them kept his place in the government till forced to resign from very shame, and there are others of smaller calibre who are still retained, —traitors in the camp.

"And we are to allow the best government in the world to be destroyed in the first hour of danger, without an effort to demonstrate that if statesmen will but do their duty it is capable of withstanding far more serious shocks than that with which it is now threatened. What mockery of statesmanship! What imbecility! What culpable wickedness! Will not the God of nations send down his thunderbolts and arrest the base wretches who are thus plotting our ruin?

"It seems now to be pretty generally conceded that the cotton States will secede, and the next thing is to avoid a conflict on that account, or the whole country will be ablaze with civil war!

"Very respectfully and truly yours,

"HORATIO KING.

"HON. JOHN A. DIX, New York."

" (PRIVATE.)

"NEW YORK, 14 Dec., 1860.

"MY DEAR SIR,—Your note received yesterday is confirmed to-day in its worst anticipations. I did not answer because I have been busy preparing an address to the people of the South, to be submitted this evening to a committee, and passed upon to-morrow at a larger but not a public meeting. I do not know that any appeal, in whatever fraternal feeling it may be made, will be of any avail, but I think we have the right to ask our Southern friends to pause and listen to us. If they refuse, I see no issue out of the present darkness but in darker strife.

"Yours cordially,

"JOHN A. DIX.

"HON. HORATIO KING."

"WASHINGTON, Dec. 14, 1860.

"MY DEAR SIR,—It may seem presumptuous in me, an humble subordinate, to address you on great matters of state, but my apology, if any is necessary, must be that I am an American citizen, with all that ardent love for my country and its government which should ever animate the true patriot, and especially in times of danger like the present.

"I am amazed that some decided action is not taken by the Government to cut itself entirely loose from disunion and disunionists. Look at the *Constitution* newspaper of to-day—and, indeed, I may say, of every issue since the Presidential election. *Its whole bearing is for disunion;* and, say what you will, the Government is held, and will be held, in a great degree responsible for it. It was the organ to which the message was confidentially intrusted, and its columns are daily filled with advertisements which it receives and can receive *only by favor of the President,* for its circulation would not secure them to it by law.

"I saw, as every person of observation must have seen, the very day after the election, that its influence was directed toward secession, and I felt myself compelled immediately to call the attention of the President to it, as I did in a letter, a copy of which I herewith inclose for your perusal.

"I know how the President is pressed by the secessionists, and I sympathize fully in all reasonable measures to be taken *within the Union* to secure the rights of the South, and consign to infamy the leaders of black republicanism at the North; but, as his devoted friend and the friend of every member of his Cabinet, I cannot restrain myself from the expression of the deepest astonishment and mortification that the Government should for one moment allow itself to occupy such a position as to afford even its enemies a pretext to charge it with giving the slightest countenance, either directly or indirectly, to secession or secessionists.

"Is it not possible to relieve the administration from the *infamy* which must attach to it for all time, so far as it is made responsible for the course of the *Constitution,* and for keeping men in responsible positions who are known and avowed disunionists? For God's sake, let us see the Government placed squarely and unequivocally on the side of the Union! With great respect,

"Very sincerely your friend,

"HORATIO KING.

"HON. J. S. BLACK, Attorney-General U. S."

"P. O. DEPT., APPT. OFFICE, Dec. 15, 1860.

"MY DEAR SIR,—Your letter to Jefferson Davis is excellent, and I have sent it forward through the P. O.

"You will see the President's proclamation and the address of the disunionists in the *Constitution* (the secession organ) of to-day.

"I need hardly say that I am desponding to the last degree.

"Very truly,

"HORATIO KING.

"NAHUM CAPEN, ESQ., P. M., Boston, Mass."

"P. O. DEPARTMENT, APPT. OFFICE, Dec. 17, 1860.

"MY DEAR SIR,—Your private letter of the 14th inst. came duly to hand. . . . I inclose, for your private eye and that of any of our friends, the copy of a letter I was addressing to General Cass at the very moment I heard of his resignation. I therefore sent it to Judge Black. You may think it injudicious, but I am determined to sustain the Union until not a hope for its continuance remains.

"The papers state the main reason of General Cass's resignation, but I know that he has long felt as I have about the course of the *Constitution* newspaper.

"Very respectfully and truly,
"HORATIO KING.
"GEN. DIX, New York."

"P. O. DEPT., APPT. OFFICE, Dec. 18, 1860.

"MY DEAR SIR,—I have read your address with great pleasure. It is cheering to read such a paper in the midst of the infamous articles and speeches of treason that have of late been so common. The *Intelligencer* of to-day has a stinging article, which I wish you would read. Let all traitors be shown up, and the solid people will assign them to their proper places. Don't let us permit their conduct to be so far winked at even as to afford a shield to black Republicans who are the original aggressors.

"Very respectfully and truly,
"HORATIO KING.
"HON. J. A. DIX, New York."

"NEW YORK, 19 Dec., 1860.

"MY DEAR SIR,—I thank you for your excellent letter to Judge Black. I am as much disgusted as you are at the encouragement given to the secessionists. I am for making all reasonable concessions. . . . But the Government should quietly and firmly maintain the central authority.

"I am glad you like the address. I have written to leading Southern men—some of them secessionists—against the right of secession, and especially against an attempt to break up the Union on the grounds assumed by South Carolina. But in a fraternal appeal intended to gain time for readjusting existing differences, I thought it not wise to introduce any topic on which our Southern brethren are sensitive. . . .

"I am very truly yours,
"JOHN A. DIX.
"HON. HORATIO KING."

"P. O. DEPT., APPT. OFFICE, Dec. 20, 1860.

"DEAR SIR,—Yours of the 18th inst. is received. I have not had time to read the proceedings or address of the solid men of Boston, but have heard it spoken of with great satisfaction.

"I think the disunionists are not having everything quite so much their own way as at first. The true friends of the country are beginning more generally to denounce the disunion *Constitution*, and to protest against disunionists being retained in office.

"To show you how I feel, I inclose the copy of a letter which I had nearly finished and intended to send to General Cass when I heard of his resignation, so I addressed it to Judge Black. It is for the private eye of friends only, of course.

"Very truly,
"HORATIO KING.

"NAHUM CAPEN, ESQ."

"(CONFIDENTIAL.)

"P. O. DEPT., Dec. 28, 1860.

"MY DEAR SIR,—I feel as though we were on the verge of civil war, and I should not be surprised if this city is under the military control of the disunionists in less than one month! There can be no doubt that the Cabinet is divided, and rumor has it that the sympathies of the President, as well as of Mr. Toucey, are with the disunionists in reference to the question of sustaining Major Anderson! Holt, Black, and Stanton are firm for the Union, there can be no doubt.

"Is there no way to bring a healthful influence to bear on the President and Governor Toucey? Northern men all seem to be dumb and paralyzed!

"In haste, yours truly,
"HORATIO KING.

"NAHUM CAPEN, ESQ."

"(PRIVATE.)

"NEW YORK, 29 Dec., 1860.

"MY DEAR SIR,—Yours is received. I see fully, without any power to prevent it, the danger in which the country is placed. I have had little faith in the conciliatory action of the Republicans in Congress, though I know there are some who think rightly. It was for this reason that I moved, in conjunction with others here, in favor of a strong appeal to our Southern friends in the States on the Gulf of Mexico and the lower Mississippi to await the issue of the change which is going on in public opinion in the North. Our appeal is to go to the Southern conventions about to assemble in Georgia, Alabama, and Mississippi. There seems but little prospect that any good will be accomplished. At Washington I fear I can do nothing. I have written to several leading Southern men, but I get no response. There is a determination on the part of leading Republicans here that a conciliatory course shall be pursued, and that reasonable compromises shall be made. It remains to be seen whether they can influence the action of their friends in Congress.

" Major Anderson, who was my lieutenant when I was a captain in the army, I have no doubt acted as any military man responsible for the lives of those under his command would have done. His conduct is approved here by all parties, even by the warmest advocates of Southern rights.

" My great fear is that the masses, North and South, who have been indoctrinated into secession views on the one hand, and abolitionism on the other, will not follow their leaders in a retrograde movement.   But I have less anxiety for the North than for the South.   We can make things right here if we can have time. . . .

" I am, dear sir,
" Yours truly,
" JOHN A. DIX.

" HON. HORATIO KING."

" WASHINGTON, Dec. 30, 1860.

" MY DEAR SIR,—I rejoice to learn that the disunionists failed yesterday in their impudent and insulting demand that the administration should remove Major Anderson or otherwise degrade him.

" It is every day becoming more and more apparent that they are determined, as far as lies in their power, to make use of the administration to strengthen themselves in their rebellious position, and, if necessary for their purpose, *to break up the Government*.   Does it require any close discernment to see that it would be fatal to follow their counsels?

" They commenced, long before the election, by getting possession of the *Constitution* newspaper, which, from the announcement of Lincoln's election, has been openly for a dissolution of the Union, and some of them have continued, and still continue, to hold office here in the Government, although known to be hostile to that very Government which feeds them !

" In a letter to the President on the 7th of November,—the day after election,—I called attention to these startling facts ; and, from that day to the present, my amazement has increased until I am, at times, almost paralyzed to see such things go unrebuked.   It is all folly for the editor of that paper to issue his pronunciamentoes that he alone is responsible . . . *so long as it is supported and kept alive by Government advertisements which it receives solely through the favor of the administration, for it is not entitled to them by law.*   Has not this fact been overlooked in the pressure of the great troubles now threatening our destruction?

" The question now is union or disunion.   An article in that paper to-day advises that Lincoln's inauguration be prevented by armed force !

Can the Government give such a paper patronage and escape the charge of treason? We must now take sides either for or against the continuance of the Union; and the sooner we know where we stand the better.

"I wrote you yesterday hastily what I regard as the clear duty of the Government in reference to Major Anderson, and I am confirmed in my opinions by everybody to whom I have spoken since, as well as by the press, several extracts of which I beg to inclose for your perusal.

"The duty of the administration, it seems to me, is very plain. It is simply to see that the laws are executed, thus maintaining, with a firm hand, the integrity of the Union. In this, rest assured, every friend of the Union will sustain you.

"I have the honor to be

"Very truly your friend,

"HORATIO KING.

"HON. I. TOUCEY See'y Navy."

"(PRIVATE.)

"P. O. DEPT., APPT. OFFICE, Dec. 31, 1860.

"MY DEAR SIR,—I am rejoiced to hear you express yourself as you do in regard to sustaining Major Anderson. But I greatly fear the Cabinet now in session may take some action against him, although if he is not sustained, you may expect to see the resignations of Black, Holt, and Stanton. The most intense excitement is felt here on the subject, and disunion men are raising heaven and earth to get the President to degrade Major Anderson. To-day we have a most unpleasant rumor that Floyd is to go back into the Cabinet. If this rumor is true, all is lost! It is known that he sent a most savage message of inquiry to Major Anderson; but the answer he got in return had the true ring to it of the *Veni, vidi, vici* stamp.

"It is said there is a secret society forming here to prevent Lincoln's inauguration!

"Very truly,

"HORATIO KING.

"HON. JOHN A. DIX, New York."

"(PRIVATE.)

"P. O. DEPT., APPT. OFFICE, Dec. 31, 1860.

"MY DEAR SIR,—In answer to your note of the 29th inst., I am sorry to say that I cannot give any assurance that the 'Jackson policy' in the present crisis will be pursued. Up to this time (12 M.), however, I believe no order has been made against Major Anderson, except that the Secretary of War (since resigned, thank God!) sent him a savage despatch, inquiring why he removed his command. But this was not sustained by the majority of the Cabinet, and he got a regular soldier's answer back, full of true metal. The Cabinet is now in session on this subject, and the most intense interest is felt here for fear that Major Anderson will not be sustained.

"The President is borne down by the disunionists, and, as well as Governor Toucey, needs support from all true friends of the Union. Pray, see that letters are poured in upon them. On Saturday, however, Governor Toucey was right, and I cannot think it possible that he will flinch. General Scott, I fear, does not have the influence he should in the counsel touching his command. . . .

"Very respect'ly and truly,
"HORATIO KING.

"NAHUM CAPEN, ESQ., Boston, Mass."

"BINGHAMTON, Dec. 31, 1860.

"MY DEAR SIR,— . . . I am filled with anxious solicitude for the fate of our country. May God avert the threatened evil !

"Sincerely yours,
"D. S. DICKINSON.

"HON. H. KING, 1st Asst. P. M. Gen'l."

"(CONFIDENTIAL.)
"P. O. DEPT., APPT. OFFICE, Jan. 3, 1861.

"MY DEAR GENERAL,— . . . Things are being brought to a point here, I think. I understand the 'Commissioners' (from South Carolina) sent an insulting communication to the President, and that he sent it back to them. We shall soon know who is for and who against the Union. At present we know not whom to trust.

"Very truly,
"HORATIO KING.

"GEN. DIX, New York.

"P. S.—That was most infamous business of Floyd at Pittsburgh. One of the 'forts' for which guns were intended is a bare sand-bar, and the other has been just commenced, having a wall about two or three feet high. He and Cobb are both traitors. Floyd's orders will be countermanded."

"(PRIVATE.)
"NEW YORK, Jan. 3, 1861.

"MY DEAR SIR,—I have been so pressed with outside business during the last ten days (trying to save the Union) that I have been unable to write to you.

"The first time we began to breathe freely was when Mr. Holt took Governor Floyd's place in the War Department. The feeling here is strong and undivided in regard to sustaining the administration in its determination to stand by Major Anderson, to protect the public property, and to enforce the revenue laws. On these points the people of the Northern States are as one man; and I am satisfied the President will have with him the conservative men of all sections of the country.

"I have been very busy corresponding with prominent men in and out of Congress. We must preserve the Union. Congress should do what is right, and the rest will be easy. Why cannot enabling acts be passed admitting Kansas and New Mexico, and like enabling acts dividing the residue of our territory by 36° 30′, and admitting two more States, at once, with no other restriction than that of 'a republican form of government,' which Congress under the Constitution is bound to guaranty? This will dispose of the whole territorial question; and all may support it without surrender of principle. What if New Mexico has a very small population? This fact should weigh nothing against restoration of harmony and preservation of the Union.

"Do not things look better? Let me hear from you.

"Yours very truly,

"JOHN A. DIX.

"HON. HORATIO KING."

"(PRIVATE.)

"P. O. DEPT., Jan. 4, 1861.

"MY DEAR SIR,—I am obliged for your favor of yesterday. I feel as though there is a slight improvement in the state of things here; but the disunionists—conspirators—are doing their utmost to head off the Government in its present efforts to right itself. Things will not go entirely satisfactory so long as Thompson and Thomas are retained in the Cabinet, and especially the latter, who, I am disappointed to learn, is a rabid secessionist. I am glad to hear that there is a committee here from your city to make a representation to the President in regard to him. For Thompson I have more compassion. He is not willingly a disunionist; and I guess he sustained the President in sending back their insulting communication to the S. C. 'Commissioners.'

"Let us press forward till we clear the Government of every disunionist.

"Very respectfully and truly,

"HORATIO KING.

"GEN. DIX, New York."

"(PRIVATE.)

"NEW YORK, Jan. 5, 1861.

"MY DEAR SIR,—Facts that have come to my knowledge give me strong hopes that the Union will be preserved. I look for a speedy movement on the part of the Republicans in Congress, and an effective one.

"In the mean time the authority of the Government must be maintained. I have written to several members of Congress, among others Governor Seward, urging the adoption of the plan I suggested to you yesterday, as one involving no sacrifice of principle or surrender of position. We can do nothing unless the Republicans act with us, and I have for the last week been pressing them here and in Congress.

"Yours sincerely,

"JOHN A. DIX.

"HON. HORATIO KING."

"P. O. DEPT., Jan'y 7, 1861.

"MY DEAR SIR,—I have yours of the 5th, and am glad to see that you are laboring in the right direction. The Republicans must yield, or all is lost.

"But the South must be reasonable. . . . Many good Union men are disgusted with their arrogance.

"Very resp'ly and truly,

"HORATIO KING.

"HON. JOHN A. DIX."

"(CONFIDENTIAL.)

"NEW YORK, Jan. 8, 1861.

"MY DEAR SIR,—Why is money to very large amounts being transferred to Washington? It may be all right, but it is unusual. Nearly a million of dollars has been sent on in specie within the last week. I write you in confidence. Are these transfers made by order of the President? Is he aware of them? These questions have suggested themselves to me. There is a good deal of uneasiness in regard to the Treasury Department. The Secretary and his assistant are known to be secessionists, and our capitalists, who furnish the Government with money, naturally feel a solicitude in regard to the disposition made of it. The transfers in specie have attracted attention and produced a good deal of unpleasant speculation. The Assistant Treasury Office is in Wall Street, and any considerable quantity of gold cannot be moved without being known. I met, a few days ago, a large number of boxes going out, and on inquiry I found $400,000 were going to Washington.

"In haste, very truly yours,

"JOHN A. DIX.

"HON. HORATIO KING."

"P. O. DEPART., Jan'y 12, 1861.

"MY DEAR SIR,—Yours of the 8th came duly to hand. I am glad to know that you have been active in your efforts to head off the conspirators here. We are progressing slowly, but surely, as I trust. The appointment of General Dix to the Treasury, and the discarding of the *Constitution* (newspaper) in the last two days, are two things most gratifying. What is doing now, however, should have been done two months ago, as you know I have been decided upon from the start.

"Who will be nominated for Secretary of War and Secretary of Interior remains to be seen. You will have seen Slidell's attack on Mr. Holt. Nevertheless, I believe if his name is sent in they will not be able to reject him. One thing I hope there will be no mistake about, and that is, that none but Union men will be allowed to go into the Cabinet, even if they have all to be taken from the North.

"Matters at Charleston are bad enough; but it is gratifying to know that Major Anderson will not need any assistance, probably, for four months to come. This was not known to the Government when the *Star of the West* was sent for his relief.

"Very truly,
"HORATIO KING.

"NAHUM CAPEN, ESQ., P. M., Boston, Mass."

"P. O. DEPT., Jan'y 21, 1861.

"MY DEAR SIR,—Yours of the 19th inst. is received.

"I presume I shall continue to act as P. M. G., as I have been doing since the 1st inst. I do not anticipate that any appointment will be sent to the Senate at least for the present.

"I cannot see that there is much if any improvement in the state of things. Yet if the Republicans would only present some reasonable proposition, and vote upon it with anything like unanimity to show that they were willing to do something, it would at once take the wind out of the sails of secession in all the border States, and this would dampen the ardor of the rebels . . . further South.

"Very resp'ly and truly yours,
"HORATIO KING.

"NAHUM CAPEN, ESQ., P. M., Boston, Mass."

"P. O. DEPT., March 5, 1861.

"MY DEAR SIR,—I have only time in this, doubtless my last communication from the 'P. O. Department,' to thank you for your kind letter of the 2d inst., and, in reply to your question, to say that I fear the proceedings of the Peace Convention will result in little, if any, good; yet it is quite possible that they may be of use at an early day before a called session of Congress. The aspect of affairs is gloomy, and it will not surprise me if we are engaged in a civil war before the end of this month, unless all the forts in the seceding States are peaceably given to the revolutionists.

"Very sincerely your friend,

"HORATIO KING.

"NAHUM CAPEN, ESQ., P. M., Boston, Mass."

On the appointment of General Dix to the Treasury, January 11, 1861, our correspondence, of course, ceased. As the more important of his letters were read by Postmaster-General Holt, who in turn showed them to the President, I have always thought they led the way to that appointment. Eminent as a patriotic statesman, his selection for the position was hailed with marked satisfaction, and he filled it with distinguished ability. With none but kindly sentiments towards the South, he at the same time held it to be the imperative duty of the Government to "quietly and firmly maintain the central authority." This, it may as well be said here, is what President Buchanan endeavored to the utmost of his power to do, while at the same time he deemed it prudent, in the cause of peace and to avoid bloodshed, to pursue a conciliatory policy towards the South. It was this forbearance that for a time led even some of his best friends to harbor slight misgivings in respect to him as well as Secretary Toucey; and to this day we sometimes hear him censured because he did not at once come down on the secessionists as General Jackson did on the nullifiers of South Carolina in 1832. These critics seem to forget that, whereas President Jackson had but a solitary little State to deal with, in President Buchanan's case all the Cotton States were united in the rebellion, and only anxious for the Government to strike the first blow, as in their view the surest and most speedy means of inducing all the border States to join them. Mr. Buchanan fully understood this; hence his extreme caution, with which it must, however, be admitted, some of his nearest friends did not always sympathize, although it is now far from certain that his was not the wiser course. Said Joseph Holt, in 1865 :

" Looking at the glorious results of the war, and remembering how wondrously Providence has dealt with us in its progress, and how sublimely the firing upon instead of from Fort Sumter seemed to arouse, instruct, and unite the nation, and to inflame its martial and patriotic spirit, we stand awe-struck and mute; and that man would be bold, indeed, who, in the presence of all that has occurred, should now venture to maintain that the policy of forbearance was not at the moment the true policy."

It is well known, and should be borne in mind when Mr. Buchanan's policy of forbearance is assailed, that, for several weeks after his inauguration, President Lincoln still " hoping [we have the testimony of Gideon Welles, his Secretary of the Navy] for a peaceful solution of the pending questions," the greatest forbearance was observed, and " a calm and conciliatory policy" pursued toward the South.

President Buchanan stood on the defensive, and, true to his oath, strove by every means in his power to protect the rights and property of the Government. He held it to be his duty to see that the laws were obeyed; but this was impossible where the local authorities were all in rebellion, and officers could not be found to enforce the execution of the laws. For instance, there was no collector of customs at Charleston, and he sent to the Senate the name of a gentleman to fill the place; but his nomination was not confirmed. In a letter to me of September 18, 1861, Mr. Buchanan said, " Had the Senate confirmed my nomination of the 2d of January of a collector for the port of Charleston, the war would probably have commenced in January instead of May."

As a further indication of his true sentiments, and as due to his memory, I venture to infringe the salutary rule (which has been so often violated since Mr. Buchanan's time in revealing what takes place in Cabinet session) by relating a little incident that happened in Cabinet on the

19th of February, 1861. I copy from my diary made on
that day:

"February 19.—In Cabinet to-day the principal matter presented was
an inquiry from Major Anderson, in charge of Fort Sumter, at Charleston, what he should do in the event of the floating battery understood to
have been constructed at Charleston being towed toward the fort with
the evident purpose of attack. The President wished time to consider.
Mr. Holt asked what he would do, or rather what Major Anderson ought
to do, in case he were in charge of a fort and the enemy should commence
undermining it. The President answered that he should 'crack away at
them.' The President, however, is very reluctant to fire the first gun.
The Peace Convention, he said, was now in session in this city, and its
president, ex-President Tyler, had this morning assured him that no
attack would be made on the fort. The President expressed the opinion
that the fort would eventually be taken."

"WASHINGTON, May 13, 1861.

"DEAR SIR,—Your letter of the 11th inst. is received. Troops continue to arrive, but what the end is to be, who can tell? It seems to me
the South has everything to lose and nothing to gain.

"Truly yours,
"HORATIO KING.

"NAHUM CAPEN, ESQ., Boston, Mass."

CHAPTER II.

PRESIDENT BUCHANAN TO ROYAL PHELPS, ESQ.

THE following letter came into my hands through the
favor of the late George Bancroft, who received it from
Mr. Phelps some time before his death. I am left free to
publish it, but the responsibility is my own. The letter
bears date December 22, 1860, two days after the secession
of South Carolina. At that time there was some hope that
Congress might agree to the Crittenden Compromise. An
act of Congress of 17th December had authorized the issue
of treasury notes; the advertisement inviting bids for them

was then out, and New York was looked to for the bulk of subscriptions to the loan. Thus we may behold *the key to the letter*. It is evident from Mr. Buchanan's appeal to his personal and political friend that he wished to convince him that it would be for the interest of New York to take the loan. Deeply regretting the attempted secession of the cotton States as Mr. Buchanan did, this and other documents show that he never had the slightest inclination to part with them.

(PRIVATE.)

WASHINGTON, 22d December, 1860.

MY DEAR SIR,—I have received your favor of the 20th inst., and rejoice to learn the change of public sentiment in your city. Still secession is far in advance of reaction, and several of the cotton States will be out of the Union before anything can be done to check their career. I think they are all wrong in their precipitation, but such I believe to be the fact.

It is now no time for resolutions of kindness from the North to the South. There must be some tangible point presented, and this has been done by Mr. Crittenden in his Missouri Compromise resolutions. Without pretending to speak from authority, I believe these would be accepted though not preferred by the South. I have no reason to believe that this is at present acceptable to the Northern senators and representatives, though the tendency is in that direction. They may arrive at this point when it will be too late.

I cannot imagine that any adequate cause exists for the extent and violence of the existing panic in New York. Suppose, most unfortunately, that the cotton States should withdraw from the Union, New York would still be the great city of this continent. We shall still have within the borders of the remaining States all the elements of wealth and prosperity. New York would doubtless be somewhat retarded in her rapid march; but, possessing the necessary capital, energy, and enterprise, she will always command a very large portion of the carrying trade of the very States which may secede. Trade cannot easily be drawn from its accustomed channels. I would sacrifice my own life at any moment to save the Union, if such were the will of God; but this great and enterprising brave nation is not to be destroyed by losing the cotton States, even if this loss were irreparable, which I do not believe unless from some unhappy accident.

I have just received an abstract from the late census.

In the apportionment of representatives the State of New York will have as many in the House (30) as Georgia, Florida, Alabama, Mississippi, Louisiana, Texas, and South Carolina united. The latter State contains 296,422 free people and 408,905 slaves, and will be entitled in the next Congress to 4 representatives out of 233.

Why will not the great merchants of New York examine the subject closely and ascertain what will be the extent of their injuries and accommodate themselves to the changed state of things?

If they will do this, they will probably discover they are more frightened than hurt. I hope the Treasury Note Loan may be taken at a reasonable rate of interest. No security can be better, in any event, whether the Cotton States secede or not. Panic in New York may, however, prevent, because panic has even gone to the extent of recommending that the great city of New York shall withdraw herself from the support of at least twenty-five millions of people and become a free city.

I had half an hour, and have scribbled this off in haste for your private use.

Your friend,
Very respectfully,
JAMES BUCHANAN.

ROYAL PHELPS, ESQ.

CHAPTER III.

OFFICIAL CORRESPONDENCE.

Honorable John D. Ashmore, Member of Congress from South Carolina, asks if he has the Right to the Franking Privilege, now that South Carolina has passed an Ordinance of Secession—A Pointed Answer.

ANDERSON, S. C., Jan. 24, 1861.

MY DEAR SIR,—I have in my possession some one thousand to twelve hundred volumes of "public documents," being my proportion of the same as a member of the thirty-sixth Congress. They were forwarded me in mail-sacks and are now lying in my library. Since the date of the ordinance of secession (December 20, 1860) of South Carolina I have not used the franking privilege, nor will I attempt to do so without the special permission of the Department. To pay the postage on these books, etc., would cost me a large sum, and one I am not prepared to expend. The books are of no use to me, but might be to my constituents, for whom they were intended, if distributed among them. Have I the right to frank and distribute them under existing relations? If so, please inform me. Having said that I have not used the franking privilege since the 20th December, I need hardly add that I shall not do so, even on a "public document," unless you authorize it.

I am, with great respect,

Truly and sincerely yours,

J. D. ASHMORE.

HON. HORATIO KING,

Acting Postmaster-General.

POST-OFFICE DEPARTMENT, January 28, 1861.

SIR,—In answer to your letter of the 24th instant, asking if you have the right, "under existing relations," to frank and distribute certain public documents, I have the honor to state that the theory of the administration is that the relations of South Carolina to the general Government have been in nothing changed by her recent act of secession; and this being so, you are of course entitled to the franking privilege until the first Monday in December next. If, however, as I learn is the case, you sincerely and decidedly entertain the conviction that by that act South Carolina ceased to be a member of the confederacy, and is now a foreign State, it will be for you to determine how far you can conscientiously avail yourself of a privilege the exercise of which assumes that your own conviction is erroneous, and plainly declares that South Carolina is still in the Union, and that you are still a member of the Congress of the United States.

I am, very respectfully,
your obedient servant,
HORATIO KING,
Acting P. M.-General.

HON. JOHN D. ASHMORE,
Anderson, S. C.

CHAPTER IV.

A FRANK ANSWER.

Hon. A. G. Jenkins,[1] Member of Congress from Virginia, informed why a Route Agent in his District was removed.

POST-OFFICE DEPARTMENT, February 22, 1861.

DEAR SIR,—Your letter of the 20th inst. is received, requesting "distinct and specific answers" to the following interrogatories,—viz. :

1. What are the grounds of the removal of Thomas J. West, late route agent on the line from Grafton to Parkers-

---

[1] Killed at the head of Confederate cavalry in Virginia early in the war.

burg, Va., and of the substitution of another person in his place?

2. Why is it that these proceedings have been carried out on my part without affording you any information of my contemplated action?

3. Upon whose suggestion was I led to remove Mr. West, and by whose recommendations was I induced to appoint his successor?

4. And, finally, whether the same policy of secretly decapitating your friends is to be acted upon hereafter as the settled rule of the Department?

These are plain questions, stated nearly in your own language, and, in view of the custom which for a number of years has prevailed in the Department, of consulting members of Congress in regard to appointments and removals in their respective districts, it is not unnatural and perhaps not unreasonable that you should ask them. But you will excuse me for remarking, in all kindness, that, in the first place, it is contrary to the rule of the Department to communicate written answers to such inquiries; and, secondly, that the right which you seem to claim, of controlling the appointments in your district, has no existence in fact. Excepting the comparatively few cases in which the law imposes this duty on the President and Senate, the power of appointing the officers of this Department rests exclusively with the Postmaster-General, who alone is responsible for its proper exercise. By courtesy, the member, when agreeing politically with the administration, is very generally consulted with respect to appointments in his district; but his advice is by no means considered as binding on the Department, nor is the Postmaster-General precluded, even by courtesy, from making removals or appointments on satisfactory information, as in the present instance, exclusively from other reliable sources. When the member is politically opposed to the administration, it is not usual to consult him.

Here I might close; but, since you have asked these questions, evidently under the honest impression that it is my duty to answer them, I will disregard the rule so far as to reply to the first, second, and fourth, simply stating, with reference to the third, that I respectfully decline giving the names of the parties by whose suggestions and recommendations I have been guided in making the change.

To the first, then, I have to inform you that Mr. West was removed for leaving his route without permission from the Department, and actively engaging in a movement the avowed object of which is to induce the withdrawal of Virginia from the Union. In other words, he was discharged for undertaking to destroy the Government from whose treasury he was drawing the means of daily subsistence and whose Constitution he had solemnly sworn to support.

Your second and fourth interrogatories may be answered together. I did not advise with you because I had good reason to believe that you were yourself, honestly, I doubt not, fully committed to the secession interest in your State. As to the policy to be pursued in the future towards your friends in office, I can speak only of what may be done in the few remaining days of this administration; and I hesitate not to assure you that if, during this short time, any other cases like the present come before me, I shall esteem it my imperative duty to pursue the course adopted in this instance.

This being not strictly an official letter, I may be pardoned for adding that I am for the Union without reservation, equally against disunionists at the South and abolitionists at the North, and for the just rights of all sections in the Union.

I have the honor to be,

Very respectfully, your obedient servant,

HORATIO KING.

HON. A. G. JENKINS,
House of Representatives.

CHAPTER V.

THE PEACE CONVENTION.

A Little Secret History—Order Calling Out the Troops on February 22, 1861—Revoked—Then Renewed.

THE strong prejudice which existed against President Buchanan at the breaking out of the civil war, and not yet entirely dispelled from the minds of many of his political opponents, may, in a great degree, be truly ascribed to a misapprehension of his real motives and modes of action. As a case in point, there is a little piece of secret history which, in justice to his memory, ought no longer to be kept concealed. It relates to a private letter of his to ex-President Tyler which was found among Mr. Tyler's papers when his house was entered by United States soldiers during the war. It was written when the Peace Convention, presided over by Mr. Tyler, was in session in Washington. The warmest relations existed between him and President Buchanan, and great hopes were based on the action of that Convention. As a matter of course, the President was anxious to avoid everything which might, in the remotest degree, disturb its tranquillity, and, in deference to Mr. Tyler's judgment and wishes, he had indicated a willingness to dispense with the usual parade of United States troops on the occasion of the celebration of Washington's birthday, the 22d of February. Meantime, as a matter of routine, the Secretary of War, Honorable Joseph Holt, had, without, of course, consulting the President, given the customary order calling out the troops on that day. Meeting the Secretary late on the evening of the 21st, the President, having committed himself to Mr. Tyler, was much concerned to learn that such an order had been issued, and that, in all probability, it was too late, as it proved, to pre-

vent its insertion in the *National Intelligencer*, to which it had
in the regular course of events been sent for promulgation.
Greatly fearing from Mr. Tyler's representations that the
people might accept the display as a menacing demonstration, especially as a troop of Flying Artillery just ordered
from the West for the protection of the capital was to
form part of the military procession, the President at once
directed that the order be countermanded, and General
Scott was so informed in time to prevent the assembling of
the United States troops on the morning of the 22d. All
this, however, was unknown to the people, who had filled
the streets and avenues in expectation of witnessing the
grand parade; and after waiting impatiently an hour or
more for the appearance of the United States troops, only
the militia of the District having come out, a startling rumor
reached the ears of the crowd that the order which had
appeared in the *Intelligencer* calling out the troops had been
countermanded; thereupon a distinguished friend of the
President (Daniel E. Sickles, M.C.) hastened to the War
Department, where he found the President and the Secretary
of War together, and in a state of great excitement inquired
if the rumor was correct. Learning that it was, his earnest
protest and representations made so deep an impression on
the President that he authorized the Secretary of War to
confer immediately with General Scott, in order to see, late
as it was, if the original order could not be carried into
effect. This was done, and, although General Scott said the
soldiers had been dismissed and all of the officers had doffed
their uniforms, rendering it doubtful whether the order could
be obeyed, nevertheless he would, if possible, see it executed.
Fortunately, he succeeded, and everything passed off well.
The next morning the *Intelligencer* said:

"The military parade was, of course, the chief feature of the day. It
might be said the double military parade, for, while that of the morning
was composed of the militia companies only, there was a subsequent
general parade, in which the United States troops formed a conspicuous

part. The artillery were the especial mark of interest, and their parade on Pennsylvania Avenue dissipated all sense of fatigue from the thousands who had been abroad from almost 'the dawn of day.' The rapidity with which the guns and magazines were manned and prepared for action was startling to those unaccustomed to artillery practice. While they were on the avenue they were at times as completely enveloped in the dust they stirred up as they would have been in the smoke of battle."

Thus we have briefly the main circumstances under which the following letter was written, on account of which letter President Buchanan has been severely censured. It was a simple explanation to Mr. Tyler of the reasons which had led him to permit the military display, that under the previous understanding would not otherwise have taken place.

"WASHINGTON, February 22, 1861.

"MY DEAR SIR,—I find it impossible to prevent two or three companies of the Federal troops from joining in the procession to-day with the volunteers of the district without giving serious offence to the tens of thousands of people who have assembled to witness the parade. The day is the anniversary of Washington's birth,—a festive occasion throughout the land,—and it has been particularly marked by the House of Representatives. These troops everywhere else join such processions in honor of the birthday of the Father of his Country, and it would be hard to assign a good reason why they should be excluded from this privilege in the capital founded by himself. They are here simply as a *posse comitatus* to aid the civil authorities in case of need. Besides, the programme was published in the *National Intelligencer* of this morning without my knowledge, the War Department having considered the celebration of this national anniversary by the military arm of the Government as a matter of course.

"From your friend, very respectfully,

"JAMES BUCHANAN.

"MR. TYLER."

Happily, as already observed, the celebration was a success; and what was especially gratifying, the presence and wonderful manœuvring of the light artillery companies, not forgetting the splendid bearing of the dragoons, and the dismounted companies, headed by Duane's detachment of sappers and miners, had the effect to allay, in a great degree, the feeling of insecurity which for some time had existed to an alarming extent, not only in Washington, but throughout the country, before the arrival of these troops.

WASHINGTON, D. C., June, 1885.

NOTE.—As confirmatory of the correctness of the foregoing, it is deemed proper to insert the following statement:

"WASHINGTON, June 26, 1885.

"MY DEAR SIR,—I am greatly indebted to you for the number of the *Magazine of History* containing your article on Mr. Buchanan, which was received this morning. I read the article carefully, and regard it as simply perfect.

"Most sincerely yours,

"J. HOLT."

CHAPTER VI.

BEAUREGARD'S REMOVAL FROM WEST POINT.

Senator Slidell's Letter of January 27, 1861, to the President, asking if this was done with his approbation—The President's Polite but Crushing Reply.

"WHEATLAND, September 18, 1861.

"MY DEAR SIR,—I am collecting materials for history, and I cannot find a note from Mr. Slidell to myself and my answer relative to the very proper removal of Beauregard from West Point. I think I must have given them to Mr. Holt. He was much pleased with my answer at the time. If they are in his possession I should be glad if you would procure me copies. They are very brief. The ladies of Mr. S.'s family never after looked near the White House. . . . From your friend,

"Very respectfully,

"JAMES BUCHANAN.

"HON. HORATIO KING."

On the receipt of this letter I immediately applied to Mr. Holt, in the hope of being able to obtain from him the desired copies, but he could not find them among his papers. Some time afterward it occurred to me that I might possibly find them in the War Department, and I remember I inquired after them there on two separate occasions. I remember this because I was refused, I thought very unnecessarily, the first time, by Secretary W. W. Belknap, who not only declined to search for, but said he would not furnish them if on file. This not very pleasant recollection was strengthened by a very polite note now before me, under date of May 6, 1878, from Secretary George W. McCrary, informing me " that a careful search of the records of the department fails to show such correspondence." Further comment is unnecessary.

I wish now to express my gratification that the letters of which the venerable ex-President desired copies, to be used in his history of his administration, have at length made their appearance. General Crawford gives them in his " Genesis of the Civil War," together with a statement of Major Beauregard's appointment on November 8, 1860, by Secretary of War Floyd, and his subsequent removal by Mr. Secretary Holt, Floyd's successor. Major Beauregard was from Louisiana, and, as General Crawford no doubt correctly states, owed the appointment to Senator Slidell, his brother-in-law. As regards secession, he had, General Crawford says, declared that the course of Louisiana was to decide his course. Mr. Slidell knew his man. He himself was among the most determined conspirators in seeking to destroy the Union; and I remember how I was startled, I think in 1859, when I met him on the occasion of a dinner at the White House, and he expressed the opinion that the Union would soon be dissolved. Seeing my surprise, " Oh, well," said he, with apparent unconcern, " it may last five or six years longer!" Of course when he heard that his secession protégé had been summarily dismissed from his snug office of Superintendent of the Military Academy at West Point, where he had put him to teach the cadets " how to shoot" Union soldiers, he was very wroth, and immediately addressed to President Buchanan the following letter:

"WASHINGTON, January 27, 1861.

"MY DEAR SIR,—I have seen in the *Star*, and heard from other parties, that Major Beauregard, who had been ordered to West Point as Superintendent of the Military Academy, and had entered on the discharge of his duties there, had been relieved from his command. May I take the liberty of asking you if this has been done with your approbation?

"Very respectfully yours,

"JOHN SLIDELL."

General Crawford is at fault, as he is in many other things in his "Genesis of the Civil War," when he says that Senator Slidell's "influence with the President was at this time potential." He apparently thought he might overawe Mr. Buchanan, but he was not long in finding out his mistake.

I have more than once heard General Holt relate what took place between him and the President at this point, and, as appeared by a foot-note, he communicated the same in a letter to General Crawford, from which I may be allowed to quote. Soon after receiving Mr. Slidell's letter the President sent for the Secretary of War and handed him the letter, saying to him, "Read this." Upon reading it General Holt, indignant at its tone, said, "Mr. President, we have heard this crack of the overseer's whip over our heads long enough. This note is an outrage; it is one that Senator Slidell had no right to address to you." "I think so myself," replied the President, "and will write him to that effect." "No," continued the Secretary, "I feel that I have a right, Mr. President, to ask that you do more than this; that you will say to Senator Slidell, without qualification and without explanation, that this is your act; for you know that, as Secretary of War, I am simply your representative, and if my acts, as such, are not your acts, then they are nothing." The President assented to this view, and without delay sent to Mr. Slidell the following answer:

"WASHINGTON, January 29, 1861.

"MY DEAR SIR,—With every sentiment of personal friendship and regard, I am obliged to say, in answer to your note of Sunday, that I have full confidence in the Secretary of War, and his acts, in the line of his duty, are my own acts, for which I am responsible.

"Yours very respectfully,

"JAMES BUCHANAN."

Speaking of this subject only a few days ago, General Holt expressed great satisfaction at the noble conduct of the President on that occasion.

WASHINGTON, February 11, 1888.

CHAPTER VII.

THE GOVERNOR'S GRIEVANCE.

An Anecdote of Secretary Holt and Governor ("Extra Billy") Smith—
The Governor wishes to know why the Guns of Fortress Monroe have
been Pointed Landward—Secretary Holt's Amusing Answer.

I HAVE heard an amusing anecdote, altogether too good to be lost, in which General Holt, Secretary of War in the latter part of Mr. Buchanan's Administration, and the late Governor William Smith, of Warrenton, Virginia, fondly known as "Extra Billy," were the principal actors. Without professing to speak "by authority," from my long acquaintance with those gentlemen I should not hesitate to declare the story to be true.

For more than fifty years up to the time of his death, in his eighty-ninth year, on the 18th of May, 1887, no man from the Old Dominion was better known or more respected in Washington than the kind-hearted and genial "Extra Billy" Smith. Above all, he was a great favorite with the ladies. I have seen him hold them delighted for an hour, while he told them, in his rich, flowing expression, of his love-affairs and other touching incidents of his early life.

It was in the month of January or February, or possibly in the beginning of March, 1861. Secretary Holt was sitting alone in his room at the War Department, meditating, no doubt, on what to do in the then agitated state of the country, when Governor Smith was announced and was at once shown in. He had hardly taken his seat when he said, with some excitement,—any one acquainted with him can recall his manner of address under the circumstances, —" Mr. Secretary, I learn that cannon have been mounted on the land side of Fortress Monroe, which I consider an outrage on the sovereign State of Virginia, and I have come to see what explanation can be made of this extraordinary proceeding."

General Holt, though sometimes exhibiting what might be regarded as rather a stern exterior, is far from cold when the ice is once broken; and he has a keen relish for genuine wit and fun. He could not help smiling, perhaps a little too broadly, when he replied : " Well, Governor, I am not a military man, and do not claim to have knowledge of the tactics or strategy of war, but I have always heard that it was the duty of the commander of a fortification to keep the muzzles of his guns turned in the direction from which he was expecting the enemy. It is possible" (he added) "that this traditional view of military duty has led, under the circumstances, to the result of which you speak."

This explanation did not seem to impress the Governor favorably, and after a few hurried words he left.

CHAPTER VIII.

LETTER TO NATHANIEL MITCHELL, ESQ., OF BOSTON.

Views of W. L. Yancey, Jefferson Davis, J. C. Breckinridge, and Howell Cobb averse to Secession prior to 1861—Alexander Hamilton and Judge Story against the Right to Secede—Pointed Comments.

WASHINGTON, October 12, 1861.

DEAR SIR,—Your letter of the 8th instant is received. I concur fully in the views expressed by you respecting the wickedness of the present rebellion and the desperate character of many of its leading spirits; nor have I any doubt that these men, who have conspired to destroy the Government, will ere long be brought to condign punishment. It cannot be otherwise. Unless all history is false, they are certain, sooner or later, to meet the traitor's doom. They stand already condemned, not only by the united voice of true loyalty everywhere, but by the testimony of some of their own chieftains. Said Mr. W. L. Yancey, at Montgomery, in 1858: "No more inferior issue could be tendered to the South upon which we could dissolve the Union than the loss of an election." Yet the election of Mr. Lincoln, admitted on all sides to have been made according to the requirements of the Constitution, is the controlling fact on which they rely as a sufficient excuse for their infamous conduct.

Mr. Yancey continues, "When I am asked to raise the flag of rebellion against the Constitution, I am asked to do an unconstitutional thing, according to the requirements of the Constitution as it now exists. I am asked to put myself in the position *of a rebel,—of a traitor;* in a position where, if the Government should succeed and put me down in the revolution, I and my friends can be arraigned before the Supreme Court of the United States, and there sentenced to be hanged for violating the Constitution and the laws of my country."

This is clear and to the point. There is no intimation that there was any way of escape except through success. Not even the favorite subterfuge of the "right of secession" seems then to have been thought of as affording any chance for relief in case of failure.

Next hear what Mr. Jefferson Davis said in Faneuil Hall, in the month of September, 1858: "But," he remarked, "if those voices which breathed the first instincts into the colony of Massachusetts, into those colonies which formed the United States, to proclaim community, independence, and assert it against the powerful mother-country —if those voices live here still, how must they feel [alluding to Northern disunionists] who come here *to preach treason to the Constitution and assail the Union it ordained and established!* It would seem that their criminal hearts would fear that those voices, so long slumbering, would break their silence, that those forms which look down from these walls, behind and around me, would come forth, and that their sabres would once more be drawn from their scabbards to drive from this sacred temple these fanatical men, who desecrate it more than did the changers of money and those who sold doves in the temple of the living God."

If the preaching of treason in Faneuil Hall by a few fanatics should, in the opinion of Mr. Jefferson Davis, thus start the dead to life, with armor on, ready to battle for the Constitution and the Union, what must be the effect of his own conduct and that of his guilty associates in now assailing that Constitution and that Union with arms in their hands? Should he not expect that, awakened by the sound of guns aimed at that glorious "flag, whose constellation," as he declared in his speech at Portland, "though torn and smoked in many a battle by sea and land, has never been stained with dishonor,"—should he not, I say, look, at such a time, to see the immortal Washington, supported by his brave compatriots in arms, rise up and smite them from the face of the earth?

Much as the leaders of the rebellion relied on their own internal strength and foreign aid, they depended yet more for success on division and dissension in the free States. Even while thus professing devotion to the Constitution and the Union, looking to the possible contingency, if not the probability, of an early rupture between the North and the South, in these same speeches from which I have quoted, Mr. Davis took occasion adroitly to inculcate his peculiar States-Rights doctrines,—affirming that fealty to the Federal Government was subordinate to State allegiance, and at Faneuil Hall he exultantly said, "And if it comes to the worst, if, availing themselves of their majority in the two Houses of Congress, they should attempt to trample upon our equality in the Union, I believe that there are here in Massachusetts States-Rights Democrats, who have not been represented in Congress for many a day, in whose breasts beats the spirit of the revolution, who can whip the black Republicans."

In the same confident tone Mr. J. C. Breckinridge, deprecating the employment of force against the revolting cotton States, in his letter of the 6th of January last to the Governor of Kentucky, held this language: "The Federal Union cannot be preserved by arms. The attempt would unite the Southern States in resistance, while in the North *a great multitude of true and loyal men* never would consent to shed the blood of our people in the name and under the authority of a violated compact."

Such, I think I am correct in saying, was the opinion of most of the prominent politicians, not to say statesmen, of the South prior to the inauguration of the war by "that ungodly and unmanly assault upon the little garrison of Sumter" (as Mr. Winthrop forcibly characterizes it); nor is it more strange that they indulged this belief than that they finally became so lost to all sense of honor as to plunge the country from the height of prosperity and happiness into a cruel civil war. By the aid of their friends in the free States they had hitherto secured nearly everything they had demanded and maintained their supremacy in the Government, and, like spoiled children, they had the presumption to think that these friends would adhere to them to the extent even of assisting to trample the flag of their country in the dust.

The more I reflect upon the atrocious conduct of these men, the more amazed do I become at the enormity of their guilt. Who, one year ago, would have believed such a spectacle possible as that which we behold to-day?—more than two hundred thousand men in arms against our Government, a Government the most beneficent the world ever saw, and all this primarily through the influence and combined action of probably less than one hundred individuals. It could not and did not take place alone from natural causes. No adequate cause nor combination of causes existed to justify it. The whole country was prosperous, and the people, in spite of the angry contentions of politicians, were generally contented and happy. Even after the conspirators succeeded in breaking up the Democratic Conventions at Charleston and Baltimore,—which, it now plainly appears, was an important step, sternly determined on and resolutely carried out, in their programme of disunion,— the great mass of the Southern people were loyal in their feeling, so much so that Mr. Yancey himself, in his public address before them, was constrained to profess a love for the Union; and Mr. Breckinridge, as a candidate for the Presidency, and especially for the extreme States-Rights party, felt compelled in the most emphatic manner to declare himself devotedly attached to the Union. Here is what he said on the occasion of being serenaded at his home in Frankfort, on the 18th of July, 1860: "Fellow-citizens,—As to the charge that the convention to which I owe my nomination, or that the friends who support me, or that I myself am tainted with a spirit of disunion, how absurd to make a response to a Kentucky audience, and in this old district, too! I am an American citizen,—a Kentuckian who never did an act nor cherished a thought that was not full of devotion to the Constitution and the Union. . . . That Constitution was framed and transmitted by the wisest generation of men that ever lived in the tide of time. It may be called an inspired instrument. It answered them at an early day. It has answered our purpose. It is good enough for our posterity to keep it pure."

Alas! Where now is this once proud and gallant Kentuckian who so recently filled the second highest office in the gift of the republic? A fugitive from his own loyal State, not merely "tainted with a spirit of disunion," but, with shame and mortification be it spoken, an open rebel and traitor, in the camp and service of the enemy.

One of the ablest and purest among Southern statesmen, Mr. J. S. Millson, late representative in Congress from the Norfolk district, in a letter dated August 21, 1860, said: "Mr. Breckinridge was, I fear, put up to be beaten, not to be elected, and to make sure, also, of the defeat of any Democratic competitor. . . . That there is a purpose to accomplish the destruction of the present Union I have much reason to fear."

But referring to the controversies then going on upon issues relating to slavery, both between the Democratic and Republican, and between the two sections of the Democratic party, he remarked: "The truth is, both quarrels relate rather to speculative differences of opinion than to evils or dangers of which there is any well-founded apprehension. I allude, of course, to evils and dangers resulting from Federal legislation. And yet the quarrel has never been fiercer than now. The explanation must be sought, not in history, *but in psychology: it is, that there*

never has been so little to quarrel about. . . . It is the Union
that is wounded and suffers with us from every blow
struck at the Constitution, and those who counsel secession
on the bare apprehension of injustice forget that to flee
from wrongs committed *against* the Union is to flee from
remedies provided *by* the Union."

In his speech delivered in the hall of the House of
Representatives of Georgia on the 14th of November last,
Mr. Alexander H. Stephens, now Vice-President of the so-
called Confederate States, declared, " frankly, candidly, and
earnestly," that he did not think the people of the South
ought to secede from the Union in consequence of the
election of Mr. Lincoln to the Presidency of the United
States.

" In my judgment," said he, " the election of no man,
constitutionally chosen to that high office, is sufficient cause
for any State to separate from the Union. It ought to stand
by and aid still in maintaining the Constitution of the
country. To make a point of resistance to the Government,
to withdraw from it because a man has been constitutionally
elected, puts us in the wrong. . . . If all our hopes are to
be blasted, if the republic is to go down, let us be found to
the last moment standing on the deck with the Constitution
of the United States waving over our heads. . . . The
President of the United States is no emperor, no dictator;
he is clothed with no absolute power. He can do nothing
unless he is backed by power in Congress. The House of
Representatives is largely in the majority against him. In
the Senate he will also be powerless. There will be a majority of four against him. . . . My countrymen, I am not
of those who believe this Union has been a curse up to this
time. . . . But that this Government of our fathers, with all
its defects, comes nearer the object of all good governments
than any other on the face of the earth, is my settled conviction. . . . Have we not at the South as well as at the
North grown great, prosperous, and happy under its op-

eration ? Has any part of the world ever shown such rapid progress in the development of wealth and all the material resources of national power and greatness as the Southern States have under the general Government, notwithstanding all its defects? . . . Some of our public men have failed in their aspirations: that is true, *and from that comes a great part of our troubles.*"

This last observation was received with "prolonged applause," and the feeling in Georgia continued, in various ways, to manifest itself strongly in favor of the Union until, as in the other revolting States, silenced for the time being by violence.

But notwithstanding the undoubted attachment to the Union of the great majority of the people of the South, the conspirators, whose head-quarters were in this city, determined, reckless of consequences, that the work of separation should go on.

"State Sovereignty," "Peaceable Secession," "No Coercion," was their cry, while they threw out the bait of "Reconstruction" to draw in the doubting and to deceive the unwary. The greatest pains seem to have been taken to impress upon the minds of Southern men holding influential positions, especially officers of the army and navy, that the allegiance due from them to their respective States was paramount to that which they owed to the United States; and in this consists the fatal error of thousands of honest Southern men. How strange to us, who feel in every pulse and nerve, in our very souls, that we are citizens,— not merely of this or that State, but *American citizens!* State sovereignty, as understood and proclaimed by Southern radicals, is a fallacy. Need we proof of this? It is abundant and conclusive; and, since I have set out by quoting freely from various sources, and as I wish to group these things, as well for my own as for your satisfaction, I will here cite a few authorities, either of which ought to put this question forever at rest. I commence with extracts

from the letter of George Washington to the President of
Congress, 17th September, 1787, presenting officially to
Congress the Constitution as passed by the Convention of
which he was President. This letter, as a writer in the
National Intelligencer remarks, was prepared and submitted
by Washington for the approval of the Convention, and was
approved by them *unanimously*, paragraph by paragraph:
" It is obviously impracticable in the Federal Government
of these States to secure all rights of *independent sovereignty*
to each, and yet provide for the interests and safety of all.
Individuals entering into society must give up a share of
liberty to preserve the rest. . . . It is at all times difficult
to draw with precision the line between those rights which
must be surrendered and those which must be reserved. . . .
In all our deliberations on this subject, we kept steadily in
our view that which appears to us the greatest interest to
every true American, the *consolidation* of our *Union*, in which
is involved our prosperity, felicity, safety, and, perhaps, our
national existence."

Chief Justice Marshall states his opinion clearly in the
next two extracts : " The Government of the Union is emphatically and truly a Government of the people.   In form
and in substance it emanates from them.   Its powers are
granted by them, and are to be exercised directly on them
and for them."

And again : " The people made the Constitution, and the
people can unmake it.   It is the creature of their will, and
lives only by their will.   But this supreme and irresistible
power to make or unmake resides only in the whole body
of the people, not in any subdivision of them.   The attempt
of any of the parts to exercise it is usurpation, and ought
to be repelled by those to whom the people have delegated
their power of repelling it."

Judge Story is not less explicit and decided in the following : " The Constitution of the United States was ordained
and established, not by the States in their sovereign capaci-

ties, but emphatically, as the preamble of the Constitution declares, by ' The People of the United States.' "

The second clause of the sixth article of the Constitution itself is in the following language : " This Constitution and laws of the United States which shall be made in pursuance thereof, and all treaties made, or which shall be made, under the authority of the United States, shall be the supreme law of the land; and the judges in every State shall be bound thereby, *anything in the Constitution or laws of any State to the contrary notwithstanding.*"

With reference to the question whether a State, under any circumstances, could rightfully secede from the Union, Mr. Madison says : " My opinion is that a reservation of a right to withdraw, if amendments be not decided on under the form of the Constitution within a certain time, is a conditional ratification; that it does not make New York a member of the new Union, and consequently should not be received on that plan. Compacts must be reciprocal; this principle would not in such a case be preserved. The Constitution requires an adoption *in toto* and *forever.*"

In a letter to Mr. Hamilton on the subject, he further says : " The idea of reserving a right to withdraw was started at Richmond, and considered as a conditional ratification, which was itself abandoned as worse than a rejection."

In the year 1850, Mr. Howell Cobb, quoting and endorsing these opinions of Mr. Madison against " the right of a State to secede and thus dissolve the Union," truthfully says : " The policy of our Government, during its whole existence, looks to the continuance and perpetuity of the Union. Its temporary and conditional existence is nowhere impressed either upon its domestic or foreign policy. . . . Now we are told that there is no obligation to observe that Union beyond the pleasure of the parties to it, and that the Constitution can be annulled by the act of any State in the Confederacy. I do not so understand our Government. I feel that I owe my allegiance to a Government possessed of more vitality and strength than that which is drawn from a voluntary obedience to the laws."

It is due to Mr. Cobb that I should state here a historical fact, which certainly ought not to be and will not be forgotten, namely, that while holding a seat in the Cabinet on a salary of $8000 a year, he prepared an elaborate and inflammatory address to the people of his State, in which he counselled an immediate resort to secession. Said he, "I entertain no doubt either of your *right* or your *duty* to secede from the Union."

I have stated that the conspirators had their headquarters in this city. I should add that many of them were under pay of the United States, and until late into the last winter, their leading newspaper organ, the *Constitution*, whose editor was a foreigner of the Hessian order, was sustained at the seat of the general Government. They were all "honorable gentlemen," and ardent advocates of "peace." Of course their request, to be "let alone," could not be disregarded without the danger of serious consequences. They retained their seats in the Cabinet and legislative halls during the day, opposing every measure intended to strengthen and protect the Government, and secretly plotted treason at night. They were keenly averse to the ordering of troops to Washington, and when, in spite of their opposition, several companies of regulars were brought here to secure the safety of the capital, some of them "gnashed their teeth in rage." Here their plans were concocted which were to carry all the slave States out of the Union and give them the city of Washington as their seat of government. They were "honorable gentlemen," and this was to be done "legally," under the authority of "State Sovereignty" and the "Sacred Right of Secession." The forts, arsenals, navy-yards, custom-houses, government deposits, etc., were to be seized only just so fast as the States in which they were located should pass their ordinances of

secession, and the city of Washington was to be taken
only when both Virginia and Maryland should be fairly out
of the Union. For a while they went on quite smoothly,
encountering scarcely the slightest opposition, much of
which success was owing to the ability and foresight of
that celebrated financier, the "honorable" J. B. Floyd, in
managing, while Secretary of War, to leave the fortifications, etc., either without garrisons, or, as in the case of
General Twiggs's command in Texas, under the charge of
officers known to be traitors at heart. True, in some instances they did not wait for the passage of the ordinances
of secession before taking possession of the public property;
and but for the presence of General McClellan and his band
of patriots, no doubt they might bring their tender con-
sciences to consent as "a military necessity" to their occupying Washington at once, notwithstanding that, owing to the
absence of some of her distinguished citizens on a visit to
Colonel Burke, of "l'Hôtel de Lafayette," in New York,
Maryland has not yet "seceded."

Seriously, is there in the history of the world to be found
an account of any rebellion which, in the enormity of its
wickedness, can begin to compare with what we now witness? There is no such record, and there never was so
great a crime committed by a people entitled to be styled
civilized, as that now being perpetrated by the rebels of the
Southern States. It is appalling to contemplate. Think of
the suffering and distress already caused and the still greater
pain and sorrow indescribable which, ere the rebellion is
subdued, must be experienced throughout the length and
breadth of the land, by this most inexcusable and savage
attempt to subvert the mildest and best Government ever
vouchsafed to mortal man.

No wonder that the loyal heart of the nation is bleeding
in agony at this awful spectacle.

No wonder that the Sons of Liberty in countless numbers
are aroused and hastening with stout hearts and strong arms

to the rescue, all resolutely declaring that "*the Union must and shall be preserved.*" Yes, and rest assured the Union will be preserved.

Welcome, thrice welcome, then, say I, to these brave soldiers. On to victory!

"Strike till the last armed foe expires,
Strike for your altars and your fires,
Strike for the green graves of your sires,
God, and your native land."

Let me not be misunderstood. I entertain no hostile feelings against the South. On the contrary, I have always been, and trust I shall ever continue to be, her steadfast friend. I would defend her to the last against every encroachment, and secure to her the uninterrupted enjoyment of all her just rights under the Constitution. Her people are our brethren, and I rejoice to know from personal observation that the feeling of friendship toward them in the North remains unshaken. It is not against them that we contend, but against a band of traitors and conspirators, their oppressors, and for their deliverance. In a word, the war which has been forced upon us, and in which we are engaged, "is not one of aggression, or conquest, or spoliation, or passion, but, in every light in which it can be regarded, it is a war of duty. The struggle is intensely one for national existence."

Very truly yours,

HORATIO KING.

NATHANIEL MITCHELL, ESQ.,
BOSTON, MASSACHUSETTS.

CHAPTER IX.

ADDRESS OF HORATIO KING ON THE WAR.

Delivered at Oxford and Paris, Maine, in August, 1862; never before
published—Vivid Sketch of the Times.

LADIES AND GENTLEMEN,—Unaccustomed as I am to public speaking, I am, nevertheless, glad of the opportunity of
giving expression here, the home of my youth, to the sentiments nearest my heart touching the wicked and uncalled-
for rebellion now threatening the destruction of the best
government upon the face of the earth.

What do we behold? A people numbering more than
twenty millions, all in a condition of unparalleled prosperity, suddenly thrown into a state of war; and for what?
Were any portion suffering under wrongs which could not
have been redressed by the peaceful means provided by the
Constitution? No; the ballot-box was still open to them,
and the loyalty of the great body of the people was yet
unshaken, when a few desperate men, who had long been
plotting the overthrow of the Government in the event of
being unable to control its action, set about to obtain possession of or destroy it by force of arms.

My friends, from that moment there have been but two
parties in this country; one for and the other against the
Union. True, men may differ as to the proper mode of
conducting the war; but all who are not now ready to lend
their countenance and support to the Government in its
efforts to put down this rebellion, I care not whether they
be North or South, are at heart traitors, and should be
treated as such.

It is too late to go into a discussion of the causes of the
war,—at least, any such discussion should be postponed
until the contest is ended. It is enough to know that the

war has been forced upon us, and that we must now either
conquer or be conquered. A permanent division is out of
the question. Were peace proclaimed to-day on the basis
of a dividing line and the acknowledgment of a Southern
Confederacy, two years would not elapse before we should
be again at war more determined and fiercer than ever.

There is in the South, I am sorry to say, a class of men
who have been educated to think themselves the superiors
of Northern men, and especially of our laboring classes,
whose intelligence they underrate and whose courage they
have heretofore doubted. This class is known as the
" Chivalry," and, having secured political control by making
politics their sole study and business, they have unfortunately had it in their power, although in a small minority,
so to shape the course of their State and county organizations as to override the more quiet and law-abiding portion
of the Southern community ; and nothing short of a severe
chastisement will serve to bring them to that state of rational
common-sense and decency which is consistent with republican equality and good neighborhood. Without a sound
drubbing, this class, which is not confined to the male gender,
will never consent to live at peace with us, unless, indeed,
we will agree to be their slaves.

No, gentlemen, there can be no peace now, except
through stern, unrelenting war ; and those among you who
cry "Peace, peace," should be regarded as no better than
rebels in disguise, if they are not so in fact.

Peace, forsooth! Yet we may have peace if we will give
up to the rebels the slave States, the District of Columbia
with its public buildings, the control of the Mississippi, raise
the blockade, and settle quietly down as " hewers of wood
and drawers of water" to this self-inflated Southern chivalry.
Nothing short of this will satisfy them ; and, if you have any
here at the North who are so blinded by partisan spite or so
degraded from innate meanness as to be willing to submit
to such a peace as this, I hope and trust it may be so man-

aged that they may be drafted and forced to go where the bullets of the enemy will put an end to their God-for-saken lives.

I have said it is not now the time to discuss the causes of the war; but I may say that, whatever these causes, they were one and all insufficient to justify this wicked assault on the flag of the Union. There was no subject of controversy which, with sensible men, could not have been adjusted without a resort to arms. The cry of "abolition," raised by the conspirators, was only a pretext. South Carolina, the leader of the rebellion, never lost a slave. The real conspirators had for years been secretly engaged in preparations to "precipitate the South into revolution." Instead of seeking to prevent the election of Lincoln, which they falsely proclaim as a reason for their infidelity, they did all in their power to secure it.

But they really had nothing to fear from his elevation to the Presidency. Had they kept their places in the halls of Congress, instead of retiring in mock dignity and leaving their seats vacant, they would, with the aid of the conservative party of the loyal States, have been able to control every important appointment under the Government, even the members of his Cabinet. Nor would it have been in the power of Congress to pass a single measure tending to interfere with slavery in any State where it exists, nor in the District of Columbia, where it is now forever abolished. Their purpose was first to embarrass and then break up or get control of the Government. Meantime, while State after State was seceding, or proclaiming secession from the Union, armed bands were taking possession of the forts, arsenals, custom-houses, and other Government property in those States, and the determination no doubt was, if possible, thus to carry every slave State out, including Maryland, when the capital itself was to fall into their hands. This they hoped to do before Lincoln's inauguration. All through the winter of 1860–61, still having their head-quarters at Washington,

they were every moment occupied in their work of conspiracy, some of their number being yet in the Cabinet,
where, professing to be entirely loyal, they were unfortunately allowed to remain to a late day. The error is plain
now: it was not so clear then, else they would undoubtedly
have been required to leave long before they did. Nor
would their political organ, the *Constitution* newspaper, have
been so long permitted there, at the very seat of Government, to counsel open rebellion, had the Government or the
people seen, as they now see, that treason, and only rank
treason, was at the bottom of all these proceedings. The
constant cry then was "Peace, peace," and few would believe
that the South would venture beyond a menace against the
Union, which, as they had indulged in this practice, though
in a milder manner, so often before, it was supposed was
resorted to merely for political effect. A great error. Some
few were for the adoption of energetic measures against the
conspirators, but the prominent sentiment, or perhaps hope,
seemed to be that if the shedding of blood could be avoided
all might yet be well. This view, of course, was favored by
all the conspirators and their satellites, who were constantly
on the alert to prevent the Government, as far as lay in their
power, from taking any measures of defence. To my certain knowledge, their utmost influence was exerted to prevent the bringing of troops to Washington, and some of
them were heard to say, when this was finally accomplished,
just prior to the inauguration, that the then Secretary of
War—the patriotic and true-hearted Joseph Holt—would
"be execrated by the South" for his action in producing
this important result, while others declared he "ought
to be placed in a strait jacket." Understand, these professedly "peace" men, or, at least, the most of them, were
not then open traitors, but were boisterous and some of them
sincere in their devotion to the Union; and as their loyalty
had not hitherto been questioned, it is not surprising that
they should have been listened to with a degree of respect.

It was not, in fact, until some time after the inauguration that anything resembling a warlike policy was adopted on the part of the national Government. Mr. Lincoln had assured the country of his stern purpose to see that the rights of the people in every section were protected, and of his earnest desire for the preservation of peace. He had offered positions in his Cabinet to prominent Southern men and given every evidence of a friendly disposition towards the South that any but base traitors could expect or demand; but all to no purpose. The rebellion had become thoroughly rooted in the hearts of the original conspirators, whose motto was "rule or ruin," and the Government and the people were at length compelled to give up all hope of peace, and now, as it were, for the first time, to look hideous war full in the face. If doubt had existed before, there was now no question as to the real purpose of the conspirators, and that the capital was actually in danger.

What was the Government to do? Was it to sit still and patiently wait the arrival of the "Southern Chivalry," who, defeated at the polls, were, Mexican-like, coming to take possession by force of arms? Is there in all the loyal States a single person, not a traitor at heart, who will proclaim himself a dastard by declaring that it was not the imperative duty of the President to make the call for the first seventy-five thousand troops when he did? Does any one now believe that if these decisive measures had not been adopted, Washington would not have fallen into the hands of the rebels? If any such there be, let me tell him he was never more mistaken. I firmly believe that it was their plan to usurp the government, and, once in possession, they relied on sufficient support from the Middle and Western States to enable them to establish themselves permanently therein, thus securing not only their ascendency but the perpetuity of their favorite institution.

And how was this call of the President received by the South? It was at once misrepresented. The people, already greatly excited, were told that, instead of the defence of Washington, "subjugation of the South" was to be the work of the troops thus called into the field. Under this delusion and deception, overawed by armed sentinels, the people of Virginia committed the, to her, fatal error of seceding from the Union. Had she remained firm and forbidden the armed traitors of the Cotton States to pollute, by their footsteps, the soil of the once glorious but now degraded Old Dominion, it is highly probable the rebellion would ere this have been crushed and the country once more united and happy.

Such, however, was not to be our lot, and it was left only for the Government to put forth its strength for a desperate struggle. Most nobly have the people rushed to the rescue. In this bloody and unexpected contest, is it strange that the Government, thus taken by surprise, should commit some mistakes? Certainly not. But, after all, is it not wonderful that so much has been accomplished in the short time we have been engaged in active warfare, considering the gigantic proportions of the rebellion and the savage character of our assailants? Endangered, as we constantly have been and are, by traitors from without and within, the enemy have nevertheless been encircled by a wall of fire, they have been defeated in many a well-fought battle, and the pressure on nearly every side is becoming more and more severe every day. Our navy, soon I trust to be in a condition "to defy the world in arms," has covered itself with glory, our brave officers and soldiers are earning for themselves undying fame, and we who remain at home have but to do our duty in contributing by every means in our power to the support of the holy cause of the Union, and there is no fear of the result.

As in the days of the Revolution, so now we rejoice to see that the gentler sex are in no wise backward in lending a helping hand. With words of encouragement, they are sending their sons, their husbands, and their brothers to the field of strife, themselves in many instances performing the work of husbands and sons and brothers in their absence. While those at home generally manifest an earnest desire to aid the good cause and are thus doing all they can to that end, many have enlisted as nurses for the sick and wounded in the army, and, go where you may in the hospitals, you will find one or more of these angels of mercy, who, by her soothing presence and patient watching, is doing all that a few years ago gave Florence Nightingale so enviable a name throughout the civilized world. All honor to the fair sex for their patriotic devotion and substantial aid in this hour of our country's trial! But what shall we say of their erring sisters of the South, who have so far forgotten what belongs to the female character as to disgrace themselves by insults to our soldiers and by other conduct most unbecoming their sex? Should they be treated as ladies? I think not. They are unworthy of the name. For my own part, I think General Butler deserves great credit in setting an example of rigid punishment for this class of persons. By this I would not be understood as exactly approving the phraseology of his now celebrated order on this subject; not that the females in question receive more punishment than they really deserve by the odious comparison conveyed by its language, but it is open to objection on the ground that it gives his enemies and the enemies of the Union an opportunity so eagerly seized upon by them of misrepresenting its true intent, and thus exciting unjust prejudice. If a woman unsexes and makes of herself a devil, I know of no reason why she should not be treated accordingly. Besides, it is an insult to all deserving the title, to speak of such a female as a "lady;" and so far as I have heard the opinion of ladies upon the order in question, they have been decidedly in its favor. That it would be misconstrued by the rebels might have been anticipated; but there is something ludicrous in the exhibition which grave members of the British Parliament made about this matter, and I am not surprised to observe that this display of holy indignation on their part regarding this and other acts of our officers has furnished a theme for our American Punch which has been well improved. Brother Jonathan, long, lank, and saucy, stands leaning upon his musket, a small black speck appearing upon one side of his nose, while John Bull, beef-fed and pursy, with cane in hand, very pompously calls his attention to this slight speck, apparently without the remotest thought of his own nasal organ, which presents itself a perfect blossom of blotches.

But we can afford to allow the British Government and the British people to entertain any views and make any comments they please in regard to our management of the war, provided they will keep on their own side of the water. We cannot, however, but feel humiliated for England when we see her so ready to extend all the aid she dares to give to the rebels, thereby plainly showing that she is not only desirous of witnessing the downfall of our Government, but the establishment of a Southern oligarchy, whose foundation corner-stone is slavery. The Queen, I am happy to see, steadily maintains her declared purpose to observe neutrality with reference to our domestic concerns. I entertain for her a high respect, and if she consults the happiness of her own people and that of her amiable son, the Prince of Wales, who is to succeed her on the throne, she will never allow of any active interference, which would be certain to bring on a war between the United States and Great Britain.

"Whom the gods would destroy they first make mad." The conspirators confidently counted both on foreign aid and on division in the free States. Hitherto they have received less of foreign assistance than they thought themselves sure of ere they plunged the South into revolution, and they have been almost wholly disappointed in respect to division at the North. They have been equally at fault in the estimate they had formed of the resources of the loyal States and of the courage of our citizen soldiers, especially of the Northern and Middle sections of the Union. It may be reasonably doubted whether they would have ventured on rebellion had they possessed correct information on all these points. But this was not possible, and, having carefully calculated their own strength, which, it must be admitted, we have ourselves underrated, and trusting to their erroneous judgment on these points, they rushed madly into revolution.

Nevertheless, if the contest is prolonged many months longer, there is great danger that their calculations respecting foreign interference and division among ourselves may yet be realized. It behooves us, therefore, to be thoroughly united and to extend our utmost aid to the Government, thus to secure a vigorous prosecution and speedy termination of the war. Let us keep in view the fact that we are fighting, not for the abolition of slavery, but for the preservation of the Constitution and the Union. The danger is that the very division on which the rebels counted may yet be produced, and everything lost by the reckless and determined pressure of certain extremists in the free States for a proclamation of immediate emancipation of the slaves throughout the South, and for the arming of the slaves to fight against their masters. Will not this class of our citizens take warning in season and cease embarrassing the Government? The President has repeatedly announced his policy on this subject, and it is such as commends itself to the favor of every intelligent and well-disposed friend of the Union. If slavery suffers or is totally destroyed as a consequence of the war, no matter; this is all right, and the slave-owners must look for redress to those who commenced the war. Wherever the slaves can be employed to advantage as laborers in the army, it should of course be done, but to think of ever raising the negro to a social equality with the white man is arrant folly.

I was struck by some remarks in a letter written a few weeks ago by the Honorable George E. Badger, of North

Carolina, and late United States Senator from that State. It is addressed to Honorable Mr. Ely, member of Congress from New York. He says:

"Mr. Ely, think a moment. We have been invaded by an enemy as unrelenting and ferocious as the hordes under Attila and Alaric, who overran the Roman Empire. He comes to rob us, to murder our people, to insult our women, to emancipate our slaves, and is now preparing to add a new element to this most atrocious aggression and involve us in the direful horrors of a civil war. He proposes nothing less than our entire destruction, the total desolation of our country, universal emancipation,—not from love of the slave, but from hatred to us; 'to crush us,' to 'wipe out the South,' to involve us in irremediable misery and hopeless ruin."

Now, so far as the United States Government is concerned, I would ask, Is there in all this really one word of truth? Let us see. In one sense it is true, the armies of the Union have 'invaded' the South. Chivalrous South Carolina pronounced it an "invasion" when the Government sought to convey, by a merchant steamer, food to the famishing little garrison at Fort Sumter, and fired upon that vessel. So, when the President first called for troops to protect the capital, the secessionists of Maryland had the effrontery to proclaim that their State was "invaded" by the transit of these troops to Washington; and our brave soldiers were stoned and shot down like dogs in the streets of Baltimore, so that, when they reached Washington, many of them were bloody and bruised and maimed, as I saw them in the city hospital the next day, while the lifeless remains of others were returned to their friends in Massachusetts, and others still left to die in Baltimore.

And so, too, the Virginia rebels cried "invasion" when a detachment of our army moved across the river to Arlington Heights and Alexandria, taking position there as the best

6

possible means of preventing the rebels from destroying the city; and, in the act of removing a secession flag from one of the public houses in Alexandria, the brave Colonel Ellsworth fell dead with a bullet through his body from the gun of a rebel, who, thanks to young Brownell, instantly paid the penalty of his crime with his own life.

In this sense, and this only, has the South been "invaded." Invasion is a hostile entrance upon the territory or premises of another, and no such invasion has been made by the United States forces, who go, not as enemies nor with hostile intent, but as friends equally of the North and the South, to assert the rights of all under the Constitution and to uphold the flag of the Union. If the people of the South would lay down their arms and submit to the Constitution and the laws, not another gun would be discharged nor sword unsheathed against them.

It is untrue that either the loyal citizens or the soldiers of the Union are "unrelenting and ferocious" toward the South. On the contrary, the almost entire absence of this feeling is one of the most remarkable features of this lamentable contest.

They do not go to "rob," nor "murder," to "insult their women," nor, as a primary object, "to emancipate their slaves." One of the most serious complaints against our army, heretofore, has been that, instead of subsisting our troops as far as possible upon the rebels,—thus making the latter bear a part of the expense required to subdue them,—our generals have kept guard over their property while our troops have been suffering for the actual necessaries of life. To speak of the act of our soldiers in taking the lives of rebels in arms as "murder" is a misnomer; and as to "insulting their women"—this charge has already been disposed of. Neither is it true that our Government, or any considerable number of our citizens, are for "universal emancipation." Let the South return to its loyalty to-day, and not a slave need be set free without the consent of his

master. Let the seceded States wheel again into line, and
instantly they will resume all their rights as sovereign and
independent States under the Constitution.

No, no, Mr. Badger, "think a moment," and see if you
are not charging the United States Government and the
brave troops who are fighting for your liberty and that of
your posterity, as well as ours, with entertaining sentiments
regarding emancipation which are common only to a small
party of extremists in the free States. I exceedingly regret
that you have even this much upon which to found your
charge, and I would fain hope that, discovering from your
own misconceptions the great injury they are inflicting on the
Union cause by their fanatical course, this party of extremists
will see the propriety of hereafter supporting the sound policy
of the national administration, instead of doing all in their
power to embarrass and turn it from the even tenor of its way.

My friends, I appear before you in no partisan spirit, for,
until the rebellion is put down, I desire to recognize no party
at the North other than the one great party of the Union.
It will then be time enough to look after party organizations,
and, if need be, settle up old scores. He who is not for us
is against us. I can hardly conceive it possible, and yet I
am told there are some, even in this State, who actually
sympathize with the rebellion and rejoice in its success.
We have in Washington many persons of this class,—some,
I have no doubt, still subsisting on the bounty of the Government; but being, as I believe without exception, of Southern
birth and generally careful to avoid exposure to arrest, they
have been tolerated there with a degree of patience, I must
say, scarcely compatible with public safety. Occasionally
one has been sent to the old capitol prison for a short time,
and with effect decidedly salutary, not only upon himself but
upon all his sympathizing friends in the city. Some should
long since have been made to join those of their brethren
who took themselves off to Richmond before the commencement of hostilities, in the fond expectation of soon returning

in triumph; but hitherto the Government has treated the great body of these rebel sympathizers with marked leniency, so they have been suffered to remain undisturbed. With Christian fortitude and patience we can bear this in the border States and the District of Columbia; but in the free States the Government should make short work of them. I care not if not only the *habeas corpus* be suspended for their benefit, but I am not sure it would not be a wholesome remedy and excellent caution, here and there, to have another kind of *suspension* practised upon them. I know that all such traitors, and they are nothing but traitors, are professedly great sticklers for the Constitution. They are awfully shocked at any act of the Government, no matter how necessary to self-preservation, which they may regard as in the least extra-Constitutional; while at the same time they have no hesitation in cheering on the bogus President and his faithful minions in their efforts utterly to annihilate the Constitution and spread destruction throughout the land. Such creatures would dance over the graves of their mothers; they should be branded with infamy, and by means either of bolts or hemp speedily put beyond the pale of decent society.

But there certainly can be few, if any, such in this State. The atmosphere is too pure for them. Judging from the alacrity with which the noble sons of Maine, led on by our distinguished generals,—Howard, Jameson, Berry, Prince, —and other able officers, have sprung to arms, it is difficult to believe that any among you are so base as to harbor even the remotest thought of sympathy with treason. One would suppose that every heart would thrill with joy and pride at the glorious spectacle of our brave troops thus marching on to duty and to victory. I shall never forget the pride and delight with which I hailed their first appearance in Washington, at a time when it seemed that any night the rebels might bring their guns to bear upon and shell the city. Honor, all honor, say I, to our brave officers and soldiers.

Let us strain every nerve to strengthen and encourage them in their holy work of restoring the Union. I have said they are marching on to victory. This cannot, must not be doubted. The Union must be preserved. Slavery or no slavery, the people of the United States are one family, the territory they occupy is their own country, and this country can have but one supreme government,—the Government of the old Union,—whose Star-spangled Banner shall ever continue a token of joy to all lovers of freedom throughout the world.

CHAPTER X.

REMINISCENCES OF THE EARLY STAGES OF THE REBELLION.

Few Persons Apprehend Serious Trouble—Only a Small Number of Active Union Men in Washington—Extracts of a Fierce Letter from John D. Ashmore, Member of Congress from South Carolina—Letters from Edward Everett and ex-President Pierce—Alarm now in the City—Resolution of the Senate appointing a Committee to Investigate Cause—Testimony of General Scott, Jacob Thompson, the Mayor, Governor Hicks, of Maryland, and others—Letters of ex-President Buchanan—Star of the West—Sharp Correspondence between Holt and Thompson—Resignation of Members of the Cabinet—Senator Yulee's Threats—Midnight Interview with General Scott.

In recurring to the horrors of the war and of the few months preceding it, as experienced by us here at the capital, it has often occurred to me that, if possible, I suffered more from the dread apprehension of the impending conflict, and the shock upon shock at the seizure of the forts, arsenals, custom-houses, post-offices, and other government property by the rebels in the last months of President Buchanan's administration, than at any subsequent period during the war. No sooner was the election of Mr. Lincoln announced —and it was known throughout the country on the evening of election-day, the 6th of November, 1860—than the threatening signs appeared in all parts of the South, and the secessionists everywhere, urged on by the *Constitution* news-paper of this city,—nominally under the editorship of William M. Browne, an Englishman, but really the mouth-piece and under the direction of the leaders of the rebellion,—set to work actively to effect a withdrawal of all the slave States from the Union.

This newspaper, having been regarded as the organ of the administration, still sustained this character to a greater or less extent, particularly as it was the continued recipient of the Government advertisements, which furnished its principal means of support; and this naturally gave rise to doubt as to the course the administration intended to pursue in the momentous crisis now at hand. But Messrs. Cobb, Floyd, and Thompson were yet members of the Cabinet, the Southern element was greatly in the ascendant here generally, and the time had not come for so decisive a step even as to withdraw from that paper the government patronage, notwithstanding I know that soon after the election it became a source of regret and mortification to many here that such a sheet should be allowed to draw its main sustenance from the Government it was seeking to destroy. When this patronage, some weeks afterward, was finally withheld by order of the President, the paper immediately ceased to exist; but so long as it was continued, it not only operated to the injury of the administration, but did great harm also to the Union cause North and South, for the reason before mentioned, that the public had come so generally to regard it as the organ of the administration.

A most remarkable fact of this period—a fact which, in making up a judgment upon President Buchanan's administration of affairs at this time, should not be forgotten—was, that few persons comparatively, either in the North or West, appeared to apprehend any serious trouble, regarding the threats and movements of the secessionists as only a repetition—in an aggravated form, to be sure—of what we had seen on former occasions, and all for political effect. Nor was this feeling confined to one party: it pervaded all the free States. Hence, while the disunionists were everywhere active, and endeavoring to disseminate the idea that they were not only in favor with the administration, but with the Democratic party at large, the great body of the true friends of the administration stood aloof, never coming near the President or offering counsel. How well I recollect that all through the month of November I thought almost everybody in the free States was asleep. Here we were, a small number then of active Union men, in the very hotbed of the conspiracy, and surrounded by a host of bold and determined disunionists bent on "rule or ruin." The great mass of those here who at heart were true to the Union were passive rather than otherwise, because they did not care to expose themselves to the charge of "Black Republicanism," which was then the potent missile levelled by the secessionists against every person who dared openly to oppose them. Was it strange, therefore, that any one, seeing and feeling the real danger ahead, should have reached out after help? that with such feelings one should cast around for patriotic statesmen to come to the rescue? Humble as I was, occupying then a subordinate position in the Post-Office Department, so impressed was I by the appalling aspect of affairs, that I seemed to be impelled by a power beyond myself to "cry aloud and spare not;" and, departing from my previous rule of appropriate modesty,—to which it may be thought I have not returned,—I made bold to address earnest appeals to distinguished men, far and near, to exert their influence toward averting the threatened outbreak. The following extract of a letter from a Southern member of Congress may be taken as a specimen of the encouragement I received from that quarter. It bears date November 5, 1860, the day before the Presidential election :

"To the latter part of your letter I reply frankly. On my entrance into Congress it was as a constitutional Union-loving man. From the days of my childhood I have loved the Union,—during youth and manhood I still loved it. . . . If Lincoln be elected, as I have no doubt he will be, and the South submit to his inauguration, then are they, in my judgment, cowards and traitors to their own rights, unworthy of any other condition than that that awaits them,—inferiors, provincialists, and subjects. Lincoln will never be the President of thirty-three confederate States. Men like myself, who for a lifetime have fought the extreme ultraisms of the South and the mad fanaticism of the North, will not permit Abe Lincoln's banner, inscribed with 'higher law,' 'negro equality,' 'irrepressible conflict,' and 'final emancipation,' to wave over us. We have and do deserve a more glorious destiny. . . . Three hundred thousand swords are *now* ready to leap from their scabbards in support of a Southern confederacy. Fort Moultrie will be in the hands of the South on the morning of the fourth day of March next. Our women and children are ready and eager for the conflict, and would kick us out of our houses if we basely and tamely yield again."

The above was evidently not intended, nor was it regarded, as strictly a private letter. All such information, when received, was promptly communicated to those in authority. It was important, of course, that the President himself should not only be kept advised of the actions of the disunionists, but that he should discountenance their nefarious proceedings, and that his hands should be strengthened by support from patriotic citizens everywhere; and to this end it was the desire to have placed before him, as far as possible, the opinions and advice of citizens in whose judgment he might confide. Here is a letter to me from the Hon. Edward Everett, who, it will be recollected, had just passed through the canvass as candidate for Vice-President on the conservative ticket, with the Hon. John Bell for President:

"BOSTON, 27th November, 1860.

"MY DEAR SIR,—I share the opinion of your correspondent as to the very critical state of public affairs, and I feel it to be the duty of every good citizen, by word and deed, to contribute his mite, however small, to rescue the country from impending peril,—by far the greatest that ever threatened it.

"The cause assigned by your correspondent as that which prevents Union men from affording the President their support and counsel in this crisis will not prevent my doing it, but ordinary self respect under the notorious circumstances of the case requires that my views should not be obtruded upon him unasked. Whenever they are specially invited by the President himself, or any one in his confidence, they will be cheerfully and respectfully given.

"I remain, my dear sir, with much regard,

"Very truly yours,

"EDWARD EVERETT."

The following letter is from ex-President Pierce. Immediately on its receipt I called on Mr. Secretary Thompson, who with his own pen prepared a preface agreeably to General Pierce's suggestion, and the letter to the Secretary appeared in the *Constitution* of the next morning:

"ANDOVER, MASS., November 28, 1860.

"MY DEAR SIR,—I have received your kind, earnest letter, and participate strongly in your apprehensions. To my vision the political horizon shuts down close and darkly. It may be that light is to break through somewhere, but I do not discern the quarter whence it is to come. I had occasion to write a friendly letter to Secretary Thompson (Interior) a day or two since, and expressed to him briefly my convictions and fears and hopes in relation to the present state of public affairs. I did not expect that letter to be published, but the blackness is gathering so fast that if anything can be done to save our glorious Union it must be done speedily, and, in my judgment, at the North chiefly. If you call on the Secretary he will show you that letter, and if he thinks the publication of it would be useful, he can use it as he pleases. The truth must appear that it was written in the course of friendly correspondence, and not with a view to publication. Among intelligent, reflecting men, alarm is evidently increasing here daily. One decisive step in the way of *coercion* will drive out all the slave-labor States. Of that I entertain no doubt. My suggestion about the tone and temper of Congress, and the importance of temperate words and actions might possibly have some degree of good influence, and there is, perhaps, more hope that the letter might be serviceable just at this juncture at the North; but it was hastily written, and my friend, the Secretary, must judge. If you call on him, show him this note.

"In haste, your friend,

"FRANKLIN PIERCE."

It was all to no purpose: the tide rolled on. Congress soon assembled, and became the arena of the fiercest declamation and conflict. Everything like coercion on the part of the general Government was denounced and resisted. Mr. Hindman, of Arkansas, said in the House, "I am willing to give gentlemen a chance to try steel if they prefer it." This was in debate on the bill to amend the acts of 1795 and 1807, so as to authorize the President to accept the services of volunteers, etc., called a "force bill." "This bill," said the chairman having it in charge, "only comes up in the morning hour." Mr. Cochrane, of New York, replied, "If you pass this bill it will be the mourning hour of this republic." "A most ill-timed, unwise, and iniquitous measure," said Mr. Botts,—not an extreme man,—from Virginia. "If there be any hope of a restoration of peace," said Mr. Babcock, from the same State, "it must be in the defeat of these force bills." And they were finally all defeated.

Treason was openly proclaimed in the Senate, if not in the House; State after State "seceded," and the members and senators thereof, with mock solemnity, resigned their seats and withdrew from the halls. The Secretary of the Treasury, Howell Cobb, resigned on the 10th of December; the Secretary of State, General Cass, on the 14th; and the Secretary of War, J. B. Floyd, on the 29th of that month, followed by the Secretary of the Interior, Jacob Thompson, on the 8th of January.

Alarm continued to increase, and on the 26th of January, 1861, the following resolution was referred to the select committee of five appointed by the House of Representatives on the 9th of that month, Hon. W. A. Howard, of Michigan, being its chairman:

"*Resolved*, That the select committee of five be instructed to inquire whether any secret organization hostile to the Government of the United States exists in the District of Columbia; and, if so, whether any official or employé of the city of Washington, or any employés or officers of the Federal Government, in the executive or judicial departments, are members thereof."

The committee say that they entered upon the investigation under a deep sense of the importance and the intrinsic difficulty of the inquiry. They took the testimony of a great many persons, including that of General Scott, ex-Secretary Jacob Thompson, Colonel Berret, mayor, Dr. Blake, Commissioner of Public Buildings, and Governor Hicks and ex-Governor Lowe, of Maryland. I had occasion, several years ago, to prepare for one of the public journals a synopsis of the report and testimony. It is a curious book, especially when viewed in the light of subsequent events. The mayor was the first witness called to the stand. He said he had not " been able to ascertain the slightest ground for any apprehension of any foray or raid upon the city of Washington." He knew about an organization called the "National Volunteers," which he said was not " a political organization;" that it was composed of citizens whom he knew to be " not only respectable," but a great many of them " stake-holding citizens, who would scorn to do anything that would bring reproach upon the city." Nevertheless, if I am not mistaken, the larger part of them, including their " senior officer," left Washington and joined the rebellion.

The Commissioner of Public Buildings also said he " could see no real ground to apprehend danger," but that he had taken care to see that the Capitol was not blown up; that examinations were made every night, " by going through it, up and down, all through the cellar and every place," and that in the daytime he had his men placed about all the main doors, " so that they might know what came in and what went out."

Ex-Governor Lowe, who afterward, I think, left his State to assist in the rebellion, denied any knowledge of an organization in the District of Columbia " having for its object the taking or holding any of the public property here, as against the United States;" but he said, " I have not the slightest doubt that, if Maryland does secede, she will claim her rights here, and I will advocate them." "So far as the possession of the District is concerned?" a member inquired. He answered, "Yes, sir,—peaceably, if possible,—forcibly only as a last resort,—that is, provided Maryland shall resume her State sovereignty."

Mr. Jacob Thompson said, "Soon after the Presidential election it was a question frequently discussed by individuals in my presence, in which discussion I participated, as to the mode by which the inauguration of Mr. Lincoln could be defeated, or, in other words, how the rights of the South could be maintained in the Union. I heard some discussion as to organizing a force by which his inauguration could be prevented," but he believed this was now given up.

Dr. Cornelius Boyle, "senior officer" of the "National Volunteers," said he knew there was no unlawful purpose whatever entertained by that organization; that it was nothing more nor less than a military company, numbering between two hundred and fifty and two hundred and eighty names, and that it was not a secret organization. He admitted that he drafted and presented a set of resolutions, the first of which declared that "we will stand by and defend the South, and that under no circumstances will we assume a position of hostility to her interests;" and the fourth that "we will act, in the event of the withdrawal of Maryland and Virginia from the Union, in such manner as shall best secure ourselves and those States from the evils of a foreign and hostile government within and near their borders."

Cypriani Fernandini and O. K. Hillard, of Baltimore, testified that there were military organizations in that city, numbering, the latter believed, not less than six thousand, whose object was to prevent armed bodies of men from passing through Maryland to the capital. Philip P. Dawson, of Baltimore, stated that he had it from good authority that it was their object also to make an attack upon the capital and prevent the inauguration of Mr. Lincoln.

General Scott's testimony tended to show that there was great concern for the capital in almost every part of the country. Many letters were received by him daily, warning him to put the city in a state of defence. Some of these professed to give the plans of the conspirators, and pointed out means of detection. He said, " These letters, from the broad surface whence they come, either prove or seem to indicate a conspiracy for one of two purposes at least,—either for mischief or creating alarm." One writer, signing himself " Union," from South Carolina, concluded his letter, " Would give my name, but if found out would have to *swing*."

Governor Hicks, on the 3d of January, issued an address to the people of Maryland, in which he said:

"I have been repeatedly warned by persons having the opportunity to know, and who are entitled to the highest confidence, that the secession leaders in Washington have resolved that the Border States, and especially Maryland, shall be precipitated into secession with the Cotton States before the 4th of March. They have resolved to seize the Federal capital and public archives, so that they may be in a position to be acknowledged by foreign governments as the United States ; and the assent of Maryland is necessary, as the District of Columbia would revert to her in case of a dissolution of the Union. The plan contemplates forcible opposition to Mr. Lincoln's inauguration, and consequently civil war upon Maryland soil, and a transfer of its horrors from the States which are to provoke it."

Again, there had been some interviews as well as correspondence between the commissioners of some of the Southern States and himself; and Governor Hicks said that much of the opinion he had formed in regard to a contemplated movement such as he had apprehended had grown out of these interviews and other corroborative circumstances. One of these commissioners, Judge Handy, from Mississippi, had said, among other things, that Mr. Lincoln and Mr. Hamlin would never be installed in office. He had also received letters from several gentlemen, and verbal statements from others in whom he had the fullest confidence, all going to convince him that he was not mistaken in his apprehensions, although he now thought that the hostile organization referred to had probably been disbanded. On the 14th of February the committee made their report, in which they said, "If the purpose was at any time entertained of forming an organization, secret or open, to seize the District of Columbia, attack the capital, or prevent the inauguration of Mr. Lincoln, it seems to have been rendered contingent upon the secession of either Maryland or Virginia, or both, and the sanction of these States." They also declared it as their unanimous opinion that the evidence produced before them did not prove the existence of a *secret* organization, here or elsewhere, hostile to the Government, having for its object, upon its own responsibility, an attack upon the capital or any of the public property here, or an interruption of any of the functions of the Government. I nevertheless believe that it was the determination of the conspirators, if possible, to take possession of the capital, a determination depending, it is quite probable, on the secession of Virginia and Maryland, both of which States they hoped to see unite their fortunes with the " Southern Confederacy." But Maryland did not come up to time; the flying artillery was brought here, and it was then too late to attempt a *coup d'état* for the possession of the capital and the public archives. Inasmuch as Mr. Buchanan refers to this subject in one of his letters, which, with the exception of a few words, I propose to give entire, I will introduce it in this place. It will be observed that he did not apprehend any serious danger to the city, although he acted wisely in ordering the troops here.

                    "WHEATLAND, April 21, 1861.

   "MY DEAR SIR,—I presume, from your letter to the *New York Times*, we shall not agree as to the existence of any serious danger to the inauguration of Mr. Lincoln on the 4th of March, 1861. The truth is, when I first heard the reports circulated in the early part of the previous session, I kept my eye upon the subject and had my own means of information.

I had no apprehension of danger for some time before the report of the committee, but the stake was so vast I yielded to the members of the Cabinet and ordered the troops to Washington. Virginia was at that time as loyal a State as any in the Union, and the Peace Convention which she originated was still in session. But we need not discuss this question. . . . While with you I should be very unwilling to fall into line under —— as a leader of the Democratic party, yet I know I shall never be condemned to such an ordeal. I am as firm and as true a Democrat of the Jefferson and Jackson school as I have ever been in my life. The principles of Democracy grew out of the Constitution of the United States, and must endure as long as that sacred instrument. I firmly believe that the Federal Government can only be successfully administered on these principles; and although I may not live to see it, yet I shall live and die in the hope that the party, purified and refined by severe experience, will yet be triumphant. Whilst these are my opinions, I obtrude them on no person, but, like yourself, have withdrawn from party politics. . . .

"Very respectfully, your friend,
"JAMES BUCHANAN."

But to return to the winter of 1861. The contest in both houses was continued daily, but I do not propose to recite further what occurred there, exept in reference to a resolution which called forth a report from the committee on military affairs of the House, of which the Hon. Benjamin Stanton, of Ohio, was chairman; and I notice this report because of the reference to it in the following letter from Mr. Buchanan:

"WHEATLAND, NEAR LANCASTER, 12th November, 1861.

"MY DEAR SIR,—You will confer a great favor upon me if you can obtain a half-dozen copies of Mr. Stanton's report from the committee on military affairs, made on the 18th of February, 1861 (No. 85), relative to the arms alleged to have been stolen and sent to the South by Floyd. This report, with the remarks of Mr. Stanton when presenting it, ought to have put this matter at rest, and it did so, I believe, so far as Congress was concerned. It has, however, recently been repeated by Cameron, Reverdy Johnson, and others, and I desire these copies to send to different parts of the Union, so that the falsehood may be refuted by the record. I am no further interested in the matter than that if the charge were true it might argue a want of care on my part. . . .

"I learn from those who read Forney's *Press* that Stanton (Edwin M.) is the counsel and friend of McClellan, who is, I trust and hope, 'the coming man.'

"I have materials put together which will constitute, unless I am greatly mistaken, not merely a good defence, but a triumphant vindication, of my administration. You must not be astonished some day to find in print portraits drawn by myself of all those who ever served in my Cabinet. I think I know them all perfectly, unless it may be Stanton.

                "From your friend, very respectfully,
                              "JAMES BUCHANAN."

A letter of somewhat earlier date refers to a controversy between Mr. Holt and Mr. Thompson:

                "WHEATLAND, 18th September, 1861.

"MY DEAR SIR,—You recollect the correspondence between Mr. Holt and Mr. Thompson. The last letter of Mr. Thompson to Mr. Holt was published in the tri-weekly *National Intelligencer* of March 19, 1861, and was dated at Oxford on March 11th. I should be much obliged to you if you could procure me a copy of this reply. . . .

"How Mr. Holt came to be so far mistaken in his letter of May 31st to Kentucky as to state that the revolutionary leaders greeted me with all-hails to my face, I do not know. The truth is that after the message of the 3rd of December they were alienated from me, and after I had returned the insolent letter of the first South Carolina commissioners to them, I was attacked by Jefferson Davis and his followers on the floor of the Senate, and all political and social intercourse between us ceased. Had the Senate confirmed my nomination of the 2nd of January of a collector for the port of Charleston, the war would probably have commenced in January instead of May. . . .

                "From your friend, very respectfully,
                              "JAMES BUCHANAN."

Some time in the latter part of February or the beginning of March, 1861, Mr. Thompson made a speech in Mississippi, in which he said: "As I was writing my resignation I sent a despatch to Judge Longstreet that the *Star of the West* was coming with reinforcements. The troops were thus put on their guard, and when the *Star of the West* arrived she received a rude welcome from booming cannon, and soon beat a retreat. I was rejoiced that the vessel

was not sunk, but I was still more rejoiced that the concealed trick, first conceived by General Scott and adopted
by Secretary Holt, but countermanded by the President
when too late, proved a failure." Mr. Holt, quoting the
above, wrote under the date of March 5 a scathing letter to
the editors of the *Intelligencer*, saying, "We have here a
distinct and exultant avowal on the part of the Honorable
Secretary, that while yet a member of the Cabinet he disclosed to those in open rebellion against the United States
information which he held under the seal of a confidence
that from the beginning of our history as a nation had
never been violated." He went on to show, by correspondence between Mr. Thompson and the President, that the
sending of the *Star of the West* was done with the President's sanction and after full consultation in the Cabinet;
that the " countermand" spoken of was not more cordially
sanctioned by the President than it was by General Scott
and himself; and the order countermanding the sailing
of that vessel was given, not because of any dissent from
the order on the part of the President, but because of a
letter received that day from Major Anderson, stating in
effect that he regarded himself as secure in his position, and
yet more because of intelligence, which late on Saturday
evening reached the Department, that a heavy battery had
been erected among the sand-hills at the entrance of Charleston harbor, which would probably destroy any unarmed
vessel (and such was the *Star of the West*) which might
attempt to make its way up to Fort Sumter. This important
information satisfied the Government that there was no
present necessity for sending reinforcements, and that when
sent they should go, not in a vessel of commerce, but in a
man-of-war.

Mr. Thompson responded March 11, indignantly denying,
not that he sent the despatch, but that he acted on official
information, or that he had divulged any Cabinet secret.
He said, " On the morning of the 8th [of January] the

Constitution newspaper contained a telegraphic despatch
from New York that the *Star of the West* had sailed from
that port, with two hundred and fifty soldiers on board,
bound for Fort Sumter. This was the very first intimation
I had received from any quarter that additional troops had
been ordered to be sent. This information to me was not
'official;' it was, in fact, conveyed with electric speed to
every part of the confederacy, known to be true by every
well-informed man in the city of Washington as soon as
known by me."

In his letter of resignation he had intimated that the *Star
of the West* expedition had been fitted out without his knowledge, in violation of an express understanding; but the
President in his reply denied this, saying that on Monday,
31st December, he had suspended orders which had been
issued by the War and Navy Departments to send the
Brooklyn with reinforcements to Fort Sumter, at the same
time promising that these orders should not be renewed
without being previously considered and decided in Cabinet.
He proceeds :

"I called a special Cabinet meeting on Wednesday, 2d January, 1861,
in which the question of sending reinforcements to Fort Sumter was
amply discussed both by yourself and others. The decided majority was
against you. At this moment the answer of the South Carolina commissioners to my communication of 31st December was received and
read. It produced much indignation among the members of the Cabinet.
After a further brief conversation I employed the following language :
'It is now all over, and reinforcements must be sent.' Judge Black said,
at the moment of my decision, that after this letter the Cabinet would be
unanimous, and I heard no dissenting voice. . . . You are certainly mistaken in saying that 'no conclusion was reached.' In this your recollection is entirely different from that of your oldest colleagues in the Cabinet.
Indeed, my language was so unmistakable that the Secretaries of War and
the Navy proceeded to act upon it without any further intercourse with
myself than what you heard or might have heard me say."

Finally, in Mr. Holt's rejoinder to Mr. Thompson's, under
date of 25th March, he spoke of the absurdity of his (Mr.

Thompson's) resigning his commission simply on an anonymous telegraphic report, adding that "such undoubted proofs (of the correctness of the report) could have been had on the 8th of January at Washington only from the President, members of the Cabinet, or others having confidential relations with the Government. . . . So far as the moral aspects of the question are concerned, I deem it wholly unimportant whether the information was derived from official or private sources. In either ease it was alike his (Mr. T.'s) duty, as a faithful officer, to have withheld it from those who sought it at his hands for purposes of hostile action against the Government of the United States."

It is but fair toward Mr. Thompson to say, that personally he and the President parted on perfectly friendly terms, although in the matter of this controversy it is equally true that Mr. Buchanan did not sustain him.

Next as to the bearing of the secessionists toward President Buchanan. In his stirring and patriotic letter of May 31, 1861, to J. F. Speed, Esq., of Kentucky, Mr. Holt held the following language: "The atrocious acts enumerated" (the seizure of forts, arsenals, etc., and the surrender of an entire military department by a general, to the keeping of whose honor it had been confided—meaning General Twiggs, in Texas, who was summarily dismissed by the order of President Buchanan "for treachery to the flag of his country") "were acts of war, and might all have been treated as such by the late administration; but the President patriotically cultivated peace,—how anxiously and how patiently the country well knows. While, however, the revolutionary leaders greeted him with all-hails to his face, they did not the less diligently continue to whet their swords behind his back. Immense military preparations were made, so that when the moment for striking at the Government of the United States arrived, the revolutionary States leaped into the contest clad in full armor."

One thing is certain, if the leaders in the rebellion did

not greet the President "with all-hails to his face," they beset him, many of them, to the last. Undoubtedly there was less of perfect freedom of communication between them after his annual message of the 3d of December, but they followed him up, and sought to control his action to the extent of their power, until his term expired.

And now about the removal of Major Beauregard from West Point. I wish I had the notes which passed between Mr. Slidell and the President on the subject, to insert here; but as it appeared that Mr. Holt could not find them among his papers, it is to be feared they are lost. It is amusing to observe that while the Secretary of War was arranging to ship some of his "big guns" to the South, Senator Slidell was equally diligent in having one at least transferred to a most important position at the North; and both came to grief in much the same way,—by running against "Old Buck." If I am not mistaken, Major Beauregard, whose rank did not entitle him to the appointment, had hardly more than reached West Point before the order for his removal was made by Secretary Holt, then recently placed at the head of the War Department, and Senator Slidell doubtless thought, when he wrote the President—as he did, I have reason to believe, in an imperious manner— that the latter would disavow the act of removal and reinstate Major Beauregard, so that he could have the opportunity of teaching the cadets at West Point not only "how to shoot," "but where to shoot." Instead, however, of disavowing it, he, no doubt, gave the Senator to understand, in no equivocal language, that he as President was responsible for it, probably without saying whether the Secretary brought the matter to his attention before the order was made or not. This, of course, was a fatal offence.

The same spirit was also manifested in reference to the postal service. Before speaking of this, however, I will refer to one other fact connected with the administration of the War Department. A short time before the withdrawal of the Florida senators, they made a communication, either to the President or to the Secretary of War, requesting to be advised as to the particulars and extent of the armament of the Government fortifications in that State. It is hardly necessary to say that Secretary Holt declined to furnish this information.

The ordinance of secession was passed in Florida on the 11th of January, and her senators withdrew about the 21st of that month; on which day the Postmaster-General made an order abolishing the post-office at Pensacola. As soon as this became known, Mr. Yulee, late senator from that State, but now a citizen of "the Southern Confederacy," called at the Post-office Department and requested to see or be served with a copy of the order of discontinuance. His request was politely refused. I do not remember whether it was on this occasion or previously that he jocosely intimated to the officer, thus unmindful of his wishes, that a rope might, at some day not far distant, be serviceable to him; but I well recollect that officer replied that he would esteem it a great favor then to be elevated in some position sufficiently commanding to enable him to proclaim to the whole country his opinion of secession and its wicked abettors.*

---

* This order may still possess interest as an item of history, and it is now for the first time brought to light, as follows: "Whereas, an armed body of men from the State of Alabama, acting under authority of its Governor and upon the invitation of the Governor of Florida, have taken possession of the navy-yard and of parts of the forts of the harbor of Pensacola, in the State of Florida, and still retain them in defiance of the rights of the Government of the United States; and whereas, the officers and troops constituting the garrison of Fort Pickens in said harbor, and who are citizens of the United States and in the service of its Government, are by said armed body of men prevented from communicating with the shore and with the post-office of Pensacola; and whereas, the Department has reliable information that attempts on the part of said garrison to correspond with the Government at Washington have been defeated by the intervention of said armed

There was another instance of like character which occurs to me. A route agent by the name of West, on one of the railroads in Virginia, having been removed, the Honorable Albert G. Jenkins, member of Congress from that State, who was afterward killed at the head of guerillas in West Virginia, demanded in writing to know distinctly and specifically the grounds of his removal. In this case the Postmaster-General was more accommodating, as will be seen by his letter to the member on a preceding page.

The postal service generally throughout the South was continued under the direction of the Government of the United States up to the 31st of May, 1861, when it was suspended by a general order of the Department. Meantime, all through the winter the leaders of the rebellion were making use of the mails, and those of them in Congress of their franking privilege also, to "fire up the Southern heart" and force the States into passing ordinances of secession, seizing the Government property, etc. One senator (Yulee), whose letter fell into loyal hands some time during the war, wrote to his State under date of January 5, 1861:

"I think by the 4th of March all the Southern States will be out, except, perhaps, Kentucky and Missouri, and they will soon have to follow. A strong government of eight States, promptly organized, with Jeff Davis for general-in-chief, will bring them to a realizing sense of the gravity of the crisis. . . . I shall give the enemy a shot next week before retiring. I say enemy. Yes, I am theirs, and they are mine. I am willing to be their master, but not their brother."

This is a fair representation of the spirit manifested by

force and by their lawless power over said post-office, whereby its freedom and integrity have been destroyed; and whereas, it is neither just nor proper that a post-office or postal service should be supported by the Government of the United States, from the use of which its own citizens, and those in its employment and obeying its commands, are excluded by the usurpations of the said Governor, or by any other cause whatever: it is ordered that said post-office at Pensacola, in the State of Florida, be and the same is hereby abolished."

the leading secessionists congregated in Washington during
the winter and spring of 1861; and when on the 15th of
April the President issued his call for seventy-five thousand
men, his demand was met by the Governors of several of
the Southern States in the same spirit of bravado and
defiance.

I have a vivid recollection of the doubt and gloom which
pervaded the city for days preceding the arrival of the first
troops called for by the President. Such, at least, was the
feeling among all those here who had resolved to stand by
the Government. Reports were rife that rebel soldiers were
moving on the Virginia side of the river—that arms had
been sent forward for them; and, as the passenger-boats
were plying every hour between Alexandria and Washington, there was great fear that this means of communication
might be seized upon to place a hostile military force
suddenly in our midst. Late one night I found myself
at the telegraph-office with my friend, Gincry Twitchell,
a representative in Congress from Massachusetts, and so
alarming were the reports in reference to the movements
of troops near us in Virginia (who, it afterward appeared,
were on their way to take Harper's Ferry) that we sent to
General Scott an urgent request to stop the running of the
Alexandria boats. It was, I think, on the following night
that, being again at the telegraph-office, Mr. Twitchell
received a despatch that another Massachusetts regiment
had reached Havre De Grace; and we immediately proceeded to communicate this information to General Scott.
It was midnight or after when we arrived at his lodgings,
and we were told that he had retired for the night. Our
message, however, was conveyed to him, and, in a few
minutes, clothed in his dressing-gown, he received us in
his office. Calm and commanding, " he looked every inch
a soldier," yet it was evident that he felt the deepest concern in view of the then threatening aspect of affairs. His
greatest anxiety at that moment was for troops to protect

Fortress Monroe and Harper's Ferry; and having called upon Massachusetts for these, he requested Mr. Twitchell to urge Governor Andrew to hasten forward two regiments for the purpose—the one for the former place to be sent by the fastest steamer possible direct to Old Point Comfort. This request was complied with, and the Massachusetts regiments for Fortress Monroe happily arrived there on the 20th of April, just in time to save that important post. Six hours later and it is believed it would have been captured. As General Scott apprehended, Harper's Ferry fell into the hands of the insurgents before the Union troops could reach that point.

WASHINGTON, April, 1872.

CHAPTER XI.

WHY WAS NOT THE REBELLION CRUSHED AT THE START?

The Southern Disunionists Prepared to Resist—Violence of the Abolitionists and Republicans, etc.

IT is no easy matter to eradicate deep-rooted prejudice. President Buchanan's is a remarkable case in point. Called to the Presidency at a period when partisan spirit was almost at its highest pitch, he encountered from the first the bitter opposition not only of the original Abolitionists, but also of the main body of the Republican party. The Southern disunionists, prepared to resist had Mr. Buchanan been defeated, were not in the best disposition for peace or quiet; and it was natural and appeared wise for the administration to endeavor to conciliate them by all reasonable means in its power. This excited Republican opposition the more; and when Mr. Lincoln came to be elected entirely by the votes of non-slaveholding States, the public mind at the South was raised to fever heat, while the sentiment of the Republican party generally was that of boastful defiance; and it was some time after that election before they came to believe that the South was really in earnest in its threats of secession. In their estimation it was only bluster and bravado for political effect, and this idea was not entirely relinquished until the attack on Fort Sumter. Although such was the opinion of the Republican party, as expressed through the press and its public speakers, up to the time and even after Mr. Lincoln's election to the Presidency, it is no uncommon thing now to hear Mr. Buchanan condemned because he did not crush the rebellion at the start; and many no doubt honestly believe that the reason why this was not done was, that, if not at heart a traitor, he failed on account of inexcusable weakness and timidity. Any such belief is wholly without foundation.

There were two circumstances which gave rise to many complaints and no little prejudice against Mr. Buchanan outside of any mere partisan considerations. The most serious of these related to his declaration that "the Constitution has conferred no power on the Federal Government to coerce a State;" and the other grew out of his being held responsible for the treasonable utterances of the *Constitution* newspaper in the fall of 1860, and until that paper was finally discontinued on the 30th of January, 1861. That newspaper, published at the seat of government, had been looked upon as the organ of the administration; and although its active editor, Mr. William M. Browne, a good-looking and well-educated Englishman, from time to time declared that he alone was responsible for its opinions, the fact that it continued to receive the advertising patronage of the Government, solely through the favor of the President, went far toward satisfying the opposition, at least, that the denial of the editor was only a weak subterfuge, especially as he sustained the President in many of his public acts, including his course touching

coercion. It is needless to deny that the best friends of
the President were embarrassed and not a little displeased
with this state of things, which existed for nearly three
months before the President rescinded his order giving
the Government advertising to that paper. It might have
been somewhat different had the paper obtained the advertising by reason of its large circulation, the law authorizing
it to be given to two of the city papers having the largest
subscription list and to such other paper as the President
might designate. I never could understand why the President so long delayed to rescind his order, except that his
forbearance came from his fixed purpose to avoid, as far as
possible, exciting Southern hostility to the end of relinquish-
ing the reins of government to his successor without bloodshed.

In his book entitled " Mr. Buchanan's administration on
the Eve of the Rebellion," speaking of the political aspect
of affairs at the time of Mr. Lincoln's election on the 6th
of November, 1860, and of the "virulence, uncommon even
in our own history," with which "his administration had
been pursued by the triumphant party from the beginning,"
—how "his every act had been misrepresented and condemned," plainly showing "that whatever course he might
pursue he was destined to encounter their bitter hostility,"
—Mr. Buchanan further truthfully remarks : " No public
man was ever placed in a more trying and responsible position. Indeed, it was impossible for him to act with honest
independence without giving offence to both the anti-slavery
and secession parties, because both had been clearly in the
wrong." Since that time a new generation has come into
active life ; and it is not strange that prejudices should have
been imbibed by the younger class, on the one side and on
the other in politics, without that full knowledge of the
causes by which such prejudices were superinduced possessed by those whose experience reaches back to the dawn
of abolitionism under the administrations of Presidents

Jackson and Van Buren. There are now living comparatively few who can remember with what disfavor the Abolitionists were then regarded by both of the great political parties of the country,—a feeling which underwent little change until after the election of James K. Polk to the Presidency in 1844. The discussion on the admission of Texas, and subsequently of California, now gave marked impetus to the Abolition party for several years; but the compromise measures of 1850, although condemned by the Garrison Abolitionists, were acquiesced in by the Democratic and Whig parties, and the public mind for the time being was quieted on the slavery question. The platform of both the great political parties in the Presidential campaign of 1852 contained resolutions in favor of maintaining that compromise, and, in the language of the Whig platform, declared that "We depreciate all further agitation of the question thus settled, as dangerous to our peace, and will discountenance all efforts to continue or renew such agitation, whenever, wherever, or however the attempt may be made." This, however, did not silence the Abolitionists, then odious to both the Whig and Democratic parties on account of their unjust interference with the constitutional rights of the South, and of their openly declared disunion sentiments. These agitators were thus characterized by Mr. Webster in his famous cabinet circular of October, 1850: "In the Northern and Eastern States," he says, "these sentiments of disunion are espoused principally by persons of heated imaginations, assembling together and passing resolutions of such a wild and violent character as to render them nearly harmless." So they appeared at the time to the great body of the people in all sections of the country opposed to them; yet their continued promulgation afforded just the fuel required to feed the flames of disunion in the slave States. In the words of Mr. Buchanan, "When Congress assembled after the election of President Pierce, on the first Monday in December, 1853, although the abolition fanatics had not ceased to agitate, crimination and recrimination between the sectional parties had greatly subsided, and a comparative political calm everywhere prevailed. . . . But how short-lived and delusive was this calm!" The "long and angry debate" upon the Kansas and Nebraska bill, introduced by Senator Douglas on the 23d of January, 1854, and its passage with a section repealing the Missouri Compromise in May following, "reopened the floodgates of sectional strife, which it was fondly imagined had been closed forever." This continued to increase "in violence and malignity" until the country became involved "in the greatest and most sanguinary civil war in history."

President Buchanan went no further in sustaining what he considered the clear constitutional rights of the South than did Mr. Webster in his great seventh of March speech. Both were alike condemned by the Republicans for the doctrines they advanced and their efforts at conciliation. In his eulogy on Daniel Webster at the Marshfield celebration, on the 12th of October, 1882, President Allen, of the Webster Historical Society, well remarked: "Who can deny to-day that the extremists of the South were as logical in their claims for the maintenance of slavery as were the Abolitionists of the North for its unconditional overthrow? Webster stood alone, but Webster was consistent. He claimed to maintain the Constitution and the laws of the land in good faith, and he acted up to his belief. . . . For this he was reviled and maltreated both in the North and South. He dreaded (and the result has proved the divinity of his prescience) that disunion would be forcibly attempted by the South, and that the country, plunged in all the horrors of a civil war, would be deluged with the blood of its citizens. Who can now say that he was not right?" Undoubtedly there are few among the reflecting of the community, especially of those conversant with public affairs as far back as 1835, who will not say he was right. Yet, how often do we hear even the Garrison Abolitionists extolled for "their work so well begun, and which finally culminated in the abolition of slavery in the United States!" It is difficult to see how their "work," which, in the judgment of the great body of the people, was treasonable and consequently highly reprehensible before the war, can now be regarded as entitling them to the gratitude of the present and future generations, unless at the same time they are to be commended for bringing on the most terrible war that ever afflicted mankind. For my own part, rather than have any share in such commendation, I feel much better satisfied to retain my true position with Daniel Webster, James Buchanan, and the million of other patriots throughout the country who also agreed with them in condemning the course of the Abolitionists, and doing everything in their power to quiet agitation and prevent bloodshed.

Said President Buchanan in his last annual message:

"The long-continued and intemperate interference of the Northern people with the question of slavery in the Southern States has at length produced its natural results. The different sections of the Union are now arrayed against each other, and the time has arrived, so much dreaded by the Father of his Country, when hostile geographical parties have been formed. I have long foreseen and often forewarned my countrymen of the now impending danger."

Who will deny the correctness of this statement?

Decided, however, as was President Buchanan in his censure of Northern interference with the question of slavery, he was equally earnest in his appeals to the Southern States not to allow this interference to drive them into secession, which he likewise condemned as wholly indefensible. In his message to Congress, he said:

"In order to justify secession as a constitutional remedy, it must be on the principle that the Federal Government is a mere voluntary association of States, to be dissolved at pleasure by any one of the contracting parties. If this be so, the Confederacy is a rope of sand, to be penetrated and dissolved by the first adverse wave of public opinion in any of the States. . . . Such a principle is wholly inconsistent with the history as well as the character of the Federal Constitution."

Nor did he consider that anything which had yet occurred would justify revolutionary resistance. "In order to justify a resort to revolutionary resistance," he said, "the Federal Government must be guilty of 'a deliberate, palpable, and dangerous exercise' of powers not granted by the Constitution." So far as the Federal Government was concerned, he urged that no act whatever had been committed, either by the executive, legislative, or judicial branch thereof, not strictly within constitutional limits; but, on the contrary, that even the fugitive slave law, so offensive to many in the free States, had been faithfully executed; it was not what Congress had done, but what it was feared it might do, that was objected to; and the Supreme Court of the United States had sustained the rights of the South in every particular touching the question of slavery. Knowing the impulsive character of most of the leading men of the South, he earnestly cautioned them against hasty action, insisting that "reason, justice, a regard for the Constitution," all required that they should "wait for some overt and dangerous act on the part of the President elect, before resorting" to extreme measures.

Thus, Mr. Buchanan found himself between two fires. "To preserve the Union," he says in his book, "was the President's supreme object, and he considered it doubtful whether it could survive the shock of civil war."

This brief summary shows how the President felt, and it is the key to much of his action for which he has been severely censured. Evidently decided not to do anything to give the South just cause of complaint, he was ready himself to suffer from what was regarded even by some of his political friends as extreme moderation toward the secessionists, rather than that any act of his should serve to increase their already inflamed passions. Hence I conclude that he deemed it prudent not at once to incur their bitter enmity by withdrawing the Government advertising from the *Constitution* newspaper.

The most cursory view of the columns of that sheet will show how inevitable it was that President Buchanan must suffer in the estimation of Union men on account of its declared disunion sentiments and character. A few brief extracts from it may not be out of place here. Its key-note was sounded in its leading editorial of the 7th of November, 1860, the first morning after Lincoln's election, when the editor said :

" We can understand the effect that will be produced in every Southern mind when he reads the news, that he is now called on to decide for himself, his children, and his children's children, whether he will submit tamely to the rule of one elected on account of his hostility to him and his, or whether he will make a struggle to defend his rights, his inheritance, and his honor."

From this time until its " suspension" on the 30th of January, the paper was filled with articles favoring secession, and, under the immediate eyes of the leaders of disunion, it was their willing mouth-piece. A month before even South Carolina passed its ordinance of secession, we find a letter from Senator Yulee informing the Legislature of his State " that upon learning, any time between this [November 20] and the 4th day of March next, of the determination of Florida to dissolve her union with the Northern States, I shall promptly and joyously return home, to support the banner of the State to which my allegiance is owing and in which my family altar is established."

Next, under date of 21st of November, we hear Senator Hammond, of South Carolina, addressing a mass-meeting at Columbus, Georgia, and saying:

"South Carolina will certainly secede from the Union on the 17th or 18th of December next. She intends to try it fully at all costs. No more compromise of any sort. She takes no *guarantee*, but will go out high and dry forever. If Georgia will back her, there will be little or no trouble."

On the following day the editor of the *Constitution* writes:

"Another and more decisive way is open to Messrs. Lincoln and Hamlin. By one bold stroke may they remove the difficulties and avert the danger. Let them resign their positions. . . . Since Mr. Lincoln cannot, in all likelihood, be more than the President of a broken Union, comparatively little philosophy may reconcile him to the sacrifice. He is simply called upon to give up gracefully what he cannot keep peacefully and usefully."

At this time it was stated that Mr. Lincoln was receiving a dozen letters a day threatening him with assassination.

Movements being now in progress with a view to the repeal of the "personal liberty acts" in those States which had declared their purpose to disregard the fugitive slave law, the editor, under date of November 24, said: "The mere repeal of the ' personal liberty acts' will not suffice to satisfy the South;" that amendments to the Constitution are demanded. Again, December 22, he wrote: "Nowhere throughout the Cotton States has a journal or a public man ventured to counsel submission to the rule of a black Republican President." And on the 25th of December he said: "The alternative is clear. You must recognize secession when ordained by the people of a State; or, dreaming of coercion, you must prepare for civil war."

Meantime, on December 20, the South Carolina Convention unanimously adopted an ordinance of secession, and on the 22d appointed three commissioners " to proceed forthwith to Washington to treat with the Government of the United States concerning the relations between the parties." The New York *Commercial Advertiser* having said that these commissioners " ought to have no notice taken of them whatever until the people who sent them to Washington have rescinded the insulting and rebellious ordinance of secession," the editor of the *Constitution*, quoting the same on the 25th of December, remarked:

"The commissioners, we submit, will be entitled to a hearing—to a friendly, candid, and intelligent hearing; and, if wisdom have any weight in the counsels of Congress, they will have it. They will be entitled to more—to a readiness to enter into negotiation for the adjustment of matters in which the State and the Union are both concerned; that, although unable to prolong former relations, they may yet be enabled to remain friends, and quietly and beneficially reciprocate the obligations and favors of neighbors."

It now appears that, seriously disturbed by this persistent opposition to his own patriotic views and purposes, President Buchanan addressed to the editor of the *Constitution* the following private letter, which was first published only on November 22, 1880, when Mr. George Ticknor Curtis, his biographer, produced it in a communication to the New York *Sun*, in which article this observation also occurs: "There is not a more remarkable instance in all history of the misconception with which a great public man may be pursued than this case of Mr. Buchanan."

[PRIVATE.]
" WASHINGTON, December 25, 1860.

"MY DEAR SIR,—I have read with deep mortification your editorial this morning, in which you take open ground against my message on the right of secession. I have defended you as long as I can against numerous complaints. You have a perfect right to be in favor of secession, and for this I have no just reason to complain. The difficulty is that the *Constitution* is considered my organ, and its articles subject me to the charge of insincerity and double dealing. I am deeply sorry to say that I must in some authentic form declare the *Constitution* is not the organ of the administration.

" Your friend, very respectfully,
" JAMES BUCHANAN.
" WILLIAM M. BROWNE, ESQ."

This rebuke doubtless drew from the editor the following article, which appeared in his paper of December 27:

8

"Notwithstanding our frequent and positive assurances to the contrary, we see it daily asserted by the opponents of the President and his administration that he is responsible for the course of this paper; that the editorial articles are written at his dictation, or submitted for his revision and approval; and that, to all intents and purposes, it is the organ through which he and his Cabinet express their opinions. We again, and for the last time, pronounce the assertion that the President, or anybody on earth but the editor and proprietor of this paper, is responsible for its opinions, to be a deliberate falsehood. While we have given, and shall continue to give, the President and his administration a hearty and zealous support, we reserve to ourselves and always exercise the right to entertain and express our own views and sentiments, no matter how widely they may differ from those of our best friends."

The "hearty and zealous support" of the administration thus promised was shown by the continued production of such articles as were calculated only to disparage the Union cause and embarrass the President in his efforts at conciliation. So infatuated were the leading secessionists with the idea of their final success, and so sure were they that the North would consent to a peaceable separation rather than go to war, that their papers, of which the *Constitution* was a conspicuous example, were jubilant over every act of disloyalty, whether of citizen or State, that in rapid succession was chronicled in their columns. Any prospect of staying the tide of secession, instead of pleasure seemed to give them only pain, and every such prospect was discredited. On the 29th of December, Senators Crittenden and Douglas received from gentlemen at Atlanta, Georgia, a despatch inquiring, "Is there any hope for Southern rights in the Union? [adding] We are for the Union of our fathers if Southern rights can be preserved in it." They answered, "We have hopes that the rights of the Southern and of every State and section may be protected within the Union. Don't give up the ship. Don't despair of the Republic."

This correspondence appeared in the *Constitution* on the following day, with remarks by the editor of a discouraging nature, and asking, "On what foundation do they [the Senators] build their hopes?"

Howell Cobb, Secretary of the Treasury, resigned on the 8th of December, and Lewis Cass, Secretary of State, on the 12th of that month, but for opposite reasons. Mr. Cobb differed with the President on the right of secession and the question of defending the public property and collecting the revenue in South Carolina; and General Cass withdrew from the Cabinet, it was understood, on account of a difference of opinion in reference to the reinforcement of Fort Sumter. I know, from an affecting interview I had with him soon after his resignation, that he thought the fort should have been put in a complete state of defence immediately after Mr. Lincoln's election.

Meantime the *Constitution* seized upon everything within its reach to encourage the secessionists to press forward in their insane movement to dissolve the Union. The withdrawal of South Carolina was proclaimed as complete and final, and in a "Song of Deliverance," one of her most gifted poets devoutly sung,—

> "The night of doom is past
> And our Freedom born at last,
> A fair immortal rises o'er the storm of doubt and dread ;
> She dawns in pomp of power,
> At the God-appointed hour,
> Youth's dewy morning in her eyes, Hope's halo round her head."

The *Charleston Mercury* published the "Doings in the Federal Congress," and other news from Washington under the head "Foreign News," and, as appears from the *Constitution*, the Rev. Mr. Dupree, in his prayer at the opening of the South Carolina Convention on the 1st of January, exclaimed: "O God, wilt thou bring confusion upon our enemies, and wilt thou strengthen the hearts and nerve the arms of our sons to meet this great trial, in the name of the God of Israel."

The Governor of South Carolina had already issued his proclamation, which appeared in the *Constitution* of the 28th of December, saying,—

"By virtue of authority in me vested [I] do hereby proclaim to the world that this State is, as she has a right to be, a separate, sovereign, free, and independent State; and, as such, has a right to levy war, conclude peace, negotiate treaties, leagues, or covenants, and to do all acts whatsoever that rightfully appertain to a free and independent State."

The secessionists could be witty, as well as solemn and devout; and, by way of variety, I venture to reproduce a specimen of their wit by transcribing from the *Constitution* of the 12th of January the following effusion, entitled—

"SECESSION CONSUMMATED.

"Yankee Doodle took a saw,
 With patriotic devotion,
To trim the Tree of Liberty
 According to his 'notion!'

"Yankee Doodle on a limb,
 Like another noodle,
Cut between the tree and him,
 And down came Yankee Doodle.

"Yankee Doodle broke his neck,
 Every bone about him,
And then the Tree of Liberty
 Did very well without him!"

The thought intrudes itself whether it were not others instead of "Yankee Doodle" that undertook thus to trim the "Tree of Liberty;" but this is all now satisfactorily settled.

As a matter of course, the editor of the *Constitution*, like all other Secessionists, was resolutely opposed to coercion; and they were all cunning enough to give the word a much broader signification than did either President Buchanan or any of his friends. While the secessionists, supported, I regret to say, in no small degree by the Republican party, chose to represent the President as holding that the Government of the United States had no power under the Constitution to use force either against a rebellious State or the individual citizens of such State to prevent the dismemberment of the Union, he used the word "coercion" expressly as against a seceding State in its corporate capacity, and not in respect to the people of a State. This is what he said in his message to Congress:

"The question, fairly stated, is, 'Has the Constitution delegated to Congress the power to coerce a State into submission, which is attempting to withdraw, or has actually withdrawn, from the Confederacy?' If answered in the affirmative, it must be on the principle that the power has been conferred upon Congress to make war against a State. After much serious reflection, I have arrived at the conclusion that no such power has been delegated to Congress or to any other department of the Federal Government."

In support of this view, he quotes Mr. Madison as saying, in the convention which framed the Constitution, that "The use of force against a State would look more like a declaration of war than an infliction of punishment, and would probably be considered by the party attacked as a dissolution of all previous compacts by which it might be bound." The clause "authorizing an exertion of the force of the whole against a delinquent State" was then, 31st of May, 1787, under consideration, and Mr. Buchanan states that it was on motion of Mr. Madison unanimously postponed, and was never, he believes, again presented.

Andrew Johnson, of Tennessee, in his speech in the Senate on the 18th of December, 1860, said, "I do not believe the Federal Government has the power to coerce a State," but "it has the right and the power to enforce and execute the law upon individuals within the limits of a State."

Mr. Buchanan justly complains of the Republican party "because they have not chosen to take the distinction between the power to make war against a State in its sov-

creign character, and the undoubted power to enforce the
laws of Congress directly against the individual citizens
thereof within its limits."

Mr. Simon Cameron, Republican Senator from Pennsylvania, when the subject was under consideration in the
Senate, said, " Coercion is the last remedy to which I would
resort.   I do not know that I should ever resort to it; but
certainly it is the last remedy that I would resort to, to
keep my brother in my family."

We have the testimony of Judge Black and General
Holt that they both agreed with the President upon the
legal proposition that the Constitution of the United States
does not confer the power upon the Federal Government to
coerce a State by force of arms to remain in the Union.
General Holt says he knows that such was the opinion also
of Secretary Stanton, and Judge Black avers that General
Cass " was strong" for " the retention" of the term " coercion" in the President's message, although he [Black]
was opposed to that expression, because, as he says, he told
the President, " it would be read superficially and misunderstood."   It is equally certain that Secretary Toucey was
opposed to coercion ; for Judge Black says he " always
agreed with the President."   Of course there is no doubt
as to the views of Secretaries Cobb and Thompson on this
subject.

In a letter to the Philadelphia *Press*, from Mr. John W.
Forney, then the Republican Clerk of the United States
House of Representatives, and reprinted in the *Constitution*
of the 28th of December, he wrote :

"Let me not be misunderstood.   The word ' coercion' should never be
used.   There is no desire on the part of the friends of the Union to
make war.   Their attitude is, and should be, to enforce the execution of
the laws,—nothing more, nothing less.   It is not intended to make an
attack on South Carolina unless South Carolina should make an attack
upon the Government.   Then that which is now secession becomes revolution, and revolution is treason, and must be rebuked as such."

It is well to remember that some time before the President's message, in which the unfortunate expression, "coercion," appeared, was sent to Congress, leading Republicans everywhere scouted the idea of using force against the Southern States; and only three days after Lincoln's election the New York *Tribune* said:

"If the Cotton States shall become satisfied that they can do better out of the Union than in it, we insist on letting them go in peace. The right to secede may be a revolutionary one, but it exists nevertheless. . . . We must ever resist the right of any State to remain in the Union and nullify or defy the laws thereof. To withdraw from the Union is quite another matter; and whenever any considerable section of our Union shall deliberately resolve to go out, we shall resist all *coercive* measures designed to keep it in. We hope never to live in a republic where one section is pinned to another by bayonets."

Similar sentiments were subsequently repeatedly enunciated by the *Tribune* as well after as before the formation of the Southern Confederacy. These and kindred articles from other sources were greedily transferred to the columns of the *Constitution*, whereby the secessionists were encouraged and the administration suffered. At length, near the end of January, 1861, the President withdrew the Government patronage from that paper, when the editor, on the 30th of that month, announced its "suspension for a short time," after which he said it would be resumed "within the limits of the Southern Confederacy, as at present constituted, hoping, as I do most fervently, that in a short time Washington and the State to which she belongs may be included within those limits." He spoke of the President's order as "official persecution," in the same breath declaring: "I advocated secession. I hoped, and still hope, that all the Southern States will secede."

The failure to reinforce the forts in Charleston harbor was another serious cause of complaint against President Buchanan. As already stated, this subject received early attention of the Cabinet; but so many difficulties intervened that no decisive action was taken in the matter until the attempt to send recruits and subsistence stores to Fort Sumter on the 5th of January, 1861, by the passenger steamer *Star of the West*, which vessel, it will be recollected, was fired upon by order of the Governor of South Carolina as she was endeavoring to approach the fort, and she was compelled to put to sea.

In an "interview" with a correspondent of the Philadelphia *Press*, in August, 1881, Judge Black said:

"Mr. Buchanan understood as well as anybody that the forts there must be kept, and was thoroughly determined not to give them up. Immediately after the election [of Mr. Lincoln] he directed Floyd, the Secretary of War, to see that the forts were fully manned and provisioned. 'If,' said he, addressing the Secretary, 'those forts should be taken by South Carolina in consequence of our negligence to put them in defensible condition, it were better for you and me both to be thrown into the Potomac with millstones tied about our necks.' Floyd replied very solemnly—that is, more solemnly than he usually spoke—that his own convictions accorded with those of the President, and said that duty should be immediately and completely performed."

It was not done, however, and the sequel shows that, while Messrs. Cass, Black, Holt, and Stanton were impatient at the delay in ordering reinforcements sent, the President came to the conclusion that it was prudent to wait. Judge Black says:

"The object of the policy which the President thought proper to pursue, and that which I urged upon him as a better one, were the same,—namely, to preserve the peace and hand over the Government in as good order as possible to the succeeding administration, and give Lincoln a chance to do that which seemed good in his own eyes. Buchanan's conviction was that Lincoln would try his best to avoid a fatal rupture, and he would be able to satisfy the Southern men of that, if only they would be quiet until the 4th of March. But if previous to that time a war should open, the Union must utterly perish, for it was very plain that the Congress then in session would not vote a man or a dollar to aid him in saving it. [This point is strongly and conclusively presented by Mr. Buchanan in his book.] If Fort Sumter should be taken, the conflict would immediately begin, with the certainty of hideous ruin to the cause of the Union. The imperious necessity of holding the forts in Charleston harbor was a point acknowledged by the whole of the administration, except those Southern members who thought they ought to be peaceably handed over to the secessionists. But we divided on the practical question of the best mode to keep them. The President was convinced that if no movement were made looking to the increase of our force at that point, the revolutionary States would await the advent of the new administration."

The correctness of this statement is fully corroborated by Mr. Buchanan, who says that he had "determined not to touch the *status quo* at Charleston as long as our troops should continue to be hospitably treated by the inhabitants, and remain in unmolested possession of the forts." Without any formal agreement not to order a reinforcement of the forts, as proposed by four of the representatives from South Carolina, who called on the President for that purpose, and who were told by him "such an agreement he would never make," there is no doubt whatever of his determination at that time (10th December) to await any hostile movement on the part of South Carolina before sending such reinforcements. Judge Black says he knows of no satisfactory evidence that there was any such agreement, and here is what General Holt says on the subject in an "interview" with the aforementioned correspondent of the Philadelphia *Press*, in August, 1881, viz.:

"I should deny emphatically that he [President Buchanan] ever had any understanding with the Southern people which would prevent him from carrying out the expressed and well-known policy of his administration, to refrain from hostile acts, if possible, but to defend the Southern forts to the last extremity if they were assailed. I have often thought while looking back over that stormy period that Mr. Buchanan acted most wisely and judiciously in his treatment of the Southern question. You must bear in mind that Mr. Buchanan was surrounded by a Congress which would not have voted a man or a dollar to strengthen the force at the command of the executive if a war should be precipitated. I firmly believe the fact that because so much of forbearance was shown to the South and that we refrained from firing first upon them, gave us great moral strength when war finally came. I am convinced that the feeling that they first fired upon the flag aroused our people to a point of enthusiasm which carried us through the war."

But there were other important reasons why it would have been unwise at this time to undertake to strengthen the military force doing garrison duty in the South. Mr. Buchanan well remarks : ·

"The Senators from the Cotton States and from Virginia, where these forts are situated, were still occupied with their brother Senators in devising means of peace and conciliation. . . . Had the President never so earnestly desired to reinforce the nine forts in question at this time, it would have been little short of madness to undertake the task with the small force at his command. . . . Had the President attempted to distribute the General's [Scott's] thousand men, as he proposed, among the numerous forts in the Cotton States, as well as Fortress Monroe, their absurd inadequacy to the object would have exhibited weakness instead of strength. It would have provoked instead of preventing collision. It would have precipitated a civil war with the Cotton States without the slightest preparation on the part of Congress, and would at once have destroyed the then prevailing hopes of compromise. Worse than all, it would have exasperated Virginia and the other border States then so intent on remaining in the Union, and might have driven them at once into hostile action."

On the 29th of December, John B. Floyd, Secretary of War, handed in his resignation, containing the charge that the administration had been guilty of a " violation of solemn pledges and plighted faith," in allowing Major Anderson to occupy Fort Sumter instead of Fort Moultrie. Two days before, on learning that Major Anderson had removed to Fort Sumter, as he claimed " against the solemn pledges of the Government," he urged upon the President, as the " one remedy now left us by which to vindicate our honor and prevent civil war," to allow him to order Major Anderson to withdraw the garrison from the harbor of Charleston altogether. His letter of resignation immediately appeared in the *Constitution*, together with the President's letter of 31st of December, accepting the same and relieving him at once from the charge of the War Department; Joseph Holt, Postmaster-General, being authorized to fill his place until his successor should be appointed. The fact is, as stated in

Mr. Buchanan's book, the authority under which Major Anderson removed his troops to Fort Sumter was given in a letter of instructions "prepared and transmitted to Major Anderson by the Secretary himself," only a few days before that removal took place. In a letter to the War Department of the 27th of December, which, Mr. Buchanan says, "unfortunately did not arrive in Washington until some days after its date," Major Anderson says: "I will add that many things convinced me that the authorities of the State designed to proceed to a hostile act" (against Fort Moultrie); "the very contingency," Mr. Buchanan says, "on which the Secretary had not only authorized but directed the Major to remove his troops to Fort Sumter, should he deem this a position of greater security." And here I may remark that I well remember with what delight Mr. Holt, coming from the Cabinet, announced at the Post-Office Department the gratifying news of Major Anderson's success in transferring the garrison to Fort Sumter. Mr. Floyd embraced the occasion to present and read his letter of resignation in Cabinet session, and we have the word of General Holt for saying that it gave rise to "a scene exceedingly dramatic. Mr. Floyd" (he says in the "interview" already referred to) "became quite violent, and, knowing he was to go out of the Cabinet on account of his advanced acceptances, he made the removal of Anderson from Fort Moultrie to Fort Sumter the pretext for language which made his further continuation in the Cabinet impossible, and it was a position in which he knew the Southern people would sustain him." It was at this or a previous Cabinet session, that, the question of giving up the forts being under discussion, Judge Black said:

"There had never been a period in the history of the English nation when any minister would propose to give up to an enemy of his Government a military post which was capable of being defended, without being brought to the block. Mr. Buchanan," he continues, "thought the expression a harsh one, but did not deny that it was true. He had no thought of yielding to Mr. Davis's solicitation [to abandon the forts in Charleston harbor]. Floyd would have done it at that time, that is to say, after he was notified that he must resign from the Cabinet for other reasons or be removed. . . . In this determination [to assert the national control of the forts, arsenals, custom-houses, and other public property] President Buchanan never wavered. He saw the drift toward war much more clearly and much earlier than any public man of whom I have knowledge."

Mr. Buchanan refers to what he thinks was " a probable cause for this strange conduct on the part of the Secretary. This was," he says, " that three days before the South Carolina commissioners reached Washington, the President had communicated to him (23d December), through a distinguished friend and kinsman of his own, a request that he should resign his office, with a statement of the reasons why this was made. When he heard this request he displayed much feeling, but said he would comply with the President's wishes. It is proper to state the reason for this request. On the night before it was made (22d December) the fact was first made known to the President that eight hundred and seventy State bonds for $1000 each, held in trust by the Government for different Indian tribes, had been purloined from the Interior Department by Godard Bailey, the clerk in charge of them, and had been delivered to William H. Russell, a member of the firm of Russell, Majors & Waddell. Upon examination it was discovered that this clerk, in lieu of the bonds abstracted, had from time to time received bills of corresponding amount from Russell, drawn by the firm on John B. Floyd, Secretary of War, and by him accepted and indorsed, and this without lawful authority. In consequence there was found in the safe where the Indian bonds had been kept, a number of these accepted bills, exactly equal in amount to $870,000. These acceptances were thirteen in number, commencing on the 13th of September, 1860, and had been received by Mr. Bailey, according to his own statement, ' as collateral security for the return of the bonds,' and as such had been placed by him in the safe.

It is remarkable that the last of them, dated on the 13th
of December, 1860, for $135,000, had been drawn for the
precise sum necessary to make the aggregate amount of the
whole number of bills exactly equal to that of the abstracted
bonds."

These bills, being unlawfully accepted, have never been
paid, leaving their innocent holders to suffer the loss of all
they paid for them, which I think was par value in the
market. The advertisement of these Indian trust bonds,
making nearly three columns, was published daily in the
Constitution for a full month, thus adding greatly to its re-
ceipts from the very Government it was at the same time
striving to destroy.

This extended explanation, touching Secretary Floyd's
resignation, is interesting, not only as an incident in history,
but it no doubt discloses the main cause, at least, of his
sudden hostility.

To give even a synopsis of all the accredited facts relating
to the matter of Fort Sumter would extend this article to
an unreasonable length. I have already furnished enough
to convince any unprejudiced person that, while there were
conflicting views on the subject in his Cabinet, there is no
question whatever that President Buchanan pursued the
course in regard to it that he honestly believed best for the
preservation of peace and the safety of the Union. It
should not be forgotten that after the removal of Major
Anderson to Fort Sumter, the administration felt that there
was no danger of the fort being taken. On this point no
more conclusive evidence need be required than what appears in the following letter of Mr. Holt, Secretary of War.
This letter, as its date shows, was sent to President Lincoln
on the 5th of March, immediately following his inauguration. I should premise, what I can do, not only from personal
knowledge and recollection, but also from Mr. Buchanan's
own statement and from notes made in my diary at the
time, that, " on the 4th of March, at the moment when Mr.

Buchanan's administration was about to expire," the Secretary of War received from Major Anderson a letter, with
inclosures, declaring "that he would not be willing to risk
his reputation on an attempt to throw reinforcements into
Charleston harbor with a force of less than twenty thousand good and well-disciplined men."   In his book, referring to this communication from Major Anderson, Mr.
Buchanan correctly says, " This was read by Mr. Holt,
greatly to his own surprise, and that of every member of
the Cabinet."   I may add that it was then and there " agreed
that Mr. Holt should prepare a letter giving a history of
what had been done by Major Anderson and the Government since his removal to Fort Sumter, and transmit it with
this last communication to President Lincoln as early as
possible to-morrow" (5th of March, 1861).   Here is Mr.
Holt's letter :

"WAR DEPARTMENT, March 5, 1861.

"SIR,—I have the honor to submit for your consideration several letters with inclosures received on yesterday from Major Anderson and Captain Forster of the Corps of Engineers, which are of a most important
and unexpected character.   Why they were unexpected will appear from
the following brief statement:

"After transferring his forces to Fort Sumter he (Major Anderson)
addressed a letter to this Department, under date of the 31st December,
1860, in which he says, ' Thank God ! we are now where the Government
may send us additional troops *at its leisure.* To be sure, the uncivil
and uncourteous action of the Governor (of South Carolina) in preventing us from purchasing anything in the city will annoy and inconvenience us somewhat; *still we are safe.*' And after referring to some defi-
ciency in his stores, in the articles of soap and candles, he adds: 'Still
we can cheerfully put up with the inconvenience of doing without them
for the satisfaction we feel in the knowledge that we can command this
harbor *as long as our Government wishes to keep it.*' And again, on the 6th
of January, he wrote : 'My position will, should there be no treachery
among the workmen whom we are compelled to retain for the present,
enable me to hold this fort *against any force which can be brought against
me ;* and it would enable me, in the event of war, to annoy the South
Carolinians by preventing them from throwing supplies into their new
posts except by the aid of the Wash Channel through Stono River.'

"Before the receipt of this communication, the Government, being without information as to his condition, had despatched the *Star of the West* with troops and supplies for Fort Sumter, but the vessel, having been fired on from a battery at the entrance to the harbor, returned without having reached her destination.

"On the 16th of January, 1861, in replying to Major Anderson's letters of the 31st of December and of the 6th of January, I said, 'Your late despatches, as well as the very intelligent statements of Lieutenant Talbot, have relieved the Government of the apprehensions previously entertained for your safety. In consequence it is not its purpose at present to reinforce you. The attempt to do so would no doubt be attended by a collision of arms and effusion of blood—a national calamity which the President is most anxious to avoid. You will, therefore, report frequently your condition, and the character and activity of the preparations, if any, which may be being made for an attack upon the fort or for obstructing the Government in any endeavors it may make to strengthen your command. Should your despatches be of a nature too important to be intrusted to the mails, you will convey them by special messenger. Whenever, in your judgment, additional supplies or reinforcements are necessary for your safety or for a successful defence of the fort, you will at once communicate the fact to this Department, and a prompt and vigorous effort will be made to forward them.'

"Since the date of this letter Major Anderson has regularly and frequently reported the progress of the batteries being constructed around him, and which looked either to the defence of the harbor or to an attack on his own position. But he has not suggested that these works compromised his safety, nor has he made any request that additional supplies or reinforcements should be sent to him. On the contrary, on the 30th of January, 1861, in a letter to this Department, he uses this emphatic language: 'I do hope that no attempt will be made by our friends to throw supplies in; their doing so would do more harm than good.'

"On the 5th of February, when referring to the batteries, etc., constructed in his vicinity, he said, 'Even in their present condition they will make it impossible for any hostile force, other than a large and well-appointed one, to enter this harbor, and the chances are that it will then be at a great sacrifice of life;' and in a postscript he adds: 'Of course, in speaking of forcing an entrance, I do not refer to the little stratagem of a small party slipping in.' This suggestion of a stratagem was well considered in connection with all the information that could be obtained bearing upon it, and in consequence of the vigilance and number of the guard-boats in and outside of the harbor it was rejected as impracticable.

"In view of these very distinct declarations, and of the earnest desire to avoid a collision as long as possible, it was deemed entirely safe to adhere to the line of policy indicated in my letter of the 16th January,

which has been already quoted. In that Major Anderson had been requested to report 'at once,' 'whenever, in his judgment, additional supplies or reinforcements were necessary for his safety or for a successful
defence of the fort.' So long, therefore, as he remained silent upon this
point the Government felt that there was no ground for apprehension.
Still, as the necessity for action might arise at any moment, an expedition has been quietly prepared, and is ready to sail from New York on a
few hours' notice, for transporting troops and supplies to Fort Sumter.
This step was taken under the supervision of General Scott, who arranged
its details, and who regarded the reinforcements thus provided for as
sufficient for the occasion. The expedition, however, is not upon a scale
approaching the seemingly extravagant estimates of Major Anderson and
Captain Forster, now offered for the first time, and for the disclosures of
which the Government was wholly unprepared.

"The declaration now made by the major that he would not be willing
to risk his reputation on an attempt to throw reinforcements into
Charleston harbor, and with a view of holding possession of the same,
with a force of less than twenty thousand good and well-disciplined men,
takes the Department by surprise, as his previous correspondence contained no such intimation.

"I have the honor to be,

"Very respectfully,

"Your obedient servant,

"J. HOLT.

"TO THE PRESIDENT."

But I must bring this imperfect sketch to a close, imperfect because there are so many more facts of like import
that might easily be given. It is, or ought to be, well
known that, for one month after President Lincoln's accession, the policy of forbearance towards the seceding States
was pursued by him to an extent far beyond anything
his predecessor had done in that direction. Mr. Gideon
Welles, his Secretary of the Navy, has publicly declared
that "at the time of Mr. Lincoln's inauguration, and for
several weeks thereafter, he and others indulged in the
hope of a peaceful solution of the pending questions, and a
desire, amounting almost to a belief, that Virginia and the
other border States might, by forbearance and a calm and
conciliatory policy, continue faithful to the Union. . . .
And to conciliate the people of Virginia and the convention

then in session, the President desired that there should be no step taken which would give offence."

This is true beyond a doubt. It was in this spirit that President Lincoln delivered his Inaugural Address, and in his message to Congress of the 4th of July, 1861, he says:

"The policy chosen looked to the exhaustion of all peaceable measures before a resort to any stronger ones. It sought to hold the public places and property not already wrested from the Government, and to collect the revenue, relying for the rest on time, discussion, and the ballot-box. It promised a continuance of the mails at Government expense to the very people who were resisting the Government, and it gave repeated pledges against any disturbance to any of the people or any of their rights. Of all that a President might constitutionally and justifiably do in such a case, everything was forborne without which it was possible to keep the Government on foot."

Need more be said to satisfy the most censorious critic of President Buchanan's loyalty and honesty of purpose? For my own part, I but follow the precepts of the Golden Rule in presenting, while I may, this humble tribute in his behalf, and thus bearing testimony, as I do, to his unsullied honor, patriotism, and fidelity. As General Holt said in his late "interview," so I declare: "I wish distinctly to say that I believe Mr. Buchanan was in all respects, and at all times, true to the Union," and that "he did the best he could under the circumstances to preserve it." Judge Black is not less explicit. Said he: "To charge him [President Buchanan] with unfaithfulness to the Union is the foulest slander that was ever uttered. To say that he was influenced by any feeling akin to personal fear, or that he ever acted or forbore to act without the sanction of his conscience, is an outrage upon truth too gross to be endured. He had faults. But what faults may not be forgiven to a man of great ability and pure integrity who spent the best years of his life in the public service? He was as honest a patriot as ever lived, and no man ever sat in the Presidential chair that knew better than he did how to enforce the respect due to himself and his office."

9

CHAPTER XII.

DOCTRINE OF COERCION.

Views of President Buchanan, Madison, and Senator Johnson—Letters of Ex-President Buchanan—Forbearance of both President Buchanan and Lincoln towards the South.

It can be no satisfaction to any true American citizen to entertain the belief that any President of the United States has ever been guilty of treason, or an inclination towards treason, either in act or thought. On the contrary, it must be a subject of congratulation to every such citizen to know, if it really be the fact, that we have never yet had a President of whom it may not be said, " He was honestly devoted to what he conscientiously believed to be the best interests of this country; in a word, he was a patriot."

In the heat of party excitement, accusations more or less grave have been made against each and all of our presidents, not excepting the Father of his Country; but probably no one of them has ever been pursued with charges more serious or with a rancor more unrelenting than James Buchanan, not only during his presidency and the subsequent years of his retirement, but since his death.

I do not propose to enter upon a discussion of the questions generally which divided the Democratic and Republican parties at and after his election, but to touch briefly upon two points only: 1. The unjust censure cast upon Mr. Buchanan in the allegation that he was opposed to coercing the seceding States; and, 2. The charge that he favored the South to an extent in its nature treasonable.

Regarding the first allegation, it would be presumption in me to attempt to offer any observations of my own after Judge Black's able exposition of this subject in the June number of *The Galaxy;* but I think it will be interesting to the general reader to hear what Mr. Buchanan himself says on this much-controverted doctrine, and, as I have his book before me, entitled "Mr. Buchanan's Administration on the Eve of the Rebellion," published in 1866, I will make a copious extract from it.

To illustrate his views, he quotes from his annual message of December 3, 1860, to Congress, going at length into facts and arguments to show that the right of a State to secede from the Union does not exist under the Constitution. He says:

"In order to justify secession as a constitutional remedy, it must be on the principle that the Federal Government is a mere voluntary association of States, to be dissolved at pleasure by any one of the contracting parties. If this be so, the Confederacy is a rope of sand, to be penetrated and dissolved by the first adverse wave of public opinion in any of the States. In this manner our thirty-three States may resolve themselves into as many petty, jarring, and hostile republics, each one retiring from the Union without responsibility whenever any sudden excitement might impel them to such a course. By this process a Union might be entirely broken into fragments in a few weeks, which cost our forefathers many years of toil, privation, and blood to establish. Such a principle is wholly inconsistent with the history as well as the character of the Federal Constitution."

After enforcing this patriotic view of the subject, demonstrating the illegality and folly as well as the wickedness of secession, he proceeds:

"Then follows the opinion expressed in the message, that the Constitution has conferred no power on the Federal Government to coerce a *State* to remain in the Union. [The italicizing is his.] The following is the language: 'The question, fairly stated, is, Has the Constitution delegated to Congress the power to coerce a State into submission which is attempting to withdraw from the Confederacy? If answered in the affirmative, it must be on the principle that the power has been conferred upon Congress to make war against a State.'

"'After much serious reflection [this and the following paragraph he quoted from his message] I have arrived at the conclusion that no such power has been delegated to Congress or to any other department of the Federal Government. It is manifest, upon an inspection of the Constitution, that this is not among the specific and enumerated powers granted to Congress; and it is equally apparent that its exercise is not necessary and proper for carrying into execution any one of these powers. So far from this power having been delegated to Congress, it was expressly refused by the convention which framed the Constitution.

"'It appears from the proceedings of that body that on the 31st May, 1787, the clause "*authorizing an exertion of the force of the whole against a delinquent State*" came up for consideration. Mr. Madison opposed it in a brief but powerful speech, from which I shall extract but a single sentence. He observed: "The use of force against a State would look more like a declaration of war than an infliction of punishment, and would probably be considered by the party attacked as a dissolution of all previous compacts by which it might be bound" Upon his motion the clause was unanimously postponed, and was never, I believe, again presented. Soon afterward, on the 8th of June, 1787, when incidentally adverting to the subject, he said: "Any government for the United States formed on the supposed practicability of using force against the unconstitutional proceedings of the States would prove as visionary and fallacious as the government of Congress," evidently meaning the then existing Congress of the old Confederation.'

"The Republican party have severely but unjustly criticised this portion of the message, simply because they have not chosen to take the distinction between the power to make war against a State in its sovereign character, and the undoubted power to enforce the laws of Congress directly against individual citizens thereof within its limits. It was chiefly to establish this very distinction that the Federal Constitution was framed. The Government of the old Confederation could act only by requisitions on the different States, and these, as we have seen, obeyed or disobeyed according to their own discretion. In case of disobedience, there was no resort but to actual force against them, which would at once have destroyed the Confederacy. To remove the necessity for such a dangerous alternative, the present Constitution, passing over the governments of the States, conferred upon the Government of the United States the power to execute its own laws directly against their people. Thus all danger of collision between the Federal and State authorities was removed, and the indissoluble nature of the Federal Union established. The Republican party have, notwithstanding, construed the message to mean a denial by the President of the power to enforce the laws against the citizens of a State after secession, and even after actual rebellion. The whole tenor, not only of this message, but of the special message of January 8, 1861, contradicts and disproves this construction. Indeed, in the first clause of the message immediately preceding that relied upon, and whilst South Carolina was rapidly rushing to secession, he expressed his determination to execute the revenue laws whenever these should be resisted, and to defend the public property against all assaults. And in the special message, after South Carolina and other States had seceded, he reiterated this declaration, maintaining both his right and his duty to employ military force for this purpose. Having proved secession to be a mere nullity, he considered the States which had seceded to be still within the Union, and their people equally bound as they had been before to obey the laws.

"The disunionists, unlike the Republicans, placed the correct construction upon both messages, and therefore denounced them in severe terms.

"The President was gratified to observe that Senator Johnson, of Tennessee, a few days after the date of the first message, placed this subject in its true light, and thereby exposed himself to similar denunciations. In his speech of December 18, 1860 ('Congressional Globe,' p. 119), he says, ' I do not believe the Federal Government has the power to coerce a State, for by the eleventh amendment of the Constitution of the United States it is expressly provided that you cannot even put one of the States of this Confederacy before one of the courts of the country as a party. As a State, the Federal Government has no power to coerce it; but it is a member of the compact to which it agreed in common with the other States, and this Government has the right to pass laws, and to enforce those laws upon individuals within the limits of each State. While the one proposition is clear, the other is equally so. This Government can, by the Constitution of the country, and by the laws enacted in conformity with the Constitution, operate upon individuals, and has the right and the power not to coerce a State, but to enforce and execute the law upon individuals within the limits of a State.'

"Sound doctrine, and in conformity with that of the framers of the Constitution! Any other might, according to Mr. Madison, have been construed by the States in rebellion as a dissolution of their connection with the other States, and recognized them as independent belligerents on equal terms with the United States. Happily, our civil war was undertaken and prosecuted in self-defence, not to coerce a State, but to enforce the execution of the laws within the States against individuals, and to suppress an unjust rebellion raised by a conspiracy among them against the Government of the United States."

Such was Mr. Buchanan's belief in regard to the power of the general Government to coerce a *State*. His official acts were made to conform to this conviction, and out of this came the charge of weakness and treachery which I will also meet, not so much by any remarks of my own as by the testimony readily at hand of other witnesses entitled to the fullest credit. The facts, however, speak for themselves. Judge Black, in the article referred to, has presented Mr. Buchanan's position in this regard clearly and truthfully, and I venture the opinion that there are few, if any, fair-minded persons of any political party whatever, who, when they bring to mind the actual state of things existing during the closing months of Mr. Buchanan's administration, will not admit that great injustice has been done him by the thoughtless accusations against him of timidity, weakness, and treachery. That he was cautious there is no doubt, and it is equally certain now that in his caution there was great wisdom. Had he been rash, instead of cautious and forbearing as he was, in all probability active hostilities would have been inaugurated in January or February, 1861. Maryland as well as Virginia would have been forced to declare for secession, the rebels would have seized and held Washington, as I firmly believe it was their intention to do, and, as was also their purpose I am just as firmly convinced, Mr. Lincoln's inauguration would have been prevented. The city was swarming with secessionists both in and out of office, and there was a feeling of insecurity fearful to contemplate, which found relief only when, through the patriotic foresight of the Hon. Joseph Holt, Secretary of War, supported by the President and the rest of the Cabinet, a well-appointed body of United States troops was brought here from the West to preserve the public peace. The policy of the Government, however, was purely defensive; and this policy and the effect of it cannot be better illustrated than by the answer made by Mr. Holt, in a publication, in September, 1865, to the false charge that the cannon of Fort Sumter had "been muzzled by treaty stipulations."

He says:

"That the batteries around Sumter were not fired upon while in course of construction, was because the President shrank from the dread responsibility of inaugurating civil war, and deemed forbearance his duty; not because he was restrained by any agreement or understanding whatever. Looking at the glorious results of the war, and remembering how wondrously Providence has dealt with us in its progress, and how sublimely the firing *upon*, instead of *from*, Fort Sumter, served to arouse, instruct, and unite the nation, and to inflame its martial and patriotic spirit, we stand awe-struck and mute; and that man would be bold indeed who, in the presence of all that has occurred, should now venture to maintain that the policy of forbearance was not at the moment the true policy."

Nor, as is well known, did this policy of forbearance cease with Mr. Buchanan's administration. It was continued for some time after Mr. Lincoln's inauguration, and to a degree much beyond anything of the kind under his predecessor. They even went so far (according to Judge Black's statement, which I have not seen contradicted) as to vote six to one in Cabinet in favor of surrendering Fort Sumter! Strange, indeed, if such were the fact! But, be this as it may, we have the undoubted testimony of the Hon. Gideon Welles, the able and courteous Secretary of the Navy during the administrations of Presidents Lincoln and Johnson, that extreme leniency was practised towards the people in the southern States up to the firing upon Fort Sumter; and this may be taken as evincing on the part of Mr. Lincoln and his Cabinet the strongest approbation of Mr. Buchanan's line of policy, much more restrained to be sure, in the same direction. Allow me to reproduce here some of Mr. Welles's observations, as given in *The Galaxy* of July last on this point. He remarks:

"At the time of Mr. Lincoln's inauguration, *and for several weeks thereafter*, he and others indulged the hope of a peaceful solution of the pending questions, and a desire, *amounting almost to a belief*, that Virginia and the other border States might, *by forbearance and a calm and conciliatory policy*, continue faithful to the Union. Two-thirds of the convention then in session at Richmond were elected as opponents of secession, and the people of that State were in about that proportion opposed to it. But the Union element in the convention and out of it was passive and acquiescent, while the secessionists were positive, aggressive, and violent; and, as is almost always the case in revolutionary times, the aggressive force continually increased in strengh and exactions at the expense of those who were peacefully inclined. It was charged that the new administration was inimical to the South, was hostile to Southern institutions, and would use its power to deprive the people and States of their rights by coercive measures. In order to counteract these unfounded prejudices and to do away with these misrepresentations, which were embarrassing to the administration just launched upon a turbulent sea, and *to conciliate the people of Virginia and the convention then in session, the President desired that there should be no step taken which would give offence,* and to prevent any cause of irritation, he desired that *not even the ordinary local political changes* which are usual on a change of administration should be made. In regard to the navy-yard at Norfolk, he was particularly solicitous that there should be no action taken which would indicate a want of confidence in the authorities and people, or which would be likely to beget distrust. No ships were to be withdrawn, no fortifications erected. . . .

" Not until the last of March did the President fully and finally decide to attempt to relieve Fort Sumter. . . .

" The attempt to relieve Major Anderson, though a military question, was a political necessity. *It became a duty of the Government after all conciliatory efforts were exhausted.*"

In allusion to his order of April 18, 1861, to Commodore Paulding, " to proceed forthwith to Norfolk and take command of all the naval forces there afloat," and " with the means placed at his command to do all in his power to protect and place beyond danger the vessels and property belonging to the United States," he says :

" This order was to repel, not to assail; *the administration continued to be forbearing,* and to the last was not aggressive. Extreme men were dissatisfied and censorious because the administration did not attack, though not prepared. On to Sumter was the word, as at a later period the cry, equally inconsiderate, was, ' On to Richmond.' "

Without specifying the many slanders promulgated against Mr. Buchanan in respect to his conduct and sentiments touching the war after its commencement and during its progress, I think the time has arrived to lay before the public extracts of letters from him in my possession, which ought to remove the false impressions that many persons have no doubt honestly entertained on the subject, from too confident a reliance upon reckless partisan statements. I shall omit, mostly, those parts of a personal or private nature, confining myself mainly to his observations upon public affairs. His first letter, which I will offer, is dated—

"WHEATLAND, NEAR LANCASTER, July 13, 1861.

"MY DEAR SIR,—My late severe illness has hitherto prevented me from acknowledging the receipt of your kind letter of May last. . . .

"The future of our country presents a dark cloud through which my vision cannot penetrate. The assault upon Fort Sumter was the commencement of war by the Confederate States, and no alternative was left but to prosecute it with vigor on our part. Up to and until all social and political relations ceased between the secession leaders and myself, I had often warned them that the North would rise to a man against them if such an assault were made. No alternative seems now to be left but to prosecute hostilities, unless the seceding States shall return to their allegiance, or until it shall be demonstrated that this object, which is nearest my heart, cannot be accomplished. From present appearances it seems certain that they would accept no terms of compromise short of an absolute recognition of their independence, which is impossible. I am glad that General Scott does not underrate the strength of his enemy, which would be a great fault in a commander. With all my heart and soul I wish him success. I think that some very unfit military appointments have been made, from which we may suffer in some degree in the beginning, but ere long merit will rise to its appropriate station. It was just so at the commencement of the war of 1812. I was rejoiced at the appointment of General Dix, and believe he will do both himself and the country honor.

　　　　　　"Very respectfully, your friend,
　　　　　　　　　　　　　　"JAMES BUCHANAN.
"HON. HORATIO KING."

　　　　　　　　　"WHEATLAND, September 18, 1861.

"MY DEAR SIR,—I think I can perceive in the public mind a more fixed, resolute, and determined purpose than ever to prosecute the war to a successful termination with all the men and means in our power. Enlistments are now proceeding much more rapidly than a few weeks ago, and I am truly glad of it. The time has passed for offering compromises and terms of peace to the seceded States. We well know that under existing circumstances, they would accept of nothing less than a recognition of their independence, which it is impossible that we should grant.

There is a time for all things under the sun, but surely this is not the moment for paralyzing the arm of the national administration by a suicidal conflict among ourselves, but for bold, energetic, and united action. The Democratic party has ever been devoted to the Constitution and the Union, and I rejoice that among the many thousands who have rushed to their defence in this hour of peril, a large majority belong to that time-honored party.

"I sat down to write you a few lines, but find that my letter has swelled into large proportions.

"From your friend,

"Very respectfully,

"JAMES BUCHANAN.

"HON. HORATIO KING."

"WHEATLAND, NEAR LANCASTER, November 12, 1861.

"MY DEAR SIR,— . . . By the by, it is difficult to imagine how it was possible to mystify so plain a subject under the laws of war as an exchange of prisoners with the rebels, so as to make it mean a recognition in any form, however remote, of their confederacy. It admits nothing but that your enemy, whether pirate, rebel, Algerine, or regular government, has got your soldiers in his possession. The exchange admits nothing beyond. The laws of humanity are not confined to any other limit. The more barbarous and cruel the enemy, the greater is the necessity for an exchange, because the greater is the danger that they will shed the blood of your soldiers. I do not apply this remark to the Confederate States, and only use it by way of illustration. I believe they have not treated their prisoners cruelly.

"They do not seem to understand at Washington another plain principle of the law of nations, and that is, that while the capture and confiscation of private property at sea is still permissible, this is not the case on land. Such are all the authorities. The Treaty of Ghent recognized slaves as private property, and therefore they were to be restored; and we paid for all our army consumed in Mexico. The rebels have violated this law in the most reckless manner. . . .

"From your friend,

"Very respectfully,

"JAMES BUCHANAN.

"HON. HORATIO KING."

"WHEATLAND, January 28, 1862.

"MY DEAR SIR,— . . . I do most earnestly hope that our army may be able to do something effective before the first of April. If not, there is great danger not merely of British but of European interference.

There will then be such a clamor for cotton among the millions of operatives dependent upon it for bread, both in England and on the Continent, that I fear for the blockade.

"From my heart I wish Stanton success, not only for his own sake but for that of the country. . . I believe him to be a truly honest man, who will never sanction corruption, though he may not be quite able to grapple with treason as the lion grapples with his prey.

"I remain, very respectfully, your friend,
"JAMES BUCHANAN.
"HON. HORATIO KING."

"WHEATLAND, NEAR LANCASTER, February 10, 1862.

"MY DEAR SIR,— . . . I trust that our late victories may be the prelude to those more decided, and that, ere the spring opens, we may be in such a condition as to afford no pretext to England and France to interfere in our domestic affairs.

"From your friend, very respectfully,
"JAMES BUCHANAN.
"HON. HORATIO KING."

I regret that from this time till near the close of the war our correspondence was suspended; but I heard from him frequently through common friends, and know that he remained faithful and true to the end. In the month of August, 1866, being in the city of Portland, Maine, I took occasion to have published in the *Eastern Argus* a highly patriotic letter which he addressed, on the 28th of September, 1861, to Samuel A. Worth, Esq., in answer to an invitation from him, "as chairman of the appropriate committee, to attend and address a Union meeting of the citizens of Chester and Lancaster Counties, to be held at Hayesville, on the 1st of October." He excused himself on account of feeble health, but said: "Were it possible for me to address your meeting, waiving all other topics, I should confine myself to a solemn and earnest appeal to my countrymen, and especially those without families, to volunteer for the war, and join the many thousands of brave and patriotic volunteers who are already in the field." He concluded by saying, that "until that happy day shall arrive [of the return of the seceding States], it will be our duty to support the President with all the men and means at the command of the country, in a vigorous and successful prosecution of the war." Under date of August 29, 1866, referring to this "Hayesville letter," as he termed it, he said in a letter to me, "I thank you for having caused it to be published. It is in perfect consistency with all I have written or said."

If he was not as prominently active during the war as might have been, the secret of it may perhaps be discovered in his reply to the following letter, the production of which in this familiar communication (since, contrary to my usual custom, I happened to retain a copy) will, I trust, be excused:

"WASHINGTON, April 22, 1865.

"MY DEAR SIR,—It is a long time since I have had the pleasure of receiving a letter from you, and, although I believe the last which passed between us was from me, I venture again to address you, for within the past week my thoughts have been frequently directed toward you and the scenes of the last few weeks of your administration. The frightful tragedy just enacted in our midst appears only as the natural sequence of the acts of the rebel conspirators in commencing first to denounce you because you resisted their efforts to take possession of or break up the Government, and next in openly assailing the Government by fire and sword after the reins had passed from your hands. I have felt a strong desire to hear from you, not only in months past, but especially in this period when the whole heart of the nation is bowed and stricken with grief. In all the letters I have from you wherein you speak of the rebellion, it is a pleasure and a consolation to know that your declarations, and hopes, and prayers are all for your country and its brave defenders, and it is reasonable to suppose that few if any of our fellow-citizens can be more deeply moved than you yourself must be at the awful assassination of President Lincoln. Why, then, may we not be favored by a word from you—possibly, in all this darkness, a word of encouragement and of hope? Whether for the public eye or not, be assured it will always afford me sincere pleasure to receive a letter from you.

"I have the honor to be, very respectfully and truly,

"HORATIO KING.

"His Excellency, JAMES BUCHANAN, Wheatland, Pa."

"WHEATLAND, NEAR LANCASTER, April 27, 1865.

"MY DEAR SIR,—Rest assured that I was much gratified to receive your favor of the 22d. If I was indebted a letter to you, I am sorry for it; because I entertain no other feeling toward you but that of kindness and friendship.

"In common with you, I feel the assassination of President Lincoln to be a terrible misfortune to our country. May God, in his mercy, ward from us the evils which it portends, and bring good out of this fearful calamity! My intercourse with our deceased President, both on his visit to me after his arrival in Washington and on the day of his first inauguration, convinced me that he was a man of a kind and benevolent heart, and of plain, sincere, and frank manners. I have never since changed my opinion of his character. Indeed, I felt for him much personal regard.

"Throughout the years of the war I never faltered in my conviction that it would eventually terminate in the crushing of the rebellion, and was ever opposed to the recognition of the Confederate government by any act which even looked in that direction. Believing, always, secession to be a palpable violation of the Constitution, I considered the acts of secession to be absolutely void, and that the States were therefore still members, though rebellious members, of the Union.

"Having prayed night and morning for the restoration of the Union, the Constitution, and our civil liberties, and fondly believing that President Lincoln was the destined instrument in the hands of Divine Providence to accomplish these inestimable blessings, the awful news of his diabolical assassination at such a moment overwhelmed me with sorrow.

"These are my heartfelt sentiments which you invite, but they are not for the public eye. When, on the first opportunity after the battle of Bull Run I expressed strong opinions to a public meeting in support of the war, I was assailed as violently for this . . . as if I had uttered treason. If I were now to write for the public, which I could do with heartfelt emotion, on the subject of the assassination, I should be treated in a similar manner.

"My health is good, considering that I was seventy-four years of age on Sunday last. I lead a tranquil and retired life; and should be very glad to welcome you once more to Wheatland.

"From your friend, very respectfully,

"JAMES BUCHANAN.

"HON. HORATIO KING."

In conclusion, let me say that I present this communication in no partisan spirit, but purely in the interest of truth and justice, without reference to party politics. Moreover, I have no hesitation in declaring that I consider it a duty plainly devolving upon me to bear this testimony, while yet I may, to the honesty, fidelity, and patriotism of Mr. Buchanan. Seldom if ever absent from his post, whether as senator, secretary of state, minister plenipotentiary, or President of the United States, he was attentive to every duty incumbent upon him. While President, if a citizen, no matter how humble, appealed from any head of a department to him for redress, he always listened with patience, and, calling for a full statement of facts of the case, investigated it thoroughly, and gave his decision in the spirit of an upright judge. No one was turned away. He acted as the President of the whole people, and as feeling that he was ultimately to be held responsible for every official act done under his administration. If matters happened to go wrong, no one regretted it more than he. His ardent desire was for everything to go right. Happy would it be for the people of this country could they be assured of always securing in the higher posts of honor and authority, men as able, conscientious, and patriotic as was James Buchanan, late President of the United States.

Washington, September, 1870.

CHAPTER XIII.

LETTER ON THE WAR.

Its Progress—The Hand of the Almighty now Apparent—Poison at the National Hotel.

WASHINGTON, Nov. 13, 1863.

REV. G. M. P. KING, PROVIDENCE, R. I.

DEAR SIR,—What you say in regard to the sentiments and conduct of some of the people in New England touching the war would have surprised me had I not in my visit there last summer heard and seen the same things. It seemed to me that many of our friends there considered it their duty, in standing up for what they called the "rights of the South," to advocate the cause of slavery with quite as much earnestness as we of the Democratic party in a spirit of generosity, when we knew less about it than at present, felt constrained to do in our political contests previous to the war. Instead of moving forward with the rest of the world, they appear to remain stationary. As an instance of this not a little amusing, I observed in a Maine newspaper, just before the late election in that State, an extract from a speech of George F. Shepley, Esq., now brigadier-general of volunteers, delivered in 1856, in which he took occasion to pay a high compliment to John C. Breckinridge, then a candidate for the Vice-Presidency, which extract was quoted to show General Shepley's present *inconsistency* in giving his hearty support to the measures of the administration for the suppression of the rebellion in which this same recreant son of Kentucky is engaged! I am pained to say that I met some who justified the South in taking up arms, and who were bitterly severe upon the administration for every shortcoming, real or supposed, while blind to the stupendous crimes and wickedness which

have characterized the boasted "chivalry" of the South
from the moment of their embracing the hideous monster,
Treason, to the present time.   Averring that the South was
fighting for republican independence as fought the heroes
of 1776, they charged that it was the purpose of the administration to prosecute the war for the abolishment of
slavery and the subjugation of her people.   They seemed
willing to ignore, if not actually to deny, the fact that,
instead of republican liberty, the leaders of the rebellion
openly proclaimed that they were contending for the establishment of a government, than which none could be more
aristocratic, and of which, as declared by their Vice-President, A. H. Stephens, *slavery* was the "corner-stone." But
the further we move onward into the heart of the South,
the clearer view do we gain, not only of the real character
of slavery, but of those who seek to found a government
upon it.   You have no doubt read a remarkable article on
this subject, which appeared in the Richmond *Examiner* of
28th May last, at a time when the rebels were flushed with
success and full of hope.   The writer of that article says,
"The establishment of the Confederacy is verily a distinct
reaction against the whole course of the mistaken civilization of the age.   And this is the true reason why we have
been left without the sympathy of the nations till we conquered that sympathy with the sharp edge of the sword.
For liberty, equality, fraternity, we have deliberately sub-
stituted slavery, subordination, and government.   Those
social and political problems which rack and torture modern
society, we have undertaken to solve for ourselves in our
own way and on our own principles." . . . "Reverently we
feel," he continues, "that our Confederacy is a God-sent
missionary to the nations, with great truths to preach.   We
must speak them boldly, and whoso hath ears to hear let
him hear."   Is it not passing strange, when we behold the
South—I mean those who control there—acting up to these
monstrous doctrines, that there should be any division of

sentiment in the free States as to the policy or importance
of subduing at once and forever a power promising or undertaking thus to subvert the principles of liberty throughout the world?   In the presence of such declarations, and
the better knowledge obtained of the institution of slavery
since the war broke out, need we marvel that intelligent
statesmen like Mr. Bright, of the English Parliament, for
instance, should say of the South, " Her object is to retain
the power to breed negroes, to lash negroes, to chain them,
to buy and sell negroes, to deny them the enjoyment of the
commonest family ties, to break their hearts by rending
them at their pleasure, to close their mental eye against a
glimpse of that knowledge which separates us from the
brute creation, for, in accordance with their laws, it is a
penal act to teach a negro to read."

These are sweeping charges, and I do not quote to en-
dorse them, although one must be very blind now to doubt
that the South is fighting to perpetuate slavery by the
establishment of a government hostile to the rights and in
denial of the dignity of labor.   Nor is it less apparent,
judging from the ferocity and heartless barbarity manifested by the traitors towards the Union prisoners in many
instances, and towards the Union people of the South, that
the effect of slavery upon them is to the last extent per-
nicious.   Still they cling to and fight for it.

But a great change is going on—greater by far in the
border States and at the South than at the North—in regard to this institution.   One of the most striking individual instances of this is to be seen in the recent address
of E. W. Gantt, a member elect to Congress, in 1860, from
Arkansas, who, until within a few months past, has held a
commission in the rebel service.   Of slavery he says, " Its
existence had become incompatible with the existence of
the Government; for while it had stood as a wall damming
up the current and holding back the people and laborers
of the North, it had, by thus precluding free intercourse

10

between the sections, produced a marked change in their manners, customs, and sentiments; and the two sections were growing more divergent every day. This wall or the Government—one must give way. The shock came which was to settle the question. I thought the Government was divided and negro slavery established forever. I erred. The Government was stronger than slavery. Reunion is certain, but not more certain than the downfall of slavery. . . . We fought for negro slavery. We have lost."

Look, too, at the wonderful strides towards general emancipation in Maryland, Missouri, and several other slave States; nor let it be forgotten with what general satisfaction immediate emancipation has been acquiesced in in this District. There was at first, to be sure, some hesitancy, and a little grumbling on the part of a few of the owners, while a smaller number declined to present their slaves for valuation and compensation, on the ground, as it was understood, that they hoped and believed that Jefferson Davis would sooner or later have permanent possession here at the capital, and would, of course, protect them in their "sacred rights." But while this latter number, which was very small, are no doubt vexed with themselves for their latent treachery, those who took advantage of the law under a sort of protest would, I doubt not, every one of them now heartily approve it, were the thing to be gone over again.

In view of these among other numerous considerations patent to every one who reads, it is unaccountable that so many of our good people at the North, as if in a spirit of magnanimity, should esteem it either their duty or good policy to brace themselves so firmly in support of this tottering institution of slavery, and especially that they should be so ready to denounce such men as General Butler, General Shepley, Daniel S. Dickinson, and others for yielding to their honest convictions, and with Joseph Holt, Andrew Johnson, Horace Maynard, and hosts of other patriotic

Southerners, saying, "God speed to universal emancipation."

Do you ask if I have turned Abolitionist? I answer that the political Abolitionism of former days differs widely from the great movements now in progress for the freedom not alone of the slaves, but of the down-trodden, laboring white population, too, of the South. I am constrained to believe with Mr. Gantt, that "the mission of slavery is accomplished." And when, as he says, he has "recently talked with Southern slaveholders from every State," that "they are tired of slavery, and believe they could make more clear money and live more peaceably without than with it," why should we of the free States longer strive for its maintenance? Mr. Boyce, of South Carolina, warned his friends that if they brought on a war against their Government it would be the death of their cherished institution. They did commence the war; let them suffer, as they are doing in many ways, its legitimate consequences.

Certainly we are not called upon to interpose any counteracting obstacle. Let the work go on. Do we not plainly see in it the hand of the Almighty? Heretofore we have, as it were, waited for the records of history to be made up before being permitted to see clearly the workings of Providence in the affairs of men. As from an eminence we looked back into the past to behold "His wonderful doings." But now we seem to feel His immediate presence and to see His all-powerful hand in the great events daily transpiring around us.

No, my friend, you well know I am beyond the influence of either official position (for I neither hold nor desire any) or partisan politics. Neither "Abolitionism," "Republicanism," nor "Democracy," in a party sense, have I anything to do with during the war. My motto is, "My country *first*—afterwards, if need be, my party." Let us give to the administration a cheerful support. Its responsibilities are immense—how tremendously oppressive we cannot fully realize until the war is ended, if, indeed, we ever can. Let us seek to strengthen, not to destroy it. If we think errors are committed, point them out in a spirit of friendship, not of carping bitterness. Let us be united. Before there can be peace the military power of the rebels must be broken and thoroughly subdued. This can be done only by exerting our united strength against them. They had been long preparing for this struggle, and had, no doubt, many times surveyed the whole field ere entering upon it in hostile array.

You have, no doubt, seen the letter of that arch-traitor, J. M. Mason, to Jefferson Davis, written in September, 1856, when the latter was Secretary of War, in which Mason informs him, through his "most private ear," that the Governors of several of the Southern States had agreed to rendezvous at Raleigh, evidently for treasonable purposes, in view of the anticipated election of Fremont to the Presidency, in which event he said he had already given it as his judgment, that the South should not pause, but proceed at once to immediate, absolute, and *eternal* separation, adding, —as he knew what he deserved,—"so I am a candidate for the first halter." The principal object of the letter, however, was to urge Davis to comply with Governor Wise's *official* request "to exchange with Virginia, on fair terms of difference, *percussion for flint muskets.*"

This, by the way, is the same "J. M. Mason" who, when the question was to be submitted to Virginia whether or not she should secede from the Union, you will recollect, had the unblushing effrontery to advise all who were opposed to secession *to leave the State!* The same, too, who, in his place in the United States Senate, in the spring of 1861, with an air of offended dignity, expressed his indignation at the quartering of United States troops in this city and the mounting of cannon on the land side of Fortress Monroe! It was, indeed, a sore thing for the conspirators, the arrival here of one or more batteries of flying artillery, and they used their utmost power to prevent it. It seriously interfered with their arrangements; for there is scarcely a doubt that their fixed purpose was to prevent President Lincoln's inauguration and take violent possession of the Government.

Again, looking farther back, it should create no surprise if, when the entire history of this infamous conspiracy finally comes to the light, it shall be found that the poisoning at the National Hotel, where Mr. Buchanan was stopping in the spring of 1857, prior to his inauguration, had for its special object quietly to put him out of the way, in order to give place to Vice-President Breckinridge, upon whom they could rely to co-operate with them, through Floyd, Cobb, and Thompson, in usurping the Government in the event of being defeated, as they were, at the polls. Such a suggestion then would have shocked the public sense; but after what we have since witnessed,—the perjuries, the thefts, the robberies, the cold-blooded murders, the savage cruelties of this traitor horde,—no act of theirs, however horrible, need startle us.

But this is diverging. The signs of an early suppression of the rebellion are auspicious. Our armies on land and water are bravely pressing onward; the rebel cause is fast losing ground in Europe, where so much pains have been taken by Southern emissaries to enlist the aristocracy and enemies of the United States in their behalf; no more piratical vessels will be constructed in England or France to prey upon our commerce; the rebels are in a straitened condition for the necessaries of life; and all that is now wanted to put an end to further bloodshed, is for the people of the loyal States at home to reinforce and support our armies in the field, in the same spirit of union and patriotism with which they rallied in defence of our flag when it was first assailed at Fort Sumter. This will ensure certain success and end the war. Then the seceded States will return to their positions under the Constitution; slavery, if not already abolished, will have been destroyed as a political power and be in a condition speedily to be annihilated by the mighty current of emancipation sweeping southwardly from the border slave States; fraternity and brotherly love will resume their sway; we shall, I trust, all feel humbled and yet exalted by our trials, and ready devoutly to exclaim, "Let the heavens be glad and let the earth rejoice: and let men say among the nations, THE LORD REIGNETH."

Very truly yours,
HORATIO KING.

NOTE.—In reference to the above, I am quite sure I shall not only be excused, but that I shall receive the thanks of every loyal reader, for giving place here to the following letter, showing, as it does, the hearty approbation of one of the ablest, most eloquent, and patriotic of American statesmen:

WASHINGTON, December 12, 1863.

MY DEAR SIR,—I return your letter, which I have read with great gratification. It is fully up to the measure of loyalty and statesmanship demanded by the stern emergencies of the times, and cannot fail to meet with a grateful and appreciative reception from all true men. As a page in the volume of your patriotic life, I am sure that in the years to come you will look back upon it with unalloyed pleasure.

Sincerely yours,
J. HOLT.

HON. HORATIO KING.

CHAPTER XIV.

PRESIDENT BUCHANAN'S RECORD.

A critic of the *Atlantic Monthly* criticised—General Dix's famous despatch—Opinions of Judge Black and General Holt.

If the spiteful, and what I cannot help characterizing as a juvenile, criticism of Mr. Curtis's " Life of Buchanan" in the November number of the *Atlantic Monthly* shall have the effect to induce the readers of that magazine to peruse his work for themselves, the labor of the critic may not fail entirely of good effect, for no one can read that work attentively without being convinced of the honesty of purpose, great ability, and wisdom of President Buchanan.

Not to enter into any lengthy discussion, let us quote a few of the critic's statements, with running remarks. Speaking of Mr. Buchanan's failure to receive the nomination for President in 1852, the writer says :

"The rejected candidate resigned himself to his disappointment and was consoled by the mission to England."

The evidence presented by Mr. Curtis clearly shows that Mr. Buchanan consented reluctantly to accept the appointment to England, and finally agreed to take it only on condition that the " seat of negotiations," especially including " the Central American questions," should be at London instead of Washington. Again, says the critic :

"There is something very pitiable, something almost tragic, in the figure of James Buchanan during those last months of his administration. . . . On Mr. Curtis's own showing—presumably the best that can be made—Buchanan failed miserably at the great crisis in the nation's life. He took the ground that he would not precipitate war by applying force to prevent a State from seceding, but that he would defend the flag and property of the United States."

The writer ought to know, what every school-boy knows who has studied the Constitution of the United States, that the President would have violated that instrument and broken his oath of office had he attempted of himself to "precipitate war by applying force to prevent a State from seceding." Moreover, his great aim and most anxious desire was to avoid an open rupture, and this policy of forbearance was also pursued by President Lincoln until all hope of a peaceful settlement had to be abandoned. Says Mr. Gideon Welles, Mr. Lincoln's Secretary of the Navy:

"At the time of Mr. Lincoln's inauguration, and for several weeks thereafter, he and others indulged in the hope of a peaceful solution of the pending questions, and a desire, amounting almost to a belief, that Virginia and other border States might, by forbearance and a calm and conciliatory policy, continue faithful to the Union. . . . And to conciliate the people of Virginia and the convention then in session, the President desired that there should be no step taken which would give offence."

In his message to Congress of the 4th of July, 1861, President Lincoln himself said:

"The policy chosen looked to the exhaustion of all peaceable measures before a resort to any stronger ones. It sought to hold the public places and property not already wrested from the Government, and to collect the revenue, relying for the rest on time, discussion, and the ballot-box. It promised a continuance of the mails at Government expense to the very people who were resisting the Government, and it gave repeated pledges against any disturbance to any of the people or any of their rights. Of all that a president might constitutionally and justifiably do in such a case, everything was forborne without which it was possible to keep the Government on foot."

The *Atlantic* censor continues:

"General Dix sent his famous order ['If any one attempts to haul down the American flag, shoot him on the spot'], and says he did not show it to the President, because he knew the latter would not have allowed it to go forth. In other words, the President of the United States would have refused to order an officer of the Government to defend the national flag. It seems hardly worth while to write a volume in defence of a man who was in such a state of cowardly panic as that. Mr. Curtis says that Buchanan had no troops, and that Congress would not do anything to help him. He had enough troops to have fought on the instant, and at the first moment the flag was touched or a public building seized. The moment a move was made by the South he should have struck hard, and, whether defeated or victorious, the next breeze that swept from the North would have brought to his ear the clash of resounding arms. Congress did nothing for him for the obvious reason that they did not trust him. They knew that he was timid and time-serving, and they then thought him a traitor. Many people in the North could not believe that the South would really secede, and the leaders who saw what was coming were simply playing for time, and waiting until they could get a president in whom they could confide. The fact was that Mr. Buchanan was a very weak man, who had been a tool of stronger forces all his life."

Now, in answer to all this tirade let me say, first, that I have no doubt General Dix was correct in the belief that President Buchanan would have objected to the sending of his famous order, although, knowing that I fully sympathized with him as regards the adoption of the most energetic measures in support of the Union, he told me of it the evening he sent it. I am free to say, too, that it met my hearty approbation. But, after all, showing the true grit, as it certainly did, may there not be some doubt of its wisdom? Not only was no attempt whatever made to carry it into effect, but I have it from Mr. William Hemphill Jones himself, to whom the order was sent, that he was obliged to steal out of New Orleans to save his own neck.

Let me conclude with the handsome tribute which General Holt, in his pamphlet already cited, pays to his old chief, under date of October 8, 1883.

"I cannot close this communication without bearing emphatic testimony to the loyalty of President Buchanan throughout the troubled and trying scenes which marked the last months of his administration. With measureless responsibilities oppressing him, badgered by traitors and by the department of the Government which owed him sympathy and a loyal support, and standing, as he did, on the brink of a great national calamity, the imminence of which was awing all hearts, he was often cast down, but never unfaithful to his duties. Amid the blinding rancor of party strife he was constantly misunderstood and constantly misrepresented. He was not an aggressive man, nor at all given to violent forms of speech or of action. He shrunk from the contemplation of civil war and the bloodshed it would involve, and sought to postpone it to the last possible moment. But in all this there was no taint of disloyalty. While, however, uniformly gentle and suave in his modes, he was not the less firm in view of the ends to be finally attained. And yet it was this very gentleness and suavity—the result in part, perhaps, of his peculiar temperament, but yet more, it may be, of the training inseparable from his diplomatic career—which often misled men who paused not to reflect that iron hands are sometimes found in silken gloves."

WASHINGTON, October 27, 1883.

CHAPTER XV.

GENESIS OF THE CIVIL WAR.

Fall of Fort Sumter—Acts of the Government and Major Anderson Preceding the Fall—Defence of Buchanan's Administration—President Lincoln's Forbearance.

AFTER all that has been written on the subject of Fort Sumter, the failure to send reinforcements to Major Anderson, in command of the forts in Charleston harbor, and the charges brought against President Buchanan's administration on that account, it seems almost superfluous to attempt any further answer to such charges. No one who will read Mr. Buchanan's own account of the matter, as related in his book, entitled "Mr. Buchanan's Administration on the Eve of the Rebellion" (1866), followed in 1883 by Curtis's clear exposition in his "Life of James Buchanan," need require more evidence to convince him that what was done, or left undone, in respect to reinforcements or supplies to those forts, affords no good ground of complaint against President Buchanan. Unfortunately, however, those books are beyond the reach of the general public; hence it is no uncommon thing to hear him severely censured because of his failure to order reinforcements sent and of the unfounded charge that he entered into an "agreement" or "understanding" with the South Carolinian authorities to withhold reinforcements so long as no attacks should be made on the forts.

One among the latest arraignments of President Buchanan, mainly on this subject, comes from Samuel Wylie Crawford, "brevet major-general, U. S. A., A.M., M.D., LL.D.," in his work, entitled "The Genesis of the Civil War." Although the above titles appear after the name of the author on the title-page, we learn from him, in the last chapter of his book, that he was assistant surgeon on the medical staff of Major Anderson, and that it was not until the return of the command from Fort Sumter to New York that he was appointed major in the Thirteenth United States Infantry, from which position, by gallant and meritorious services in various battles, he rose to his present rank. His book of 469 octavo pages relates almost exclusively to the action of the South Carolina authorities, of the Government at Washington, and of Major Anderson, touching Fort Sumter and the other forts and United States arsenal at Charleston. Whoever shall read this book will, I think, be surprised at two things at least: the first is, that he has given such prominence to the acts and sayings of leading secessionists, notably the "narrative of William H. Trescot," who was assistant Secretary of State under Buchanan, serving, according to his own statement, until the 17th of December, three days only before the passage of the secession ordinance of South Carolina. For weeks before severing his official connection with the Department of State he had, according to his own admission and from letters now published, been acting as confidential agent of "the leaders of the (secession) movement in his own State," and immediately thereafter "he became the agent of his State at Washington until his return to South Carolina in February, 1861," when "he made a record of his impressions of the events which have been the subject of so much controversy, and the truth about which is of essential importance to the future history of the country. A record thus made [General Crawford continues] may well be considered a valuable contribution to the materials of that future history. It is from this manuscript the writer has drawn largely, and oftentimes the clear and vigorous narrative has been inserted in the terse and graphic words of the author himself."

Surely General Crawford is to be congratulated on being able to bring to his aid so astute and valuable an assistant, whose name, from the amount of matter furnished by him, might not have been out of place on the title-page of this remarkable "Genesis of the Civil War." In a matter relating to secession and the rebellion, such a witness in the case of a gallant Union officer and historian striving to convict the President of the United States of a dereliction of duty appears, in his estimation, to have been considered more credible and of much greater weight than any testimony of the President himself, or that of any member of his Cabinet. The latter is not less explicit and abundant than the former, and was ready at hand.

By way of parenthesis, I may remark that the private secretaries to President Lincoln, in their one-sided, partisan "history," have resorted to this same "narrative" of Mr. Trescot, as well as to the testimony of other distinguished secessionists, with a view to present President Buchanan in an unfavorable light, if not actually as a traitor, before the country. It would be interesting to know whether or not this sort of aid on the part of Mr. Trescot to the Republican cause was the inspiring motive which led Mr. Blaine, when Secretary of State, to select him for one or more important diplomatic appointments.

One other thing that must strike the reader of General Crawford's work is the conflicting estimates which he, unwittingly perhaps, places on the character, if not the motives, of President Buchanan.

After narrating what he holds the President had done or left undone in regard to South Carolina, he goes on to say:

"The failure on the part of the President to reinforce the Southern forts, or any of them, . . . had produced its legitimate result. . . . Had such relief been promptly sent . . . the situation might have been far different. . . . It is true that the organized force legitimately under his command, as reported by Lieutenant-General Scott, was small ; but it was at the time at least sufficient to show the purpose of the Government and to hold Fort Sumter until Congress could come to the rescue of the country. But the President did nothing. His fear that by his own act he might inaugurate hostilities and so bring on civil war, sustained by his political convictions that the Union could not be preserved by a war between the States, his overwhelming desire for peace, and his hope to keep the border States, amounted to a timidity which ' wholly incapacitated him for action.' . . . When history shall come to pen the record of the close of his career it will judge him not from what he did, but what, from his great opportunities and grave responsibilities, he utterly failed to do."

Now, before turning back to his previous record, let it be observed that General Crawford gives the sentiment he quotes against President Buchanan—"Wholly incapacitated him for action"—as his own; but he does not tell us from whom the language came. We might infer from his introduction that it was from his principal witness, although Martin J. Crawford, one of the Confederate commissioners from Montgomery, is credited by the author with having employed similar language in speaking of the President. Mr. Crawford had resigned his seat as a member of Congress from Georgia, and, coming on the 3d of March fresh from the new-fledged Confederate Government, he probably flattered himself that he might induce the President to take some action by which they could avail themselves to their advantage in their proceedings with the incoming administration. Finding, as he wrote home, that he had become "fully satisfied that it would not be wise to approach Mr. Buchanan with any hope of his doing anything which would result advantageously to our [Confederate] Government," in his chagrin, he added that he found him " wholly disqualified for his present position." Therefore, " he would not attempt to open negotiation with the outgoing administration."

Our author is entitled to as much of the testimony of his peculiarly qualified witnesses from the Confederate side as I can possibly find room for.

But to return. Mr. Lincoln was elected on the 6th of November, prior to which time it was generally supposed, certainly by all Union men, that his election would be acquiesced in, North and South. It was not until the threatening attitude of South Carolina and rumblings of disunion on the part of secessionists in other Southern States and in Washington that much, if anything, was said on the importance of strengthening either our military or naval defences. " Meantime [says General Crawford] the Government at Washington was not indifferent to the movements in South Carolina," where, " as soon as the result of the election was known, the Governor called for the services of the Washington Light Infantry, and stationed them as a guard over the United States arsenal, in the city of Charleston, on the 12th of November." An inventory, afterward taken, placed the value of this property at $400,000, all of which was seized and appropriated to the use of the State.

At this period Secretary Floyd, while holding to the right of secession, professed opposition to its exercise, but believed it injudicious to attempt to reinforce the Southern forts, while General Cass and Judge Black (Trescot states) were in favor of it, and the President also " then informed him that he had determined to reinforce the garrison in Charleston harbor, upon which a very animated discussion arose." Floyd said " that he would cut off his right hand before he would sign an order to send reinforcements to the Carolina forts. Thompson, Secretary of the Interior, agreed with him perfectly ;" and " the President consented to suspend his decision until General Scott could reach Washington." It was now proposed that Mr. Trescot call on the President and announce his determination to resign, and proceed at once to Columbia "to lay the facts before the executive of South Carolina" should the determination to reinforce be insisted on. "I would be in Columbia, he said, in thirty-six hours, and upon such information there could be no earthly doubt that the forts would be occupied in the following twenty-four," before reinforcements could reach them. Merely the sending of ordinary supplies to Fort Moultrie, he "believed, would lead to the occupation of Fort Sumter in forty-eight hours."

Under date of November 15, 1860, "a special order was issued by command of Lieutenant-General Scott, directing Major Robert Anderson, First Artillery, to proceed to Fort Moultrie and immediately relieve Brevet-Colonel John L. Gardiner, lieutenant-colonel First Artillery, in command thereof." Colonel Gardiner, it appears, had, on the 7th of November, sent to the arsenal at Charleston—"a matter of ordinary routine"—for a quantity of military stores, and "to avoid observation, it was thought advisable to put the soldiers detailed for the duty in citizens' dress." Nevertheless, "the movements of the men were watched—information was sent at once to Charleston," whose authorities prevented the execution of the order. That effort of Colonel Gardiner, General Crawford says, "cost him his position," but there is nothing to show that even General Scott, through whom the order for his removal was made, was advised of its impelling motive; and it is not at all probable that the President was consulted or knew anything about it. Mr. Trescot was in the secret. The adjutant-general, S. Cooper, was in the interest of the secessionists, and afterwards filled the same position under Jefferson Davis, while Floyd, although still claiming to be a Union man, "on his arrival at Richmond [our author states] announced 'that he had, while Secretary of War, supplied the South with arms in anticipation of the approaching rebellion'—a confession that he had proved treacherous to his former high official trust. He succeeded.

He was taken into favor and was subsequently appointed to the rank of brigadier-general in the Confederate army."

We may add here that on the 20th of December, without the knowledge or consent of the President, he ordered to the forts at Ship Island and at Galveston—" in no condition to receive their armaments!"—one hundred and thirteen columbiads and eleven 32-pounders. Fortunately, the order was revoked by his successor, Joseph Holt, before the guns could be shipped.

On his appointment, "Major Anderson proceeded at once to his post, and, on the 23d of November, recommended that Fort Sumter—the key of entrance to the harbor—should be garrisoned at once." This was as quickly communicated to the South Carolina authorities, for the city was full of secession spies, always on the alert, and there was no possibility of any movement being made by the Government for protection against treason without its being immediately known at Charleston. Colonel R. B. Rhett, Jr., a prominent and influential citizen of South Carolina, urged upon the Governor " that a large steamer of the Boston line should be chartered, five hundred riflemen put on board, and the ship anchored abreast of the fort [Sumter] commanding the entrance of the inner harbor."

Instead of going to the President, as at first proposed, with a notice of his determination to resign and hasten to Columbia, should the President determine to reinforce the garrison at Charleston, it was decided that he should write to Governor Gist—" tell him that the President was under very strong apprehensions that the people of Charleston would seize the forts; that in consequence he felt bound to send reinforcements; that the Southern members of the Cabinet would resist this policy to resignation, but they thought that if he felt authorized to write a letter assuring the President that if no reinforcements were sent, there would be no attempt upon the forts before the meeting of the convention," etc.   On the 29th of November, in a letter marked " strictly confidential," he proceeds to execute this trust, assuring the Governor that he wished him " distinctly to understand that there is no possibility of such an order being issued without the dissolution of the Cabinet and your receiving ample notice."   This, observe, was from the Assistant Secretary of State.   The Governor answered Mr. Trescot November 29 : " I have found great difficulty in restraining the people of Charleston from seizing the forts, and have only been able to restrain them by the assurance that no additional troops would be sent to the forts, or any munitions of war."   In a letter marked " confidential," of same date, Governor Gist wrote to Mr. Trescot to "ask if you [he] have any objections, in the event of your connection with the Federal Government ceasing, to remain in Washington and act as confidential agent for this department."   He takes occasion also to remark : " If there is any inquiry as to the course South Carolina will pursue, you may safely say that she will not permit any increase of troops or munitions of war in the forts or arsenals, and, considering it an evidence of intention to coerce and an act of war, she will use force to prevent it, and a collision must inevitably ensue."

General Cass's letter of resignation was handed to the President on the 15th of December, " the President [as Mr. Buchanan himself states in his book, page 167] having determined not to disturb the status quo at Charleston as long as our troops should continue to be hospitably treated by the inhabitants, and remain in unmolested possession of the forts."   " Meantime [says General Crawford] a despatch had arrived from Major Anderson stating that he felt secure in his position.   This, in connection with the influence exercised by the Southern members of the Cabinet, induced the President to change his purpose, and reinforcements were not sent."   Major Anderson had been informed by the adjutant-general that it was

11

"believed, from information thought to be reliable, that an attack will not be made on your command. . . . . The increase of the force under your command, however much to be desired, would, the Secretary thinks, judging from recent excitement produced on account of an anticipated increase, as mentioned in your letter, but add to the excitement, and might lead to serious results."

On the 9th of December, John McQueen, William Porcher Miles, M. L. Bonham, W. W. Boyce, and Lawrence M. Keitt, members of Congress from South Carolina, after a conference with the President by four of them, deprecating any attempt at reinforcements, addressed a letter to him expressing their "strong convictions" that the forts would not be either attacked or molested "previous to the act of the convention, and we hope and believe, not until an offer has been made through an accredited representative to negotiate for an amicable arrangement of all matters between the State and the Federal Government; provided that no reinforcements shall be sent into these forts, and their relative military status shall remain as at present."   The President objected to the word "provided" in their statement, "lest, if he should accept it without remark, it might possibly be construed into an agreement on his part not to reinforce the forts.   Such an agreement, he informed them, he would never make."   Still he had no present design, under the circumstances, to change the condition of those forts.   In their report of this interview to the convention, Messrs. Miles and Keitt said that the President promised, in the event of his changing his policy for any reason, he would return the paper to them—that "the impression made upon the delegation was that the President was wavering, and had not wholly decided as to what course he would pursue."   They do not pretend or even intimate that there was any pledge on either side.

Provision had been made "for the reinforcement of the

forts in case of need," when, on the 11th of December, the following instructions were conveyed to Major Anderson by Assistant Adjutant-General D. C. Buell, who was despatched to Fort Moultrie for that purpose by the Secretary of war,—viz. :

"You are carefully to avoid every act which would needlessly tend to provoke aggression, and for that reason you are not, without evident and imminent necessity, to take up any position which could be construed into the assumption of a hostile attitude; but you are to hold possession of the forts in this harbor, and, if attacked, you are to defend yourself to the last extremity. The smallness of your force will not permit you, perhaps, to occupy more than one of the three forts, but an attack on or attempt to take possession of either of them will be regarded as an act of hostility, and you may then put your command into either of them which you may deem most proper to increase its power of resistance. You are also authorized to take similar steps whenever you have tangible evidence of a design to proceed to hostile acts."

When a copy of this order was laid before the President he gave directions for its modification as regards the instruction "to defend himself to the last extremity," Major Anderson being advised that "it was sufficient for him to defend himself until no reasonable hope should remain of saving the fort."

About the 17th of December Captain Foster took from the arsenal forty muskets and placed them in the magazines at Fort Sumter and Castle Pinckney. "The act," says General Crawford, "occasioned an excitement that ought to have been foreseen." The military storekeeper informed Captain Foster of this, "and assured him that some violent demonstration was certain unless the excitement could be allayed," and he asked the immediate return of the muskets. Captain Foster declined, but was willing to refer the matter to Washington. Mr. Trescot's services were now called into requisition by a telegram asking him "to have the arms instantly returned, or a collision may occur at any moment." The result was an order from the Secretary of War directing Captain Foster to return the arms instantly, which was done; and J. J. Pettigrew, aide-de-camp, telegraphed back to Trescot, " The Governor says he was glad of your despatch [conveying the order], for otherwise there would have been imminent danger. Earnestly urge that there be no transfer of troops from Fort Moultrie to Fort Sumter, and inform the Secretary of War."

General Crawford states that " the sending of Major Buell and the object of his mission were known in Washington, and on the 13th of December the principal newspaper of Charleston published from its correspondent in Washington the following despatch:

" Major Buell and several other officers of the army have been sent to Fort Moultrie to look after the forts. Keep a sharp lookout upon them. They were sent for no good to us. See that they make no change in the distribution of soldiers so as to put them all in Fort Sumter; that would be dangerous to us."

Meantime, the difficulties of Anderson's position at Fort Moultrie increased daily.

The President had now definitely determined upon a policy (says our author) which he maintained until the last.

At midnight on the 18th of December (General Crawford states) Governor Pickens (Governor Gist's successor) sent for Captain Charles H. Simpson, who, with his Washington Light Infantry, had been guarding the arsenal to prevent the removal of ammunition or stores to the forts, and ordered him, " with such men from his company as he could rely upon, to cruise between the two forts" of Moultrie and Sumter, to prevent the evacuation of the former and taking possession of the latter. He said that he had heard of such intention, and that it must be prevented " at all hazards." He was to hail every boat passing between the forts. If he found that any were boats with United States troops on board, he was to prevent their passage, and, should the officers persist, he was to sink their boats and then immediately take Fort Sumter.

In a letter to Governor Pickens, dated December 18, President Buchanan informed him of sending Caleb Cushing to hold communication with him in his own behalf. He "assumes the fact that the State of South Carolina is now deliberating on the question of seceding from the Union, and he considers it his duty to exert all the means in his power to avert so dread a catastrophe." Governor Pickens said to Mr. Cushing that he would return no reply to the President's letter, except to say, "very candidly, that there was no hope for the Union, and that, as far as he was concerned, he intended to maintain the separate independence of South Carolina, and from this purpose neither temptation nor danger should for a moment deter him." The ordinance of secession having passed on the 20th of December, a committee of both houses of the legislature invited Mr. Cushing to be present on the evening of that day, when the ordinance was to be signed. It is hardly necessary to say that he declined the invitation and returned at once to Washington.

On the evening of December 26, Major Anderson addressed a short letter to Adjutant-General Cooper, saying: "I have the honor to report that I have just completed, by the blessing of God, the removal to this fort [Sumter] of all my garrison, except the surgeon, four non-commissioned officers, and seven men. . . . The step which I have taken was, in my opinion, necessary to prevent the effusion of blood."

General Crawford states that orders had been given to Captain Foster, who was left in charge of Fort Moultrie, "that if there should be any attempt to interfere with the passage of the boats upon the part of the guard-boat, he was to fire upon her." Fortunately, the guard-boat did not make her appearance until just after the transference, and "the night passed without incident."

Meantime three commissioners—Robert W. Barnwell, James H. Adams, and James L. Orr—were appointed from

South Carolina "to treat with the Government of the United States," and they arrived in Washington on the day of Major Anderson's removal to Fort Sumter. Before they were ready to present their credentials to the President, the news of that unexpected movement was, on the morning of the 27th of December, brought to him by Senators Hunter, of Virginia, and Davis, of Mississippi, Mr. Trescot also accompanying them. Here is Mr. Trescot's account of the interview, as quoted by our author :

"'Have you received any intelligence from Charleston in the last few hours?' asked Colonel Davis. 'None,' said the President. 'Then,' said Colonel Davis, 'I have a great calamity to announce to you.' He then stated the facts, and added, 'And now, Mr. President, you are surrounded with blood and dishonor on all sides.' The President exclaimed, 'My God, are calamities (or misfortunes, I forget which) never to come singly! I call God to witness, you gentlemen, better than anybody, know that this is not only without, but against my orders. It is against my policy.'"

The Cabinet was immediately called together, when, as our author states, at the suggestion of Judge Black, the order conveyed to Major Anderson by Major Buell on the 11th of December, which order "seemed to be ignored or forgotten," was sent for, and its import brought into special notice. Until now, General Crawford observes, the President had "possibly regarded it as a matter of routine only."

The South Carolina commissioners had their first and only interview with the President on the 28th of December. "He received them courteously and as private gentlemen alone. He listened [continues General Crawford] to their statement, but informed them that it was to Congress they must look, at the same time expressing his willingness to lay before Congress any 'propositions' they might make to him." Mr. Barnwell acted as the chairman, and "brought to the attention of the President the arrangement which had been made early in December between him and the South Carolina delegation; that it had been observed in good faith by the people of South Carolina, who could at any time, after the arrangement was made, up to the night when Major Anderson removed to Sumter, have occupied Fort Sumter and captured Moultrie with all its command; that the removal of Anderson violated that agreement on the part of the Government of the United States, and that the faith of the President and the Government had been thereby forfeited." They persistently demanded that Major Anderson should be at once ordered back to Fort Moultrie. General Crawford furnishes this further account of the interview from a letter of Mr. Orr, one of the commissioners present, written to him September 21, 1871, over ten years after the interior took place.

"The President made various excuses why he should be allowed time to decide the question. . . . Mr. Buchanan still hesitating, Mr. Barnwell said to him, at least three times during the interview, 'But, Mr. President, your personal honor is involved in this matter; the faith you pledged has been violated, and your personal honor requires you to issue the order.' Mr. Barnwell pressed him so hard on this point that the President said, 'You must give me time to consider—this is a grave question.' Mr. Barnwell replied to him for the third time, 'But, Mr. President, your personal honor is involved in this arrangement.' Whereupon Mr. Buchanan, with great earnestness, said, 'Mr. Barnwell, you are pressing me too importunately; you don't give me time to consider.' . . . The interview terminated without eliciting an order from the President to restore the status of the troops in Charleston harbor."

We will let General Crawford speak again :

"Whatever agreement or understanding may have been entered into between the Government at Washington and those who acted for the State of South Carolina in regard to the existing status in the harbor of Charleston, it is evident that Major Anderson had not been informed of it. When he heard almost daily that his position in Fort Moultrie would be attacked, and saw the nightly watch upon him lest he should transfer his command to the stronger and safer position of Fort Sumter,—it was the latter action, wholly in violation of any agreement that might have been made, that impressed him beyond all others and mainly influenced his actions,—and he resolved to take advantage of the 'tangible evidence' and remove his command."

In his letter of December 27 to the War Department, Major Anderson says: "I will add that many things convinced me that the authorities of the State designed to proceed to a hostile act."

In their letter to the President the South Carolina commissioners renewed their demand that Major Anderson should be ordered to remove his command back to Fort Moultrie, and insisted that "the removal to Fort Sumter was made in violation of the pledges given by the President." On this point, while the President freely expressed his surprise and regret at the removal, as likely to operate injuriously against his policy for the preservation of the peace, he positively denied the existence of any pledge, on his part, tying his hands. "As to the alleged pledge" (he himself says) "we have already shown that no such thing existed." Nevertheless, strange to say, our Union general (Crawford) seems to take the opposite side of this question, and introduces his secession witnesses in support of it. Says he :

"Anderson's action, while not inconsistent with the position of his message nor the official action of his Cabinet, was wholly in violation of the policy that the President had pursued. For a time the President was undetermined as to what course to take, but he had eventually prepared a draft of an answer to the South Carolina commissioners which yielded the point at issue, when, by the firm and decided action of his Secretary of State, the consequence of such action upon his part was presented in so clear a light as to induce him to change his purpose." Says Trescot: "For a moment he wavered. But he could take no other course. . . . His Secretary of State and his Attorney-General said to him, 'Decide; whatever you may have done, we are uncommitted. Keep the word which the South says you have pledged, and we resign.'"

Right at this point I beg to introduce as a witness one whose testimony ought to have nearly, if not quite, as much weight as any presented in "Trescot's Narrative"—no less a witness than Judge Black himself. He was writing upon his "memorandum" touching the paper above referred to, which the President had hastily drawn up in reply to the commissioners of South Carolina. He had remarked that had the President refused to adopt his views, equally approved by Messrs. Holt and Stanton, as expressed in his (Judge Black's) "memorandum" thereon, both he and Stanton "would have resigned. Mr. Holt" (he adds) "perhaps would have done the same, but he did not say so. There never was any talk, or suggestion, *or threat*, absolute or conditional, of resignation by any Northern member of the administration than what is here stated."

It does not appear on whose authority General Crawford makes the following statement, but presumably on that of his assistant editor. He writes:

"In regard to any 'understanding' or 'agreement,' the President had acknowledged it, and claimed that he was affected by it personally. 'You do not seem to appreciate, Judge Black,' said he, 'that my personal honor as a gentleman is involved.' 'Such an understanding,' said Judge Black, 'is impossible. You could not make it, or any agreement with any one that would tie your hands in the execution of the laws, and if you did make it you must retire from it.' Finally the President yielded his objections and committed the paper which he had submitted to his Cabinet into the hands of his Secretary of State."

It would appear from this that the supposition or allegation that the President acknowledged he had bound himself by an "understanding" or "agreement," as charged, is based on something he may have written in that paper, which he placed in "the hands of his Secretary of State." It is certain that General Crawford did not receive from either Judge Black, Mr. Stanton, or Mr. Holt any such admission, however he may have tried to obtain it from the former, as indicated by the following marginal note, saying:

"On the 22d of March, 1882, I had a long and earnest conversation with Judge Black upon the subject of the interview between the President and the congressional delegation of South Carolina, as to the understanding or arrangement agreed upon at that interview. The details of his interview with the President when the commissioners of South Carolina were in Washington were stated, when, at the end, I said, 'Well, then,

Judge Black, there appears to be but one conclusion to be reached—the President did make that agreement.' The judge rose, and, looking steadily at me for a moment, said, ' Remember, that is *your* conclusion.' "

Mr. Trescot, in his " Narrative," represents Attorney-General Stanton as saying to him (Trescot), " You say the President has pledged himself. I do not know it. I have not heard his account, but I know you believe it."

Referring to this subject, Mr. Blaine, in his political history, makes the charge that " Mr. Buchanan prepared an answer to their (the South Carolina commissioners') request, which was compromising to the honor of the executive and perilous to the integrity of the Union." Mr. J. Buchanan Henry, the President's nephew and private secretary, called General Holt's attention to and asked his opinion particularly on that statement. In his answer, May 26, 1884, General Holt goes into a lengthy and unanswerable vindication of Mr. Buchanan, which paper will form an important chapter in the history of his administration. I will give place only to this paragraph, which of itself is a sufficient answer to Mr. Blaine's false and ill-judged charge. Says General Holt, " While unable, at this late day, to recall all the details of the answer to the commissioners drafted by the President, my recollection is distinct that it contained nothing, properly understood,—that is, as the President himself understood it and wished it to be understood by others,—which could be held to be ' compromising to the honor of the executive and perilous to the integrity of the Union.' Mr. Buchanan had so guarded his personal honor through a long life that, at its close, there was found upon it neither stain nor trace of stain; with equal solicitude, and, in my belief, with equal success, did he watch over the honor of the great office he held."

The publication of the " Memorandum," or " Judge Black's Protest," as he styled it when he first promulgated it through the Lancaster (Pa.) *Intelligencer* of July 7, 1874, has no doubt given rise to very erroneous as well as unjust criticisms upon Mr. Buchanan, and it is due to the memory of Judge Black to express the charitable belief that had he known that the well-intentioned paper against which he so excitedly entered his "protest" was no longer in existence, he never would have given his comments to the press. Speaking of it, General Holt, in his letter just mentioned, says, "The judge did nothing by halves, and in the fervor of his loyalty to the Union he commented on what had been evolved in the Cabinet, *but much more* elaborating and intensifying his strictures by the vigor of speech for which he was so distinguished."

Suffice it to say, in the language of General Holt, "the President unhesitatingly directed that an answer should be prepared in accordance with the changes desired, and this was accordingly done." The letter, so perfected, was sent to the commissioners, whose reply was so insulting that it was instantly returned, with this indorsement: "This paper, just presented to the President, is of such a nature that he declines to receive it." Commenting on this matter, Judge Black remarks: "Mr. Buchanan had always felt in full the deep responsibility which rested upon him. He was anxious to avoid a collision which would prevent accommodation, hurry the border States out of the Union, and precipitate a civil war, for which the Government was totally unprepared. But he had never for a moment willingly contemplated the surrender of the forts at Charleston. On the contrary, he had uniformly declared, before the election and after, that if those forts should be given up he would 'rather die than live.'"

After all was over, Mr. Buchanan himself, in writing in the third person on this subject, said, "The President believed it to be impossible to garrison the numerous forts of the United States in time of peace; that to attempt this would have been a confession of weakness, as the force at his command was absurdly inadequate to the object in view, and that it would have provoked instead of preventing col-

lision. He therefore considered it his duty to refrain from
any act which might provoke or encourage the Cotton
States into secession, and to smooth the way for congressional compromise."

Major Anderson was now, as he believed, firmly in-
trenched in Fort Sumter, and delegation after delegation,
sent by Governor Pickens, demanding his surrender or
return to Fort Moultrie was courteously dismissed with the
undeniable statement that he " had removed his command
from Fort Moultrie to Fort Sumter, as he had a right to do,
being in command of all the forts in the harbor." He said
he had not been informed of any " understanding" which
the Governor claimed he had violated,—that his position
was threatened every night by the troops of the State,—and
that he was apprehensive of a landing on the island. " To
prevent this," said he, earnestly, " I removed on my own
responsibility, my sole object being to prevent bloodshed."
He said at the same time, " In this controversy between the
North and the South, my sympathies are entirely with the
South."

Says General Crawford, " Anderson now felt strong in
his position, and he frequently remarked to the writer that
he controlled the situation. His whole effort was to effect,
as far as it lay in his power, a peaceful solution of the difficulties." " He had reported the progress of batteries in
construction around him, but as late as the 30th of January
he had urged with emphasis that he hoped that no attempt
would be made by friends to throw supplies in, and that
their doing so would do more harm than good." " Two
days after his entrance into the work he had informed his
Government that, God willing, he would in a few days be so
strong that the South Carolinians would hardly be foolish
enough to attack [me] him. He thought that the city was
entirely in his power ; that he could cut off its communications by sea and close its harbor by destroying its light-
houses, and he believed in his ability to do it." On the

31st of December he wrote to the War Department, saying, "Thank God, we are now where the Government may send us additional troops at its leisure." The Government having decided to sustain Major Anderson in his present position, Secretary Floyd made it a pretext to offer his resignation, which was instantly accepted, as the President, through Vice-President Breckinridge, had requested it some days before.

Now came the firing upon the *Star of the West*, on the 9th of January, 1861, the circumstances of which are too well known to require repetition here. In a letter to Governor Pickens, demanding to know if the firing was by his order, Major Anderson characterized it as an act "without a parallel in the history of our country or of any other civilized government," that "if not disclaimed, he must regard it as an act of war," and after a reasonable time for the return of his messenger, he should not permit any vessel to pass within the range of his guns. As Mr. Buchanan remarks, "Had he adhered to his purpose, the civil war would then have commenced." Governor Pickens replied to Major Anderson, saying, "The act is perfectly justified by me." Major Anderson concluded to despatch Lieutenant Talbot to Washington and await instructions.

"On the 11th of January, the same day [General Crawford says] upon which the hulks of four vessels were sunk across the channel at the entrance of the harbor," Governor Pickens made another demand for the surrender of Sumter, having previously seized all the other forts, as well as the United States arsenal at Charleston, with its nearly half a million of stores. The result was the despatching of Lieutenant Hall to Washington with instructions from Major Anderson, and the Governor appointed Isaac W. Hayne, his attorney-general, to accompany him. Meantime the State authorities continued their active work on the fortifications. I need not give the particulars of Mr. Hayne's mission; they are of public record, and it is sufficient to say that the Governor's proposition to "buy Fort Sumter and con-

tents as property of the United States, sustained by a declaration in effect that if she is not permitted to make the purchase she will seize the fort by force of arms," was, of
course, declined as wholly inadmissible, the ground of this
decision being clearly and ably stated in the letter of February 6, 1861, from the Secretary of War (Holt) to Mr.
Hayne. Mr. Holt closes his letter with the following
solemn warning: "If, with all the multiplied proofs which
exist of the President's anxiety for peace, and of the earnestness with which he has pursued it, the authorities of
that State (South Carolina) shall assault Fort Sumter, and
peril the lives of the handful of brave and loyal men shut
up within its walls, and thus plunge our common country
into the horrors of civil war, then upon them and those
they represent must rest the responsibility."

As early as the 31st of December provision had been
matured for the sending of reinforcements to the forts in
Charleston harbor by the war ship *Brooklyn*, but it was
deemed advisable to substitute the *Star of the West* for that
vessel—we have seen with what result. This did not deter
the Government from making other preparations for the
relief of Fort Sumter, but the plan for such relief, for
various reasons, was not carried into effect.

On the 16th of February, Major Anderson wrote to the
War Department asking what course it would be proper for
him to take if, without a declaration of war or a notice of
hostilities, he should see the floating battery of the South
Carolina authorities approaching his fort, seeing they might
"attempt placing it within good distance before a declaration of hostile intentions." I was present when this question was presented in Cabinet. The President, still anxious
to avoid firing the first gun, wished time to consider. The
Secretary of War asked him what he would do, or, rather,
what Major Anderson ought to do, in case he were in
charge of a fort and the enemy should commence undermining it. The President promptly answered that he

"should crack away at them." This, according to my memorandum made at the time, was on the 19th of February. On the 23d of that month, replying to Major Anderson, Mr. Holt repeated his instructions of the 10th of January, which were "to act strictly on the defensive, and to avoid, by all means compatible with the safety of your command, a collision with the hostile forces by which you are surrounded," and added, "The policy thus indicated must govern your conduct. The President is not disposed at the present moment to change the instructions under which you have been heretofore acting, or to occupy any other than a defensive position. If, however, you are convinced by sufficient evidence that the raft of which you speak is advancing for the purpose of making an assault upon the fort, then you would be justified on the principle of self-defence in not awaiting its actual arrival there, but by repelling force by force on its approach."

The length of my article reminds me that I should bring it to a close by the mention of only a few things more relating to President Buchanan's administration, with a brief allusion to the beginning of the administration of Mr. Lincoln.

On the 4th of March, at the moment when the thirty-sixth Congress and Mr. Buchanan's administration were about to expire, the Secretary of War laid before the Cabinet a letter that morning received from Major Anderson, which, as Mr. Buchanan correctly states, "was read by Mr. Holt, greatly to his own surprise and that of every other member of the Cabinet. In this the major declares that he would not be willing to risk his reputation on an attempt to throw reinforcements into Charleston harbor with a force of less than twenty thousand good and well-disciplined men." On the evening of the 4th, Mr. Buchanan, whose term as President had expired at 12 M., called the members of his Cabinet together at the office of District-Attorney Ould, over Corcoran and Riggs's Bank, when, after full consultation, it was agreed that Mr. Holt should prepare a letter to President Lincoln, giving a detailed account of what had been done touching Major Anderson's occupation of Fort Sumter, and send it to him with Major Anderson's letter and accompanying papers as early as possible on the next day.

At noon on the 5th another meeting was held, as per agreement, at the War Department, Mr. Buchanan and all the members of his Cabinet except Judge Black being present, when Mr. Holt's letter, which he had prepared, was read, discussed, and, with slight alterations, unanimously approved. This letter forms an important chapter in the history of President Buchanan's administration.

Now, with two or three more quotations from our author (not Trescot, but Crawford), and a forcible expression of Judge Black, I pass to a brief mention of Mr. Lincoln's policy of treating the great question of the day.

General Crawford states truthfully and manfully that " it was not denied that the President was powerless. No one claimed that he could, by virtue of his office, make war, or that, without additional and special legislation, he could properly or efficiently act; and yet the Congress of 1860–61 simply and persistently refused to pass any act or adopt any resolution either to preserve the Union by peaceful measures or to grant to the executive the power of aggression, or to increase and define his power of defence." " And yet Mr. Buchanan desired and strove to serve his country. He had asked Congress for those powers necessary to meet the unprecedented condition of things, but whose exercise without the action of Congress he deemed impossible. To all of his appeals for such powers Congress treated him with indifference, if not with contempt." " Upon one point he was inflexible, and from it he never wavered, and that was his determination never, under any pressure of circumstances, to surrender the forts at Charleston, and to this resolve he adhered to the last."

Shortly before his death, in August, 1883, Judge Black, writing in answer to a letter of Mr. Jefferson Davis, said, "The demand for the evacuation of Fort Sumter and the surrender into the hands of South Carolina was, take it all in all, the most impudent in the history of the world."

President Lincoln had no sooner taken his seat than he was beset with the same difficulties which had caused his predecessor so much concern and trouble. The Montgomery commissioners, with Associate Justice James A. Campbell, of Alabama, who shortly afterwards resigned his seat on the Supreme Bench, and many other pronounced secessionists, were on hand, all demanding the evacuation of Fort Sumter. Justice Campbell, who had used his influence with President Buchanan in trying in vain to get him to disavow the act of Major Anderson in removing his command to Fort Sumter, sought still, also "by his personal influence with the new administration, to bring about a peaceful solution of the difficulties," and the first step towards that most desirable end was, they insisted, the relinquishment of Fort Sumter into the possession of the Montgomery government.

"A warlike construction [says General Crawford] of the inaugural of Mr. Lincoln was placed upon it by the Southern element at Washington." On the 6th of March, General Beauregard assumed command of the troops at Charleston. "Friends at Washington kept him fully informed of any possible movement. On the same day Commissioner Crawford reported to his government that 'the selections made of the advisers of the President would prove beneficial to the Confederate States,' and that it was the determined purpose of the Secretaries of State and War (Seward and Cameron) to accept and maintain a peace policy." He deemed it advisable to support Mr. Seward's policy of peace, because he felt confident it would tend to "cement the Confederacy and put it beyond the reach of either his arms or his diplomacy." "On the 11th of March, Senator

12

Wigfall informed the Confederate general by telegraph that it was believed that 'Anderson will be ordered to evacuate Sumter in five days, and that this was certainly informally agreed upon in Cabinet Saturday night.'" General Beauregard thereupon wrote Major Anderson that he had been informed that Mr. Lamon, the authorized agent of the President, had, after seeing Major Anderson, informed Governor Pickens that the command was to be transferred in a few days to another post. He added that "all that would be required of him would be his word of honor as an officer and gentleman that the fort, with its armament and all public property, should remain without any arrangements for its destruction; that company and side arms might be taken, and the flag saluted."

Major Anderson replied that "if he could leave this fort only upon such a pledge he would never, 'so help him God, leave this fort alive.'"

There were fears that the fort would be undermined, and the New York *Commercial Advertiser* said, "If Sumter must be abandoned, let it be a shapeless mass of ruins."

Commissioner Crawford professed great impatience at the delay, as did also the authorities at Charleston. Said the former, "The evacuation of Sumter is imperative." Still, Judge Campbell advised patience. On the 15th of March he drew up the following memorandum, which "received the approval of Mr. Justice Nelson," who, with him, was striving for peace, "and its contents having been communicated to the Secretary of State, was handed to the commissioner, who at once advised the authorities at Montgomery."

"I feel perfect confidence in the fact that Fort Sumter will be evacuated in the next five days, and that this is felt to be a measure imposing vast responsibility upon the administration.

"I feel perfect confidence that no measure changing the existing status of things prejudicially to the southern Confederate States is at present contemplated.

" I feel entire confidence that any immediate demand for an answer to the communication of the commissioners will be productive of evil and not of good. I do not believe that it should be pressed.

" I earnestly ask for a delay until the effect of the evacuation of Fort Sumter can be ascertained, or at least for a few days,—say, ten days."

Hon. John Bell, of Tennessee, we are told, strongly urged Mr. Lincoln " not to disturb the Confederate States. He had assured him that any attempt to collect the revenue or to interfere with its government would be the signal for the secession of every border State."

" The reluctance manifested upon the part of the committee to yield to any delay," it appears, was " largely assumed," as General Crawford states that Colonel Forsyth, one of the committee, told him in 1870 that their secret instructions from Montgomery were " to play with Mr. Seward to delay and gain time until the South was ready."

On the same day (15th of March) President Lincoln wrote to each of his Cabinet officers, asking a written answer to the following question : " Assuming it to be possible to now provision Fort Sumter, under the circumstances is it wise to attempt it ?"

Mr. Seward answered by a long letter, from which I make the following extracts :

" If it were possible to peacefully provision Fort Sumter, of course I should answer that it would be both unwise and inhuman not to attempt it. But the facts of the case are known to be that the attempt must be made by the employment of a military and marine force, which would provoke combat and probably initiate a civil war, which the Government of the United States would be committed to maintain through all changes to some definite conclusion.

" Influenced by these sentiments, I have felt that it is exceedingly fortunate that to a great extent the Federal Government occupies thus far not an aggressive attitude but practically a defensive one, while the necessity for action, if civil war is to be initiated, falls on those who seek to dismember and to subvert the Union.

" The policy of the time, therefore, has seemed to me to consist in conciliation, which should deny to disunionists any new provocation or apparent offence, while it would enable the unionists in the slave States to maintain with truth and with effect, that the alarms and apprehensions put forth by the disunionists are groundless and false.

" If it be indeed true that pacification is necessary to prevent dismemberment of the Union and civil war, or either of them, no patriot and lover of humanity could hesitate to surrender party for the higher interests of country and humanity.

" Partly by design, partly by chance, this policy has been hitherto pursued by the late administration of the Federal Government and by the Republican party in its corporate action. It is by this policy thus pursued, I think, that the progress of dismemberment has been arrested after the seven Gulf States had seceded, and the border States yet remain, although they do so uneasily, in the Union.

"Suppose the expedition successful. [For the reinforcement of Sumter.] We have then a garrison in Fort Sumter that can defy assault for six months. What is it to do then ? Is it to make war by opening its batteries and attempting to demolish the defences of the Carolinians? Can it demolish them if it tries ? If it cannot, what is the advantage we shall have gained ? If it can, how will it serve to check or prevent disunion ? In either case, it seems to me, that we will have inaugurated a civil war by our own act, without an adequate object, after which reunion will be hopeless, at least, under this administration."

The Secretary of War had given the subject careful consideration, and he was " reluctantly forced to the conclusion that it would be unwise now to make any such attempt."

A like opinion was expressed by the remaining members of the Cabinet, with the exception of the Secretary of the Treasury, Mr. Chase, and the Postmaster-General, Mr. Blair. Mr. Chase expressed himself as "in favor of some attempt being made to relieve Fort Sumter, although he was not now, nor had he previously been, decided in his expressions to that effect."

Postmaster-General Blair availed himself of the occasion to enter into a tirade against the Democratic party and the late administration, charging that, " to the connivance of the late administration, it is due alone that this rebellion has been enabled to attain its present proportions. . . . The action of the President in 1833 (he said) inspired respect, while in 1860 the rebels were encouraged by the contempt they felt for the incumbent of the Presidency."

He strongly urged that the attempt should be made. "I believe (he said) that Fort Sumter may be provisioned and relieved by Captain Fox with little risk. No expense or care should therefore be spared to achieve this success."

Immediately after the Cabinet meeting when this subject was considered, it is stated, on the authority of Mr. Blair, that, the President being called on by Mr. Blair's father, Francis P. Blair, and asked "If it had been determined to withdraw Anderson from Fort Sumter, the President replied that it had not yet been fully determined upon, but that the Cabinet were almost a unit in favor of it,—'all except your son,' said he,—and that he thought that such would be the result." This story, General Crawford says, "was so believed in the country."

I remember myself hearing Postmaster-General Blair say in his office, probably at about this time, that a force of twenty-five thousand men could easily put down the rebellion. The result shows how mistaken he was, and how unfit for Cabinet counsel. I have good reason to believe, also, that his spiteful fling at President Buchanan was superinduced not by any patriotic impulse but from personal pique. It is apparent that there was "no love lost" between Mr. Buchanan and the Blairs. I have before me a letter from Mr. Buchanan in which, remarking that he had long known them, he says: "Montgomery had not the ability to make a respectable advocate of the Government in the Court of Claims." .

General Crawford states that Captain G. V. Fox, Postmaster-General Blair's brother-in-law, was sent, with the approval of the President, to confer with Major Anderson, arriving at Charleston on the 21st of March. He had suggested a scheme for the relief of Sumter. On their meeting, Major Anderson "at once earnestly condemned any proposal to send him reinforcements," as he had repeatedly done as far back as the time when Floyd was removed. "He asserted that it was too late; he agreed with General

Scott (who, in the belief that the surrender of Fort Sumter had been determined upon, advised the surrender also of Fort Pickens) that an entrance by sea was impossible, and he impressed upon Captain Fox his belief that the reinforcements coming would at once precipitate a collision and inaugurate civil war."

Not five only, but fifteen days had now passed since the date of Judge Campbell's "memorandum." The South Carolina authorities "had been impatient at the delay. The promise made to them by the agent, Lamon, that he would shortly return to remove the garrison from Fort Sumter had not been fulfilled."

On the 30th of March, Governor Pickens telegraphed the facts of Colonel Lamon's visit to the commissioners at Washington, and they at once communicated with Judge Campbell. "On that day the Secretary (Seward) informed Justice Campbell that 'the President was concerned at the contents of the telegram;' that 'the question involved a point of honor, and that Lamon had no commission or authority from him, nor any power to pledge him by any promise or assurance.'"

"Mr. Seward said to Justice Campbell that he did not think the President would attempt to supply Fort Sumter, and that there is no intention to reinforce it." Judge Campbell urged immediate evacuation. Mr. Seward said, "I must see the President." He returned with the modified answer, "I am satisfied the Government will not undertake to supply Fort Sumter without giving notice to Governor Pickens."

April 10, Secretary Seward informed the commissioners that "the Secretary of State is not at liberty to hold official intercourse with them," and they communicated this decision to the authorities at Montgomery. They left the city the next day, but before their departure a telegram was received from General Beauregard informing them "of the arrival of a special messenger with the notice of the President of the United States that Fort Sumter was 'to be provisioned either peaceably or otherwise forcibly.'"

It should be remarked that at no stage of these troubles was Justice Campbell recognized in any other capacity than that of a private gentleman, nor did he profess to have any official agency. On the 13th of April fire was opened on Fort Sumter, when he wrote the Secretary of State, charging "equivocating conduct" and "systematic duplicity," as having been practised upon the authorities at Montgomery through him, and that "such equivocating conduct of the administration was the proximate cause of the great calamity."

At length the fleet intended for the relief of Fort Sumter put out to sea, and "before daylight on the 12th (April) the rendezvous agreed upon was reached off the Charleston bar." "As they approached the land the firing was heard, and the smoke and shells of the batteries 'were distinctly visible.'"

The first gun upon the national flag had now been discharged and actual hostilities commenced by the enemies of the Union. Little did they anticipate the terrible results of their folly and rashness in firing that fatal shot which both Presidents Buchanan and Lincoln had so earnestly sought, by forbearance and peaceful measures, to avoid,—the latter pursuing, as he did for nearly six weeks, the same conciliatory policy practised by his predecessor,—nay, in some respects even greater moderation and forbearance until "forbearance ceased to be a virtue." I doubt if he thought for one moment that peace would be preserved for another day after he notified the Governor of South Carolina of his order for the relief of Fort Sumter. After this there was not the remotest prospect or possible reason to hope for any other result. As he himself says, in his message to Congress, the 4th of July, 1861, "The policy chosen looked to the exhaustion of all peaceful measures before a resort to any stronger ones. . . . It promised the continuance of the mails (and they were continued until the 31st of May) at the Government expense to the very people who were resisting the Government, and it gave repeated pledges against any disturbance to any of the people or any of their rights. Of all that a President might constitutionally and justifiably do in such a case, everything was forborne without which it was possible to keep the Government on foot."

How true it is, as Joseph Holt has pointedly written, "That the first shot in the rebellion came from the enemy was due wholly to this policy of procrastination, then so severely censured; and yet it was this first shot, and the fact that it was fired not *from*, but *upon*, Fort Sumter and the flag floating over it that inflamed and united the country, and gave to the national patriotism a fervor and resistless impetus which carried our armies and people in triumph and glory through the war. Had the first shot come from the batteries of Sumter, the fierce party passions then raging would have been swift to denounce the administration as making war upon the South, and fatal dissensions among ourselves might have ensued. Could, therefore, the short-sighted carpers of that day have been able to see the end from the beginning, the reproaches which they heaped upon President Buchanan would have turned to blessings on their lips."

It is time to bring this long paper to a close. When I began, I had no idea of extending it to so great a length It was not my purpose to undertake a regular review of General Crawford's highly interesting volume, but by unimpeachable evidence, including not a little from his own pen, to show not only that, in the general treatment of his subject, he has done great injustice to President Buchanan and members of his Cabinet who stood by him, but also to demonstrate, as I believe I have done indisputably, that never at any time did he give any pledge not to send relief to the garrison in Charleston harbor; and that, as the result has proved, his steady precaution in guarding against any and every step which the secessionists might have seized on as an overt act on his part, was the wisest course that could possibly have been adopted, looking to the fearful difficulties by which he was surrounded and the grave responsibility resting upon him to preserve the peace, if, by any means short of dishonor, war could be averted. It was this moderation and forbearance that carried the Government over to President Lincoln without bloodshed, and, as we have seen, he pursued the same policy until it was apparent, beyond doubt or hope, that the only alternative now was national disgrace or civil war. Forced to decide, he chose the latter alternative and laid down his life, a martyr to the sacred cause of the Union.

Now, talk as you will—censure Presidents Buchanan and Lincoln as you may—touching their action in regard to the forts at Charleston, which it was but natural every loyal person should have wished to see strengthened, and hence the futile attempts to respond to their patriotic impulse; but I venture the assertion that after the election of Lincoln there never was a day prior to Major Anderson's removal to Sumter, when those forts would not have fallen into the hands of the secessionists before any reinforcements could have reached them, no matter how secretly ordered. As to secrecy, such a thing, as we have seen, was impossible, with secession spies in and out of Government office, everywhere around us.

WASHINGTON, February 2, 1888.

NOTE.—It is due to history that I should state here that the foregoing article was written at the desire of General Holt, who, before General Crawford's book was published, had learned from conversation with him that he intended to make some strictures upon President Buchanan's course in regard to Fort Sumter that were unjust. Shortly after the book appeared I read it carefully, and when I had finished the article I sent for General Holt to come to my house for the purpose of submitting it to him. I handed him paper and pencil with request to note the number of any page in which he might wish to make any change. He listened attentively to the end without a pencil mark or a single word, and, rising to take his leave, he said, in an earnest and emphatic manner, "You have exhausted the subject," thus expressing entire acquiescence in and approval of the narrative.   H. K.

CHAPTER XVI.

JOHN A. DIX.

How it happened that General Dix was made Secretary of the Treasury —The Coe-Spaulding Letters—Names of Secession Senators who voted against Mr. Holt's Nomination for Secretary of War—Plot to Poison President Buchanan.

DOUBTLESS not many have seen the remarkable correspondence between Mr. George S. Coe, of New York City, and Hon. E. S. Spaulding, formerly a member of Congress, of Buffalo, New York, relating to the removal of Philip F. Thomas, and the appointment of John A. Dix, Secretary of the Treasury, in January, 1861.

Mr. Coe writes under date of February 14, 1888, and, premising that "all incidents of the civil war are now of historic interest," says he "recalls very vividly the fact of meeting you [Mr. Spaulding] one morning at the Bank of Commerce to confer about the payment of the Government loan, which our bank in New York had taken in connection with Baring Bros. & Co., of London, and had paid in part, when it was discovered that Thomas [then Mr. Buchanan's Secretary of the Treasury] was to transfer the money into the Confederate region, where it would be captured by the enemy. The question for us to consider was, whether we should pay or default upon the balance. Upon that question we sent Mr. Moses Taylor, John C. Green, and A. A. Lowe to Washington to confer with Mr. Buchanan. I feel quite confident that you were the trusted agent to confer with us on the subject, and it resulted in the appointment of General Dix to be Secretary of the Treasury when we paid the money."

Mr. Spaulding's answer is dated February 17. He says, what is well known, that soon after the assembling of Congress in December, 1860, " Howell Cobb resigned the office of Secretary of the Treasury, leaving the disloyal deputy Philip Clayton, of Georgia, in charge of the Treasury Department. President Buchanan then appointed Philip F. Thomas, of Maryland, Secretary to fill the vacancy, and John J. Cisco, who was loyal to the Union, continued to act as Sub-Treasurer in the city of New York, while the Assistant Secretary at Washington was disloyal, and apparently acted with a view to discredit the bonds and financial credit of the United States."

Mr. Spaulding proceeded to give an account of the course now taken to raise " more money to pay current expenses and the interest on the bonds," supposed to be the bonds about to be offered under act of Congress of December 17, 1860, for a loan to the Government. As the record which I have examined shows, Secretary Thomas, who came in soon after Mr. Cobb resigned on the 8th of December, issued an advertisement, under date of December 18, inviting sealed proposals " until the 28th December for the issue of any portion or the whole of $5,000,000 in treasury notes in exchange for gold coin of the United States within five days from the acceptance of such proposals," under the authority of the aforesaid act. " After this loan was made [Mr. Spaulding states] it became apparent that more money was being transferred to the Southern States than was necessary, and that the United States army was to a large extent located in the Southern States. One or more of the instalments was paid on the bids on the last of December, 1860. The financial situation became more and more alarming at the attitude of the disloyal men in Mr. Buchanan's Cabinet. Mr. Buchanan was himself in some degree vacillating and undecided, but was generally believed to be loyal to the Union.

"Three of his Cabinet—viz., Jeremiah Black, Edwin M. Stanton, and Joseph Holt—were known to Mr. Seward and others to be loyal to the Union, and were ready to co-operate in preserving the finances and other important measures until Mr. Lincoln should be inaugurated on the 4th of the following March."

Under these circumstances Mr. Spaulding says that he went from Washington—he was then in Congress—to New York " to consult the brokers who had bid for the loan with a view to have them hold back the payment of further instalments until the new Secretary of the Treasury could be selected and appointed by Mr. Buchanan, and General Dix was mentioned as a good man for the place in the emergency." The result was that through the influence, as he states, of a committee of distinguished gentlemen who returned with him to Washington, in conference with Senator Seward and the loyal members of the Cabinet, the President " finally, in a very few days, removed Mr. Thomas and appointed John A. Dix Secretary of the Treasury in his place. General Dix came to Washington and took possession of the Treasury Department. The remaining instalments on the loan were paid, and the Treasury Department was thereafter well managed."

In this connection, not wishing to cast the least doubt as to the correctness of Mr. Spaulding's narrative, it seems apropos that I should relate the substance of what I wrote to the New York *Tribune* on the 3d of May, 1879, published in that paper near that date. I had seen it stated that Judge Black had written to the Philadelphia *Times* that " General Dix was not appointed Secretary of the Treasury by Mr. Buchanan in consequence of a pressure from New York capitalists, as has been said, and that only one person mentioned his name to the President before the appointment was made." Quoting this, I said that I had good reason to believe that President Buchanan invited General Dix to Washington not to take charge of the Treasury De-

partment, but with a view to his appointment as Secretary
of War. At that time, January 1, 1861, Postmaster-General Holt, by designation of the President, was Secretary of
War *ad interim*, vice John B. Floyd. Under the law this left
me as acting Postmaster-General. Philip F. Thomas was
Secretary of the Treasury, having succeeded Howell Cobb.
The more ardent Union men near the President were not
satisfied to have Mr. Thomas in the Cabinet, and when General Dix was sent for, Mr. Stanton, Attorney-General, requested me to meet General Dix on his arrival at the depot,
and, if possible, obtain his acquiescence in the plan, which I
was to divulge to him, of inducing the President to appoint
him Secretary of the Treasury. These instructions I carried
out with alacrity. I had a carriage ready, and before General Dix reached his lodgings at Willard's Hotel, he had
heartily agreed to the proposition. Taking leave of him
for the night—he arrived by the evening train—I was
driven at once to Mr. Stanton's residence on C, near Four-
and-a-half Street. Having company in the parlor, he met
me in the hall, and when I informed him that all was as he
desired, he was so filled with delight that he seized and
embraced me in true German style. General Dix was
immediately appointed to the Treasury, vice Thomas, and
confirmed by the Senate January 11, 1861.

It is proper to remark here that some time after I wrote
as above to the *Tribune*,—it may have been a year or two,
more or less,—meeting Judge Black in Washington, he
intimated to me, somewhat darkly, that this account of
mine was not the true history of the case. I did not understand him as doubting my narrative, but he appeared
disinclined to tell me wherein it was erroneous, if it were
so, and greatly to my regret I never afterwards had an
opportunity of speaking with him, as I intended to do, on
the subject.

I am reminded by this correspondence, also, of a private
letter written on the 22d of December, 1860, by President

Buchanan to Royal Phelps, Esq., of New York, which, with explanatory remarks, was published in the *Magazine of American History* for July, 1887. A copy of that letter was given by Mr. Phelps, some time before his death, to a gentleman of world-wide fame, George Bancroft, who, in speaking of it to me, expressed the opinion that it looked as though President Buchanan had made up his mind to let the Cotton States go. I was startled by this remark, when he offered to read the letter to me. I listened, almost breathlessly, to its close, when, naturally relieved, I said that I saw nothing whatever in it to justify any construction unfavorable to Mr. Buchanan. It showed his great anxiety to have the loan just advertised "taken at a reasonable rate of interest," and argued that such investment would be perfectly safe even "should the Cotton States withdraw from the Union." Said he, "Trade cannot easily be drawn from its accustomed channels. I would sacrifice my life at any moment to save the Union, if such were the will of God; but this great and enterprising and brave nation is not to be destroyed by losing the Cotton States, even if this loss were irreparable, which I do not believe unless from some unhappy accident."

The explanation appeared to satisfy my distinguished friend, and he afterward gave me a copy of Mr. Buchanan's letter, leaving me free to publish it, but on my own responsibility—which I did not hesitate to assume—accompanying the letter with an explanatory key.

To the contemporaries, certainly, of Messrs. Coe and Spaulding, it must seem a little strange to hear Mr. Spaulding say that "three of his [Buchanan's] Cabinet—viz., Jeremiah Black, Edwin M. Stanton, and Joseph Holt—were known to Mr. Seward and others to be loyal to the Union." We can afford to pass by the oft-repeated remark of President Buchanan's "vacillating" and indecision. No doubt he was generally believed to be "loyal to the Union."

As regards those three members of his cabinet, two were

from Pennsylvania and the third, although from Kentucky, needed no stronger proof of his loyalty than was demonstrated when his nomination for Secretary of War came up for confirmation and the following senators voted against it,—viz., Bayard (father of the now Secretary of State), Benjamin, Bragg, Clingman, Green, Hemphill, Hunter, Iverson, Lane, Mason, Polk, Slidell, and Wigfall. "Many of the conspirators had previously withdrawn from the Senate," else this proof had been still stronger.

I well remember that Philip Clayton was one of the most rabid and outspoken disunionists in Washington, and at the period referred to by Mr. Spaulding the city was full of them. All that appeared to be necessary for their triumphant success in the last days of 1860, provided they could have controlled Vice-President Breckinridge, which is doubtful, was that the hellish plot to poison President Buchanan at the National Hotel, in the spring of 1857, prior to his inauguration, had succeeded, in which event the Vice-President would have been in the Presidential chair. Of course neither Mr. Breckinridge nor any but base wretches like the assassins of Lincoln, knew of or would have countenanced such an infamous proceeding, but with a Southern man not opposed to secession in the chair of State, who knows that he might not have deemed it wise, as well as merciful, to have favored a *coup d'état, à la* Napoleon III., and withheld the reins from Lincoln, with a view to the preservation of peace? They (the disunionists) had Congress and the Supreme Court almost in their power, and with all branches of the Executive Government also in their hands, thus controlling the Treasury, the army, and the navy, what could the people have done but submit to fate?

Was the thought of such plot chimerical? It may be, but since I first ventured to express it in a letter published in the Providence *Journal* of December 3, 1863, I have met many well-informed persons who have said they fully believe it, but the only public confirmation of it I have seen is the following extract from the private journal of the late H. J. Raymond, editor of the New York *Times*, published in *Scribner's Monthly Magazine* for March, 1880, as follows:

"THURSDAY, March 5 [1863].

"At lunch to-day I had a talk with Mr. Forbes [the celebrated war correspondent, who married General M. C. Meigs's daughter]. He said he had very good reasons for saying that the famous disease at the National Hotel, in Washington, in 1857, from which so many persons suffered, was the result of an attempt on the part of the Southern disunionists to poison Buchanan, in order to bring in Breckinridge as President, who was in their councils, and would throw the power of the Government into their scale. He said that soon after he visited a prominent Southern politician, living at Culpepper Court House, in Virginia, and that from what there transpired he was convinced he was in the plot. He did not mention his name, and I did not think it proper to ask it."

WASHINGTON, February 24, 1888.

CHAPTER XVII.

THE "STOLEN ARMS."

Letter from ex-President Buchanan—The Real Facts of the Case—Investigation in Congress—Secretary J. B. Floyd's Order for Columbiads revoked by his Successor.

IN looking over the things of the past I have thought an interesting chapter might be introduced on the controverted subject of the "stolen arms." A great deal was said and written on the subject in the early days of the rebellion, and, as may be seen by the letter of November 12, 1861, of ex-President Buchanan, in Chapter X., the matter was fully investigated by the Committee on Military Affairs of the United States House of Representatives. Hon. Benjamin Stanton, the chairman of that committee, who made the report, was a Republican member from the State of Ohio.

I obtained and sent to Mr. Buchanan the desired copies of Mr. Stanton's report, and the following observations of the venerable ex-President, as copied from his book, entitled "Mr. Buchanan's Administration on the Eve of the Rebellion," will show the use he made of it. The spicy correspondence between him and General Scott relative to the efforts to reinforce Fort Sumter, etc., will doubtless be remembered by the intelligent reader. After giving a full history of his own action in that matter he says:

"The general deemed it wise to escape from his awkward position by repeating and endorsing the accusation against Secretary Floyd in regard to what have been called 'the stolen arms,' although this had been condemned as unfounded more than eighteen months before by the report of the Committee on Military Affairs of the House of Representatives. This was that the Secretary, in order to furnish aid to the approaching rebellion, had fraudulently sent public arms to the South for the use of the insurgents. This charge chimed in admirably with public prejudice at the moment.

"Although the committee, after full investigation, had, so long before as January, 1861, proved it to be unfounded, yet it has continued, notwithstanding, to be repeated and extensively credited up till the present moment. Numerous respectable citizens still believe that the Confederate States have been fighting us with cannon, rifles, and muskets thus treacherously placed in their possession. This delusion presents a striking illustration of the extent to which public prejudice may credit a falsehood not only without foundation but against the clearest official evidence. Although the late President has not been implicated as an accessory to the alleged fraud, yet he has been charged with a want of vigilance in not detecting and defeating it.

"The pretext on which General Scott seized to introduce this new subject of controversy at so late a period (November, 1862) is far-fetched and awkward." Mr. Buchanan, while repelling the charge in the general's report to President Lincoln that he had acted under the influence of Secretary Floyd in refusing to garrison the Southern fortifications, declares that "all my Cabinet must bear me witness that I was the President myself, responsible for all the acts of the administration; and certain it is that during the last six months previous to the 29th of December, 1860, the day on which he resigned his office, after my request, he exercised less influence in the administration than any other member of the Cabinet."—*Letter to National Intelligencer*, October 28, 1862.

Whereupon the general, in order to weaken the force and impair the credibility of this declaration, makes the following insidious and sarcastic remarks :

"Now, notwithstanding this broad assumption of responsibility, I should be sorry to believe that Mr. Buchanan specially consented to the removal by Secretary Floyd of one hundred and fifteen thousand extra muskets and rifles, with all their implements and ammunition, from northern repositories to southern arsenals, so that on the breaking out of the maturing rebellion they might be found without cost, except to the United States, in the most convenient positions for distribution among the insurgents. So, too, of the one hundred and twenty or one hundred and forty pieces of heavy artillery, which the same secretary ordered from Pittsburg to Ship Island in Lake Borgne, and Galveston, Texas, for forts not yet erected." . . .

"But to proceed to the report of the committee, which effectually disproves the general's assertions. . . . The committee made their first report on the 9th of January, 1861. With this they presented two tables (Nos. 2 and 3) communicated to them by Mr. Holt, then the Secretary of War, from the Ordnance Bureau, exhibiting 'the number and description of arms distributed since the 1st of January, 1860, to the States and Territories, and at what price. Whoever shall examine Table No. 2 will discover that the Southern and Southwestern States received much less in the aggregate instead of more than the quota of arms to which they were justly entitled under the law for arming the militia. Indeed, it is a remarkable fact that neither Arkansas, Delaware, Kentucky, Louisiana, North Carolina, nor Texas received any portion of these arms, though they were army muskets of the very best quality. This arose simply from their own neglect, because the quota to which they were entitled would have been delivered to each of them on a simple application to the Ordnance Bureau. The whole number of muskets distributed among all the States, North and South, was just eight thousand four hundred and twenty-three. Of these the Southern and Southwestern States received only two thousand and ninety-one, or less than one-fourth.

"Again, the whole number of long-range rifles of the army caliber distributed among all the States in the year 1860 was one thousand seven hundred and twenty-eight. Of these, six of the Southern and Southwestern States—Kentucky, Louisiana, Mississippi, North Carolina, Tennessee, and Virginia—received in the aggregate seven hundred and fifty-eight, and the remainder of those States did not receive any.

"Thus it appears that the aggregate of rifles and muskets distributed in 1860 was ten thousand one hundred and fifty-one, of which the Southern and Southwestern States received two thousand eight hundred and forty-nine, or between one-third and one-fourth of the whole number. Such being the state of the facts, well might Mr. Stanton have observed, in making this report, much to his credit for candor and fairness, that 'there are a good deal of rumors and speculations and misapprehensions as to the true state of facts in regard to this matter.' "—*Congressional Globe,* 1860–61, p. 294.

The report of the committee and the opinion expressed by its chairman before the House, it might have been supposed, would satisfy General Scott that none of these muskets or rifles had been purloined by Secretary Floyd. But not so. The ex-President had stated in his letter to the *National Intelligencer* of November 7, 1862, that "the Southern States received in 1860 less instead of more than the quota of arms to which they were entitled by law." This statement was founded on the report of the committee, which had now been brought fully to his notice. He, notwithstanding, still persisted in his error, and in his letter to the *National Intelligencer* of the 2d of December, 1862, he says: "This is most strange contrasted with information given to me last year, and a telegram just received from Washington and a high officer now of the Ordnance Department, in these words and figures: 'Rhode Island, Delaware, and Texas had not drawn at the end of 1860 their annual quotas of arms for that year, and Massachusetts, Tennessee, and Kentucky only in part. Virginia, South Carolina, Georgia, Florida, Alabama, Louisiana, Mississippi, and Kansas were, by the order of the Secretary of War, supplied with their quotas for 1861 in advance, and Pennsylvania and Maryland in part.' "

" It is in vain that the general attempts to set up an anonymous telegram against the report of the committee. . . . There is a mysterious vagueness about this telegram, calculated, if not intended, to deceive the casual reader into the belief that a great number of these arms had been distributed among the enumerated States, embracing their quotas not only of 1860, but for 1861. From it no person could imagine that these eight States in the aggregate had received fewer muskets and rifles than would be required to arm two full regiments.

" The next subject investigated by the committee was, had Secretary Floyd sent any cannon to the Southern States ? This was a most important inquiry. Our columbiads and 32-pounders were, at the time, considered equal, if not superior, to any cannon in the world. It was easy to ascertain whether he had, treacherously or otherwise, sent any of these formidable weapons to the South. Had he done this it would have been impossible to conceal the fact and escape detection. The size and ponderous weight of these cannon rendered it impracticable to remove them from the North to the South without the knowledge of many outside persons in addition to those connected with the Ordnance Bureau. The committee reported on this subject on the 18th of February, 1861. There was no evidence before them that any of these cannon had actually been transmitted to the South. Indeed, this was not even pretended. From their report, however, it does appear that Secretary Floyd had attempted to do this on one occasion a very short time before he left the Department, but that he had failed in this attempt in consequence of a countermand of his order issued by Mr. Holt, his successor in the War Department.

" It requires but a few words to explain the whole transaction. Secretary Floyd, on the 20th of December, 1860, without the knowledge of the President, ordered Captain (now Colonel) Maynadier, of the Ordnance Bureau, to cause the guns necessary for the armament of the forts on Ship Island and Galveston to be sent to those places. This order was given verbally, and not in the usual form. It was not recorded, and the forts were far from being prepared to receive their armaments. The whole number of guns required for both forts, according to the statement of the Engineer Department to Captain Maynadier, was one hun-

dred and thirteen columbiads and eleven 32-pounders.
When, late in December, 1860, these were about to be
shipped at Pittsburg for their destination on the steamer
Silver Wave, a committee of gentlemen from that city first
brought the facts to the notice of President Buchanan.
The consequence was that, in the language of the report
of the committee, 'Before the order of the late Secretary
(Floyd) had been fully executed, by the actual shipment of
said guns from Pittsburg, it was countermanded by the
present Secretary.' This prompt proceeding elicited a vote
of thanks on the 4th of January, 1861, from the Select and
Common Councils of that city, 'to the President, the Attorney-General (Black), and the acting Secretary of War
(Holt).' . . .

" The committee then, in the third place, extended back
their inquiry into the circumstances under which Secretary
Floyd had a year before, in December, 1859, ordered the
removal of one-fifth of the old flint-lock muskets from the
Springfield armory, where they had accumulated in incon-
venient numbers, to five Southern arsenals. The committee, after examining Colonel Craig, Captain Maynadier,
and other witnesses, merely reported to the House the testimony they had taken, without in the slghtest degree im-
plicating the conduct of Secretary Floyd. . . .

" The United States had on hand four hundred and
ninety-nine thousand five hundred and fifty four—say five
hundred thousand—of these muskets. They were in every
respect inferior to the new rifle muskets, with which the
army had for some years been supplied. They were of the
old caliber, .69 of an inch, which had been changed in 1855
to that of .58 in the new rifle muskets. It was one hundred
and five thousand of these arms that Secretary Floyd ordered to be sent to the five Southern arsenals; 'sixty-five
thousand of them were percussion muskets of the caliber
of .69, and forty thousand of this caliber altered to percussion.' By the same order ten thousand of the old per-

cussion rifles of the caliber of .54 were removed to these arsenals. These constitute the one hundred and fifteen thousand extra muskets and rifles, with all their implements and ammunition, which, according to General Scott's allegation, nearly three years thereafter, had been sent to the South to furnish arms to the future insurgents. We might suppose from this descripton—embracing ' ammunition,' powder, and ball, though nowhere to be found except in his own imagination—that the secessionists were just ready to commence the civil war. His sagacity, long after the fact, puts to shame the dulness of the Military Committee. While obliged to admit that the whole proceeding was officially recorded, he covers it with an air of suspicion by asserting that the transaction was ' very quietly conducted.' And yet it was openly conducted according to the prescribed forms, and must have been known at the time to a large number of persons, including the general himself, outside either of the War Department, the Springfield armory, or the Southern arsenals. In truth, there was not then the least motive for concealment, even had this been possible."

The general pronounces these muskets and rifles to have been of an " extra" quality. It may, therefore, be proper to state from the testimony what was their true character.

In 1857 proceedings had been instituted by the War Department under the act of 3d March, 1825, " to authorize the sale of unserviceable ordnance, arms, and military stores." The inspecting officers under the act condemned one hundred and ninety thousand of the old muskets " as unsuitable for the public service," and recommended that they be sold. In the spring of 1859 fifty thousand of them were offered at public sale. " The bids received," says Colonel Craig, " were very unsatisfactory, ranging from $10\frac{1}{2}$ cents to $2, except one bid for a small lot for $3.50. In submitting them to the Secretary I recommended that none of them be accepted at less than $2.

An effort was then made to dispose of them at private sale for the fixed price of $2.50. So low was the estimate in which they were held that this price could not be obtained, except for thirty-one thousand six hundred and ten of them in parcels. It is a curious fact that, although the State of Louisiana had purchased five thousand of them at $2.50, she refused to take more than two thousand five hundred. On the 5th of July, 1859, Mr. II. G. Fant purchased a large lot of them at $2.50 each, payable in ninety days, but in the mean time he thought better of it, and, like the State of Louisiana, failed to comply with his contract; and Mr. Belknap, whose bid at $2.15 for one hundred thousand of them, intended for the Sardinian government, had been accepted by the Secretary, under the impression that it was $2.50, refused to take them at this price after the mistake had been corrected. Colonel Craig, in speaking of these muskets generally, both those which had and those which had not been condemned, testified that " It is certainly advisable to get rid of that kind of arms whenever we have a sufficient number of others to supply their places, and to have all our small-arms of one caliber. The new gun is rifled. A great many of those guns (flint-locks), altered to percussion, are not strong enough to rifle, and, therefore, they are an inferior gun. They are of a different caliber from those now manufactured by the Government."

" Had the cotton States at the time determined upon rebellion what an opportunity they lost of supplying themselves with these condemned ' extra muskets and rifles,' of General Scott !"

Before dismissing this subject, the space devoted to which, I trust, will not be deemed unreasonable, since there has been so much doubt about it in the public mind, it may not be out of place to say that I took occasion, about three years ago, to examine the records in the Ordnance Office, particularly as to the quantity of arms, accoutrements, etc., distributed to the Southern States in advance for 1861, and it appeared that the whole quantity to Virginia was equal to four hundred and fifty muskets; South Carolina, three hundred and thirty-five; Georgia, five hundred and seventy-six; Florida, one hundred; Alabama, four hundred and ten; Louisiana, two hundred and seventy-three, for W. T. Sherman's military school; Mississippi, two hundred and twelve; Arkansas, one hundred and eighty-two; and to Maryland, one hundred; total, two thousand six hundred and thirty-eight. Pennsylvania also received a supply equal to nine hundred and five in advance for that year. It should be observed here that all ordnance stores, including accoutrements as well as muskets, were charged as so many muskets at thirteen dollars each; therefore, in the above aggregate of two thousand six hundred and thirty-eight, for instance, there may have been, and probably was, actually less than two thousand muskets and rifles altogether. Neither of the States of Delaware, Kentucky, Tennessee, North Carolina, nor Missouri received any ordnance stores in advance for 1861, for the reason, no doubt, that they did not apply for them. The yearly quota for each State was very small, and the orders for distribution were made from time to time, in the ordinary course of business, as the applications were received.

These applications, I understand, if correct as to quantity of stores, were never declined; but for years before the war some of the States, either from having no suitable place for the storage of arms, or from apprehension of their seizure by the negroes, to be used in a servile insurrection, omitted to apply for their quotas, and did not, therefore, receive them. I did not take time to make a very thorough examination, or to compare one year with another; but, while some of the States south may have been a little earlier or a little more prompt than formerly in securing their quotas for 1860 and 1861, I am bound to say that I have seen no evidence to show that the report of the Committee on Military Affairs is not substantially correct. It may be that, so far as the small number of arms distributed in advance for 1861 are concerned, had the Secretary of War sympathized with the free instead of the slave States, he would have withheld those supplies; although it might have done more harm than good thus early to have indicated in this manner a want of confidence in the honor and loyalty of the States applying. Be that as it may, however, there was nothing whatever in these transactions touching small-arms which could in the remotest degree reflect on either the patriotism or the watchfulness of President Buchanan; and, as to Secretary Floyd, it is quite apparent that, leaving muskets and rifles out of sight, he had enough to answer for simply in regard to the one hundred and thirteen columbiads and the eleven 32-pounders, about which there never has been any dispute. He was no doubt greatly chagrined at the revocation of his extraordinary order by his successor.

August 19, 1874.

PART II.

CHAPTER I.

The Author's Appointment as Commissioner to Free the Slaves in the District of Columbia—General Scott and Mr. Holt—F. P. Blair—Judge Woodbury—General Cameron's Bank—Politics in Pennsylvania—General Dix.

WHEATLAND, NEAR LANCASTER, 1st May, 1862.

MY DEAR SIR,—I have received your favor of the 27th inst. With my opinions steadily maintained for more than a quarter of a century, I could not have advised you to accept the appointment of appraiser of the negroes [of the District of Columbia] under the late Emancipation Act [of April 16, 1862, the wisdom of which was doubted by many at the time], yet I feel much gratified with the token of friendly regard manifested by your letter. If you have done wrong by accepting, you shall never be upbraided by me for it. On the contrary, I ardently hope you may never have occasion to regret it.

We lately had a visit from our friend, Dr. Blake, of Washington. It was quite refreshing to us to learn so much news and so many things relating to our friends in that city.

I sincerely trust that your daughter enjoys good health and is happy.

I have a debt due me in Maryland of a highly meritorious character; but the debtor, after years of delay, now says he cannot be touched on account of an act of the

202

Legislature suspending all proceedings against debtors in that State up till November next. If convenient, I would thank you to send me a copy of this act (of course not certified) or the substance of it.

With my kind regards to Mrs. King, I remain

Very respectfully,

Your friend,

JAMES BUCHANAN.

HON. HORATIO KING.

WHEATLAND, 5th October, 1865.

MY DEAR SIR,—I have received your favor of the 26th ultimo with the two copies in pamphlet of Mr. Holt's reply to Montgomery Blair, and, although I had read this before in the newspapers, I received it with pleasure as a token of your friendly regard.

If Mr. Holt had appreciated General Scott as I did upon my first interview with him after I had unfortunately invited him to Washington, he would not have addressed him the letter of the 31st August, 1865, though every fact stated therein, *and more*, is literally true. He ought to have known that the general would not frankly admit them, notwithstanding the preface of praises to his " great name." He ought to have stated the well-known fact, which could not be denied, without any such reference, and thus escaped the evasive and unsatisfactory answer. By the bye, as I was not perfectly certain who the person was that induced General Scott to substitute the *Star of the West* for the *Brooklyn*, then prepared for the occasion, I have not named him in my book.

I know and have long known the Blairs perfectly well, or, rather, old Francis P. Blair, for Montgomery had not the ability to make a respectable advocate of the Government in the Court of Claims. If President Johnson should fall into their hands, which some think probable, I shall not say what I apprehend, though I agree with him on his plan of restoration.

I thought at the time that Mr. Holt's report of the 18th February, coming four days after that of Mr. W. A. Howard, from the select committee, expressed unnecessary alarm. If you have never read this report, especially the long testimony of General Scott, I would advise you to read it as a curiosity. You may find it in vol. ii., "Reports of Committees of the House, 1860–61, No. 79." I think you will agree with me that the testimony justifies the unanimous conclusion of the committee, a majority of which were Republicans.

I forgot to mention that, according to my best recollection, I did not remove Montgomery Blair, but suffered him to remain in office until he should think proper to resign, on account of regard for the memory of Judge Woodbury. I well recollect that I received his apparently cordial thanks for my forbearance. His conduct towards me since is a characteristic of the family. Some day, in passing, you might look whether he did not resign.

I am always glad to hear of the welfare of Annie and her mother; and I hope you will remember me to them with great kindness.

I believe my book will be published in the course of the present month. It has been delayed much longer than I desired or expected.

My own health, thank God! continues remarkably good considering my age, and I have excluded myself entirely from any part in party politics, still believing, however, in the Democratic creed,—more, if possible, than ever.

Miss Lane desires to be kindly remembered to you.

From your friend,
Very respectfully,
JAMES BUCHANAN.

HON. HORATIO KING.

WHEATLAND, 21st April, 1866.

MY DEAR SIR,—I was happy to receive and peruse your favor of the 12th instant. I am glad to infer, from the mule ride of your daughter on the hot ashes of Mount Vesuvius, that she is in excellent health. May she continue healthy and happy for many, very many years!

I am happy to learn your favorable opinion of my book, as well as that of Mr. Holt. As you have loaned your copy away so much, I shall embrace the first opportunity of presenting you another. . . . .

With my kind regards to the members of your family, I remain

Very respectfully,
Your friend,
JAMES BUCHANAN.

HON. HORATIO KING.

P. S.—[Referring to his last interview with Colonel Benton]. The Jacobs letter was, I know, published in the *Constitution;* but the copy he sent me is from another paper, perhaps the *Intelligencer,*—I know not.

WHEATLAND, 23 June, 1866.

MY DEAR SIR,—I am pleased to learn that you arrived safely at home the day you left us. You left very kind remembrances of you behind. Indeed, the Sabbath when all the company were together was passed charmingly, but I fear not much to Christian edification.

I have read your poem ["Employment Necessary to Happiness"]. There is much good sense in it and it is better than the common run of American poetry. Still, I think you were more distinguished as Assistant Postmaster-General and as the chief of the department than you will ever become as a poet. Notwithstanding, I read your poem with great pleasure and interest.

I have not yet obtained a copy of the letter I promised to send you.   It shall be forthcoming in good time.

We have no news worth mentioning.   The four ladies desire to be kindly and cordially remembered to you, and we all desire to see you again whenever this may meet your convenience.

From your friend,

Very respectfully,

JAMES BUCHANAN.

HON. HORATIO KING.

WHEATLAND, 14 July, 1866.

MY DEAR SIR,—I have received yours of the 9th instant, and now send you a copy of my Hayesville letter,* which I received this morning from the *Daily Express* (Republican) of Lancaster, in which it was published on the 2d October, 1861.

"Old Blair," in his letter to the public of August 15, 1856, against my election, makes a point of my recommendation of General Cameron's bank at Middleton as a safe depository of a portion of the public money.   This, he asserts, was made a short time before Mr. Polk's election in 1844, and during Mr. Tyler's administration, when the deposit bank system was, unfortunately, in full operation.   I have not the least recollection of any such recommendation, but if it exists, as I suppose it does, then General Cameron, my neighbor, and at that time my political friend, must have called upon me for it, and I gave it as a matter of course.

Should you be at the Treasury Department I should like

---

* Letter addressed to Samuel A. Worth, Esq., expresses the "deep interest he feels in the present condition of our country."   He says "the war has become inevitable by the assault of the Confederate States upon Fort Sumter," and that until the Union is restored, "it will be our duty to support the President with all the men and means at the command of the country, in a vigorous and successful prosecution of the war."

to have a copy of this letter, which Blair says was written in November, 1844; but I say in sincerity I care little for it, and do not give yourself much trouble about it.

The three girls left me on yesterday morning, and the house is now quiet. I enjoyed their society very much.

From your friend,

Very respectfully,

JAMES BUCHANAN.

HON. HORATIO KING.

WHEATLAND, 29th August, 1866.

MY DEAR SIR,—Presuming that by this time you are in Oxford [Me.], I write you to that place to thank you for your kind letter of the 17th instant, and especially for the *Portland Argus* containing my Hayesville letter. I thank you for having caused it to be published. It is in perfect consistency with all I have written or said.

The Democratic party of this State are now in high spirits, and feel much confidence that Clymer will be elected Governor. This will be rendered certain if even a moderate number of the Republicans should reinforce the Democratic army and sustain the President's policy.

I do not like the progress to Chicago. I think it is ill-judged. Mr. Seward can never obtain the confidence of the Democracy of this State, and the identification of the President with the repeal of the Missouri Compromise and the doctrine of "Squatter Sovereignty," the two great measures of Mr. Douglas, will not add to his strength. Judge Black's powerful and conclusive reply to the "little giant" does not seem to have produced any effect on the President.

I approve the proceedings of the Philadelphia Convention as far better than the programme of the Radicals. . . .

Mrs. Johnston is now with me on a visit. She is in fine health and excellent spirits. I have had much agreeable company during the summer, and enjoy my usual health.

I need not say that I shall always be happy to see you at Wheatland whenever you may be able to come.

From your friend,
Very respectfully,
JAMES BUCHANAN.

HON. HORATIO KING.

WHEATLAND, 2d May, 1867.

MY DEAR SIR,—I have received yours of the 29th ultimo, informing me of your intended departure for Europe. May you have a prosperous voyage and a happy and useful visit to the Old World. My best wishes will attend you wherever you may go.

You will, of course, meet General Dix in Paris, from whom I have not heard for a long time. I believe you were present in Cabinet and heard his denunciation of —— when his name was mentioned in connection with the mission to Turin. How changed he must be, because he and his lady have since been on friendly and visiting terms with —— and his family. It is even reported that Miss Dix is to be married to ——'s son. The last is gossip; the first is true.

I am rejoiced to learn that your pecuniary affairs are so prosperous.

With my kindest regards to Annie Augusta,

I remain very respectfully,
Your friend,
JAMES BUCHANAN.

HON. HORATIO KING.

WHEATLAND, 1st February, 1868.

MY DEAR SIR,—I have received your favor of the 28th ultimo, and cordially congratulate you on your return to your country after your European tour. It may be called a flying visit, considering the number of places visited. I have no doubt you enjoyed yourself very much and derived profit and improvement from it. The meeting with your daughter and your little grandchild must have been peculiarly agreeable, and I trust that the trip may prove advantageous to Henry, who was doubtless delighted with it.

My own health, thank God! is now good for a man of my age, and I live in tranquillity and contentment. I trust that on some occasion on your way to New Hampshire you may visit me and talk over events both foreign and domestic. . . . .

Always your friend,

JAMES BUCHANAN.

HON. HORATIO KING.

WHEATLAND, 7th Feb., 1868.

MY DEAR SIR,—I have received yours of the 5th, and know not how I came to write you down as a New Hampshire man, for I was well aware you had been born in Maine. I am glad of the mistake, however, as it has caused you to send me the biographical sketch of yourself by Mr. Merriam. I have read it with much pleasure. It is well written, and it is no more than just to the subject of it. It omits the date of your birth. . . . .

I have no news to give you. Thank God! I am very well, and always remain, sincerely and respectfully,

" Your friend,

JAMES BUCHANAN.

HON. HORATIO KING.

CHAPTER II.

HON. ROBERT C. WINTHROP AND THE WASHINGTON NATIONAL MONUMENT.

ROBERT C. WINTHROP was appointed by resolution of Congress as the orator on the occasion of the dedication of the Washington National Monument on the 22d of February, 1885, but, owing to a serious illness a few weeks prior to that time, he was not able to be present to deliver the grand oration he had prepared.

14

Near the end of June, 1884, he received formal notice of
his appointment from Senator Sherman, chairman of the
commission designated by Congress to make the necessary
arrangements for the dedication.   He was then residing at
his palatial seat in Brookline, Mass., and he immediately
drove over to see me at my summer home in West Newton, five or six miles distant.   He came to tell me, as
secretary of the Monument Society, of his embarrassment
at having so heavy a task before him.   I observed at once
that he was very nervous.   He said that this matter had
weighed upon him for a month past, and that he was sorry
to have come to the conclusion that he ought not to render
himself responsible for a long formal oration, adding that
he should immediately break down under such an effort
and do but poor justice to himself or to the occasion.   He
also said if he were called on only to unite with others in
the addresses of the occasion, he should be encouraged to
make a brief discourse, but should not dare to promise an
oration.   Recent infirmities, he said, warned him against
undertaking it, that his family all advised him to decline,
and, deeply regretting to disappoint his friends of the
association, he felt constrained to avoid so great a responsibility.

He seemed much relieved when I assured him that I
believed, under the circumstances, an address of fifteen or
twenty minutes would be satisfactory, and that everybody
would cheerfully excuse him from any labor either of
preparation or delivery likely to worry or fatigue him.
He seemed to seize on this idea, and said, possibly the
commission may make arrangements for having three or
four addresses instead of one oration.   In such an arrangement, he added, he would willingly take part with Mr.
Edmunds and Mr. Carlisle, as President of the Senate and
Speaker of the House, respectively, or with Mr. Sherman
himself.   It would give, he thought, variety and attraction
to the ceremonies.   Finally, he said, "All I can do now

is to decline a formal oration, as it is to this only I am
invited." I promised to write both Senator Sherman and
Dr. James C. Welling, of the commission, advising them
of Mr. Winthrop's deep concern about the matter, and of
the assurances I had given him. Both immediately answered, confirming my assurance.

Senator Sherman said: "You may say to Mr. Winthrop
that the commission would very much regret if he should
be either unable or unwilling to be present, and that he is
entirely at liberty to speak as much or as little as his
health will permit, and we will adapt the other arrangements to suit his convenience."

Dr. Welling said: "I should deeply lament any over-
taxing of the health or strength of our venerable friend in
his preparation for that event; that while the committee
are naturally anxious that he should be the central figure
among the speakers on that occasion, I am sure that in their
anxiety to make sure of this most desirable end they would
cheerfully defer to his own comfort and convenience in all
that relates to the length of the address."

On receipt of these letters, I immediately informed Mr.
Winthrop, who made the following gratifying reply:

"BROOKLINE, MASS., 28th June, 1884, Saturday evening.

"MY DEAR MR. KING,—I will not let the week end without having thanked you, as I do sincerely, for your kind
and most effective intervention. Your two notes of the
26th and 27th reached me successively. The latter contained the note of Senator Sherman, which was everything
I could have desired, and which afforded me great satisfaction and relief. His remark that I might say 'as much
or as little as his health will permit' dispels at once all my
doubts and difficulties, and has taken a load off my mind.
This evening I have received a similar assurance from him
in reply to my own letter, and I shall dismiss all further
anxiety. Accept my grateful acknowledgments. . . . .

"I return Senator Sherman's note to you, but have kept a copy of it as a remembrancer.

"Believe me very sincerely and gratefully yours,

"Rob't C. Winthrop.

"Hon. Horatio King."

All now seemed to augur well for the future. Thus encouraged, Mr. Winthrop proceeded to write his oration. The following letter will show that he was in good spirits, and that he was no longer oppressed by the task before him :

"Boston, 2d Dec., 1884, 90 Marlborough Street.

"Dear Mr. King,—I have just been reading the two letters of my friend Stuart, of Virginia [ex-Secretary of the Interior], in the *Sunday Herald*, which you kindly sent me. I think he has established a fair claim, though unconsciously on his own part, to have the pretty triangle [opposite the National Theatre] called by his name. But, at all events, he deserves a grateful remembrance in Washington, as having led the way to the improvements which have so adorned the capital. I owe you my acknowledgments, too, for several other papers, telling me of the progress of the great monument. The little aluminum (or is it aluminium ?) capstone is particularly interesting. When that is fairly in place, I shall begin to feel that it is time for my own preparation to be finished. But I never finish anything until the last moment. You will have observed that the 22d comes on Sunday. I hope that my part in the ceremonies will be arranged for Saturday. Indeed, I doubt extremely the expediency of allowing the celebration to occupy more than one day. Congress cannot spare two days at this short session, and the people who come from a distance will not stay over Sunday. Two hours are enough for the procession, and the exercises in the hall ought to begin by half-past one or two o'clock. I hope a chaplain will be selected who will not make such an unconscionably long prayer as Mr. McJilton made in 1848. I trust, too, that the Marine Band will be warned against such long, unmeaning interludes as they gave at the unveiling of the Marshall Statue. A brief prayer and a few patriotic melodies are all that should come before the oration.

"I am fairly established in my winter quarters, and am trying to catch some inspiration for an hours' discourse. I do not believe I can say what I ought to say in less than an hour. But 'sufficient unto the day is the evil thereof,' and I will not indulge in any forebodings. I only hope the newspapers will not have exhausted the theme, and used up all the material before the day arrives.

"One of the papers said that the capstone was put in place last Saturday at 12 o'clock, but since then it has been stated that the capstone was still in Philadelphia! 'Grace to it,' wherever it is!

"Kind regards to Mrs. King.
                              "Yours very truly,
                                   "ROB'T C. WINTHROP.
"HON. HORATIO KING."

Most unfortunately, about the middle of December, Mr. Winthrop was prostrated by "a sudden and insidious attack of pneumonia, which seized him, most unexpectedly, on Thursday last [his son, Mr. Robert C. Winthrop, Jr., writes, December 18, 1884]. On Friday he was so ill we did not think he would live twenty-four hours. On Saturday he rallied, and we were encouraged to some slight hope." On the 22d of December he writes: "My father continues about the same, and while his physicians do not wholly reject the possibility of his recovery, yet the chances are much against it. . . . In no possible event would he be able to be in Washington by February next, and he is so feeble at present that it would be impossible to consult him about having his address read by somebody else." On the 25th of December he writes that his father continues "slowly, very slowly, to improve;" that he will "feel highly flattered at their [the committee of arrangements']

decision to abide by his oration, even if he cannot deliver
it in person;" and that "all he has ever said on the subject
is that, when first taken ill, he remarked to me, "my monument address is substantially finished. I might have
altered it a little, but I dare say I should not have bettered
it." January 3, 1885, Mr. Winthrop, Jr., writes: "My
father, though still very feeble, is now able to sit up a portion of each day, and occasionally has letters and newspapers read to him. . . . To-day I read him your letter of
January 1, received this morning. He replied: "Tell Mr.
King that, if I had an ounce of strength in my body, I
should make haste to write him in person, to thank him for
his many expressions of kindness, but I cannot hold a pen.
Tell him I still cling to the hope of being in Washington
on the 21st of February, but I realize how very, very improbable it is that I shall be strong enough to do so."

"BOSTON, 90 Marlborough Street, 14th Feb., 1885.

"HON. HORATIO KING,

"Sec'y Washington Monument Association.

"MY DEAR SIR,—I sent the first letter written by my own
hand since my illness to Senator Sherman yesterday, telling
him that I had been compelled to abandon the last hope
of being at Washington next week. This will be a disappointment to you and others, perhaps even to Congress and
the country; but certainly to myself, beyond all others. I
had hoped for some weeks past to be able to be present at
the great ceremonial, and to pronounce a few opening sentences of my oration before handing it to Governor Long.
But 'man proposes and God disposes,' and I will not
murmur at what I am sure has been ordered wisely. My
physician and my family forbid my thinking of leaving home
at present. Indeed, I have not left my house and hardly my
chamber as yet, and I should have been utterly unable to un-
dergo the fatigue of a journey to Washington, or to deliver
any part of my oration if I had reached there.

" My son has communicated to me, from time to time, your kind letters, and I thank you for them. I trust all will go off well. It is a great satisfaction to me that Governor Long has so kindly consented to read the oration. I hope that our friends will be satisfied with it. If it shall revive some impressions of the real grandeur of Washington's character, to which neither obelisks nor orations can do full justice, it will have answered the main purpose I had in view.

" But I have tried also to do justice to the builders of the monument, including the association and Colonel Casey. But it will speak for itself, and I will say no more about it.

" Believe me, dear Mr. King,

" Very truly yours,

" ROB'T C. WINTHROP."

I add an extract from another letter referring to an accidental omission, and to the tablet containing the names of persons, to be placed in the monument.

" BOSTON, March 9th, 1885, 90 Marlborough Street.

" DEAR MR. KING,—Your favor of the 26th ult. was duly welcomed. . . . .

" If I can anywhere introduce Dr. [John B.] Blake's name or Senator Sherman's [in official edition of the oration] I shall do so with pleasure. I am sorry that Colonel Casey has been disappointed in the action of Congress. I hope no tablets will be affixed on the inside of the monument of an extravagant size, or with too many names. I should think a small tablet, giving the date of the dedication, with the names of those concerned in the proceedings, is all that could be wisely adopted. . . . .

" Thanks for all your pains in my behalf. I congratulate you on the success of the inauguration ceremonies.

" Yours very truly,

" ROB'T C. WINTHROP.

" HON. HORATIO KING."

PART III.

CHAPTER I.

THE TRENT AFFAIR.

Excitement in Washington—Discussion of the Neutrality Laws—British Precedent—Edward Everett justifies the seizure—George Ticknor Curtis disapproves—Admiral Wilkes reports—Banquet in Boston to the Admiral—Secretary Welles's Congratulations—Mason and Slidell in Custody—The London *Times* Moderate—Earl Russell demands the Release of the Confederate Commissioners—Mr. Seward's Masterly Diplomacy—The Ambassadors liberated—Public Acquiescence in the Decision.

I SHALL never forget my delight, October 16, 1861, when, on meeting Senator John P. Hale in Pennsylvania Avenue, opposite the White House, he informed me in a jubilant manner that James M. Mason and John Slidell, Confederate Commissioners to England and France respectively, had been captured on board the British mail steamer *Trent* by Captain Charles Wilkes, of the United States steamer *San Jacinto*, and brought into Hampton Roads, Virginia. Old Point Comfort was electrified by the tidings, and the announcement was no sooner sent over the wires than expressions of joy were heard from every quarter of the Union outside the seceded States. The Baltimore *American* said: "Two of the magnates of the Southern Confederacy, two, perhaps, who have been as potent for mischief as any that could have been selected (out of South Carolina) from the long list of political ingrates, have 'come to grief' in their persistent attempts to destroy the noble government to which they owe all the honorable distinction they have hitherto enjoyed."

216

Neither press nor people waited for the particulars of the capture before proceeding to discuss at length the question of its legality. The Baltimore *American*, while apparently justifying the act, expressed the opinion that it was "a violation of the laws of neutrality, strictly considered;" but, later, the editor said he thought the character of the question was "beyond the reach of mere diplomacy," and that the Government had no other alternative than to adhere to the position it had already assumed. "In numerous ways Government and people have fully endorsed the act of Captain Wilkes, and the verdict will never be reversed although all Europe, with England at its head, demand it." The *National Intelligencer* said: "The proceeding of Captain Wilkes is fully justified by the rules of international law, as those rules have been expounded by the most illustrious British jurists and compiled by the most approved writers on the laws of nations." In support of this position many British authorities were cited. In the declaration of war by Great Britain against Russia, promulgated on the 28th of March, 1854, the following language was used: "It is impossible for Her Majesty to forego her right of seizing articles contraband of war, and of preventing neutrals from bearing enemies' despatches."

There was a British precedent during the Mexican War: General Paredes, a bitter enemy of the United States, was arrested in 1846, at the beginning of the war, and, being in Europe, was brought to Vera Cruz on the 14th of August, 1847, in the British mail steamer *Treviot*. Secretary Buchanan made complaint in a letter to Mr. Bancroft, our Minister to England, saying, "A neutral vessel, which carries a Mexican officer of high military rank to Mexico for the purpose of taking part in hostilities to our country, is liable to confiscation, according to the opinion of Sir William Scott"—high British authority, whom he quotes. Mr. Bancroft wrote to Lord Palmerston, who admitted the justice of the complaint, and the commander of the *Treviot*,

Captain May, was ordered to be suspended for what the British Government unhesitatingly acknowledged to have been a violation of the belligerent rights of the United States. Dr. Robert Phillimore, Advocate of Her Majesty in her office of Admiralty as Judge of the Cinque Ports, held that "it is indeed competent to a belligerent to stop the ambassador of his enemy on his passage." The Washington *Evening Star*, November 9, said, "The British Government should direct Lord Lyons to return the thanks of Her Majesty to the United States Government for its forbearance in not having seized the steamer *Trent*, brought her into port, and confiscated ship and cargo for an open and flagrant breach of international law. The Queen's proclamation of May last acknowledged the rebel States to be belligerents—enemies of the United States—and by their own principles of international law, British ships were thereafter to abstain from carrying despatches, or doing any act that favored the Confederates, under penalty of seizure and confiscation. Slidell and Mason should be held in rigid custody until they can be tried and punished for their crimes against the Government of the United States. Their sham character of ambassadors affords no protection. It is a lawful right of belligerents to seize an ambassador as soon as any other person, if he can be caught at sea. The minister appointed by the Continental Congress to Holland, Henry Laurens, was captured on the 3d of September, 1780, by a British frigate, on his passage to Holland near Newfoundland, was taken to England, and, after examination, committed a close prisoner in the Tower of London on a charge of high treason. Indulgence would be thrown away on arch-traitors like Slidell and Mason."

Hon. Edward Everett, before the Middlesex Mechanic's Association at Lowell, justified the capture of Messrs. Mason and Slidell as perfectly lawful—their confinement in Fort Warren perfectly lawful—and said they "would no doubt be kept there until the restoration of peace, which we all so much desire,"—and "we may, I am sure, cordially wish them a safe and speedy deliverance." Mr. George Sumner, a well-read lawyer, said in the Boston *Transcript* of November 18: "The act of Captain Wilkes was in strict accordance with the principles of international law recognized in England, and in strict conformity with English practice." Even the British Consul at New Orleans, Mr. Muir, it was authoritatively stated, justified the seizure and supplied legal authority to appear in a leading editorial of one of the city papers.

Mr. George Ticknor Curtis and Mr. George S. Hillard, of Boston, however, among others, pointed out the irregularity of the seizure in not carrying the *Trent* in for judicial condemnation. The New York *Herald* said: "It will not probably enter the mind of a single American for a moment, even after reading the news in our columns to-day, that Mason and Slidell will be surrendered to the English Government." There were some discordant voices. For instance, the New Orleans *Crescent* said this "high-handed interference with a British mail steamer by the Lincoln Government will either arouse John Bull to the highest pitch of indignation, or it will demonstrate that there has been an understanding between the two governments for a long time—that England has been and is assisting the Abolition Government to the detriment of the South."

Then, from the other side of the line, the Toronto *Globe* and Toronto *Leader* both condemned the act. The *Globe* denounced it as "an outrage on the British flag and an infraction of international law;" and the *Leader* declared it was "the most offensive outrage which Brother Jonathan has dared to perpetrate upon the British flag." Immediate liberation of the prisoners and apology, they claimed, should be demanded. At the same time it was proposed to raise an English subscription in New York to prosecute the captain of the *Trent* in the English law courts for violating the Qecen's proclamation, in case of delay of the Queen's attorney-general to bring suit, or the owners of the vessel should decline to prosecute him.

Such was the general drift of public sentiment immediately after the news of the capture was received. The circumstances attending the seizure are briefly told. The *San Jacinto*, which had been attached to the United States African squadron, left St. Paul de Loanda on the 10th of August, in temporary command of Lieutenant (now Rear-Admiral) D. M. Fairfax, with orders to wait at Fernando Po for Captain Wilkes, who took command there. On arrival at Cienfuegos, he learned that the steamer *Theodora* from Charleston, South Carolina, with Messrs. Slidell and Mason on board, had run the blockade, and he determined to pursue and intercept her if possible. On reaching Havana, he found she had left that port on her return, and that the Confederate Commissioners were waiting to take passage to Europe in an English vessel. He then conceived the bold plan of intercepting the British mail steamer and, in the event of their being on board, to make them prisoners. He cruised in the Old Bahama channel where he encountered the *Trent* on the morning of the 8th November. The account reads : " We were all ready for her, beat to quarters, and, as soon as she was in reach of our guns, every gun of our starboard battery was trained upon her. A shot from our pivot gun was fired across her bow. She hoisted English colors, but showed no disposition to slacken her speed or heave to. We hoisted the star-spangled banner, and as soon as she was close upon us fired a shell across her bow, which brought her to." Captain Wilkes hailed her, and said he would send a boat. Thereupon he ordered Lieutenant Fairfax to board her. Under date of November 12, Lieutenant Fairfax reports the particulars to Captain Wilkes, on board the *San Jacinto*, as follows : " At 1.20 P.M. on the 8th instant, I repaired alongside of the British mail packet in an armed cutter, accompanied by Mr. Houston, second assistant engineer, and Mr. Grace, the boatswain. I went on board the *Trent* alone, leaving the two officers in the boat, with orders to wait until it became necessary to show some force. I was shown up by the first officer to the quarter-deck, where I met the captain and informed him who I was, asking to see his passenger list. He declined letting me see it. I then told him that I had information of Mr. Mason, Mr. Slidell, Mr. Eustis, and Mr. McFarland having taken their passage at Havana in the packet to St. Thomas, and would satisfy myself whether they were on board before allowing his steamer to proceed.

"Mr. Slidell, evidently hearing his name mentioned, came up to me and asked if I wanted to see him. Mr. Mason soon joined us, and then Mr. Eustis and Mr. McFarland, when I made known the object of my visit. The captain of the *Trent* opposed anything like a search of his vessel, nor would he consent to show papers or passenger list. The gentlemen above mentioned protested also against my arresting and sending them to the United States steamer near by. There was considerable noise among the passengers just about that time, and that led Mr. Houston and Mr. Grace to appear on board with some six or eight men, all armed. After several unsuccessful efforts to persuade Mr. Mason and Mr. Slidell to go with me peaceably, I called to Mr. Houston and ordered him to return to the ship with the information that the four gentlemen named in your order of the 8th inst. were on board, and force must be applied to take them out of the packet. About three minutes after there was still greater excitement on the quarter-deck, which brought Mr. Grace with his armed party. I, however, deemed the presence of any armed men unnecessary, and only calculated to alarm the ladies present, and directed Mr. Grace to return to the lower deck, where he had been since first coming on board. It must have been less than half an hour after I boarded the *Trent* when the second armed cutter, under Lieutenant Green, came alongside (only two armed boats being used). He brought in the third cutter, eight marines and four machinists, in addition to a crew of some twelve men. When the marines and some armed men formed just outside the main-deck cabin, where these four gentlemen had gone to pack up their baggage, I renewed my efforts to induce them to accompany me on board. Still refusing to accompany me unless force was applied, I called to my assistance four or five officers, and first taking hold of Mr. Mason's shoulder, with another officer on the opposite side, I went as far as the gangway of the steamer and delivered him over to Lieutenant Green to be placed in the boat. I then returned for Mr. Slidell, who insisted that I must apply considerable force to get him to go with me. Calling in at least three officers, he also was taken in charge and handed over to Mr. Green. Mr. McFarland and Mr. Eustis (the secretaries of Mason and Slidell), after protesting, went quietly into the boat. They had been permitted to collect their baggage, but were sent in advance of it, under charge of Lieutenant Green."

Lieutenant James A. Green says: "When Lieutenant Fairfax gave the order for the marines to be brought in, he heard some one call out 'shoot him.' As the marines advanced, the passengers fell back. Mr. Fairfax then ordered the marines to go out of the cabin, which they did, Mr. Slidell at the same time jumping out of a window of a stateroom into the cabin, when he was arrested by Mr. Fairfax, and was then brought by Mr. Hall and Mr. Grace to the boat, into which he got." Lieutenant Green further states that Commander Williams, the mail agent, said the Northerners "might as well give up soon." Lieutenant Green adds that, with the exception of the captain, who was "reserved and dignified," the officers of the vessel generally showed an undisguised hatred for the Northern people and a sympathy for the Confederates, denouncing Lieutenant Fairfax and his men as "pirates, villains," etc. He says he was informed by one of the crew of the *Trent* that Commander Williams was advising the captain to arm the crew and passengers of his ship, as Williams threatened that "the English squadron would break the blockade in twenty days after his report."

On his arrival at Hampton Roads, Captain Wilkes came ashore, and at once sent Lieutenant Taylor with his report to Washington. He had a long conversation with General Wool, then in command there, who expressed the opinion that he had done right, and said that, "right or wrong, he could only be cashiered for it." Wilkes's report to Secretary Welles, of the Navy, bears date Hampton Roads, November 15, 1861. He wrote: "I have found it impossible to reach New York, my coal being exhausted. I shall procure sufficient in a few hours to proceed forthwith to my destination, New York, where I hope to receive your instructions relative to the Confederate prisoners I have on board this ship. I have determined to send Commander Taylor, United States Navy, who is a passenger from the coast of Africa, to Washington by the boat, as a bearer of despatches, and have given him orders to report to you in person."

On receipt of Captain Wilkes's report, November 16, the Secretary of the Navy sent to Commodore H. Paulding, Commandant of the Navy Yard, New York, the following telegram: "You will send the *San Jacinto* immediately to Boston, and direct Captain Wilkes to deliver the prisoners at Fort Warren. Let their baggage be strictly guarded and delivered to the colonel at Fort Warren for examination. The *San Jacinto* will be paid off at Boston. Send amount of money required. Answer per telegraph."

On the same day William H. Seward, Secretary of State, united with Secretary Welles in the following telegram to Robert Murray, United States Marshal, New York: "You will proceed in the *San Jacinto* to Fort Warren, Boston, with Messrs. Mason and Slidell and suite. No persons from shore are to be permitted on board the vessel prior to her departure from New York." We next hear of the *San*

Jacinto at Newport, Rhode Island, 21st November, where Captain Wilkes was obliged to stop on account of the stress of weather and for coal. Meantime it appears his prisoners had united in a request that they might be permitted " to remain in custody at Newport, on account of the comparative mildness of climate and the delicate health" of one of their number. They said they were "willing to pledge themselves not to make any attempt to escape, nor to communicate with any person while there unless permitted to do so." This request being sent by telegram to Secretary Welles, he replied same day, November 21: "The Government has prepared no place for confinement of the prisoners at Newport. The Department cannot change destination of the prisoners."

On November 22, the Secretary of the Navy telegraphed to Captain William L. Hudson, Commandant Navy Yard, Boston: "Direct Captain Wilkes immediately on his arrival to have the effects of the rebel prisoners on board the *San Jacinto* thoroughly examined, and whatever papers may be found to send them by special messenger to the Department. Answer per telegraph." November 24, Captain Wilkes reported his arrival at Boston, after having to put into Holmes's Hole, on the morning of the 22d, on account of fog.

On her way from Hampton Roads to Fort Warren, the *San Jacinto* encountered a terrible gale, which old sailors said had not been surpassed off Cape Cod for twenty years, and she was so much delayed that she was obliged, as already stated, to put into Newport for coal, which was sent to her in lighters. The Confederate commissioners and their secretaries occupied the captain's cabin, and messed with him at table. He had, when they first came on board, tendered the offer of his cabin for the accommodation of their families, but this was declined, and the latter proceeded on their way in the *Trent*. All political talk was prohibited by Captain Wilkes. Colonel Dimmick, in command at Fort Warren, received the prisoners; their baggage was landed and examined, consisting of six or eight trunks, six valises, several cases of brandy, wines, and liquors, a dozen or more boxes of cigars, and two cases (pints and quarts) of ale, and conveyed in two carts. No despatches were found. These all went on with the ladies of the prisoners, and reached England from St. Thomas in the British steamer *La Plata*. Shortly after going on board the *San Jacinto*, the prisoners joined in a letter to Captain Wilkes, in which they gave their version of the circumstances of their arrest and transfer to his ship, and requested that it be forwarded to Washington with his report, which was done. They afterwards also united in a note to him, acknowledging the courtesy with which they had been treated on board.

There was a banquet at the Revere House, in Boston, in honor of Captain Wilkes, Hon. J. Edmunds Wiley presiding. His act was highly applauded by Mr. Wiley, Governor Andrew, and Chief-Justice Bigelow. Captain Wilkes and Lieutenant Fairfax made speeches, briefly describing the capture. Captain Wilkes said he "had read in the law books that despatches from an enemy were contraband of war, and he took it for granted that ambassadors were the embodiment of despatches." In his report to the Secretary of the Navy, he called them "live despatches." Governor Andrew said he was in the office of the Secretary of War when the despatch came announcing the capture, and that he joined heartily in the cheer led by the Secretary. He pronounced the act as "not only wise judgment, but also manly and heroic success."

On November 30, Secretary Welles wrote Captain Wilkes at Boston: "I congratulate you on your safe arrival, and especially do I congratulate you on the great public service you have rendered in the capture of the rebel emissaries. Messrs. Mason and Slidell have been conspicuous in the conspiracy to dissolve the Union, and it is well known that when seized by you they were on a mission hostile to the Government and the country. Your conduct in seizing these public enemies was marked by intelligence, ability, decision, and firmness, and has the emphatic approval of this department. It is not necessary that I should in this communication—which is intended to be one of congratulation to yourself, officers, and crew—express an opinion on the course pursued in omitting to capture the vessel which had these public enemies on board, further than to say that the forbearance exercised in this instance must not be permitted to constitute a precedent hereafter for infractions of neutral obligations."

The news of the seizure reached the Lords Commissioners in London on the 27th of November, and by their order was immediately communicated to Earl Russell. At the same time a public meeting was called there, and a resolution presented calling on the Government " to assert the dignity of the British flag by requiring prompt reparation for this outrage." On the suggestion of Mr. John Campbell, one of the speakers, that the capture might have been justifiable in view of British law on the subject, the resolution was laid over.

The London *Times* was at first quite moderate. It fully admitted the right of search, and said the British Government " had established a system of international law which now tells against us." It quoted Lord Stowell, who held that " the only security that nothing is to be found inconsistent with amity and the law of nations, known to the law of nations, is the right of personal visitation and search to be exercised by those who have an interest in making it." It also cited the opinion of Chancellor Kent, wherein he declared that " The duty of self-preservation gives to belligerent nations this right. The doctrine of the English Admiralty Courts on the right of visitation and search and on the limitation of the right, has been recognized in its fullest extent by the courts of justice in this country" (the United States). But the *Times* claimed that when these decisions were given a different state of things existed. There were then no mail steamers or vessels " carrying letters wherein all the nations of the world have immediate interest." Hence England did then what they would not now do nor allow others to do. It was not aware of any authority to show that the commissioners " were contraband of war; and in any event it was not a question to be adjudicated on by a naval officer and four boats' crews. The legal course would have been to take the ship itself into port, and to ask for her condemnation, or for the condemnation of the passengers, in a Court of Admiralty."

Under date of November 30, Earl Russell directed the Lords Commissioners of the Admiralty to instruct Vice-Admiral Sir A. Milne to communicate fully with Lord Lyons, British Minister at Washington. He speaks of the " act of wanton violence and outrage," and says the commander should " look to the safety of Her Majesty's possessions in North America," and " not to place his ships in positions where they may be surprised or commanded by batteries on land of a superior force." Arrangements for increasing the military force in Canada were at once made. Twenty thousand picked troops, the flower of the British army, were mustered and passed in review, for embarkation via Halifax. The large ship *Melbourne* was being loaded at Woolwich with Armstrong guns, some eighty thousand Enfield rifles, a large amount of ammunition, and other war materials. Greater activity could not have been displayed had war already been declared. Neither night nor Sunday was allowed to suspend the work of preparation at Woolwich.

A well-informed correspondent of the New York *Commercial Advertiser* wrote from Paris, December 6 : " The sudden despatch of arms and men to Halifax, the outfit of numerous heavy ships of war, the violent language of the

British press, and concurrence of the French press, are events out of proportion to the nominal cause of them, and indicate a secret design and foregone conclusion." He thinks the British Government from the first " was disposed to aid the rebellion for the purpose of dissolving the Union." He advises that our Government accept at once the objection to form taken by the British Government, and release Mason and Slidell, thus depriving that Government of the pretext on which it rests.

November 30, 1861, which seems to have been fraught with many important communications concerning this affair, Secretary Seward took the precaution to write to Mr. Charles Francis Adams, our minister at London, a confidential letter, with permission to read it to Lord Palmerston, " if deemed expedient," in which letter, referring to the matter, he said : " It is proper that you should know one fact in the case without indicating that we attach importance to it,— namely, that in the capture of Messrs. Mason and Slidell on board the British vessel, Captain Wilkes having acted without any instructions from the Government, the subject is, therefore, free from the embarrassment which might have resulted if the act had been specially directed by us. I trust that the British Government will consider the sub- ject in a friendly temper, and it may expect the best dispo- sition on the part of this Government."

Earl Russell was prompt to communicate with Lord Lyons on this important subject. His letter to him bears date, also, November 30, and after reciting the circumstances of the capture as reported to him, he says : " It thus appears that certain individuals have been taken from on board a British vessel, the ship of a neutral power, while such vessel was pursuing a lawful and innocent voyage—an act of vio- lence which was an affront to the British flag and a vio- lation of international law. Her Majesty's Government, bearing in mind the friendly relations which have long subsisted between Great Britain and the United States, are willing to believe that the United States naval officer who committed the aggression was not acting in compliance with any authority from his Government, or that, if he conceived himself to be authorized, he greatly misunderstood the instructions which he had received. For the Government of the United States must be fully aware that the British Government could not allow such an affront to the national honor to pass without full reparation, and Her Majesty's Government are unwilling to believe that it could be the deliberate intention of the Government of the United States unnecessarily to force into discussion between the two governments a question of so grave a character, and with regard to which the whole British nation would be sure to entertain such unanimity of feeling.

"Her Majesty's Government, therefore, trust that, when this matter shall have been brought under consideration of the Government of the United States, that Government will, of their own accord, offer to the British Government such redress as alone could satisfy the British nation,—namely, the liberation of the four gentlemen and their delivery to your Lordship, in order that they may again be placed under British protection, and a suitable apology for the aggression which has been committed. Should these terms not be offered by Mr. Seward, you will propose them to him."

Bearing upon this highly important letter of Earl Russell, we find in Martin's "Life of the Prince Consort" a significant and interesting private history, showing that the Queen was not satisfied with the draft submitted for her approval, and that it was, at her suggestion, divested of its harsher features, and very much softened in other respects, to guard against giving offence to our Government. The draft was returned with a memorandum drawn by the Prince Consort and corrected with the Queen's own hand, indicating the changes she would have made. The letter, as sent, shows that her recommendation was followed in every particular.

Thus it is more than probable that her wisdom and good will towards the United States saved the two countries from a state of open hostilities, if not actual war. It is well known that the Prince Consort was in accord with her, and it is sad to think that the memorandum referred to was the last political writing from his pen. He was then seriously indisposed, and when he handed the paper to the Queen, "he told her that he could scarcely hold the pen while writing it." He died on the 14th of December, 1861.

At a public dinner given to Commander Williams in London, 12th December, he made what appears to have been not inaptly characterized as "a braggadocio speech," in which he gave his account of the action of himself, Lieutenant Fairfax, and others on board the *Trent*. He said he and Lieutenant Fairfax asked each other's pardon for anything which might have been said or done offensive on either side, so far as they themselves were concerned. He declared that one of Mr. Slidell's daughters branded an officer of the *San Jacinto* "to his face with his infamy, having been her father's guest not ten days before." He likewise averred, with an appeal to Heaven, that "the marines made a rush towards Miss Slidell with fixed bayonets." He said, "she did strike Mr. Fairfax, but not with the vulgarity of gesture attributed to her. Miss Slidell [he continues] was in the cabin with her arms encircling his neck, and she wished to be taken to prison with her father. Mr. Fairfax attempted to get into the cabin—I do not say forcibly, for I do not say a word against Mr. Fairfax so far as his manner is concerned—he attempted to get her away by inducements. In her agony, then, she did strike him in the face three times." He said that "when the marines made a rush for Miss Slidell, she screamed, for her father snatched himself away from her to break the window of his cabin, through which he thrust his body out. But the hole was so small that I hardly thought it would admit the circumference of his waist. It was then the lady screamed. When the marines rushed on with the point of the bayonet, I had just time to put my body between their bayonets and Miss Slidell, and I said to them, 'Back, you —— cowardly poltroons.'"

The excitement in England, instead of abating, continued to increase, although there was a conservative undercurrent there not unfavorable to the United States. For instance, Mr. John Bright counselled moderation, and the Sheffield Foreign Affairs Committee petitioned the Queen to punish Captain Moir and Commander Williams of the *Trent* for disobeying her proclamation of 13th of May, by carrying "officers" of the Confederate States and their "despatches."

The New York *Tribune* of 3d December said: "England is almost beside herself, is the tenor of the latest and most trustworthy private letters. They say that passion has swept away reason in a manner to an extent unknown since 1831, and that the national sympathy with the South developed by recent events is startling." Some now thought the President might propose to submit the matter to arbitration; but the New York *Journal of Commerce* suggested that, "if the British Government wanted only an adjudication by a Court of Admiralty, they could be easily accommodated by a return of the prisoners on board of the *Trent* at the point of capture, and then Captain Wilkes could fire a gun across her bow and bring her into port according to law."

There appeared to be no thought on the part of the people or press of the United States that the prisoners would be given up. Secretary Welles, in his annual report, had referred to "the prompt and decisive action of Captain Wilkes," as having "merited and received the emphatic approbation of the Department;" and a resolution of thanks to him had been passed by the House of Representatives immediately on coming together. Nevertheless, near the close of December, to the amazement of many, it began to be whispered about that our Government, considering discretion the better part of valor, had concluded to yield to the demands of Great Britain. The New York *Herald*, referring to this "silly rumor," said there "was not the slightest truth in the report."

But now came the unexpected dénouement. Having taken several days to digest Earl Russell's despatch, a copy of which had been left with him by Lord Lyons, Mr. Seward proceeded, December 26, to reply to it. He commenced by reciting its principal points, and, saying it had been submitted to the President, added: "The British Government has rightly conjectured, what is my duty now to state, that Captain Wilkes acted upon his own suggestions of duty without any direction or instruction, or even foreknowledge of it on the part of the Government." He corrects some of Earl Russell's statements to the effect that the round shot was fired in a direction obviously so divergent from the course of the *Trent* as to be "quite as harmless as a blank shot, while it should be regarded as a signal." So, also, we learn that the *Trent* was not approaching the *San Jacinto* slowly when the shell was fired across her bow, but, "on the contrary, the *Trent* was, or seemed to be, moving under a full head of steam, as if with a purpose to pass the *San Jacinto*." Also, that Lieutenant Fairfax "did not board the *Trent* 'with a large armed guard,' but left the marines in his boat when he entered the *Trent;*" that "the captain of the *Trent* was not at any time or in any way to go on board the *San Jacinto*," as Earl Russell had stated. Mr. Seward described the character of the prisoners, saying their despatches were carried to emissaries of the rebel government in England. He said, "The question before us is, whether this proceeding was authorized and conducted according to the law of nations. It involves the following inquiries:

"1st. Were the persons named and their supposed despatches contraband of war?

" 2d. Might Captain Wilkes lawfully stop and search the *Trent* for these contraband persons and despatches?

" 3d. Did he exercise that right in a lawful and proper manner?

" 4th. Having found the contraband persons on board and in presumed possession of the contraband despatches, had he a right to capture the persons?

" 5th. Did he exercise that right of capture in the manner allowed and recognized by the law of nations?

" If all these inquiries shall be resolved in the affirmative, the British Government will have no claim to reparation."

Addressing himself to these inquiries, he disposes of the first four in the affirmative. Taking up the fifth, he says : " It is just here that the difficulties of the case begin. In the present case, Captain Wilkes, after capturing the contraband persons and making prize of the *Trent* in what seems to us a perfectly lawful manner, instead of sending her into port, released her from capture, and permitted her to proceed with her whole cargo upon her voyage."

Captain Wilkes (quoted by Mr. Seward) says he " forbore to seize her (the *Trent*) in consequence of his being reduced in officers and crew, and the derangement it would cause innocent persons" on board. These reasons, Mr. Seward declared, were satisfactory to the Government, so far as Captain Wilkes was concerned. Finally, Mr. Seward rested on the old American rule that in case of capture from search, the question must " be carried before a legal tribunal, where a regular trial may be had, and where the captor himself is liable to damage for an abuse of his power." " If I decide this case," continued Mr. Seward, " in favor of my own Government, I must disavow its most cherished principles and reverse and forever abandon its essential policy. The country cannot afford the sacrifice. If I maintain those principles and adhere to that policy, I must surrender the case itself. It will be seen, therefore, that this Government

would not deny the justice of the claim presented to us in
this respect upon its merits. We are asked to do to the
British nation just what we have always insisted all nations
ought to do to us. . . . I prefer to express my satisfaction
that, by the adjustment of the present case upon principles
confessedly American, and yet, as I trust, mutually satisfactory to both of the nations concerned, a question is finally
and rightly settled between them, which heretofore exhausted not only all forms of peaceful discussion, but also
the arbitrament of war itself; for more than half a century
alienated the two countries from each other, and perplexed
with fears and apprehensions all other nations. The four
persons in question are now held in military custody at Fort
Warren, in the State of Massachusetts. They will be cheerfully liberated. Your Lordship will please indicate a time
and place for receiving them."

Lord Lyons replied to Mr. Seward on the 27th December,
saying he would, without delay, send a copy of his " important communication" to Earl Russell, and would confer
with him (Mr. Seward) on the arrangements for the delivery of the " four gentlemen" to him (Lord Lyons). The
rest is soon told. On December 30, Lord Lyons wrote to
Commander Hewett of the *Rinaldo*, an English sloop-of-
war, to proceed with his vessel to Provincetown, Massachusetts, and receive the released prisoners, adding: " It is
hardly necessary that I should remind you that these gentlemen have no official character. It will be right for you
to receive them with all courtesy and respect as gentlemen
of distinction; but it would be improper to pay them any
of those honors which are paid to official persons;" and
their transfer should be " effected unostentatiously."

Being conveyed from Fort Warren to Provincetown by
the tugboat *Starlight*, the " four gentlemen," with their lug-
gage, were quietly transferred to the *Rinaldo* on the evening
of January 1, 1862, remarking that their " only wish was to
proceed to Europe;" and that vessel at once set sail for St.

Thomas, whence these emissaries of treason pursued their weary way to their original respective destinations, cowed and humiliated in no slight degree. Doubtless they knew that only a cool reception awaited them.

The London *Star* said : " When Mason and Slidell have been surrendered to us, it will surely be time to declare in what capacity we, as a nation, are to receive them—whether as the envoys of Mr. Jefferson Davis, or as inoffensive visitors to a country where the rebel slave-owner and fugitive negro are welcome alike to the protection of the law." The London *Times* exulted over what it called " a great victory," but said : " Mason and Slidell are about the most worthless booty it would be possible to exact from the jaws of the American lion. The four American gentlemen who have got us into our late trouble, and cost us probably a million apiece, will soon be in one of our ports. What they and their secretaries are to do here passes our conjecture. They are personally nothing to us."

Not the least wonderful thing in this extraordinary affair was the sudden acquiescence in and approbation of the act of our Government in surrendering the " Confederate ambassadors," on the part of the people and press of the United States, as soon as Mr. Seward's masterly state paper was published. Nor were our people alone in their satisfaction at so happy a settlement of a vexed question which alarmed and threatened to disturb all the maritime nations of the world.

CHAPTER II.

PRESIDENT LINCOLN AT GETTYSBURG.

Conflicting Accounts of his Speech at the Cemetery Dedication—Ex-Governor Curtin's Statement to the Writer—A Wonderful Effort—Mr. Everett's Peroration—The Dirge by B. B. French.

THERE have been so many conflicting statements about President Lincoln's Gettysburg speech that I have taken pains to bring some of them together with a view to see if there is any way to get at the truth. In the first place, as to the manner of its writing and delivery.

The reporter of the New York *Times*, as quoted by the Springfield *Republican*, says Mr. Lincoln spoke from manuscript, referring to it as often as once for each sentence; that he spoke in a loud voice and was loudly applauded. He says that when the President had finished, it is related that Mr. Everett, the orator of the day, who had spoken before him, grasped Mr. Lincoln's hand warmly and said, in substance, "What I have said here will be forgotten, but your words will live."

Mr. John Russell Young, who, as reporter for the Philadelphia *Press*, was also present, states that Mr. Lincoln "took the single sheet of foolscap, held it almost to his nose, and, in his high tenor voice, without the least attempt for effect, delivered that most extraordinary address. There were four or five thousand people present. Very few heard what Mr. Lincoln said, and it is a curious thing that his remarkable words should have made no particular impression at the time."

Let us next hear what Colonel Ward H. Lamon, one of Mr. Lincoln's most intimate associates before as well as after his election, says, in the Philadelphia *Times*, October 4, 1887:

"A day or two before the dedication, Mr. Lincoln told me he would be expected to make a speech on the occasion; that he was extremely busy, with no time for preparation, and that he greatly feared he would not be able to acquit himself with credit, much less to fill the measure of public expectation. From his hat (the usual receptacle of his private notes and memoranda) he drew a page of foolscap, closely written, which he read to me, first remarking that it was a memorandum of what he intended to say. It proved to be in substance, and, I think, *in hæc verba*, what was printed as his Gettysburg speech. After its delivery, he expressed deep regret that he had not prepared it with greater care. He said to me on the stand, immediately after concluding the speech, 'Lamon, that speech won't scour. It is a flat failure, and the people are disappointed.' . . . On the platform from which Mr. Lincoln made his address, and only a moment after its conclusion, Mr. Seward turned to Mr. Everett and asked him what he thought of the President's speech. Mr. Everett replied, 'It was not what I expected from him: I am disappointed.' In his turn, Mr. Everett asked, 'What do you think of it, Mr. Seward?' The response was: 'He has made a failure, and I am sorry for it. His speech is not equal to him.' Mr. Seward then turned to me and asked, 'Mr. Marshal, what do you think of it?' I answered, 'I am sorry to say it does not impress me as one of his great speeches.' In the face of these facts it has been repeatedly published that this speech was received with great éclat by the audience; that, amid the tears, sobs, and cheers it produced in the excited throng, the orator of the day, Mr. Everett, turned impulsively to Mr. Lincoln, grasped his hand, and exclaimed, 'I congratulate you on your success!' adding, in a transport of heated enthusiasm, 'Ah, Mr. President, how gladly would I give all my hundred pages to be the author of your twenty lines!' All this unworthy gush, it is needless to say, is purely apocryphal. Nothing of the kind occurred. . . . As a matter of fact, Mr. Lincoln's great Gettysburg speech fell on the vast audience like a wet blanket. . . . It was then [after Mr. Lincoln's death] that we began to realize that it was indeed a masterpiece, and it then dawned upon many minds that we had entertained an angel unawares, who had left us unappreciated."

Now listen to what Andrew G. Curtin, the distinguished war Governor and statesman of Pennsylvania, says. Remembering to have heard him relate the story of the writing and delivery of Mr. Lincoln's extraordinary address, which now "belongs to the classics of literature"—it was in May, 1885, while riding with him and others over the battle-field, and when he pointed out to me the house of Mr. Willis, in the village, where, he says, he saw Mr. Lincoln engaged in writing it—I called on him at his hotel in this city a few days ago, and, with pencil in hand to make sure of his exact words, asked him to repeat the account. He said:

" I saw Mr. Lincoln writing his address in Mr. (now Judge) Willis's house, on a long yellow envelope. He may have written some of it before. He said, ' I will go and show it to Seward,' who stopped at another house, which he did, and then returned and copied his speech on a foolscap sheet. The people outside were calling now on Mr. Lincoln for a speech, and he got me to go and speak for him. Mr. Lincoln rode on horseback to the field, where a temporary stand had been erected. After the oration of Mr. Everett and the singing of a dirge by the Baltimore Glee Club, Mr. Lincoln proceeded to speak. He rose and presented himself in a most dignified manner, becoming a President of the United States. He pronounced that speech in a voice that all the multitude heard. The crowd was hushed into silence because the President stood before them. But at intervals there were roars of applause. My God! it was so impressive! It was the common remark of everybody. Such a speech, as they said it was! Everett and all went and congratulated the President, shaking him by the hand."

Governor Curtin, on the former as well as on the present occasion, expressed extreme regret that he had not secured that envelope on which he most positively declares he saw Mr. Lincoln writing his address, as above described.

Finally, I am happy to be able to add one more item, not less interesting, touching this controverted subject. I have the statement from General Joseph Holt direct, that a day or two after Mr. Lincoln's return from Gettysburg, while signing some papers which he (General H.), as Judge-Advocate-General, had brought for his signature, the President looked up with lively satisfaction and remarked, " I have just received a letter from Mr. Everett, in which he says that I had said more in my little speech than he had said in his whole oration."

Having presented the above rather conflicting testimony, I believe I will submit the case " to the jury"—my readers—

without either "summing up" or "argument," premising, however, that I am inclined to stand by the grand old war Governor. Besides I want the room for further illustration of this little historical sketch.

It may be interesting to know that among the distinguished persons on the platform at the dedication were, according to the Philadelphia *Press*, the following: Governor Bradford, of Maryland; Governor Curtin, of Pennsylvania; Governor Morton, of Indiana; Governor Seymour, of New York; Governor Parker, of New Jersey; Governor Todd, of Ohio; ex-Governor Dennison, of Ohio; John Brough, Governor-elect of Ohio; Major-Generals Schenck, Stahl, Doubleday, and Couch; Brigadier-General Gibbon and Provost-Marshal-General Fry. The reporter must have also seen among them Secretary Seward and Marshal Lamon, if not others, equally distinguished, including the late Major Benjamin B. French, author of the dirge which follows.

The ceremonies were opened with prayer by Rev. Thomas H. Stockton, Chaplain of the House of Representatives. A correspondent, " D.," of the Philadelphia *Press*, states that the reverend gentleman " concluded with the Lord's prayer, and during the delivery of these eloquent words there was scarcely a dry eye in all that vast assemblage." The populace, " gathered within a circle of great extent around the stand, were so quiet and attentive" (Mr. Young says) " that every word uttered by the orator of the day (Edward Everett) must have been heard by them all."

Here is Mr. Everett's peroration:

" ' The whole earth,' said Pericles, as he stood over the remains of his fellow-citizens who had fallen in the first year of the Peloponnesian war, —' the whole earth is the sepulchre of illustrious men.' All time, he might have added, is the millennium of their glory. Surely I would do no injustice to the other noble achievements of the war, which have reflected such honor on both arms of the service, and have entitled the armies and the navy of the United States—their officers and men—to the warmest thanks and the richest rewards which a grateful people can pay. But they, I am sure, will join us in saying, as we bid farewell to the dust of these martyr heroes, that wheresoever throughout the civilized world the accounts of this great warfare are read, and down to the latest period of recorded time, in the glorious annals of our common country, there will be no brighter page than that which relates THE BATTLE OF GETTYSBURG."

THE DIRGE.

"'Tis holy ground—
This spot where, in their graves,
We place our country's braves
Who fell in Freedom's holy cause
Fighting for Liberties and Laws—
  Let tears abound.

"Here let them rest—
And summer's heat and winter's cold
Shall glow and freeze above this mould—
A thousand years shall pass away—
A nation still shall mourn this day,
  Which now is blest.

"Here where they fell,
Oft shall the widow's tear be shed,
Oft shall fond parents mourn their dead—
The orphan here shall kneel and weep,
And maidens, where their lovers sleep,
  Their woes shall tell.

"Great God in heaven!
Shall all this sacred blood be shed—
Shall we thus mourn our glorious dead,
Or shall the end be wrath and woe,
The knell of Freedom's overthrow—
  A country riven?

"It will not be.
We trust, O God! Thy gracious power
To aid us in our darkest hour.
This be our prayer, 'O Father, save
A people's Freedom from the grave—
  All praise to Thee!'"

PRESIDENT LINCOLN'S ADDRESS.

" Fourscore and seven years ago our fathers brought forth on this continent a new nation, conceived in liberty and dedicated to the proposition that all men are created equal.

" Now we are engaged in a great civil war, testing whether that nation, or any nation so conceived and so dedicated, can long endure. We are met on a great battle-field of that war. We have come to dedicate a portion of that field as a final resting-place for those who here gave their lives that that nation might live. It is altogether fitting and proper that we should do this.

" But, in a larger sense, we cannot dedicate—we cannot consecrate—we cannot hallow this ground. The brave men, living and dead, who struggled here, have consecrated it far above our poor power to add or detract. The world will little note nor long remember what we may say here, but it can never forget what they did here. It is for us, the living, rather, to be dedicated here to the unfinished work which they who fought here have thus far so nobly advanced. It is rather for us to be here dedicated to the great task remaining before us; that from these honored dead we take increased devotion to that cause for which they gave the last full measure of devotion ; that we here highly resolve that these dead shall not have died in vain; that this nation, under God, shall have a new birth of freedom ; and that government of the people, by the people, for the people, shall not perish from the earth."

WASHINGTON, February 17, 1888.

CHAPTER III.

PRESIDENT LINCOLN AND GENERAL McCLELLAN.

The President visits the General—His Accidental Detention—Mr. Lincoln declares he would not consent to sign the Death-Warrant of a Soldier for failing to go where his legs refused to carry him—Called these " Leg Cases."

HERE is a little historical item which, as far as it goes, ought to be known in explanation, possibly, of what has been publicly brought against General George B. McClellan as an unpardonable act of rudeness, not to say insult

16

to President Lincoln. This act was the keeping President Lincoln waiting for a considerable time on one occasion when he called on McClellan at his head-quarters. Referring to this a few days ago, in conversation with General Henry J. Hunt, chief of artillery at the battle of Gettysburg, and now governor of the Soldiers' Home near Washington, I inquired if he thought it possible that the story could be true. Hesitating a moment, in evident belief of its falsity so far as General McClellan was concerned, and appearing never to have heard of its publicity, he answered, "Yes—with a reservation." He said that one day when he himself called at McClellan's head-quarters he found General Barry there in a great rage on account of what he regarded as a gross insult to President Lincoln, who had called to see General McClellan and had been kept waiting in the anteroom ; but whether through the fault of the Irish door-keeper or the neglect of the general, he did not appear to know. He had, however, observed that when Mr. Lincoln passed up stairs the door-keeper or orderly—whatever his appellation —gave a clownish burst of expression, as if in derision of the President.

How can the exact truth ever be known ? One thing is certain, instead of going to McClellan, the President should have sent for him to come to the White House whenever he wished to see him; and this, I presume, was his usual custom.

While writing of President Lincoln, I will relate another singular incident not generally known, I think, and which comes to me on equally undoubted authority (Joseph Holt, President Lincoln's Judge-Advocate-General). At the beginning of the war, oftener probably than later in the fearful struggle, sometimes, in going into battle, a soldier who had "never smelt gunpowder" would falter, shrink away, and may be throw down his arms, utterly unable, from cowardice, to proceed, thus rendering himself liable to the penalty of death. When these cases came before President Lincoln and the necessity of making an example of such culprits was pointed out to him, he invariably pleaded off. By way of convincing him not only of the imperative necessity of strictly enforcing the law as a restraining influence against cowardly instincts but also of its reasonableness and justice, it was urged that, the soldier seeing before him two dangers, —on the one hand, sure death if he acted the coward, on the other, a reasonable chance of escape if he pressed forward in battle,—he would naturally choose the lesser of the two and thus save his honor at least, if not his life. But it was all to no purpose, Mr. Lincoln solemnly declaring that he never could consent to sign the death-warrant of a soldier *for failing to go where his legs refused to carry him;* and he never did. He consigned to pigeon-holes without his signature scores, if not hundreds, of these cases, where they now lie buried at the War Department. He called them " Leg Cases."

WASHINGTON, December 1, 1886.

CHAPTER IV.

A REMINISCENCE.

Ex-President Buchanan—His Last Interview with Colonel Thomas Hart Benton—Controversy between William Carey Jones and Francis P. Blair, Sr.—Interesting Incidents in the Life of Colonel Benton—His Death and Funeral.

IN one of Ex-President Buchanan's letters to me, dated at Wheatland, 21st April, 1866, he wrote as follows:

" By-the-by, I wish to impose upon you a task which I do not think will be uncongenial. Old Mr. Blair attempted to misrepresent the scene between Colonel Benton and myself on the evening preceding his death, which was as kind and affectionate on his part as if he had been my dear brother. His noble daughter, who was alone present, voluntarily, and without my previous knowledge, contradicted him, and made and published a true statement of the occurrence, signed by her husband, Governor Jacob. The date of that letter is at Clifton (Kentucky), August 2, 1858. I had much difficulty in finding it, but at last obtained it from Governor Jacob. He informs me there was a pamphlet published at the time by William Carey Jones, the son-in-law of Colonel Benton, which I ought to have, but it is not in his possession. Now I have thought that this might be procured through my old friend Peter Force. I would give any reasonable price for it, as I wish to leave behind me some interesting reminiscences."

Sincerely desirous of obliging Mr. Buchanan, I at once endeavored to procure the pamphlet referred to, calling at all our book-stores for it, as well as upon Mr. Force, who, though then a very old man, was still living in apparently good health. It was all in vain. I could find it nowhere. Mr. Force told me it might be, and probably was, in his library, but that his pamphlets were not generally classified or arranged, and that a search for it there would be nearly hopeless. I was obliged to give it up for the time being, intending, however, some time or other to find it if possible, and I have at length succeeded, it having recently come to light among the books and pamphlets of the late Peter Force's library in the library of Congress. It bears no title, but is addressed "To the People of the United States." It is very severe on Mr. Blair, Sr., and refers likewise to Mr. Francis P. Blair, Jr. The controversy arose from the appearance, in the first instance, of a communication attributed to Mr. Blair, Sr., or as having been inspired by him, from which the following is an extract. The writer professed to give an account of an interview with Colonel Benton just before his death, saying :

"The inspiration of this theme (the Compromise of 1850) fired the languid blood and reanimated for a moment the failing frame of the dying patriot. In energetic whispers he told his visitor that the same men who had sought to destroy the republic in 1850 were at the bottom of this accursed Lecompton business. . . . He warmly praised the intrepid and incorruptible Douglas Democrats who had resisted the power and wiles of a corrupt and deluded administration."

Here is Mr. Jones's account of the interview, in allusion to said communication:

"About eighty hours before the death of Colonel Benton, F. P. Blair, Sr., of Silver Springs, Md., entered the sick-room. The orders of Colonel Benton were that no visitors should be admitted. Mr. Blair's long intimacy in the house allowed him to pass the hall-door, and, when he had ascended the second story and his voice was heard, Colonel Benton said, 'Yes, let him come in a moment.' Mr. Blair, when he came in, saw this: Colonel Benton on his dying bed; on one side of it his eldest daughter, attending to the wants of her father, and catching the faintest word from his lips; on the other side of the bed the writer of this, seated at a small, narrow table writing at the dictation of Colonel Benton. Mr. Blair remained some time. Two days after there was published in the New York *Tribune* an anonymous letter, giving a daguerreotype, as it were, of what was seen, only substituting for Mr. Blair's person an imaginary person called a friend from Missouri, and mentioning by name both my wife and myself. What was seen being thus depicted, the narrative went on to falsify and defame what was said by the dying man. A month afterward, only that such a defamation should not go into record history, with apparent assent of the witnesses vouched to it, I made a contradiction, but did not mention any names."

Touching the assertion that Colonel Benton employed opprobrious terms in speaking of the Lecompton business, Mr. Jones, in reply to Mr. Blair, said, "You know that Colonel Benton did *not* die with anything accursed or denunciatory on his lips, but with only good and kind words for all to whom or of whom he had occasion to speak."

Mr. Jones says that the last lines intended for publication in his "Abridgment of the Debates of Congress," that Colonel Benton wrote, were to accompany a debate in the Senate of 17th of June, 1850, and a short, energetic speech by Mr. Webster, from which the following is an extract: "I am against agitators, North and South; I am against local ideas, North and South, and against all narrow and local contests. I am an American, and I know *no locality* in America; that is *my country*."

In commenting upon this, Colonel Benton observed that

"It is impossible to read the speeches of this session, and hear, as it were, the last words of the last great men of that wonderful time, without having the feelings profoundly moved by the deep danger to the Union which stood before them, and the patriotic attempts they made to avert that danger. This brief speech of Mr. Webster is a noble illustration of the feelings of the patriotic sages of that portentous day. They labored to save their country, and believed [that they had done it.]"

Mr. Jones remarks : " Colonel Benton, at the time (April 5) that he wrote this note, was physically very feeble, in bed, and suffering acute pain. The paper that he wrote on being filled, he desired me, in copying, to add the concluding words. His strength failed him to add more at the moment, and he continued his work of abridgment."

On the 6th of April Colonel Benton dictated to Mr. Jones, who wrote a note to be appended to a debate in the Senate of July 22, 1850, in which the concluding speech was by Mr. Clay. In this he speaks of Mr. Clay as " the great champion of the measure (the Missouri Compromise), which he adheres to as the crowning principle in the measures, of 1850, and renews his testimony to it as a Southern measure of thirty years' duration."

In this connection it may not be out of place to introduce the following extract from a patriotic speech made by Colonel Benton himself in the course of the great debate in June, 1850 : " I recognize no such parties—no two halves in the Union. I know no North and I know no South, and I repulse and repudiate as a thing to be forever contemned this first attempt to establish geographical parties in this chamber by creating a committee formed on that principle."

I cannot avoid observing here, by way of parenthesis, how different might have been the condition of the United States to-day had the patriotic sentiments and advice of these great statesmen—Webster, Clay, and Benton—pre-

vailed from the start. I am not too young to remember
well when it was the common sentiment, and no offence to
express the opinion anywhere North or South, that negro
slavery was an evil which should be removed as soon as it
could be done reasonably and safely. Virginia was moving
in important measures toward gradual emancipation, and
the same thing was taking root and commanding the attention of the better classes in the other border States, when
the whole South was aroused by the aggressive and apparently unfriendly action of the original Abolitionists, one of
whose principal leaders did not hesitate to proclaim, "The
Union is a lie; the American Union is an imposture, a cove-
nant with death and an agreement with hell. . . . I am for
its overthrow." This note of warning put a stop at once
to all steps looking toward gradual emancipation, and the
South found itself powerless to act except on the defensive.
(Understand, these interjected remarks relate particularly
to times and action long prior to the repeal of the Missouri
Compromise or the formation of the Free-soil party.)
Were the Abolitionists right? Who knows that, instead
of thus exciting the baser passions, had brotherly love and
kindness been allowed full sway, the abolishment of slavery
might not have been accomplished by peaceful means, and
our civil war, with all its attendant and consequent destruction, death, and woe unparalleled, averted? With a great-
hearted president like Abraham Lincoln, who knows that,
with the ancient harmony between the North and South
undisturbed, the peculiar institution might not have been
extinguished in the same manner and with the same general satisfaction that it was terminated in the District of
Columbia?

These questions have often arisen in my mind. It may
be unpopular, but is it a crime to ask them? I will not
pronounce the Abolitionists as intentionally dishonest, but
rather believe they were governed by pure motives. I did
not, however, believe either in their object or in their course

of action; hence I need not say that I am not now ready
to admit that the great mass of the people—the two great
political parties of the country, with whom I was in accord
on this subject—were all sinners, and only the Abolitionists
saints.   I refer, now, to the disposition, prominently manifested on the part of some of the survivors of the old Abolition party, to canonize their leaders.   Let them, if they
please, extol one another's deeds in the cause of abolition
—let them have their tea parties and recall their many exploits, their sacrifices, and their sufferings; but when they
assume all the credit of freeing the slave, if it be a credit
that he should have been freed by war and bloodshed, instead of by peaceful means, may I not, in all charity, say,
let them not forget to hold themselves answerable, also, in
conjunction with kindred spirits at the South, for their full
share of the terrible consequences of the war?

But to return to my history.   In a letter in the New
York *Tribune*, 23d July, 1858, Mr. Blair, Sr., said:

" When he died, Colonel Benton, like Clay and Jackson, left written
testimonials declaring the forfeiture of his confidence by Mr. Buchanan.
In the sketch of his life, submitted to his revision, and sent to the press
by him just before his fatal illness, he says that he had supported Mr.
Buchanan against his own son-in-law, Colonel Fremont, and assigns as
the reason the confidence that Mr. Buchanan, if elected, would restore
the principles of the Jackson administration, and the apprehension that
the success of Colonel Fremont would engender sectional parties fatal to
the preservation of the Union; but adds that, soon after, he had reason
to change both opinions."

Mr. Jones positively denies that Colonel Benton ever
approved of the sketch referred to by Mr. Blair, and avers
that he [Colonel Benton] "specially repudiated the whole
piece," and "wrote with his own hands an entire substitute
for the caricature that had been prepared for him in the
Blair interest, getting out of his bed for the purpose one
month before his death, when he was suffering the agonies
of a thousand deaths."

It may serve to elucidate the subject somewhat to state that, at this time, Francis P. Blair, Jr., was a candidate for Congress in Missouri, and Mr. Jones refers to the father as speaking of "my son and his Missouri canvass." Indeed, he intimates that the whole thing was intended "specially for Missouri consumption."

On the other hand, Mr. Blair, Sr., who, everybody knows, was an "ugly customer" to encounter with the pen, did not hesitate to affirm that, "In taking possession of Colonel Benton's sick room, he [Jones] became a very convenient exponent to suit his [Colonel Benton's] views to the necessities of the administration. But probabilities must be concerted to give countenance to favorable reports. It was arranged that President Buchanan and his premier [General Cass] should sit by the death-bed."

"'Arranged' by whom?" Mr. Jones exclaimed, with fierce invective.

There can be no doubt that it was at the special request and desire of Colonel Benton that both President Buchanan and General Cass called to see him a few hours only before he died. Mr. Jones, who returned from a foreign mission about the 29th of March, 1858, says that, having mentioned to Colonel Benton the fact of his calling immediately to pay his respects to the President and Secretary of State, Colonel Benton said to him, "I wish you to go again; to take in person my card to each of them; before long, I wish to see them." But the circumstances attending the invitation and the visit of Mr. Buchanan are succinctly stated in Governor Jacob's letter, already referred to, as follows: "Mrs. Jacob wrote the note requesting the President to call and see her father; and the writing was delayed some time for the reason that it was Colonel Benton's wish that she should call in person and make the invitation, but she was unwilling to leave her father for that length of time.

"Mr. Buchanan came at once, and had an interview of

some length with Colonel Benton, Mrs. Jacob being the only other person present. The interview was wished for by Colonel Benton for several reasons : First, to thank Mr. Buchanan for an act of kindness to one of his children, performed twelve years ago, which fact Colonel Benton was not made acquainted with until three days before his death; secondly, to exhort him to try to preserve the Union, looking to God for strength and knowledge of the right course; and, lastly, to assure him of his personal friendship and good-will in those his last moments. It is *with those words* we now have to deal. He took the President's hands in his, and said, in clear tones, ' Buchanan, we are friends; we have differed on many points, as you well know, but I always trusted in your integrity of purpose. I supported you in preference to Fremont, because he headed a sectional party, whose success would have been the signal for disunion. I have known you long, and I knew you would honestly endeavor to do right. I have that faith in you now, but you must look to a higher power to support and guide you. We will soon meet in another world; I am going now; you will soon follow. My peace with God is made, my earthly affairs arranged; but I could not go without seeing you and thanking you for your interest in my child.' Much more was said that is too sacred to repeat. Colonel Benton was much exhausted, and Mr. Buchanan frequently urged him to spare himself. Mr. Buchanan remarked to members of his family that nothing had ever given him greater pleasure. When Mrs. Jacob returned to her father's room, he called her to him, and said, ' My child, you are a witness of what has passed this evening; think of it, and remember it. I am glad Mr. Buchanan came; all is peace with me, and I can rest.' "

The Washington *Union* of April 11, 1858, said, " The President, hearing of the extreme illness of his ancient compeer, called upon him Friday evening. The dying statesman declared afterward his exceeding gratification at the visit. The interview is said to have been protracted."

Mr. Jacob Hall, of Missouri, between whom and Colonel Benton a warm personal friendship had existed for many years, said, in a letter to William Carey Jones, under date of June 17, 1858, referring to an interview with Colonel Benton, which took place a short time prior to Mr. Buchanan's visit, that "He (Colonel Benton) expressed himself in unmistakable terms of friendship toward the President, commending his honesty and uprightness of purpose. He remarked more than once that he would die without an unkind feeling toward any human being. He gave me a verbal message for the President in accordance with these sentiments, which he requested that I should deliver to him. This I did according to his request and my recollection of the same."

Colonel Benton died on the morning of April 10. Up to almost the last moment he was engaged upon his great work, dictating its closing chapter. "His daughter, Mrs. Jones, sitting beside the bed, received it, sentence by sentence, whispered in her ear, and repeated it aloud to her husband, who wrote it down. It was then read over to Colonel Benton and received his corrections. Surely this indomitable energy and courage in the very face of the "King of Terrors" was most remarkable. I thought so at the time, nor do I remember ever having heard, before or since, of so wonderful a death-bed scene.

In announcing the demise of Colonel Benton, the *National Intelligencer* had also this touching notice : "It is a curious and affecting circumstance that the youngest and the oldest of the family should have died within a few hours of each other under the same roof. An infant grandson of Colonel Benton, the child of Mr. William Carey Jones, died in the house of his grandfather yesterday morning (11th of April), and the nursling and the grandfather now lie side by side in death on the same bier."

On the 8th of April Colonel Benton addressed the following note to Samuel Houston, Esq., Senator in Congress from the State of Texas, and George W. Jones, Esq., Representative in Congress from the State of Tennessee,—viz.:

> "C Street, Washington, April 8, 1858.
>
> 'To you, as old Tennessee friends, I address myself, to say that in the event of my death here I desire that there should not be any notice taken of it in Congress. There is no rule of either house that will authorize the announcement of my death, and if there were such a rule I should not wish it to be applied in my case, as being contrary to my feelings and convictions long entertained.
>
> "Your old Tennessee friend,
>
> "Thomas H. Benton."

In the Senate, on Monday, the 12th of April, Mr. Polk, of Missouri, said it was known to the members of the Senate that Colonel Benton had requested that no public demonstration should be made in Congress in consequence of his death, but he deemed it proper to move an adjournment to give members an opportunity to attend the funeral. Mr. Clark, of Missouri, made a similar announcement in the House, and both houses adjourned accordingly.

There was a large attendance at the funeral, including the President, heads of departments, foreign ministers, members of Congress, and other distinguished persons. Only two of his daughters, Mrs. Jones and Mrs. Jacob, with their husbands, were present; of the other two, Mrs. Fremont was at the time on her way to California, and Mrs. Boileau was in Calcutta. "The grandsire and the grandchild reposed in death side by side, and friendly hands had strewn their common bier with choice flowers—some in mature bloom, others just budding into beauty."

The pall-bearers were General Jesup, General Houston, Governor Floyd, W. W. Seaton, James B. Clay, W. H. Appleton, Jacob Hall, and John C. Rives, none of whom survives, unless it be Mr. Appleton.

The place of sepulture at St. Louis is now indicated by a fine bronze statue of the illustrious Senator.

Rev. Byron Sunderland, who conducted the funeral ceremonies in this city, said, " During the last week of Colonel Benton's life I had several interviews with him at his own request. Our conversation was mainly on the subject of religion, and in regard to his own views and exercises in the speedy prospect of death. In these conversations he most emphatically and distinctly renounced all self-reliance and cast himself entirely on the mediation of the Lord Jesus Christ as the ground of his acceptance with God. His own words were, ' God's mercy in Jesus Christ is my sole reliance.' "

As early as in September, 1857, Colonel Benton had a severe attack of what he supposed to be colic, when Dr. J. F. May, his physician, pronounced his disease (cancer of the bowels) incurable, and so informed him. This Dr. May states in a letter under date of April 13, 1858, to Mr. William Carey Jones. Dr. May proceeds : " Before he was relieved, in the attack just spoken of, he had given up all hope of life. He told me he was satisfied the hour of his dissolution was near at hand, that it was impossible for him to recover, and that his only regrets at parting with the world were in ' separating from his children, and in leaving his great work undone; that death had no terrors for him, for he had thought on that subject too long to feel any.' "

In the intervals of his visits to him during the last week of his illness, Dr. May said he ascertained that he was in the habit of correcting proof-sheets, and " I recollect one occasion [said he] when I did not suppose he could stand, he suddenly arose from his bed, and, in the face of all remonstrance, walked to his table at some distance off, and corrected and finished the conclusion of another work on which he was engaged. His unconquerable will enabled him to do it, but when done he was so exhausted I had to take the pen from his hand to give it the direction. As soon as he recovered from the immediate danger of this attack he labored, as he had done for years before, constantly at his task, rising at daylight, and writing incessantly, with the exception of the hour he usually devoted to his afternoon ride on his horse, which he seemed to think was a benefit to him, and at this labor he continued from day to day until about a week before his death, when, no longer able to rise from weakness, he wrote in his bed, and when no longer able to do that dictated his views to others.

"Thus, it may be truly said of him, he literally died in harness, battling steadily, from day to day, with the most formidable malady that afflicts humanity, his intellect unclouded, and his iron will sustaining him in the execution of his great national work to the last moment of his existence."

Thus ended the life of one of the ablest and most distinguished men of his day. I have given place to these interesting accounts of his last hours because such detailed descriptions of the closing scenes in the lives of great personages always possess a charm for me, more especially as they offer encouragement in that I think I behold in bold relief the stamp of immortality upon souls thus animated as they pass out of mortal sight.

Colonel Benton was born in Hillsborough, N. C., March 14, 1782, and consequently was in his seventy-seventh year when he died. He was a student at Chapel Hill College, in that State, studied law in William and Mary College, Virginia, served one or two years as lieutenant-colonel in the army, and in 1811 commenced the practice of the law at Nashville, Tenn., removing finally to St. Louis about the year 1815. He was elected Senator from Missouri in 1820, anterior to the formal admission of that State into the Union. He retired from the Senate in 1851, but subsequently served as a Representative from the St. Louis district in the Thirty-Third Congress. At the beginning of his senatorial career he was a member of the Committee on Military Affairs, of which General Jackson was chairman. When a resident of Tennessee there had been a serious encounter between them, but, being brought together upon this committee, "their friendly intercourse was here renewed." We are also assured that "the early alienation was never alluded to between the two friends, until one or two evenings before General Jackson's departure from Washington for the Hermitage, in March, 1838, when a very solemn and affecting conversation occurred, the nature of which we may well conjecture, but which, of course, has never transpired."

But for the fact that almost a new generation has grown up since we had the happiness in this country to pay for our daily marketing in gold coin, it would doubtless still be fresh in the memory of all that the pet name for such money was "Benton mint-drops," in acknowledgment of his known character and influence as a "hard-money man," himself being not unfrequently spoken of as "Old Bullion." He became famous, likewise, for his celebrated declaration, "Solitary and alone I set this ball in motion." This he made in the Senate on the 17th of January, 1837, at the close of the debate on his resolution for expunging from the "Journal of the Senate" Mr. Clay's resolution of three years before condemning General Jackson for the removal of the public deposits from the old Bank of the United States.

I could add many more interesting incidents in the life of Colonel Benton, but my article is already sufficiently lengthy. Although of a proud and ostentatious bearing, in social intercourse he was usually mild and fascinatingly agreeable. Especially fond of his family, he was a most devoted husband and father. His wife preceded him to the tomb but a short time, and his son-in-law, William Carey Jones, has been dead several years, while the demise of his youngest daughter, Madame Boileau, occurred in France only a few months ago.

In conclusion, let me say that in referring to the Kansas trouble and to ex-President Buchanan's remark about the elder Mr. Blair, it is far from my purpose to revive any controversy relating to differences growing out of the exciting subject of slavery, or to reflect upon any person whomsoever. The feeling among the parties concerned arose, no doubt, out of political considerations alone, and I have sought to give truly and fairly only what each has said for himself.

August 2, 1874.

CHAPTER V.

ASSASSINATION OF PRESIDENT LINCOLN.

Terrible Shock and Intense Excitement at the Shooting of the President and Murderous Attack on Secretary Seward and his Son—Official Bulletins of the Fearful Particulars—Death of the President—Troops in the District of Columbia ordered out—Rewards offered for Arrest of the Assassins—The Cabinet notifies Vice-President Johnson—Ceremony of his Inauguration—The Assassin Payne's Arrest, and with Atzerodt, Herold, and Surratt condemned to Death—Evidence of Guilt of Mrs. Surratt and Others—Stanton's Impressive Remarks when the President ceased to breathe.

WERE it possible to photograph the scenes which took place on the night of the 14th of April, 1865, and the succeeding several days in the city of Washington, it would make a picture surpassing in horror and consequent excitement anything of the kind, perhaps, in the history of the world. A correspondent of the Boston *Advertiser*, under date of Washington, April 14, 11.15 P.M., truthfully wrote: "A shock from heaven, laying half the city in ruins, would not have startled us as did the word that started out from Ford's Theatre half an hour ago, that the President had been shot. It flew everywhere in five minutes, and set five thousand feet in swift and excited motion on the instant."

The description of the shooting is familiar to most readers, but no person, not present in the city, could possibly form any true conception of the horror, mingled with apprehension of threatened danger, which prevailed here at the time. No sooner was the terrible report of the assassination of President Lincoln spread abroad than the rumor came that attempts had been made also upon the lives of members of his Cabinet and of Vice-President Johnson. The early morning of the 15th was full of these and kindred startling rumors, and every one was holding his breath, not knowing what next to expect. Some relief was felt on learning that the members of the Cabinet, as well as the Vice-President, were all safe, except Mr. Seward, Secretary of State, who, with his son Frederick, it was feared, had been fatally wounded. Major Augustus Seward, an older son, and George F. Robinson, a soldier, nurse of Secretary Seward, were also reported as seriously wounded.

The following official bulletins, varying in no essential particular from the actual facts, will always possess an historical interest :

"WAR DEPARTMENT, WASHINGTON, April 15, 1.30 A.M.

"MAJOR-GENERAL DIX, New York.

"Last evening, at 10.30 P.M., at Ford's Theatre, the President, while sitting in his private box with Mrs. Lincoln, Miss Harris, and Major Rathburn, was shot by an assassin who suddenly entered the box. He approached behind the President. The assassin then leaped upon the stage, brandishing a large dagger or knife, and made his escape by the rear of the theatre. The pistol-ball entered the back of the President's head. The wound is mortal. The President has been insensible ever since it was inflicted, and is now dying.

"About the same hour an assassin, either the same or another, entered Mr. Seward's house, and, under pretence of having a prescription, was shown to the Secretary's chamber. The Secretary was in bed, a nurse and Miss Seward with him. The assassin immediately rushed to the bed, inflicted two or three stabs on the throat and two on the face. It is hoped the wounds may not be mortal. My apprehension is that they will prove fatal. The nurse alarmed Mr. Frederick Seward, who was in an adjoining room, and hastened to the door of his father's room, where

17

he met the assassin, who inflicted upon him one or more dangerous wounds. The recovery of Frederick Seward is doubtful.

" It is not probable that the President will live through the night.

" General Grant and wife were advertised to be at the theatre this evening, but the latter started for Burlington at six o'clock, last evening.

" At a Cabinet meeting, at which General Grant was present, to-day, the subject of the state of the country, and the prospects of speedy peace, was discussed. The President was very cheerful and hopeful, spoke very kindly of General Lee and others of the Confederacy, and the establishment of government in Virginia. All the members of the Cabinet, except Mr. Seward, are now in attendance upon the President. I have seen Mr. Seward, but he and Frederick were both unconscious.

" EDWIN M. STANTON,

" Secretary of War."

" WAR DEPARTMENT, WASHINGTON, D. C., 3 A.M., April 15.

" MAJOR-GENERAL DIX, New York.

" The President still breathes, but is quite insensible, as he has been ever since he was shot. He evidently did not see the person who shot him, but was looking on the stage, as he was approached behind.

" Mr. Seward has rallied, and it is hoped he may live. Frederick Seward's condition is very critical. The attendant who was present was stabbed through the lungs, and is not expected to live. The wounds of Major Seward are not serious.

" Investigation strongly indicates J. Wilkes Booth as the assassin of the President. Whether it was the same or a different person that attempted to murder Mr. Seward remains in doubt.

" Chief-Justice Cartter is engaged in taking the evidence. Every exertion has been made to prevent the escape of the murderer. His horse has been found on the road near Washington.

" EDWIN M. STANTON,

" Secretary of War."

" WAR DEPARTMENT, WASHINGTON, D. C., April 15, 4.10 A.M.

" MAJOR-GENERAL DIX, New York.

" The President continues insensible, and is sinking. Secretary Seward remains without change. Frederick Seward's skull is fractured in two places, besides a severe cut upon the head. The attendant is still alive, but hopeless.

" Major Seward's wounds are not dangerous. It is now ascertained with reasonable certainty that two assassins were engaged in the horrible crime : Wilkes Booth being the one that shot the President ; the other, a companion of his, whose name is not known, but whose description is so clear that he can hardly escape.

"It appears, from a letter found in Booth's trunk, that the murder was planned before the 4th of March, but fell through then because the accomplice backed out until Richmond could be heard from. Booth and his accomplice were at the livery-stable at six o'clock last evening, and left there with their horses about ten o'clock, or shortly before that hour. It would seem that they had for several days been seeking their chance, but for some unknown reason it was not carried into effect until last night. One of them has evidently made his way to Baltimore, the other has not been traced.

"EDWIN M. STANTON,
"Secretary of War."

General C. C. Augur, in command of the Military Department of Washington, as soon as he learned that the President had been shot, ordered out the troops in the District, and "in a few moments the city was encircled with pickets, stationed at a distance of about fifty feet apart. Cavalry was placed on all the roads leading from Washington, and mounted men and military detectives proceeded to scour the country in every direction, with orders to arrest any suspicious parties that they might find."

General Augur at the same time issued an order offering $10,000 reward "to be paid to the party or parties arresting the murderer of the President, Mr. Lincoln, and the assassin of the Secretary of State, Mr. Seward, and his son." This was followed by the offer of a reward of $20,000 by the city government, and supplemented by the further offer by the Secretary of War of $100,000, for the arrest of the assassins.

Early on the morning of the 15th of April the following communication was presented by the Attorney-General to the Vice-President:

"WASHINGTON CITY, D. C., April 15, 1865.

"SIR,—Abraham Lincoln, President of the United States, was shot by an assassin last evening at Ford's Theatre, in this city, and died at the hour of twenty-two minutes after seven o'clock.

"About the same time at which the President was shot, an assassin entered the sick-chamber of the Hon. William H. Seward, Secretary of State, and stabbed him in several places in the throat, neck, and face, severely, if not mortally, wounding him. Other members of the Secretary's family were dangerously wounded by the assassin while making his escape. By the death of President Lincoln, the office of President has devolved, under the Constitution, upon you. The emergency of the government demands that you should immediately qualify according to the requirements of the Constitution, and enter upon the duties of President of the United States. If you will please make known your pleasure such arrangements as you deem proper will be made.

" Your obedient servants,

" HUGH McCULLOCH,

" Secretary of the Treasury.

" EDWIN M. STANTON,

" Secretary of War.

" GIDEON WELLES,

" Secretary of the Navy.

" WILLIAM DENNISON,

" Postmaster-General.

" J. P. UPSHER,

" Secretary of the Interior.

" JAMES SPEED,

" Attorney-General.

"To ANDREW JOHNSON, Vice-President of the United States."

Mr. Johnson requested that the ceremony should take place at his rooms in the Kirkwood House, corner of Pennsylvania Avenue and Twelfth Street, at ten o'clock A.M., and, accordingly, Chief-Justice Chase was present at that hour and administered the oath, the following named gentlemen also being in attendance,—viz., Hugh McCulloch, James Speed, F. P. Blair, Sr., Montgomery Blair, Senators Foot, of Vermont, Ramsay, of Minnesota, Yates, of Illinois, Stewart, of Nevada, Hale, of New Hampshire, and General Farnsworth, of Illinois.

From a number of newspaper accounts before me, written at the time of the assassination, I supplement my own recollections of this tragical event.

The play on the boards that fatal night was " Our American Cousin," and it was progressing smoothly to its climax. The only character on the stage was that of Lord Dundreary (Sothern), Laura Keene being the other star of the evening. Suddenly the report of a pistol was heard. " The audience had not time to wonder what new incident of the play was thus heralded, when there came another and stranger interruption. A dark, lithe form vaulted over the railing of the President's box, which was canopied with the American flag. As the intruder struck the stage, he fell forward, but soon gathered himself up and turned erect in full view of the audience." At the moment of jumping, or as soon as he recovered himself after reaching the stage, he cried out, "*Sic semper tyrannis;*" and one statement is that either just before or immediately after those words, he cried, loud enough to be heard all over the house, " The South is avenged." Captain Rathburn, who was in the President's box, attempted to arrest him, when the assassin turned quickly, and, drawing a knife, dealt him a severe blow. The slight defence, however, had the effect to cause the spur of the murderer to catch in the fringe of the flag, and he fell, striking his right knee and thigh, and dragging the flag from its fastening down upon the stage with him, detaching the spur, which he left behind him. He had already heard his name pronounced by a score of lips when he rushed across the stage and made his escape through the back alley, where he had a horse in waiting for him.

Meantime a scream of distress was heard from Mrs. Lincoln, and the greatest confusion ensued. Everybody knew now that the President had been shot. He had sunk down without a groan or a struggle; and after her first outcry, Mrs. Lincoln had fainted. The theatre was immediately cleared, and the dying President was tenderly borne to a house on the opposite side of the street, where he expired on the 15th of April, at seven o'clock and twenty-two minutes A.M.

The murderous attempt on the life of Secretary Seward
has been often described. This part of the conspiracy was
assigned to a miscreant whose real name was found after-
terwards to be Powell, but whose alias was Lewis Payne.
He made his way into Mr. Seward's house on the pretext
that he was the bearer of a prescription or medicine from
his physician; but his bloody purpose was immediately disclosed by his attack upon the servants who stood in his way,
and nothing stopped him from reaching the Secretary's
room, where the latter was lying seriously hurt from being
thrown out of his carriage a short time previously. Robinson, the soldier nurse, stated that Frederick Seward,
Major Augustus Seward, and Mansell, one of the servants,
were all wounded on or near the stairway. The assassin
held in his hand a long knife, the blade of which appeared
to be twelve inches in length and one inch in width. Major
Seward was cut in several places, but not dangerously. One
statement is that Frederick Seward met the assassin at the
door and was then felled to the floor by blows administered
with a navy pistol with such force as to break the pistol and
separate the chambers from the barrel. In the struggle,
Robinson received a wound in his forehead. The knife
glanced off, and the assassin's hand came down upon Robinson's face and felled him to the floor. He then leaped to
the bed where Mr. Seward lay, apparently in a helpless condition, and gave a tremendous blow at his face, but missed
and almost fell across the bed. Miss Seward escaped from
the room and ran to the front window screaming murder.
By this time Robinson had recovered and caught hold of
the assassin's arm, but failed to keep him back, and he
again struck Mr. Seward with his dagger, first on one side
of his face or neck, and then on the other, when the Secretary rolled in the bedclothes out upon the floor. They continued to struggle until the enraged fiend, having, as he had
reason to believe, finished his deadly work, forced his way
out of the house, without his hat, and rode away. He

threw his knife into the street, where it was picked up and afterwards presented, presumably by the Government, to Robinson, who had been mistakenly reported as fatally wounded, and it is still in his possession.   Some years later he received the appointment, which he still holds, of pay-master in the navy, in recognition of his bravery in saving the life of Mr. Seward.

The following current account of Payne's arrest I believe to be authentic.   It is worth preserving here.   The Surratt house stands, as it did in 1865 and many years before, with-in one square of mine, No. 707 H Street, N. W., where I have resided ever since 1846.   It had been noticed that sev-eral persons were in the habit of going into a house in the heart of the city of Washington and coming out again with their clothes changed, and that other suspicious movements since the assassination of the President made it possible that the inmates might have some connection with that melancholy event.   On Monday night, April 17, Colonel Welles, provost-marshal, ordered the arrest of the inmates, who turned out to be Mrs. Surratt, the mother of one of the alleged assassins, his sister, and two other persons.   While preparing to remove them to head-quarters for examination —evidences of their deep sympathy with the assassins being discovered—there was a slight knock at the front door. What followed is thus related :

The door was opened by Major Morgan, Major Smith and Captain Wermeskirch standing by, with their pistols ready to be used if necessary.   At the door was a young-look-ing man, about five feet eleven inches in stature, of light complexion, with peculiarly large gray eyes, and hair that had evidently been dyed.   He wore a gray cashmere coat and vest, fine black cloth pantaloons, and fine boots.   His boots and pantaloons were covered with mud almost to the knees, and his whole appearance was that of one who had been lying out in the rain.   He had a pickaxe on his shoul-der.   When the door was opened, he exclaimed, " I believe

I am mistaken," and turned to go away. He was asked by Major Morgan whom he wanted to see. He answered, " Mrs. Surratt." Major Morgan said, " Mrs. Surratt lives here; she is at home; walk in." He then came in, and was ushered into the parlor. After being seated he was closely interrogated as to his business at that time of night, twenty minutes after eleven, his occupation, etc. In reply, he stated that he was a laboring man, and had been sent for by Mrs. Surratt to dig a gutter, and had called to know at what time next morning she wished him to come to work. Major Morgan stepped to the door of the parlor, and said, " Mrs. Surratt, will you step here for a moment?" Mrs. Surratt came, and Major Morgan asked, " Do you know this man?" She said, raising her hand, " Before God, I do not know him and have never seen him." The stranger went on to say that he had been for some time past employed on the Baltimore and Ohio Railroad as a laborer; that he was at work on the road on Friday last, and slept that night with the other road hands; that he had no money, and earned his living with his pickaxe. He confusedly attempted to tell where he had slept on Sunday night, and where he had been since Saturday morning, but often contradicted himself, and broke down completely in this part of his narrative. During the investigation he produced a certificate of the oath of allegiance, purporting to have been taken by Lewis Payne, of Fauquier County, Virginia, and claimed that was his name; but when questioned about it, evidently did not know anything about the date of the certificate. He asserted frequently that he was a poor man, and could neither read nor write, and earned his living by his daily labor; but his language was that of a man of education, and his feet and hands were small and well-shaped, the latter being delicate, white, as soft as a woman's, and unstained with any mark of toil. He wore on his head a sort of Scotch skull-cap, which on examination was found to have been made by cutting off the arm of a stockinet shirt, or the leg of drawers of the same material, the top of the cap being formed by tying a string around one of the ends.

Upon searching his pockets they were found to contain a comb, hair- and tooth-brushes, a pot of pomatum, a package of pistol cartridges, a new pocket compass, and twenty-five dollars in greenbacks. After the preliminary examination, he was taken, in charge of officers Sampson and Devoe, to General Augur's head-quarters, where, upon further examination, he gave an account of himself quite different from the one previously given. It was evident that he was in disguise, and had been completely taken by surprise in finding the officers at the house where he expected to find a welcome and refuge. The facts disclosed in the examination induced the belief that he was the blood-thirsty villain who had attempted the life of Secretary Seward on Friday night. He was placed in a room with two other strangers. The light was made dim, as nearly as possible in imitation of the condition of the light in Mr. Seward's room on that eventful night, and the domestics of Mr. Seward were sent for. Upon entering the room, the porter, a. colored boy about seventeen years of age, threw up his hands with an exclamation of horror, and, pointing to the man, said, "That is the man! I don't want to see him; he did it; I know him by that lip!" The servant had already described some peculiarity about the upper lip of the man whom he had admitted to commit the foul and murderous deed at Secretary Seward's, and testimony had been procured tracing him step by step, from the time of his separation from Booth until he entered Mr. Seward's house. The chain of evidence was complete and fastened upon him as the perpetrator of the horrid crime which had shocked the whole community. The villain was heavily ironed, and placed in confinement on one of the gunboats.

J. Wilkes Booth and David E. Herold, it is well known, succeeded in making their way over the Eastern Branch of the Potomac into Maryland, stopping there at Dr. Samuel A. Mudd's to have Booth's leg set, broken in jumping from the President's box at the theatre; then they were chased through the swamp in St. Mary's County across the Potomac to Garrett's farm, near Port Royal, Virginia, on the Rappahannock, where they were brought to bay in Garrett's barn on the 26th of April. Herold surrendered, but Booth refusing to surrender, after a long parley, the barn was set on fire. The flames rose rapidly, firing the whole building, when Booth ran to where the fire was kindled, and with pistol raised, was peering through the darkness, but seemed unable to see any one. He then turned, gazed upon the flames, and suddenly started for the door, when Sergeant Corbett, in violation of orders, left the line, and, going close to the wall before him, fired his pistol through a crack, shooting Booth in the neck, causing his death in about three hours.

G. A. Atzerodt, whose assignment was to kill the Vice-President, was arrested on the 18th of April, near Germantown, Montgomery County, Md. Samuel Arnold, charged with conspiracy to kidnap the President, Michael O'Laughlin, believed to have been chosen to murder General Grant, Dr. Samuel A. Mudd, Edward Spangler, who held Booth's horse in the alley leading from the theatre, and Mrs. Surratt were all soon in custody. John H. Surratt, another of the conspirators, left the city immediately after the tragedy, and, going first to Canada, went from there to Italy, where he was found in the military service of the pope, arrested in December, 1866, and brought back for trial, but escaped conviction.

Payne, Atzerodt, Herold, and Mrs. Surratt were declared guilty by a military commission, and were hanged on the 7th of July, 1865. O'Laughlin, Arnold, and Mudd were sentenced to imprisonment at hard labor for life. Spangler was let off with six years like imprisonment, and all four were sent to serve their sentence at the Dry Tortugas.

Mudd was pardoned February 8, 1869, and Arnold and Spangler on the 1st of March, 1869. O'Laughlin died of yellow fever, September 23, 1867, while in confinement at Fort Judson, Florida.

The purpose of the assassins was believed to be to take the lives also of Secretary Stanton, the Vice-President, and General Grant, the latter of whom was advertised to attend the theatre with the President, but left early in the evening for Burlington, N. J., returning immediately, however, the next morning, on learning of the assassination.

It was currently reported that, on the evening of the assaults, two gentlemen, who went to apprise the Secretary of War of the attack on Mr. Lincoln, met at the residence of the former a man muffled in a cloak, who, when accosted by them, hastened away without a word. It was evident, therefore, as was remarked at the time, that the aim of the conspirators was to paralyze the nation by at once striking down the head, heart, and arm of the country.

I did not intend in this paper to say another word about Mrs. Surratt, but when it was nearly finished I happened to mention it to one of the oldest and most distinguished United States senators, who remarked that a great deal had been said by her apologists against her execution, claiming that it was unjust and cruel, since, if guilty at all, it was only in conspiring to kidnap the President, which he believed she herself had confessed; but, said he, even were this the extent of her guilt, there is not another Government in the world that would not, for such a crime, have condemned her to death.

But whether there was ever a plot to kidnap or not, is it not simply preposterous to suppose that Booth and Herold alone were to attempt it, or that Mrs. Surratt was ignorant of the final purpose to assassinate the President? Why did she go twice to Surrattville, first on the 11th, and the second time on the afternoon of the 14th of April, when she made of John M. Lloyd, who kept the Surratt House, particular inquiry about two carbines and some ammunition left there in concealment five or six weeks previously, by John H. Surratt, in company with Herold and Atzerodt, as testified by Lloyd, who was there and her friend, and who was thrown into the old capitol prison on suspicion of being implicated with them? Weichman, another witness, who drove Mrs. Surratt both times to Surrattville, testified that, on the last occasion, they returned to Mrs. Surratt's about half-past nine or ten on the night of the 14th, and that a few minutes thereafter Mrs. Surratt answered the door-bell, and he "heard footsteps going into the parlor and immediately going out." Was it Booth, who had called to make sure that the two carbines and ammunition were in readiness for him and Herold? Lloyd testified that he thought Mrs. Surratt, on both visits, spoke of the carbines, which she called "shooting irons," and he is positive she did so on the last, when she said to him, "Mr. Lloyd, I want you to have the shooting irons ready; some parties will call for them to-night."

I will conclude with a remarkable incident which comes to me from good authority, touching Mr. Stanton. It is known, of course, that there was a time when he did not hesitate to speak contemptuously of Mr. Lincoln, and that, not infrequently, while a member of his Cabinet, his bearing toward the President was highly disrespectful, as it was, likewise, toward some of his subordinate chiefs and officers of the army. He is sometimes called the "Great War Secretary," and in many respects he doubtless was entitled to that distinction; nor would I detract one iota from the value of the great services he rendered the country during the war. But in some respects, certainly, he was a strange man, not easily comprehended. Few among his intimate acquaintances felt that they really knew him. Even President Buchanan was not sure on this point. In a letter to me of 12th of November, 1861, the ex-President, referring to his intention to write a history of his administration, said, "You must not be astonished some day to find in print portraits drawn by myself of all those who ever served in my Cabinet. I think I know them all perfectly, unless it may be Stanton."

Visitors at the War Department will remember seeing there Mr. Stanton's portrait, a perfect likeness, which represents him leaning on his elbow, the forefinger of his right hand against his cheek, and his thumb under his chin. This was the position chosen by the artist for his picture, it being Mr. Stanton's exact pose when looking with mournful anxiety on the face of the dying President; and at the moment he breathed his last, when the attending physician, with hand on Mr. Lincoln's pulse, announced that it had ceased to beat, Mr. Stanton, with deep feeling, said, "He now belongs to the ages."

It is pleasant to find that, even in this late and last hour, Mr. Stanton was brought to realize the true grandeur of the illustrious man whose martyrdom will bear precious fruit through the centuries to come.

December 1, 1893.

CHAPTER VI.

GENERAL HOLT AND THE LINCOLN CONSPIRATORS.

Triumphant Refutation of the Charges of allowing Mrs. Surratt to be manacled, and of his withholding from President Johnson the Recommendation for Commutation of her Sentence to Life Imprisonment.

In the New York *Tribune* of September 2, 1873, there appeared an anonymous communication written from Washington under the signature of "Truth," so grossly calumnious of General Joseph Holt, Judge-Advocate-General in the trial of the assassins of President Lincoln, that he demanded the name of the author, who proved to be John T. Ford, of Ford's Theatre, where the fearful tragedy was

enacted, and who, at the time, was committed to the Carroll
Prison, where he was kept—on suspicion, it is presumed—
over a month, when he was liberated without being brought
to trial.   Naturally enough, perhaps, he harbored a strong
prejudice against General Holt, and sought to defame his
character under cover through the press.   Among other
things he accused General Holt with having kept Mrs.
Surratt "heavily manacled during her trial, and also of
virtually depriving her of reputable counsel,"—referring to
the Hon. Reverdy Johnson, who, as clearly appears by his
argument, which was upon the question of jurisdiction, voluntarily withdrew, leaving the case in the hands of his associate counsel, Messrs. Clampitt and Aiken.   General Holt
met the other charge by a letter, addressed to him, under
date of September 4, 1873, from General J. F. Hartranft,
who, referring to Ford's article in the *Tribune*, said:

> "I think it proper, in justice to you, to declare publicly that its state-
> ments, so far as they relate to occurrences within my own observation,
> are absolute falsehoods.   As marshal of the court before whom the con-
> spirators were tried, I had charge of Mrs. Surratt before, during, and
> after the time of her trial, in all a period of about two months, during
> which she never had a manacle or manacles on either hands or feet; and
> the thought of manacling her was not, to my knowledge, ever entertained
> by any one in authority."

One would suppose that proof so conclusive ought to set
forever at rest the "manacle" charge; and, as regards the
reference to Reverdy Johnson, it is plain beyond doubt that,
"had he desired to continue in the case, assuredly there
was no power that could have prevented him from doing so."

Yet, notwithstanding this and the overwhelming testimony on the other more serious and wanton charge against
General Holt of withholding from President Johnson the
recommendation of five members of the court that the
sentence of Mrs. Surratt be commuted to imprisonment in
the penitentiary, John T. Ford appears again in the *North
American Review* for April, 1889, in an article reiterating

the falsehoods of his anonymous communication, and trying
to show that General Holt was guilty of withholding from
President Johnson the aforesaid recommendation of Mrs.
Surratt to mercy.

Now, in as brief a manner as possible, I will recite some
of the stronger evidence, clearly proving the falsity of this
last charge, made first before President Johnson's term
expired, and afterwards by Johnson himself, when he was
seeking "to curry favor with the South in the hope of
being elected to the Presidency." He did not dare to make
the charge while he was at the head of the Government,
because he knew if he did that General Holt would instantly
demand, as he did ask for in 1866, a court of inquiry, which
the President declined to order, and that all the facts and
circumstances of the case would come out. General Holt,
I think, took little, if any, public notice of this slander until
he found it had received the indorsement of ex-President
Johnson, when, in a communication published in the Washington *Daily Chronicle* of August 26, 1873, he produced the
most incontrovertible proof that "President Johnson had
knowledge of, considered, and commented on the recommendation of Mrs. Surratt to clemency by members of the
court before her execution." It had been publicly asserted
that President Johnson approved the findings of the court
"without having seen the recommendation or known of its
existence," although it was known, of course, to every
member of the court, and it was also made known to Secretary Stanton, both by General Holt and by Judge Bingham, one of the special judge-advocates in the trial, immediately after the close of the trial. In his answer to
General Holt (see Washington *Daily Chronicle* of November
12, 1873), Mr. Johnson undertakes to support his assertion
that he never saw the recommendation by showing that
it was omitted in Pitman's authorized publication of the
proceedings of the trial. But this omission was fully ex-
plained. It arose simply from the fact, as stated by General

II. L. Burnett, special judge-advocate, who superintended the publication, that " the recommendation to mercy constituted properly no part of the record of the trial," and was not, therefore, furnished by him to Pitman for his book.   In a letter of December 22, 1873, to General Holt (see Washington *Daily Chronicle*, December 1, 1873) Mr. Pitman also says, " The recommendation in favor of Mrs. Surratt was not inserted in my book for the reason that it formed no part of the proceedings of the trial; it was not mentioned at any open session."

Judge Bingham says:

" Before the President had acted on the case I deemed it my duty to call the attention of Secretary Stanton to the petition for the commutation of sentence upon Mrs. Surratt, and did call his attention to it before the final action of the President. . . . After the execution I called upon Secretaries Stanton and Seward and asked if this petition had been presented to the President before the death sentence was by him approved, and was answered by each of these gentlemen that the petition was presented to the President and was duly considered by him and his advisers before the death sentence upon Mrs. Surratt was approved, and that the President and the Cabinet, upon such consideration, were a unit in denying the prayer of the petition ; Mr. Seward and Mr. Stanton stating that they were present."

Attorney-General James Speed, in a letter to General Holt, March 30, 1873, says :

" After the finding of the military commission that tried the assassins of Mr. Lincoln, and before their execution, I saw the record of the case in the President's office, and attached to it was a paper, signed by some of the members of the commission, recommending that the sentence against Mrs. Surratt be commuted to imprisonment for life ; and, according to my memory, the recommendation was made because of her sex. I do not feel at liberty to speak of what was said in Cabinet meetings. In this I know I differ from other gentlemen, but feel constrained to follow my own sense of propriety."

James Harlan, Secretary of the Interior, states positively that " after the sentence and before the execution of Mrs. Surratt, I remember distinctly the discussion of the ques-

tion of the commutation of the sentence of death pronounced on her by the court to imprisonment for life, had
by members of the Cabinet, in the presence of President
Johnson." He thinks there were only three or four members present, and when he entered the subject was under
warm discussion. He does not remember hearing read in
Cabinet meeting any part of the record of the trial or the
recommendation of clemency, but says he was "told that
the whole case had been carefully examined by the Attorney-General and the Secretary of War," the two Cabinet
officers more immediately concerned, officially, in the
matter. At this period Mr. Harlan was the editor of the
Chronicle, and in reference to the recommendation to mercy
he said, "Had such a paper been presented, it is, in our
opinion, hardly probable that it would, under the circumstances, have induced him to interfere with the regular
course of justice."

James M. Wright, at the time Chief Clerk of the Bureau
of Military Justice, states that when President Johnson
sent a messenger to General Holt requesting him to bring
the papers before him for his action, the recommendation
for mercy was among them, in plain sight, and that when
the case came back through the Adjutant-General's office
it remained attached to the other papers.

General R. D. Mussey, President Johnson's private secretary, says, "On the Wednesday evening previous to the
execution (which was Friday, July 7, 1865) Mr. Johnson
said to me that he was going to look over the findings of
the court with Judge Holt, and should be busy and could
see no one." Two or three hours afterwards, Mr. Johnson
came out of the room where he had been in conference with
General Holt and said to him [General Mussey] that "the
papers had been looked over and a decision reached."
General Mussey continues:

"I am very confident, though not absolutely assured, that it was at
this interview Mr. Johnson told me that the court had recommended Mrs.

18

Surratt to mercy on the ground of her sex (and age, I believe). But I am certain he did so inform me about that time, and that he said he thought the grounds urged insufficient, and that he had refused to interfere; that if she was guilty at all, her sex did not make her any the less guilty; that he, about the time of her execution, justified it; that he told me that there had not been 'women enough hanged in this war.'"

General James A. Ekin, one of the commissioners in the trial, relates, under date of August 26, 1867, a conversation he had with General Holt soon after the trial, in which he states that General Holt told him that the entire case, including all papers, had been placed before the President, and that his particular attention had been directed to the recommendation of certain members for the commutation of the sentence of Mrs. Surratt; that the President had carefully scrutinized and fully considered the case, including the recommendation to mercy on behalf of Mrs. Surratt; but that he could not accede to or grant the petition, for the reason that there was no class in the South more violent in the expression and practice of treasonable sentiments than the rebel women, etc.

General H. L. Burnett, in an address before the Loyal Legion, New York, on the 3d of April, 1889, published in the New York *Tribune* of the next day, in giving an account of the trial and explaining why the recommendation for clemency to Mrs. Surratt did not appear in Pitman's book, said:

" When I reached my office from the War Department on June 30, or possibly on the morning of July 1, I attached the petition for mercy to the findings and sentences, and at the end of them. I carried the findings and sentences, and the petition or recommendation, and delivered them to the Judge-Advocate-General in person; and I never saw the record again until many years after,—I think in 1873 or 1874. After Judge Holt's interview with the President, on July 5, the former came to Mr. Stanton's office in the War Department. I was with Mr. Stanton when Judge Holt came in. He said, 'I have just come from a conference with the President over the proceedings of the military commission.' ' Well,' asked Mr. Stanton, 'what has he done?' ' He has approved the findings and sentence of the court,' replied Judge Holt. ' What did he say about the recommendation to mercy of Mrs. Surratt?' 'He said that she must be punished with the rest; that no reasons were given for his interposition by those asking for clemency in her case except age and sex.' "

Now, is there a fair-minded person living who would require more or better proof that the recommendation for the commutation of the sentence of Mrs. Surratt to imprisonment for life was in President Johnson's office, and that the question was fully considered by him in conference with several, if not with all, of the members of his Cabinet before the day of execution?   True, no one states that he actually saw it in the President's hands, though Judge Bingham says both Secretaries Stanton and Seward told him it was presented to him and duly considered before the death sentence was approved.   But Attorney-General Speed, a direct eye-witness, could, had he chosen to speak, have made this fact certain beyond doubt or cavil.   Mr. Ford professes amazement at General Holt's anxiety for more detailed testimony from Mr. Speed, as indicated by their correspondence on the subject in the *North American Review* for July, 1888.   I am myself free to confess that I do not think any additional proof whatever is at all necessary for General Holt's complete vindication; but Mr. Speed had been a life-long friend of his, and knowing that he saw the aforesaid recommendation in the President's own hands, is it strange that he should insist that he should tell him so?   He may be and is, I think, over-sensitive.   In his preface to Pitman's book of the trial, Major Ben: Perley Poore, who unwittingly repeats the false newspaper manacle story, observes, " General Holt is an inflexibly upright administrator of justice, yet humanities have a large place in his heart;" and General Mussey, speaking of the call made by General Holt at the White House on the morning of the execution, when Miss Surratt was there and the President had refused to see her or any one in her mother's behalf,—overruling, also, at the same time, Judge Wylie's writ of habeas corpus,—says, "I shall never lose the impression made upon me of your [General Holt's] deep pity for her [Miss Surratt] and of the pain which her distress caused you." But will Mr. Ford or any other of General Holt's persistent calumniators be so kind as to state why General Holt should have been so anxious for Mr. Speed to tell the whole truth, had he not known, beyond the remotest question, that it would have been conclusive testimony in his favor? Would he have asked Mr. Speed to say more than he did say, if he had had the least doubt on that point? Surely not.

It is not the purpose of this article to go into the evidence regarding Mrs. Surratt's guilt or innocence; but I cannot refrain from brief comment on the following quotation from Mr. Ford's article, wherein, referring to Mrs. Surratt, he says:

"The very man of God who shrived her soul for eternity was said to be constrained to promise that she should not communicate with the world. As the poor martyr walked in her shroud to the scaffold, it is also said that she begged the priest by her side to let her tell the people 'she was innocent.' She was told that 'the Church was permitted only to prepare her soul for eternity; that already she was dead to all else.'"

This looks strange, to say the least; and I am reminded by it that it was just this which the late John M. Brodhead, Second Comptroller of the Treasury, once told me was, in his view, conclusive proof of Mrs. Surratt's guilt. He believed that, had not the priest known from her confession that she was guilty, he would never have prohibited her from declaring her innocence, but would himself have insisted on it to the last moment. One thing is certain, there was no man living who more firmly believed in her guilty participation in the assassination of Abraham Lincoln than President Johnson, who, in commenting on the appeals made to him for clemency, said at the time to Rev. J. George Butler, of St. Paul's Church, Washington, that "he could not be moved; for, in his own significant language, ' *Mrs. Surratt kept the nest that hatched the egg.*' "

I have observed that General Holt at one time asked for a court of inquiry. It was in September, 1866. In his answer, November 14, 1866, Edwin M. Stanton, Secretary of War, wrote to Brevet Major-General Holt, Judge-Advocate-General, as follows:

"Your letter of the 11th of September applying for a court of inquiry upon certain imputations therein mentioned as made against you, of official misconduct in relation to the prosecution of Mrs. Surratt and others charged with the assassination of the late President, Abraham Lincoln, and in the preparation of testimony against Jefferson Davis and others, charged with complicity in said crime, has been submitted to the President (Johnson), who deems it unnecessary for your vindication to order a court of inquiry.

"In communicating the President's decision, it is proper for me to express my own conviction that all charges and imputations against your official conduct are, in my judgment, groundless. So far as I have any knowledge or information, your official duties as Judge-Advocate-General in the cases referred to, and in all others, have been performed fairly, justly, and with distinguished ability, integrity, and patriotism, and in strict conformity with the requirements of your high office and the obligations of an officer and a gentleman."

WASHINGTON, D. C.

[NOTE.—I called on General Joseph Holt to-day (October 17, 1892), and referring to the false charges made against him touching the trial and execution of Mrs. Surratt, he said, "That summary of yours (in the *Century Magazine* for April, 1890) is worth everything that has been published."] H. K.

CHAPTER VII.

THE STORY OF "THE PEACEMAKER."

The Bursting of the Big Gun on the Princeton—Five Instantly Killed and Several Wounded.

THE 28th of February, 1844, was a beautiful day. The United States steamer *Princeton*, Captain R. F. Stockton, United States navy, lay off Alexandria, then a part of the District of Columbia; and, proud of her splendid appearance, Captain Stockton had issued a large number of invitations for a grand gala day in an excursion down the river.

Never, perhaps, was there a more brilliant and delighted company than the four or five hundred people who responded to this invitation. It embraced the very *élite* of the capital, of both sexes, including the President and his Cabinet, Senators and Representatives, foreign ministers, and other distinguished citizens and temporary residents.

A grand collation was provided, and everything arranged for a day of unalloyed pleasure. One of the attractions of the occasion, and an important feature in the vessel's armament, was what was then considered an extraordinarily large gun, recently constructed, and carrying a ball of two hundred and twenty-five pounds. It was named "The Peacemaker."

As soon as the company was well on board, orders were given for the ship to start, and in a few minutes all were sailing gayly and joyously toward Mount Vernon. On the passage down, this immense gun was discharged two or three times in the presence of the crowd of visitors who lined the deck. The trial and exhibition were entirely satisfactory, and it was near four in the afternoon before the order was given to return.

The ladies had been served with ample refreshments of the choicest kind, and the gentlemen next found room at the table. The vessel was now opposite Fort Washington, when Captain Stockton ordered another discharge of " The Peacemaker," and many persons took positions near the gun, better to witness the operation of firing. Fortunately, the ladies were all between decks, and a large part of the gentlemen had not yet left the lunch table, otherwise many more doubtless might have been on the gun-deck. Instantly upon the discharge, and before the smoke had passed off, the most frightful shrieks and groans startled and almost paralyzed every living being on board. The gun had burst into many pieces, and the dead and wounded lay prostrate around it.

Death had chosen shining marks for his fatal arrows, and those who were instantly killed were Mr. Upshur, Secretary of State; Mr. Gilmer, Secretary of the Navy (both from Virginia); Commodore Kennon, of the navy; Mr. Virgil Maxcy, of Maryland, ex-minister to the Hague; and Mr. Gardner, a distinguished citizen of New York, whose daughter afterwards became the second wife of President Tyler, and presided gracefully at the White House. Among those who were stunned by the concussion were Senator Thomas H. Benton, Captain Stockton and Lieutenant Hunt, of the *Princeton*, and Mr. W. D. Robinson, of Georgetown. Seventeen seamen were wounded more or less seriously, and a colored servant of the President almost immediately died from his wounds. The wonder was that President Tyler escaped.

Sorrowfully, and with her colors at half-mast, the *Princeton* slowly continued her way back toward Washington, and when the news of the terrible disaster reached the city, the greatest excitement prevailed. Never before had such a shock been felt at the capital. It was not until near evening when the vessel arrived off the navy-yard, and the bodies of the dead statesmen were retained on board overnight.

The next morning, being placed in their coffins, they were conveyed in solemn procession (during the progress of which minute-guns were fired) to the President's House, and placed in the East Room, where thousands on thousands of citizens and strangers gathered to view them. I can never forget the impression this fearfully sad sight made upon me. On the assembling of Congress at twelve o'clock, the President sent a message to the two Houses, referring in appropriate terms to the terrible disaster, and announcing the death of the two secretaries by name. Upon the reading of the message in the Senate, Mr. William C. Rives made a short address, from which the following is an extract. Said he, "Surely, Mr. President, never in the mysterious providences of God has a day on earth been marked in its progress by such startling and astounding contrasts—opening and advancing with hilarity and joy, mutual congratulations and patriotic pride, and closing in scenes of death and disaster, of lamentation and unutterable woe. It was my sad fortune, Mr. President, to be an eye-witness of these never-to-be-forgotten events. If I had language to describe them, the power of speech would fail me."

Mr. Hopkins, of Virginia, made the leading speech in the House, and upon the adoption of resolutions to attend the funeral, etc., both branches adjourned from the 29th of February till Monday, the 4th of March. On the evening of the 29th of February, the remains of Mr. Maxcy were removed to the house of his son-in-law, Mr. Francis Markoe, and thence, on the following morning, to the family residence in Maryland.

The funeral was held at the President's House on the 2d of March. Assembling in their respective halls, the members of the Senate and House proceeded thence in a body to the funeral, the religious ceremonies at which were conducted by Rev. Mr. Hawley, of St. John's church; Rev. Dr. Laurie, pastor of the Presbyterian church, then occupying the building since converted into Willard's Hall, on F

Street; and Rev. Mr. Butler, of the Trinity church, corner of C and Third Streets. The East Room was filled to its utmost capacity, while still greater crowds assembled in the adjoining halls and in front of the edifice outside. The funeral escort under command of General Scott was most imposing. Besides the volunteer troops and a battalion of marines, there was a squadron of cavalry, troops of United States artillery, etc., and many officers of the navy as well as of the army. There were pall-bearers to each hearse. The President and surviving members of his Cabinet, the Senate and House of Representatives, with their officers, foreign ministers, judges of the courts, and officers of the executive departments, various societies and private citizens joined in the procession to the Congressional Cemetery. Never before, probably, except on the occasion of President Harrison's funeral, in April, 1841, when I remember Major-General Macomb was in command, had so large a funeral procession been seen at the capital.

In returning from the cemetery, the President's horses took fright near the Capitol, and ran with fearful speed along Pennsylvania Avenue a distance of nearly one mile, when, fortunately without collision, they were finally arrested by a resolute colored man, and the distinguished occupants of the carriage escaped unhurt.

These scenes are impressed almost as vividly on my memory as though they were of yesterday. I might go to the records to show how few of the prominent actors in public life of that time still survive; but it would only add another mournful shadow to the picture.

WASHINGTON, D. C.

CHAPTER VIII.

MY FIRST AND LAST SIGHT OF PRESIDENT LINCOLN.

His Secret Arrival in Washington—Calls with Seward on the President and Cabinet—Lee's Surrender—Great Rejoicing—The Serenade—Star-Spangled Banner and Dixie—The President's Speech.

THERE is no more vivid or apparently indelible impression on the tablet of my memory than my first and last sight of President Lincoln; and the circumstances connected therewith are equally well remembered. The first occasion was when he called on President Buchanan, in company with Senator Seward, on the 23d of February, 1861, and the last was when he excused himself from making a speech at the Executive Mansion on the evening of April 10, 1865, the next day after Lee's surrender.

It is generally known that Mr. Lincoln arrived in Washington, unannounced, several hours before he was expected by the public at large. It was supposed that he would rest at Harrisburg overnight, and probably not more than three or four persons were cognizant of his intention to come directly through without stopping. Indeed, it was stated at the time that he kept this intention entirely to himself, but it was doubtless known to his travelling companions, Mr. Lamon, afterwards marshal of the District of Columbia, and Mr. E. J. Allen, as well as to Senator Seward. None of the railroad officials on the train, either from Harrisburg to Baltimore, or from Baltimore to Washington, knew he was on board. Great preparations for his reception had been made, both at Baltimore and Washington; and as late as eleven o'clock, after his arrival in the morning of the 23d, active preparations were in progress to send the contemplated extra train for him to Baltimore. Shortly before six o'clock of that morning, somewhat to the wonder of the few around at that early hour, Senator Seward was seen waiting at Willard's Hotel, where rooms had been quietly engaged for Mr. Lincoln the previous day. He had not long to wait before Mr. Lincoln arrived, and was immediately escorted to his rooms by Mr. Seward, who left him alone for rest. At nine o'clock A.M., Mr. Lincoln received his breakfast in his private parlor, and his presence was so little known in the city that it was one o'clock in the afternoon before any callers came to see him.

About eleven in the morning, in company with Mr. Seward, Mr. Lincoln went to pay his respects to the President. There was a special meeting of the Cabinet that forenoon, and it was in session when the door-keeper came in and handed the President a card. With a look of pleasant surprise, Mr. Buchanan said, " Uncle Abe is down-stairs !" and immediately went to meet him in the Red Room.* In the course of fifteen or twenty minutes he returned with Mr. Lincoln and Governor Seward, who were presented to the members of the Cabinet, and, after a few minutes' conversation of no special importance, the visitors left to call on General Scott. Although I was living in Washington while Mr. Lincoln was a member of Congress, I had no recollection of having ever seen him before. I was at once struck by his tall, lank figure, towering, as it did, almost head and shoulders above Senator Seward, and even overtopping President Buchanan, as they entered the room. I was equally impressed, also, by his quiet, unaffected manner and placid disposition. I did not observe in him the least sign of nervousness or deep concern ; and there is good reason to believe that, " with malice towards none, with charity for all," he felt confident of being able to gain the good-will of the Southern malcontents and of soon bringing the seceding States back to their proper relations in the Federal Government. The Peace Convention was then in

* The writer was one of the members of President Buchanan's Cabinet at the time.

session, and hopes of an amicable settlement had not yet been abandoned. But, alas! alas!! Instead of allowing wisdom to assert its control, the madness of folly bore sway, and for four long years the country was deluged in blood!

The news of Lee's surrender was received at the War Department just before nine o'clock Sunday evening, the 9th of April, 1865, and ere the dawn of day the citizens were awakened by the sound of cannon proclaiming the joyful tidings. Soon crowds of people, accompanied by bands of music, passed through the streets, singing the "Star-Spangled Banner," "Rally Round the Flag, Boys," and other patriotic songs. The courts met and adjourned, and nearly all business was suspended. The clerks in the various offices were dismissed for the day, and hundreds of them, augmented by throngs of other citizens, gathered on the south steps and sidewalk of the Interior Department, and unitedly raised their voices to the grand old tune of "Old Hundred" in singing

"Praise God from whom all blessings flow."

Never in my life had I heard those words sound so sweetly or seem to touch the heart so tenderly. I was on my way to the Post-Office Department, where I found Postmaster-General Dennison in the main hall of the second story making a congratulatory address to a crowd assembled around him. About ten o'clock, a line, composed of nearly two thousand persons, mostly from the Navy Yard and vicinity, and constantly increasing, passed along Pennsylvania Avenue, headed by the Marine Band, and with two small howitzers in the rear, which were fired at intervals. On reaching the White House, after several airs by the band, loud calls were made for the President, when he shortly appeared at a front chamber window, and was greeted with hearty cheering. The band now struck up the stirring tune "America," and was joined vocally in the words,

"My country, 'tis of thee I sing,"

by the assembled multitude. It was some minutes before order was restored, when, after a moment's stillness, Mr. Lincoln said:

"I am greatly rejoiced, my friends, that an occasion has occurred on which the people cannot restrain themselves. I suppose arrangements are being made to appropriately celebrate this glorious event this evening or to-morrow evening. I will have nothing to say then if it is all dribbled out of me now. I see you have a band. I propose having this interview closed by the band performing a patriotic tune, which I will name. Before this is done, however, I wish to mention one or two little circumstances connected with it. I have always thought that 'Dixie' was one of the best tunes I had ever heard. Our adversaries over the way, I know, have attempted to appropriate it. [Applause.] I referred the question to the Attorney-General, and he gives it as his legal opinion that it is now our property. [Laughter and applause.] I now ask the band to favor us with its performance."

The band responded most heartily, to the delight of all present, and the crowd proceeded to call on Secretary Stanton, who declined speaking on the plea of ill-health. He, however, introduced General Halleck, who said:

"Always ready as I am to obey the orders of my superior officer, the Honorable Secretary of War, I hardly think he will go so far as to require me to become a stump-speaker. [Laughter, cheers, and cries, 'The people require it; it is a military necessity!'] Stump-speaking, my friends, is something in which I have never indulged. I can only say that our congratulations and thanks are due to General Grant and our brave generals and soldiers in the field for the great victory announced this morning, and for the blessing of peace, of which it is the harbinger." [Applause.]

Secretary Welles was next called on at his house, when he appeared and merely bowed his thanks for the honor.

About five o'clock in the afternoon, several hundred persons assembled in and around the portico of the White House in expectation of a speech from the President. After repeated calls, Mr. Lincoln appeared at the centre window over the front door, and, as soon as the cheering with which he was received ceased, he spoke substantially as follows:

"I appear, my friends, in response to your call, for the purpose of saying that if the present company have assembled by appointment, there is some mistake. More or less people have been gathered all day, and in the exuberance of good feeling—all of which was greatly justifiable—have called on me to say something. I have said what was proper to be said for the present. Some mistake has crept into the understanding, if you think a meeting was appointed for this evening. [Voices: 'We want to hear you now.'] I have appeared before larger audiences than the present during the day, and have said to them what I now desire to repeat. With reference to the great good news, I suppose there is to be some further demonstration, and perhaps to-morrow would suit me better than now, as in that case I should be better prepared. I would therefore say that I am willing, and hope to be ready, to say something then. [Applause.] Occupying the position I do, I think I ought to be particular, as all I say gets into print. A mistake hurts you and the country, and I try not to make mistakes. [A voice: 'You have never made any.'] If agreeable to have a general demonstration to-morrow evening, I will try and say something, in which, at least, I shall be careful to avoid making any mistakes."

Thanking those present for the call, the President bade them good-night, and retired amid the cheers of the assemblage. I never saw him again. Throughout this brief address his face wore a benignant and satisfied expression, which told plainly of the unspeakable relief the surrender of Lee had brought to him. I could but remark the great change from his usually sad look to one, I might say, almost angelic; and I am fortunate to possess his photograph taken while in this happy state of mind at that time. He delivered his contemplated speech to an immense crowd on the following evening—his last public address on earth.

CHAPTER IX.

HISTORY OF THE DUEL BETWEEN JONATHAN CILLEY AND WILLIAM J. GRAVES.

THE report, not long ago, that Major William Preston Graves was "dying at Little Rock, where he had been stationed with his regiment, the Second Artillery, the past two years," recalls the deplorable duel in which Jonathan Cilley, of Maine, fell at the hands of Major Graves's father, the late William J. Graves, of Kentucky, on the 24th of February, 1838. The report goes on to say, truly, that, "next to the duel between Alexander Hamilton and Aaron Burr, no event of the character ever attracted more attention, and it might have said greater condemnation, than that between Graves and Cilley." It also repeats what was erroneously stated at the time, and which has been repeatedly denied from certain knowledge, that "Cilley was noted as one of the most skilful shots of the day." I shall have occasion to refer again to this assertion. When this unnatural combat took place, I resided in my native State of Maine, and was at Augusta, where the Maine Legislature was in session, when the news of Mr. Cilley's death was received. I well remember the wide-spread excitement and condemnation which immediately followed. Few people are now living who shared in or were witnesses to that excitement, and who remember the circumstances leading to and attending that appalling tragedy.

Some fourteen or fifteen years ago I prepared an account of it, which the late ex-Governor of Maine, H. J. Anderson, who was familiar with all the facts, pronounced the most complete ever written of the whole affair; but unfortunately it was printed in a local magazine that never reached its second number. As it would be new to the majority of readers now, and could hardly fail to possess a melancholy interest for all, I propose to reproduce it in substance, adhering strictly to the facts of the narrative as originally presented.

Both combatants were representatives in Congress, and hitherto they had been warm personal friends, notwithstanding Cilley was a Democrat and Graves a Whig. A charge of corruption against a Senator in Congress, made by "The Spy in Washington," Matthew L. Davis, correspondent of the New York *Courier and Enquirer*, was the basis of the trouble which led to the fatal rencounter. He was the intimate friend and biographer of Aaron Burr, and while acting as correspondent at the capital, he was excluded, I remember, from the ladies' gallery on account of alleged gross immorality there. In a letter to his paper the charge referred to was set forth as follows:

"The more brief my statement the better it will be understood. It is in my power, if brought to the bar of either house, or before a committee, and process allowed me to compel the attendance of witnesses, to prove by the oath of a respectable and unimpeachable citizen, as well as by written documentary evidence, that there is at least one member of Congress who has offered to barter his services and his influence with a department or departments for a compensation. 'Why, sir,' said the applicant for a contract, 'if my proposition has merit, it will be received; if it has not, I do not expect it will be accepted.' And what do you think was the answer of the honorable member? I will give it to you in his own emphatic language: 'Merit?' said he; 'why, things do not go here by merit, but by pulling the right strings. Make it my interest and I will pull the strings for you.' "

The editor of the *Courier and Enquirer*, James Watson Webb, vouched for the character and standing of his correspondent, and called upon Congress promptly to initiate the investigation thus challenged, both as an act of justice to itself and the country. Whereupon Henry A. Wise, of Virginia, offered in the House of Representatives, on the 12th of February, a motion for a committee of inquiry, embodying in the preamble of his resolution both the above extract and the editorial comments thereon. The resolution gave rise to a warm debate, and resulted in a determination to bring Mr. Davis before the bar of the House. He appeared accordingly, and, having declared that the person alluded to in his letter was not a member of the House, he was discharged.

On the 13th of February, John Ruggles, Senator from Maine, addressed a letter to the Washington *Globe*, stating that he had been informed that the charge referred to " was a blow aimed at him." In explanation, he said that a Mr. Jones, of New Jersey, had applied to him to draw up a specification and claim for a patent for a trunk-lock. He had consented to do it, " as it was a strictly professional matter." Subsequently he had agreed to take an assignment of one-fourth part of the patent for his services; the papers were drawn and assented to by Jones, but never executed, nor had any compensation ever been allowed for his services.

On the 16th of February, at Mr. Ruggles's request, a committee to investigate the charge against him was appointed in the Senate, and he was entirely exonerated.

In the debate on Mr. Wise's resolution, Mr. Cilley said:

" As the course proposed to be pursued on this occasion was novel and extraordinary, he hoped the House would pause before it embarked in this business on such authority as was produced. This charge comes from the editor of a newspaper, and we all know that in a country where the press is free, few men can expect to escape abuse and charges of a similar description. Ordinarily, when we are about entering upon a business of this kind before a magistrate, a conservator of the peace, the charges submitted are obliged to be made distinctly, clearly, and under the solemnity of an oath; and why should we now depart from this well-known and well-settled rule? He knew nothing of this editor, but it was the same editor who had made grave charges against an institution of this country (the old United States Bank in 1831), and afterwards was said to have received facilities to the amount of fifty-two thousand dollars from the same institution and gave it his hearty support; he did not

19

think his charges were entitled to much credit in an American Congress. If he has charges to make, let him make them distinctly and not vaguely; let him make them under the solemnity of an oath, and then it will be quite time enough to act. He trusted the House would not go into an investigation of this kind on a mere newspaper statement without any proof."

It was the subject of pointed comment at the time that, whereas, the remarks of Mr. Cilley were published in the *Globe* of the 12th, Mr. Webb waited until the 21st of February before demanding an explanation. Therefore, the presumption was, and it was distinctly charged, that " the offence was taken at Washington, the plot arranged there, and Mr. Webb sent for, after full consultation, and notified that he must take offence at Mr. Cilley's remarks. This supposition was the more readily credited not only because the same imputation against Mr. Webb had " been thousands of times made on innumerable occasions in Congress" without his ever resenting it in any such manner, but also from the fact that Mr. Cilley's ability and fearless bearing in debate had aroused a determination on the part of certain Southern gentlemen, if possible, to intimidate him and destroy his influence. As an illustration of this feeling the following extract from the *Democratic Review* is in point. Referring to the discussion upon Mr. Wise's resolution, above mentioned, the editor, J. L. O'Sullivan, afterwards United States minister to Portugal, and who, I am glad to know, still survives, said:

" An altercation of a very acrimonious character on the part of Mr. Wise arose upon this occasion. In reply to Mr. Cilley, Mr. Wise, among general remarks upon the opposition of the friends of the administration to all investigation without specific charges, etc., remarked, ' Every man careful of his honor, when such charges as these are made, will not wait to have them specifically framed,' and in the present instance he would say to the gentleman from Maine that a member of the party (Democratic) to which that gentleman belongs should be the last man to oppose the investigation of a charge like this, for it was much more likely to be him that was meant by the author of the charge than himself (Mr. W.).

'I, sir,' said Mr. Wise, 'have no influence with the executive or any of its branches, to sell for a price,'" etc.

Afterwards, in the course of the debate, the following altercation took place, as we find it reported in the *Intelligencer:*

"'But now, because he (Mr. C.) had stood up to defend the character of the House against that anonymous imputation, he was to hear the basest charges against himself.

"'Mr. Wise here asked if the gentleman from Maine meant to say that he (Mr. W.) had made base charges in relation to himself?

"'Mr. Cilley would explain. He did feel that it was ungenerous for that gentleman to have said that the presumption was rather that it was he (Mr. C.) than himself (Mr. W.) to whom this charge alluded.

"'Mr. Wise had made no personal charge against the member from Maine, false or true, none whatever; and he again asked that gentleman if he meant to say that he had insinuated base charges against him.

"'Mr. Cilley responded in substance what he had said. .

"'Mr. Wise. Then the gentleman from Maine designs deliberately to insult me.

"'Mr. Cilley certainly did not; he had not made any charge against the gentleman from Virginia. He knew his rights and those of his constituents on that floor.

"'Mr. Wise understood, and did not understand the gentleman from Maine as disclaiming the charge, that he had made base charges against that gentleman.

"'Mr. Cilley said that he had distinctly remarked that the gentleman from Virginia had said he (Mr. C.) was more obnoxious to the charge contained in the resolution before the House than he (Mr. W.) was; and he could say no less than he had said, fearless of all consequences, but he had no intention to insult any one. The gentleman from Virginia just remarked that he had been informed of the name of the member alluded to; why not disclose it?

"'Mr. Wise rose and said that he could never again treat that gentleman with confidence who could rise in his place and repeat to the House what a member had said in private conversation in his seat.

"'Mr. Cilley had not intended to violate confidence. The gentleman from Virginia had said openly in his seat that he knew the name of the member meant.

"'Mr. Wise. But it was in reply to an express question of another member.

"'Some further explanation then took place between Mr. Cilley and Mr. Wise,' etc.

"The report of it is here cut off. Mr. Cilley sustained himself with perfect firmness and dignity to the end, his manner being, according to our information, in highly advantageous contrast with that of his assailant. The latter concluded by the following remark, spoken so openly and loud as to be heard at some distance, a remark which Mr. Cilley never affected to notice or to hear: ' But what is the use of bandying words with a man who won't hold himself personally accountable for his words ?' "

Fully to appreciate this scene, one needs to have known its principal actors and observed the calm, firm, and dignified manner of Cilley in contrast with the fierce look and aggressive bearing of his opponent, as the writer more than once saw him in debate in the House during the winter of 1838–39, while Graves, looking sad and desponding, was also still a member of that body.

We will next present the correspondence, etc., as it appeared in a paper signed by the seconds in the duel, George W. Jones, of Iowa, and Henry A. Wise, of Virginia, which they published as their

"STATEMENT.

"WASHINGTON CITY, D. C., February 26, 1838.

"The following is a statement of the facts of the duel between the Honorable William J. Graves, of Kentucky, and the Honorable Jonathan Cilley, of Maine, agreed upon by George W. Jones and Henry A. Wise, the seconds of the parties, committed to writing between the hours of 10.30 o'clock A.M., February 25th, and 12 o'clock M. this day. The seconds propose, first, to state the correspondence which occurred before the challenge and which was communicated through others than themselves, neither second having borne any message, verbal or written, to or from either of the principals, until Mr. Wise bore the challenge and Mr. Jones bore the acceptance. This correspondence, as it has been placed in the hands of the seconds, is as follows, to wit:

" *Mr. Graves to Mr. Cilley.*

"HOUSE OF REPRESENTATIVES, February 21, 1838.

"In the interview which I had with you this morning, when you declined receiving from me the note of Colonel J. W. Webb, asking whether you were correctly reported in the *Globe* in what you are there represented to have said of him in this House upon the 12th instant, you will please say whether you did not remark, in substance, that in declining to receive the note, you hoped I would not consider it in any respect disrespectful to me, and that the ground on which you rested your declining to receive the note was distinctly this: That you could not consent to get yourself into personal difficulties with conductors of public journals for what you might think proper to say in debate upon this floor, in discharge of your duties as a representative of the people, and that you did not rest your objection in our interview upon any personal objection to Colonel Webb as a gentleman.

"Very respectfully your obedient servant,

"W. J. GRAVES.

"HONORABLE JONATHAN CILLEY.

"*Mr. Cilley to Mr. Graves.*

"HOUSE OF REPRESENTATIVES, February 21, 1838.

"The note which you just placed in my hands has been received. In reply I have to state that in your interview with me this morning, when you proposed to deliver a communication from Colonel Webb, of the New York *Courier and Enquirer*, I declined to receive it because I chose to be drawn into no controversy with him. I neither affirmed nor denied anything in regard to his character; but when you remarked that this course on my part might place you in an unpleasant situation, I stated to you, and now repeat, that I intended by the refusal no disrespect to you.

"Very respectfully, your obedient servant,

"JONA. CILLEY.

"HONORABLE W. J. GRAVES.

"*Mr. Graves to Mr. Cilley.*

"HOUSE OF REPRESENTATIVES, February 22, 1838.

"SIR,—Your note of yesterday, in reply to mine of that date, is inexplicit, unsatisfactory, and insufficient; among other things in this, that in your declining to receive Colonel Webb's communication, it does not disclaim any exception to him personally as a gentleman. I have therefore to inquire whether you declined to receive his communication on the ground of any personal exception to him as a gentleman or a man of honor? A categorical answer is expected.

"Very respectfully,

"WILLIAM J. GRAVES.

"HONORABLE J. CILLEY.

"*Mr. Cilley to Mr. Graves.*

"HOUSE OF REPRESENTATIVES, February 22, 1838.

"SIR,—Your note of this date has just been placed in my hands. I regret that mine of yesterday was not satisfactory to you, but I cannot admit the right on your part to propound the question to which you ask a categorical answer, and therefore decline any further reponse to it.

"Very respectfully,
"JONATHAN CILLEY.

"HONORABLE W. J. GRAVES.

"Here follows the first paper borne by Mr. Wise:

"As you have declined accepting a communication which I bore to you from Colonel Webb, and as, by your note of yesterday, you have refused to decline on grounds which would exonerate me from all responsibility growing out of the affair, I am left no other alternative but to ask that satisfaction which is recognized among gentlemen. My friend, Honorable Henry A. Wise, is authorized by me to make the arrangements suitable for the occasion.

"Your obedient servant,
"W. J. GRAVES.

"HONORABLE J. CILLEY.

"Mr. Wise states that he presented the foregoing challenge to Mr. Cilley in the parlor at Mr. Birth's boarding-house a few minutes before twelve o'clock, on Friday, the twenty-third instant.

"In addition to the foregoing correspondence the seconds propose to relate only such facts and circumstances as occurred within their joint knowledge, after their own participation in the melancholy affair.

"On the evening of the twenty-third instant, about the hour of five o'clock, Mr. Jones, the second of Mr. Cilley, delivered to Mr. Graves in the room of Mr. Wise, and in his presence, the following note, which was the first paper borne by Mr. Jones, to wit:

"WASHINGTON CITY, February 23, 1838.
"HONORABLE W. J. GRAVES:

"Your note of this morning has been received. My friend, General Jones, will 'make the arrangements suitable to the occasion.'

"Your obedient servant,
"JONA. CILLEY.

"Immediately upon the preparation of the acceptance of the challenge, Mr. Graves retired, leaving Mr. Jones with Mr. Wise, who submitted to Mr. Wise the following propositions for the arrangement of the meeting, to wit:

"WASHINGTON CITY, February 23, 1838.

"SIR,—Mr. Cilley proposes to meet Mr. Graves at such place as may be agreed upon between us to-morrow at twelve o'clock M. The weapons to be used on the occasion shall be rifles; the parties placed side to side at eighty yards distance from each other; to hold the rifles horizontally at arm's length downward; the rifles to be cocked and triggers set; the word to be, 'Gentlemen, are you ready?' after which, neither answering 'no,' the words shall be in regular succession, 'Fire, one, two, three, four.' Neither party shall fire before the word 'fire,' nor after the word 'four.' The positions of the parties at the ends of the line to be determined by lot. The second of the party losing the position shall have the giving of the word. The dress to be ordinary winter clothing and subject to the examination of both parties. Each party may have on the ground, besides his second, a surgeon and two other friends. The seconds, for the execution of their respective trusts, are allowed to have a pair of pistols each on the ground, but no other persons shall have any weapon. The rifles to be loaded in the presence of the seconds. Should Mr. Graves not be able to procure a rifle in the time prescribed, time shall be allowed for that purpose.

"Your very obedient servant,
"GEORGE W. JONES.

"HONORABLE HENRY A. WISE.

"About nine o'clock P.M., at Mr. Jones's room at Dawson's, Mr. Wise returned to him the following answer, to wit:

"WASHINGTON CITY, February 23, 1838.

"SIR,—The terms arranging the meeting between Mr. Graves and Mr. Cilley, which you presented to me this evening, though unusual and objectionable, are accepted with the understanding that the rifles are to be loaded with a single ball, and that neither party is to raise his weapon from the downward horizontal position until the word 'fire.'

"I will inform you, sir, by the hour of eleven o'clock A.M. to-morrow whether Mr. Graves has been able to procure a rifle, and, consequently, whether he will require a postponement of the time of meeting.

"Your very obedient servant,
"HENRY A. WISE.

"HONORABLE GEORGE W. JONES.

"About eight o'clock A.M. on the twenty-fourth instant, Mr. Jones left at Mr. Wise's room the following note, to wit:

"WASHINGTON CITY, February 24, 1838.

"SIR,—I will receive at Dr. Reilly's, on F Street, any communication you may see proper to make me until eleven o'clock A.M., to-day.

"Respectfully, your obedient servant,
"GEORGE W. JONES.

"HONORABLE H. A. WISE.

" DR. REILLY'S, F STREET, February 24, 1838, 10 A.M.

"SIR,—I have called at this place in conformity to your note of this morning, to inform you that Mr. Graves has not as yet been able to procure a rifle and put it in order, and cannot be ready by twelve o'clock M. to-day. He is desirous, however, to have the meeting to-day, if possible, and I will inform you by half-past twelve o'clock M. to-day what time he will require to procure and prepare a weapon.

"Very respectfully, etc.,

"HENRY A. WISE.

"HONORABLE GEORGE W. JONES.

"Afterwards Mr. Jones left at Mr. Wise's room the following note, to wit:

"WASHINGTON, 10.30 A.M., February 24, 1838.

"SIR,—Your note, dated at ten o'clock to-day, is received. In reply I have the pleasure to inform you that I have in my possession an excellent rifle, in good order, which is at the service of Mr. Graves.

"Very respectfully, etc.,

"GEORGE W. JONES.

"HONORABLE H. A. WISE.

"Afterwards Mr. Jones sent to Mr. Wise's room the following note, to wit:

"WASHINGTON, February 24, 1838, 11 A.M.

"SIR,—Through the politeness of my friend Dr. Duncan, I now tender to you, for the use of Mr. Graves, the rifle referred to in my note of ten o'clock this morning.

"Respectfully, your obedient servant,

"GEORGE W. JONES.

"HONORABLE H. A. WISE.

" And with this note a rifle and powder-flask and balls were left at Mr. Wise's room.

"After the reception of this note from Mr. Jones, Mr. Wise called on him at Dr. Reilly's and informed Mr. Jones that Mr. Graves had procured a rifle other than that left at his room by Dr. Duncan, and would be ready for the meeting at three o'clock P.M. It was then agreed that the parties should meet at the Anacostia bridge, on the road to Marlborough, Maryland, between the hours of half-past one and half-past two o'clock P.M., and if either got there first he should wait for the other, and that they would thence proceed out of the District. Accordingly the parties met at the bridge, Mr. Cilley and his party arriving there first, and all proceeded, about two o'clock P.M., to the place of meeting. On arriving at the place, Mr. Jones and Mr. Wise immediately proceeded to mark off the ground. They then decided the choice of positions. Mr. Wise won the position, and consequently Mr. Jones had the giving of the word. At the time Mr. Jones was informed by Mr. Wise that two gentlemen (Mr. Calhoun, of Kentucky, and Mr. Hawes, of Kentucky) were at some distance off, spectators, but they should not approach upon the ground. Mr. Jones replied that he objected to their coming on the ground, as it was against the articles of the meeting, but he entertained for them the highest respect. Mr. Wise informed Mr. Jones that, contrary to the terms, he had brought on the ground two rifles; that if he (Mr. Jones) required him to do so, he would immediately send one of them away. Upon Mr. Jones finding that the rifle was unloaded, he consented that it should remain in one of the carriages. There were, it is proper to remark, several persons on the ground (besides the hackdrivers and the two gentlemen at a distance before mentioned) who were there without the authority or consent of either party or their friends, as far as is known either to Mr. Jones or Mr. Wise, and one of these persons was supposed to be the owner of the field. Shortly after the hour of three P.M. the rifles were loaded in the presence of the seconds; the parties were called together; they were fully instructed by Mr. Jones as to their positions, and the words were twice repeated to them as they would be and as they were delivered to them in the exchange of shots. After they were ordered to their respective positions, the seconds assumed their places, and the friends accompanying the seconds were disposed along the line of fire to observe that each obeyed the terms of meeting. Mr. Jones gave the word distinctly, audibly, and in regular succession, and the parties exchanged shots without violating in the least a single instruction. They both missed. After which Mr. Wise called upon the friends generally to assemble and hear what was to be said. Upon the assembling of the friends, Mr. Jones inquired of Mr. Wise whether his friend (Mr. Graves) was satisfied. Mr. Wise immediately said in substance, 'Mr. Jones, these gentlemen have come here without animosity towards each other; they are fighting merely upon a point of honor; cannot Mr. Cilley assign some reason for not receiving at Mr. Graves's hands Colonel Webb's communication, or make some disclaimer which will relieve Mr. Graves from his position?' Mr. Jones replied, in substance, 'Whilst the challenge is impending, Mr. Cilley can make no explanation.' Mr. Wise said, in substance, 'The exchange of shots suspends the challenge, and the challenge is suspended for the purpose of explanation.' Mr. Jones therefore said he would see Mr. Cilley, and did go to him. He returned and asked Mr. Wise again, 'Mr. Wise, do I understand aright that the challenge is suspended?' Mr. Wise an-

swered, 'It is.' Mr. Jones was then about to proceed, when Mr. Wise
suggested that it was best, perhaps, to give the explanation or reason in
writing. Mr. Jones then said, in substance, 'Mr. Wise, if you require
me to put what I have to say in writing, I shall require you to put what
you have said and may say in writing.' Mr. Wise replied, 'Well, let us
hear the explanation beforehand, as it may not be necessary to put it in
writing.' Mr. Jones then proceeded, as he now thinks, substantially to
say, 'I am authorized by my friend, Mr. Cilley, to say that, in declining to receive the note from Mr. Graves, purporting to be from Colonel
Webb, he meant no disrespect to Mr. Graves, because he entertained for
him then, as he now does, the most kind feelings; but that he declined
to receive the note because he chose not to be drawn into controversy
with Colonel Webb.' Mr. Wise thinks this answer of Mr. Jones's was,
in substance, as follows: 'I am authorized by my friend, Mr. Cilley, to
say that, in declining to receive the note from Mr. Graves purporting to
be from Colonel Webb, he meant no disrespect to Mr. Graves, because
he entertained for him then, as he does now, the highest respect and
most kind feelings, but my friend refuses to disclaim disrespect for
Colonel Webb, because he does not choose to be drawn into an expression
of opinion as to him.' Such is the substantial difference between the
two seconds as to the answer of Mr. Jones. The friends on each side,
with the seconds, then retired from each other to consult upon this
explanation. After consultation, Mr. Wise returned to Mr. Jones and
said, 'Mr. Jones, this answer leaves Mr. Graves precisely in the position
in which he stood when the challenge was sent.' Much conversation
then ensued between the seconds and their friends, but, no nearer
approach to reconciliation being made, the challenge was renewed and
another shot was exchanged in a manner perfectly fair and honorable to
all parties. After this the seconds and their friends again assembled
and the challenge was again withdrawn, and very similar conversations
to that after the first exchange of shots again ensued. Mr. Jones then
remarked, 'Mr. Wise, my friend, in coming to the ground and exchanging
shots with Mr. Graves, has shown to the world that in declining to receive
the note of Colonel Webb he did not do so because he dreaded a controversy. He has shown himself a brave man, and disposed to render satisfaction to Mr. Graves. I do think he has done so, and that the matter
should end here.' To this Mr. Wise replied, in substance, 'Mr. Jones,
Mr. Cilley has already expressed his respect for Mr. Graves in the written
correspondence, and Mr. Graves does not require of Mr. Cilley a certificate of character for Colonel Webb; he considers himself bound not
only to preserve the respect due to himself, but to defend the honor of
his friend, Colonel Webb.' These words of Mr. Wise Mr. Jones recol-
lects, and Mr. Wise thinks he added the words, 'Mr. Graves only insists

that he has not borne the note of a man who is not a man of honor and not a gentleman.' After much more conversation and ineffectual attempts to adjust the matter, the challenge was again renewed, and, whilst the friends were again loading the rifles for the third exchange of shots, Mr. Jones and Mr. Wise walked apart, and each proposed to the other anxiously to settle the affair. Mr. Wise asked Mr. Jones 'if Mr. Cilley could not assign the reason for declining to receive the note of Colonel Webb, that he did not hold himself accountable to Colonel Webb for words spoken in debate?' Mr. Jones replied, that 'Mr. Cilley would not assign that reason, because he did not wish to be understood as expressing the opinion whether he was or was not accountable for words spoken in debate.' Mr. Wise then, according to recollection, asked Mr. Jones whether Mr. Cilley would not say that 'in declining to receive the note of Colonel Webb he meant no disrespect to Mr. Graves, directly or indirectly?' To which Mr. Jones replied affirmatively, adding, 'Mr. Cilley entertains the highest respect for Mr. Graves, but declines to receive the note because he chose to be drawn into no controversy with Colonel Webb.' After further explanatory conversation the parties then exchanged the third shot, fairly and honorably as in every instance. Immediately previous to the last exchange of shots Mr. Wise said to Mr. Jones, 'If this matter is not terminated this shot, and is not settled, I will propose to shorten the distance.' To which Mr. Jones replied, 'After this shot, if without effect, I will entertain the proposition.'

"After Mr. Cilley fell, Mr. Wise, for Mr. Graves, expressed a desire to Mr. Jones to see Mr. Cilley. Mr. Jones replied to Mr. Wise, 'My friend is dead,' and went on to Mr. Graves and told him that there was no objection to his request to see Mr. Cilley. When Mr. Jones approached Mr. Graves and informed him that his request should be granted, Mr. Graves inquired, 'How is he?' The reply was, 'My friend is dead, sir.' Mr. Graves then went to his carriage. Mr. Wise inquired of Mr. Jones before leaving the ground whether he could render any service, and tendered all the aid in his power. Mr. Wise and Mr. Jones concur that there were three shots exchanged.

"Such is the naked statement of all the material facts and circumstances attending this unfortunate affair of honor, which we make in justice to our friends, to ourselves, and to all concerned, the living and the dead ; and it is made only for the purpose of allaying excitement in the public mind, and to prevent any and all further controversy upon the subject, which already is full enough of woe. We have fully and substantially stated wherein we agree and disagree. We cordially agree, at all events, in bearing unqualified testimony to the fair and honorable manner in which the duel was conducted. We endeavored to discharge our duties according to that code under which the parties met, regulated by magnanimous principles and the laws of humanity. Neither of us has taken the least exception to the course of the other; and we sincerely hope that here all controversy whatever may cease. We especially desire our respective friends to make no publication on the subject. None can regret the termination of the affair more than ourselves, and we hope again that the last of it will be the signatures of our names to this paper, which we now affix.

"GEORGE W. JONES.
"HENRY A. WISE."

Vain hope! Instead of this being "the last of the affair," the supposed instigators of it were met on all sides with a perfect storm of indignation, and an almost universal demand for a searching investigation of the matter and punishment of the guilty; and the more the circumstances of the tragedy became known the fiercer the cry for retribution. Before proceeding, however, to depict this feeling, I will introduce the sworn statement of William H. Morrell and Daniel Jackson, two chosen friends of Colonel Webb, who, according to their testimony, "said that it was utterly impossible that a meeting could be permitted to take place between Messrs. Graves and Cilley until Mr. Cilley had first met him (Webb), and that he was determined to force such a meeting upon Mr. Cilley, be the consequences what they might." It was accordingly agreed that Colonel Webb, with two friends "properly armed, should repair to Mr. Cilley's room, when Mr. Webb should offer to Mr. Cilley the choice of his duelling pistols with the following alternatives: either then and there to settle the question or pledge his word of honor that he would give Colonel Webb a meeting before Mr. Graves at such a place and time and with such weapons as Mr. Cilley might appoint; and in the event of doing neither, then to expect the most serious consequences on the spot. Mr. Webb then added: "Should he refuse either to fight me at the time, or give the pledge required, I shall have no alternative left but to shatter his right arm and thereby prevent his meeting my friend." Before this plan could be carried out, it was found that Mr. Cilley had left his lodgings for the duelling ground, understood to be Bladensburg, to which place Colonel Webb and his two friends immediately repaired. On their way, Colonel Webb designated the following order of proceedings:

" 'On reaching the parties,' said he, 'I'll approach Mr. Cilley and tell him this is my quarrel, and he must fight me, and that, if he aims his rifle at my friend, I'll shoot him on the spot. We know that, upon this, Messrs. Graves and Wise will interfere, and that we will be ordered off the ground; but I shall tell them that we have come prepared to lose our lives or prevent the meeting, and that it cannot proceed without first disposing of us. From our knowledge of the parties, it is probable that some one of them will then raise his weapon at me, when I shall instantly shoot Cilley, and we must proceed to defend ourselves in the best way we can.' "

After stating that they drove to the usual duelling ground and several other places without being able to find the parties, the witnesses say: "It is unnecessary to add what would have been the course of Colonel Webb if Mr. Graves, instead of Mr. Cilley, had been injured. Suffice it to say that his determination was sanctioned by us, and, however much we deplored it, we could not doubt but the extraordinary position in which he would then have been placed would have warranted the course determined upon."

Alluding to the dark intimation in the last paragraph, an able editor, at the time holding a high position under the United States government, remarked, "Thus, then, it seems if Cilley had escaped from the field with his life, he would have been, doubtless, assassinated by Webb and his associates."

Colonel Schaumbourg, a friend of Mr. Cilley, states that before the meeting, Mr. Cilley said to him:

" Mr. Graves has taken upon himself to demand of me to say, and that in language dictated by himself, that James Watson Webb is a gentleman and a man of honor. Now, that is what I am not going to disgrace

myself by saying. I see into the whole affair. Webb has come on here
to challenge me because he and perhaps others think that, as I am from
New England, I am to be bluffed, and Mr. Webb will proclaim himself a
brave man, having obtained an acknowledgment on my part that he is a
gentleman and a man of honor. But they have calculated without their
host. Although I know that the sentiment of New England is opposed
to duelling, I am sure that my people will be better pleased if I stand the
test than disgrace myself by humiliating concessions. Sir, the name I
bear will never permit me to cower beneath the frown of mortal man. It
is an attempt to browbeat us, and they think that because I am from the
East, I will tamely submit."

Besides the two seconds, the friends of each party on the
ground were, on the part of Mr. Cilley, Jesse A. Bynum,
member of Congress from North Carolina, Colonel W.
Schaumbourg, of Pennsylvania, and Alexander Duncan
(surgeon), member of Congress from Ohio; and, on the part
of Mr. Graves, John J. Crittenden, Senator, and Richard
H. Menifee, member of Congress from Kentucky, and Dr.
J. M. Foltz, surgeon, of Washington City. These gentlemen were quite as free from censure in the affair as were
some others not present. The greater weight of " public
opprobrium and disgust" fell upon Mr. Wise and Colonel
Webb, as will appear from quotations we will see from the
public records and the press.

Mr. Cilley's death was announced in the House of Representatives on the 26th of February by the Hon. John
Fairfield, of Maine, and in the Senate, the same day, by
the Hon. Reuel Williams, of Maine, and appropriate resolutions provided for the appointment of a committee of
seven members to investigate the causes which led to Mr.
Cilley's death and the circumstances connected therewith;
also to inquire whether, in the matter, there had been any
breach of the privileges of the House. The resolutions,
after considerable opposition, were passed by yeas one hundred and fifty-two, nays forty-nine, and this committee was
composed of the following gentlemen: Isaac Toucey, of
Connecticut, W. W. Potter, of Pennsylvania, George Grin-

nell, Jr., of Massachusetts, F. H. Elmore, of South Carolina, A. D. W. Bruyn, of New York, S. Grantland, of Georgia, and J. Rariden, of Indiana. The committee were divided in opinion, and made three reports, Mr. Toucey, afterward Senator and member of both President Polk's and President Buchanan's Cabinet, presenting that of the majority. It embraces the material facts and circumstances of the duel, and, among other things, declares that " It is a breach of the highest constitutional privileges of the House, and of the most sacred rights of the people in the person of their representative, to demand in a hostile manner an explanation of words spoken in debate."

The committee submitted resolutions for the expulsion of William J. Graves, Henry A. Wise, and George W. Jones. Finally, after a long debate, the whole subject was laid on the table by a vote of one hundred and two to seventy-six, a vote of censure merely being passed.

High as party feeling ran at the time, indignation and denunciation were by no means confined to one side in politics. "Never," said Charles G. Green, editor of the Boston *Post*, "was there a more dastardly murder than that of the unfortunate Cilley. The nation should echo with indignation at this horrible outrage, this cold-blooded assassination." Naming two of the principal actors (Webb and Wise) in the affair, the same editor calls the one " the miserable poltroon," and the other " the wretch," adding, " both of them are equally a disgrace to human nature, and will receive the execration of mankind ; we hope that the penitentiary or the gallows will soon relieve society of their baneful presence." A Washington correspondent of the *Journal of Commerce* is quoted as saying that, " After Jones returned the last time, from the conference, with Wise's reply, Mr. Cilley said, in a calm and collected tone, 'They thirst for my blood!'" In a previous conference, as reported by the seconds, Mr. Cilley said that " in declining to receive the note from Colonel Webb, he meant no disrespect to Mr. Graves, because he entertained for him then, as he now does, the highest respect and most kind feelings." "But," as remarked by the *Democratic Review*, published by Langtree and O'Sullivan, at the time, " all this was without avail."

Making due allowance for poetical license, the following poem, written by the present writer and published in the *Eastern Argus* very soon after this deplorable affair, expresses what I know was the feeling, particularly in New England :

" WITHOUT AVAIL.

" ' Without avail !'   Infernal plot !
　The thirst for blood was there ;
　Else had the noble-minded lived
　The statesman's wreath to wear.

" ' Without avail !'   In hate conspired—
　At heart the murderers' aim—
　To take his life, or deep disgrace
　To stamp upon his name !

" In vain avowals of respect—
　Of kindly feeling, where
　The base intent was fix'd—
　The thirst for blood was there !

" Revenge and private malice deep,
　In hearts as foul as hell,
　In open day demanded blood !
　Hence Freedom's champion fell !

" But though with blood their hands are stained,
　Though stiff the limbs and chill
　In death the heart of him who fell—
　Yet live the murderers still !

" Strange may it seem—the wretches live !
　But on each murderer's head
　Forever rests a Nation's curse ;
　A Nation's heart hath bled !

" The wretches live; the cause behold:
  Stern justice hath decreed
That they may reap in misery long
  The fruits of their vile deed.

" Aye, ever, wheresoe'r they roam,
  In silence awful—dread,
Before their harass'd eyes shall stand
  The spectre of the dead !

" Serene and joyful though the day
  To others may appear,
Their ears the aged mother's sighs
  In ev'ry sound shall hear !

" And ev'ry breeze to them shall bear—
  Around them e'er shall rise
The stricken widow's piteous wail
  And helpless orphans' cries!

" Their way, with piercing thorns hedg'd round,
  Shall lead them but to meet
At every step, in hideous shape,
  Mad vipers at their feet.

" Thus, until struck by death's cold darts,
  Their bitter fate shall be;
And o'er their memory e'er shall roll
  The fire of infamy !"

Mr. Cilley fought under disadvantages which (says the *Journal of Commerce*) must have been well known to those on the other side, and which induced some persons to say that his seconds ought never to have suffered him to fight under them at all.   These disadvantages were stated to be that Mr. Cilley, being, as was personally known to the present writer, very near-sighted, could not see to shoot at the distance measured off, which was alleged to be greater by twenty yards than that agreed on ; that his rifle was so light—only about one-half the calibre of that of his antagonist—that it would not carry that distance with accuracy; that he was shooting against the wind, which was blowing a gale; and that he stood on rising ground in open light, presenting a plain mark, while his antagonist was shaded by a copse of wood. Under all these disadvantages, after disclaiming all enmity to Graves, and after technical requisition preliminary to accommodation in honorable duelling, and even after he had declared that he did not wish to take Graves's life, but entertained for him "the highest respect and the most kind feelings," Mr. Cilley was shot down! "What," asked the *Eastern Argus*, "does this prove but that he was foully murdered?"

At a great public meeting, held at the capital of Maine, on the 9th of March, 1838, "for the purpose of noticing in a suitable manner the atrocious murder of Hon. Jonathan Cilley," a series of resolutions were unanimously adopted, declaring, among other things, that the duel was "the result of a foul conspiracy, concerted and approved among a few political leaders, to take advantage of Mr. Cilley and draw him into a quarrel, in order that they might seize upon the opportunity afforded to gratify personal feelings of private malice and revenge, and remove out of the way an opponent every day becoming more and more formidable, whose eloquent appeals and retorted sarcasms it would be more easy to silence by the pistol than answer in debate; that in the course pursued by Henry A. Wise in managing and conducting the incidents of the duel after the first fire, there is evidence of deep and vindictive malignity; and that he stands justly chargeable before the world, upon his own showing, of having violated every recognized principle of chivalry by availing himself of his position and the occasion to glut his own feelings of private grudge and ill-will against Mr. Cilley for a former supposed offence given by the deceased, not to his principal, Graves, but to himself, Wise, a course of conduct worthy only of a recreant and a dastard; that the studied attempt made by Henry A. Wise to palliate and gloss over his conduct during the duel, apparent in the imperfect but official account, so called, of the doings, and the special desire expressed in the account, that those who witnessed the scene should make no publication on the subject, afford strong presumptive evidence of a consciousness that there were deeds of darkness and treachery in the history of the conflict which would not bear to be told; while, on the other hand, the careful insertion in that account of a statement that Mr. Wise inquired of Mr. Jones, before leaving the ground, 'whether he could render any service, and tendered all the aid in his power,' the murder having been already perpetrated, and the lifeless corpse of Mr. Cilley then lying stretched out before him, is a derision and a mockery upon the better feelings of our nature, worthy only of the man who could coolly triumph over the fallen victim of his own foul machinations; and that in the transaction which terminated in the death of Mr. Cilley, considered under the mildest and most mitigated features given to it by those who took part in it, there is presented to the people of Maine a case of ruthless assassination—of preconcerted and cold-blooded murder of one of their representatives, for having boldly and fearlessly done his duty, and being resolved to continue to do so."

The editor of the *Democratic Review*, in a position to obtain the most correct information on the subject, was very severe in his comments upon the whole affair, and particularly with reference to Wise's course in insisting, after the second shot, either that Mr. Cilley should " acknowledge Webb to be a gentleman and a man of honor," or that " blood should flow !"

"It is not enough that he (Mr. Cilley) has said nothing to the disparagement of Mr. Webb—that he is free in expression of the highest respect and best feeling toward Graves; it is not enough that two shots have been interchanged on this flimsy punctilio of honor, in the language of one of the gentlemen on the field, in his remonstrance, ' based on an abstraction and assumed upon an implication ;' it is not enough that all persons on the ground—the second, the surgeon, and consulting friends

of the challenged party, the surgeon and one at least of the friends of
the challenging side (Mr. Crittenden)—are unanimous in opinion that
all has been done that the most fastidious honor can require; it is not
enough that he (Wise) has put a distinct proposition, in decisive terms,
as if an ultimatum, from an anxiety to bring an end to the combat, that
acknowledgment shall be made that no disrespect was meant to Mr.
Graves, directly or indirectly, and that it was, in terms, answered affirmatively : nothing whatever will suffice but a degrading acknowledgment
contrary to the conscience and truth of the party, and to the well-known
majority of society, and entirely extraneous to the relation between the
parties in the field—an acknowledgment which nothing but a trembling
cowardice, widely unlike the brave bearing of poor Cilley, could yield
under such circumstances—an acknowledgment which he knew, and
could not but have known, could not and would not be conceded. No,
nothing will suffice but this abject and impossible submission—or blood !
The spirit of malignant evil that ruled the ascendant of that dark hour
triumphed, and the kind-hearted, the generous, the peaceful, the manly,
the noble, the true, the brave, lay weltering in his own blood !"

The following, says the editor of the *Review*, are substantially the views of the matter which Mr. Cilley expressed freely to his friends on the morning of the fatal
encounter :

"I am driven to this meeting by a positive compulsion. I have done
all that an honorable man could do to avert it. Why should I acknowledge that man to be a gentleman and a man of honor? In truth and
conscience I could not do so, and still less can I have it so unreasonably
extorted from me by force and threat. I have no ill-will nor disrespect
toward Mr. Graves. He knows it, and I have repeatedly and fully
expressed it. I abhor the idea of taking his life, and will do nothing
not forced upon me in self-defence. The pretext of the challenge is
absurd. I understand the conspiracy to destroy me as a public man.
But New England must not be trampled on, my name must not be disgraced, and I go to this field sustained by as high a motive of patriotism as ever led my grandfather or my brother to battle, as an unhappy
duty, not to be shrunk from, to my honor, my principles, and my
country."

On the evening before the duel he charged one of his lady
friends, should he not survive, to say to his wife that he

" had endeavored to pursue that course in all things which she would approve and his own conscience dictated."

In a biographical sketch of Mr. Cilley, published in the *Democratic Review* for September, 1838, Nathaniel Hawthorne says:

"A challenge was never given on a more shadowy pretext; a duel was never pressed to a fatal close in the face of such open kindness as was expressed by Mr. Cilley; and the conclusion is inevitable that Mr. Graves and his principal second, Mr. Wise, have gone further than their own dreadful code will warrant them, and overstepped the imaginary distinction which, on their own principles, separates manslaughter from murder."

Mr. Wise was not a man to rest silent under such opprobrium. On the 16th of March, 1838, he issued a long address to his constituents in which he gave his own account of the duel so far as he himself was concerned. He began by saying that "the catastrophe had brought upon him much odium and reproach," but claimed that he was bound to act for Mr. Graves, because, said he:

"I felt obliged to do for him what I would have called on him to do for me. It is said that I myself was hostile to his antagonist. If so, I may have been incompetent, but I solemnly deny that I was hostile to Mr. Cilley. There had been a slight misunderstanding between us in debate, which passed off with the moment and left no trace of animosity behind. But hostile to him or not, and though hostility might, perhaps, have incited another to take his life—dark and deadly such hate must have been—yet my conduct proves that I did earnestly endeavor to prevent the shedding of blood by reconciling his difference with my friend; and the history of the tragedy proves that not only I but two other gentlemen of known character and standing, who were never accused of hostility to him, and who might have overruled me by their voices and influence, could not reconcile that difference or prevent its result."

He says, also, that he rebuked Graves for bearing the note from Mr. Webb, and that he told him that Mr. Cilley's reasons, as repeated by Mr. Graves, for refusing to receive the note " were very proper," and his answer, " certainly satisfactory." Here is what he said Mr. Graves represented

Mr. Cilley had in substance verbally declared: That, " in declining to receive the note he hoped it would not be thought disrespectful to him (Mr. Graves); that he declined on the ground that he could not consent to be involved in personal difficulties with conductors of public journals for what he had thought proper to say in debate upon the floor, and that he did not decline upon any personal objection to Colonel Webb as a gentleman." Mr. Wise appears to have assented to the propriety of Mr. Graves requiring this answer to be put in writing, and so came the challenge, the terms of which Mr. Wise said were regarded as " barbarous and such as might properly be declined; but it was thought they were intended to intimidate; that the distance was so great as in some measure to mitigate the severity of the weapon, and therefore I was advised that they should be accepted." It was likewise suggested that the challenged party might be the first to fly from these terms.

He speaks of his difficulty in procuring a suitable rifle for Mr. Graves, and admits that he had asked Mr. Jones to assist him in that particular. At the same time he says, " I wished to gain time not only to procure a fit rifle, but to afford an opportunity, if possible, to prevent the meeting."

He quotes from Mr. Jones's note the passage in which he said to Mr. Wise that he had the pleasure to inform him that he had an excellent rifle in good order which was at the service of Mr. Graves, and remarks that, without waiting for an answer, Mr. Jones tendered to him " for the use of Mr. Graves, the rifle referred to," and its appendages. Thus, Mr. Wise says, " A weapon, not one of a pair, was tendered for the use of Mr. Graves in a manner that was considered taunting." Leaving it be inferred, of course, that one preferred to it had been reserved for Mr. Cilley. He contends, too, that Mr. Cilley " precipitated the time of meeting when the second of Mr. Graves was avowing a want of preparation and a desire for delay."

He proceeds to say:

"The distance appointed was eighty yards. It is my firm belief that the distance stepped off by Mr. Jones and myself, which we did *pari passu*, was nearer one hundred yards than eighty. The ground was measured before the choice of positions, and I believe that we both stepped with a view of preventing the parties from hitting each other. I kept my eye on Mr. Cilley. It was my duty to see he obeyed the rules. At the first exchange of shots I thought he fired, though perfectly fair, too hurriedly, and his ball did not reach Mr. Graves, because he did not raise his rifle sufficiently high. Mr. Graves fired after Mr. Cilley."

At the second shot, he says:

"Mr. Graves's rifle went off quickly, and, as he told me afterwards, accidentally, and into the ground. Mr. Cilley drew up very deliberately, aimed, I feared, a deadly shot, and fired. I thought he had hit Mr. Graves. It was very apparent to me that Mr. Cilley had shot at the life of Mr. Graves. If, when Mr. Graves's rifle went off, without harm to him, he had discharged his in the air or reserved his fire, the fight would have been at an end."

Nevertheless, Mr. Cilley's friends said that, even admitting that Mr. Wise was correct in his assertion that Mr. Cilley fired after the discharge of Mr. Graves's rifle, it was equally true, according to his own statement, that Mr. Graves, on the first exchange of shots, had done the same thing toward Mr. Cilley. It does not appear how Mr. Wise could reconcile his allegation in this regard with his official statement, conjointly with Mr. Jones, that the second shot was exchanged "in a manner perfectly fair and honorable to all parties," and that they bore their unqualified testimony to the fair and honorable manner in which the duel was conducted.

Between the second and third shots, in making the proposition he did, that Mr. Cilley should say that "in declining to receive Colonel Webb's note, he meant no disrespect to Mr. Graves, either directly or indirectly," Mr. Wise says he went beyond his instructions; and that he understood Mr. Jones to say that "Mr. Cilley would not say these words alone, nor without adding words which did away the effect of the word 'indirectly,' and which left the parties exactly where they were when they came upon the ground." He says, " It was at the instance of Mr. Graves himself that I remarked to Mr. Jones, immediately previous to the last exchange of shots, 'If this matter is not terminated this shot, and is not settled, I shall propose to shorten the distance.' "

Later—February, 1839—Mr. Wise availed himself of an opportunity to present his defence before the House of Representatives. I was there and heard it. He was wildly excited and defiant. Said he:

"I am ready to be tried. Put me at your bar, and I will plead instantly. I am ready to say on the spot, I did on that occasion just what I will do again under similar circumstances. Let Puritans shudder as they may, I proclaim that I belong to the class of Cavaliers, not to the Roundheads! You shall not taunt me. What are you doing? You have passed a penitentiary act [the anti-duelling law]. You are then bound to take the defence of character into your own hands, as you have taken arms from the hands of the cavalier. Will you do it? No! I call upon you, I call upon society, either to defend me or give me back my arms. In the face of an approaching election, I say to my good constituents. . . . If you are determined I shall not defend myself when assailed, like a true knight, do not send me to Congress, for I shall just as surely fight, if occasion is given, as you send me; and so I shall ever continue until the holy religion of the Cross takes possession of my soul, which may God grant right early."

Up to this time, and for nearly two years afterwards, Mr. Wise, in public estimation, stood out prominently as the one individual altogether the most deserving of censure in this matter. As he himself said in an appeal "to the public," in March, 1842, "The whole weight of an almost insupportable odium fell upon my reputation for my conduct in the affair."

But in the winter of that year, or earlier, the relations of some of the parties to the transaction had become changed. Mr. Wise had espoused the cause of President Tyler, thus separating himself from his old friend Henry Clay, who was a candidate for the presidency, and to whose fortunes

Messrs. Graves and Webb, with the Whig party generally, adhered. It began to be whispered about that Mr. Clay had been consulted and exercised a controlling influence in the affair of the duel, and a direct charge to this effect brought out Mr. Graves, on a call from Mr. Clay, in explanation. I will not extend this narrative by going at length into the particulars of the correspondence which followed, and in which Messrs. Wise, Graves, Clay, Reverdy Johnson, and Charles King took part. Suffice it to say that, except so far as Wise was concerned, all was said that could be to exculpate Mr. Clay, but, as must be admitted, not with entire success. It came out that he was early consulted by all these gentlemen, and that he actually "drew the form of challenge which was finally adopted." It was a modification of the form submitted to him by Wise and Graves, and the latter states that "it was rather calculated to soften the language and not so completely to close the door to an adjustment of the difficulty." Mr. Wise says that when he and Mr. Graves called on Mr. Clay, in discussing the terms of the duel, which he (Wise) " protested against as unusual and barbarous," Mr. Clay remarked that Mr. Graves was "a Kentuckian, and that no Kentuckian could back out from a rifle."

Mr. Wise stated that—

"Mr. Clay's friends particularly were very anxious, for obvious reasons, not to involve his name especially in the affair. Thus many confidential facts remained unknown on both sides. Mr. Clay himself, it is true, while all his friends were trembling lest the part he took in it should be disclosed, boldly came to me and said, 'Sir, it is a nine days' bubble! If they want to know what I did in the matter, tell them to call me before them and I will tell them.' This excited my admiration at the time, and was effectual to prevent me from unnecessarily bringing his name before the committee."

After all, I think public sentiment, as at first expressed, was not materially modified by these later developments, and that it remains unchanged as regards Wise's great culpability, notwithstanding Graves, in the course of their correspondence, declared to him, "I always have, and now do, most emphatically exempt you from all blame or censure growing out of your connection with the affair. I, and I only, am justly responsible for whatever was done by myself or those representing me as my friends on that occasion."

One of the most stinging accusations against Mr. Wise was made by ex-President John Quincy Adams, in the House of Representatives on the 26th of January, 1842, when a resolution, offered by Mr. Gilmer, of Virginia (killed by the bursting of the "Peacemaker" on the "Princeton," in February, 1844), was under discussion, declaring that Mr. Adams had justly incurred the censure of the House in presenting for its consideration an abolition petition for the dissolution of the Union. Mr. Wise took a leading part in the discussion, in the course of which the venerable ex-President was led to say that, "four or five years ago, there came to the House a man [Wise] with his hands and face dripping with the blood of a murder, the blotches of which were yet hanging upon him." This, in nearly the same language, he twice repeated, and at the same time said: "I never did believe but he [Wise] was the guilty man, and that the man who pulled the trigger was but an instrument in his hands. This was my belief in the beginning."

Of the actors in this deplorable affair, the only survivor (December, 1891) is George W. Jones, of Iowa, Mr. Cilley's second. Mr. Graves, after long and intense suffering, both mental and physical, died in Louisville, Ky., on the 27th of September, 1848, aged forty-three years.

Jonathan Cilley was born at Nottingham, N. H., on the 2d of July, 1802, and was, therefore, at his death in the thirty-sixth year of his age. He was a man of fine personal appearance, in size and weight about medium, and of rather dark complexion. He was a graduate of Bowdoin

College.   His friend Nathaniel Hawthorne describes him, while at college—

"As a young man of quick and powerful intellect, endowed with sagacity and tact, yet frank and free in his mode of action; ambitious of good influence; earnest, active, and persevering, with an elasticity and cheerful strength of mind which made difficulties easy and the struggle with them a pleasure.   In the summer of 1837 I met him for the first time since our early youth, when he had been to me almost an elder brother.   In his person there was very little change, and that little was for the better.   He had an impending brow, deep-set eyes, and a thin and thoughtful countenance, which, in his abstracted moments, seemed almost stern ; but in the intercourse of society it was brightened with a kindly smile that will live in the recollection of all who knew him."

One who had been a bosom friend and constant companion through an acquaintance of sixteen years says of him :

"He was the kindest and gentlest of human beings, with a constant and happy flow of animal spirits and the innocence of a child, while at the same time as independent, courageous, and firm in his purposes as he was clear in his judgments and upright in his every thought."

Mr. Cilley left a wife and three children,—two sons and a daughter, the latter an infant whom he never saw.   It is a singular fact that on the Sunday succeeding the Saturday on which he fell, Mrs. Cilley, wholly unconscious of the terrible news already on its way to her, was so impressed from reading the well-known hymn, commencing with the lines—

"Far, far o'er hill and dale on the winds stealing,
List to the tolling bell, mournfully pealing,"

that she was induced to mark it with a pencil.   The second and third stanzas read :

"Now, through the charmed air slowly ascending,
List to the mourner's prayer solemnly bending:
    Hark! hark! it seems to say,
    Turn from those joys away
    To those which ne'er decay,
For life is ending.

" O'er the father's dismal tomb see the orphan bending,
　　From the solemn churchyard's gloom hear the dirge ascending :
　　　Hark ! hark ! it seems to say,
　　　How short ambition's sway,
　　　Life's joys and friendship's ray,
　　In the dark grave ending !"

Alas ! the soul-chilling, heart-rending news of the tragic death of the husband and father was soon to place beyond doubt the sad reality of what seemed to have been thus mysteriously foretokened. Mrs. Cilley never entirely recovered from the fearful shock. She died on the 15th of October, 1844.

CHAPTER X.

THE BATTLE OF BLADENSBURG—BURNING OF WASHINGTON IN 1814.

PRIOR to the late civil war, during many years, we had for Second Assistant Postmaster-General Mr. William H. Dundas, who was somewhat of a wag, and who delighted in rallying the mild and staid John Smith, one of the clerks of the Department, on having served in a militia company at the battle of Bladensburg, otherwise reproachfully called " the Bladensburg races." Said he, " The red-coats got a little the better of you at the start, but you beat them *in the long run.*"

There having been so many meagre and often conflicting stories about this famous battle and the fall of Washington, I determined, if possible, to sift the various accounts, and present within reasonable limits an intelligible record. To this end I examined the files of many of the prominent newspapers of the day, and read all I could find on the subject in books. It appears that no serious fears were felt for the safety of the capital until within a few days of its capture. We can imagine what consternation prevailed among the citizens when the danger suddenly became imminent. The Boston *Centinel* of August 24, 1814, contained a letter from Washington, dated August 16, saying, " We are all in alarm here. The enemy are said to be in great force in the Chesapeake. It is apprehended this city is their object, and that they will land in the Patuxent or near Annapolis, near which several of their ships have been seen. It is expected the President will issue another proclamation, directing Congress to assemble at some other place except Washington,—say Lancaster, Pennsylvania." President Madison had already summoned Congress (August 8) to meet on the 19th of September. Another item in the *Centinel* of a later date was, " The public papers began to be removed from Washington 21st August, and all the horses, carriages, and drivers are pressed. The roads are crowded with women and children, and the greatest distress prevails." A correspondent of the Baltimore *Patriot* wrote from Washington that, " On Sunday (21st) the public officers were all engaged in packing and sending off their books, and the citizens their furniture. On Monday this business was continued with great industry, and many families left the city. The specie was removed from all the banks in the District." A gentleman wrote from Washington at one o'clock in the morning of the day of the battle, "I cannot find language to express the situation of the women and children, who are running the streets in a state bordering on distraction; their husbands, fathers, and brothers all under arms, scarce a man to be seen in the city. Enemy reported to be thirteen thousand strong."

The British squadron under command of Vice-Admiral Cockburn entered Chesapeake Bay on the 16th of August. On the 18th a part of their ships with the British troops, under General Ross, then estimated, as one account states, "at from five thousand to ten thousand, probably rising

seven thousand," entered the Patuxent River, and a part
ascended the Potomac,—in all then reported to be "composed of fifty sail, including transports." It was known
that the troops were largely made up from the army of the
Duke of Wellington—tried veterans in the regular service
—whose embarkation for the United States our Government had been advised of as early as the month of June
succeeding the triumphant entry of the allied forces into
Paris, March 30, when Napoleon abdicated to give place to
Louis XVIII. (on the 6th of April, 1815), and the pacification of Europe. The report soon came that these British
troops were landing at Benedict, twenty-seven miles east
of Washington, on the Patuxent, and that they were preparing to march to Washington, although there was great
uncertainty as to whether Washington, Annapolis, or Fort
Washington, on the Potomac, was their objective point.
Meantime more active preparations for defence were hastily
made by calling out all the available militia and regular
United States troops in the District of Columbia, as well as
from Baltimore and other sections not far distant. General
W. H. Winder was ordered to the command, and under
date of August 20 issued two "General Orders," calling on
his soldiers "to do their duty without regard to sacrifice
and privation," and upon the people within or contiguous to
his command "to rally round the standard of their country
in defence of the capital and their own firesides." These
orders were supplemented by a similar stirring appeal from
James H. Blake, the mayor of Washington.

There is undoubted evidence that President Madison
was early alive to the importance of adopting effective
measures for the safety of the capital. At a special Cabinet
meeting called for this purpose on July 1, 1814, the subject
was fully discussed and a plan of defence agreed on, which,
had it been carried out, might have proved successful. But
this failed, it appears, through the inefficiency or indifference, or both combined, of General Armstrong, Secretary

of War, who could not or would not believe, until the enemy was seen on his march to Bladensburg, that Washington was his destination; who seemed to think it far more probable that he was going either to Baltimore or Annapolis, that he "would never be so mad as to make an attempt on Washington, and that it was therefore totally unnecessary to make any preparations for its defence." As late as the day of the battle, the New York *Evening Post* received information from Washington that, although the British had disembarked at Benedict, they had not marched thitherward, and that the militia had collected in such numbers in and near the capital as to insure its safety in case of attack. The result, however, was that, "only eleven days before the enemy entered the city, the commanding general had under his orders but little more than one thousand men," and with his utmost exertions he had succeeded in collecting not more than half the force it was intended by the President he should have when the day of battle came. Even then, a regiment of some eight hundred men from Virginia, who arrived in the city the day before, could not join the army for want of necessary equipments, for which the War Department had made little or no provision. General Winder, in his official report, says, "About five thousand men, including three hundred and fifty regulars and Commodore Barney's command (about five hundred men), was all that he was able to interpose at Bladensburg. Much the larger part of this force, he says, arrived on the ground when the enemy were in sight, and were disposed of to support in the best manner the position which General Stansbury had taken with his command from Baltimore. They had barely reached the ground before the action commenced."

For several days before the British ventured up the Patuxent, detachments were from time to time landed from their vessels and engaged in committing depredations on the unoffending planters, burning their dwellings and seizing tobacco and other products, not omitting to supply themselves with provisions, the most delicate within their reach. Commodore Barney had moved his flotilla up the Patuxent above Nottingham. It consisted, he said, " of fourteen open row-boats (not gun-boats) and one tender, having crews amounting in the whole to five hundred and three men." On Friday, August 19, Colonel Monroe, Secretary of State, with Captain Thornton's troops from Alexandria, made a reconnoissance, and discovered that the enemy was debarking at Benedict. A letter from Washington, in the Richmond *Enquirer* of August 23, states that Colonel Monroe was near being captured at Nottingham, but that he escaped from one side of the town while the British were marching in at the other. Mr. George R. Gleig, a British subaltern present, thus describes the debarkation: " As soon as the dawn began to appear on the morning of the 19th, there was a general stir throughout the fleet. A gun-brig had already taken her station within one hundred and fifty yards of a village called St. Benedict's, on the left bank of the river, where it was determined that the disembarkation should be effected. Her broadside was turned toward the shore, and her guns, loaded with grape- and round-shot, were pointed at the beach to cover the landing of the boats; and being moored fore and aft with spring cables, she was altogether as manageable as if she had been under sail. . . . By three o'clock in the afternoon the whole army was landed, and occupied a strong position about two miles above the village."

On Saturday, August 20, General Winder despatched Lieutenant-Colonel Tilghman, with his squadron of dragoons, " by way of the Wood Yard (about fifteen miles from Washington), to fall down upon the British, to annoy, harass, and impede their march by every possible means, to remove or destroy forage and provisions from before the enemy, and gain intelligence. Captain Caldwell, with his troop of city cavalry, was despatched with the same views toward Benedict by Piscataway, it being wholly uncertain what route the enemy would take if it was his intention to come to Washington." Other smaller detachments were sent to different points to watch the movements of the enemy and give information. At that time, being pretty well convinced that it was the intention of the enemy to proceed directly to Washington, General Winder gave orders to Colonel Scott and Major Peter to retire and occupy the first eligible position between the junction of two roads leading thither and the Wood Yard. After a great deal of reconnoitring and some skirmishing, in which shots were exchanged with little effect, the British forces continued slowly to advance and ours to fall back towards the eastern branch of the Potomac and Bladensburg. Commodore Barney's flotilla was lying near Mt. Pleasant, about nine miles from Nottingham, when, on the approach of the British fleet, August 21, the commodore, with four hundred of his men, abandoned their boats, leaving the rest of the crew with orders to blow them up, which they did on the following day, and all joined the army. The capture or destruction of this flotilla, which could not have been very formidable, was undoubtedly the first object the enemy had in view, and so soon as its destruction was thus accomplished, they were left free to decide whether to take the road to Washington, Annapolis, or Baltimore. While resting within a few miles of Nottingham, squads of British soldiers were sent out to scour the neighboring woods, where it had been represented by some of the country people, probably slaves impressed as guides into the service of the enemy, " numerous detached bodies of riflemen lay in ambush amid the thickets;" and Mr. Gleig relates "a little adventure," which he says occurred to himself on one of these excursions, premising that it illustrates what he was pleased to style "the low cunning which forms a leading trait in the American character." He says they surrounded two men dressed in black coats, and armed with bright firelocks and bayonets, sitting under a tree. " As soon," he says, " as they observed me, they started up and took to their heels, but, being hemmed in on all sides, they quickly perceived that to escape was impossible, and, accordingly, stood still. I hastened toward them, and, having got within a few paces, I heard the one say to the other, with a look of the most perfect simplicity, ' Stop, John, till the gentlemen pass.' There was something so ludicrous in this speech, and in the cast of countenance which accompanied it, that I could not help laughing aloud; nor was my mirth diminished by their attempts to persuade me that they were quiet country people, come out for no other purpose than to shoot squirrels. When I desired to know whether they carried bayonets to charge the squirrels, as well as muskets to shoot them, they were rather at a loss for a reply; but they grumbled exceedingly when they found themselves prisoners and conducted as such to the column."

During the night of August 21 the enemy remained at Nottingham,—their boats and tenders were anchored there, —and the next day, soon after daybreak, the whole moved forward again; but in such a way, first on one road and then on the other, or by dividing their forces, some taking the road toward Fort Washington and some toward Annapolis, as to keep General Winder in the dark respecting their real purpose, as well as to weary out his troops by constant watching. As the enemy advanced, our troops retired. By two o'clock on the afternoon of August 22, General Ross, supported by Rear-Admiral Cockburn, had reached Marlborough, " where he remained until the same hour next day, having, of course, abundant time to rest and refresh his troops, and being perfectly unmolested." Late in the afternoon of the 22d, General Winder, with the cavalry of observation, retired to the Long Old Fields, ten miles from Bladensburg, where his troops were encamped. Here " he was informed that the President and heads of departments had arrived at a house one mile in the rear of the camp." About two o'clock in the morning of the 23d his troops were roused by "a false alarm from a sentinel, were formed in order of battle, and, when dismissed, were ordered to hold themselves ready for their posts at a moment's warning." This was the second night in succession in which they had been deprived of their rest. Before nine o'clock in the forenoon they were under arms again, and were reviewed by the President and suite. General Stansbury was now at Bladensburg in command of the Baltimore troops. The enemy still pressing forward toward the Long Old Fields, General Smith had, agreeably to orders, sent off the baggage across the Eastern Branch, and his troops, together with Commodore Barney's men, were drawn up ready to receive the enemy should he make an attack. Orders had been sent to the city for the removal of the public records, and the most important of these in the State Department, and probably also in the War Department, both being in the same building, were taken first to an unoccupied mill on the Virginia side, near the Chain Bridge, a few miles above Georgetown, and soon afterward to Leesburg.

The head of the enemy's column, by three o'clock in the afternoon of the 23d, was about five miles from Marlborough and within three miles of General Winder's position, where they halted. This being "at a point from whence they could take the road to Bladensburg, to the Eastern Branch bridge, or to Fort Washington, indifferently, or it might be to cover their march upon Annapolis," great doubt was yet entertained which course the British meant to pursue. Their force was still "very imperfectly known, opinions and representations varying, General Winder says, from four to twelve thousand, the better opinion fixed it at from five to seven thousand," while his force at Long Old Fields numbered only about twenty-five hundred. In this state of doubt and uncertainty, after waiting for the enemy until sundown, General Winder determined, he said, to retire

over the lower Eastern Branch bridge, and, Commodore
Barney concurring, they retired with their respective commands accordingly, and encamped in the city that night,
when by his order the upper bridge over the Eastern
Branch was destroyed. The President and heads of departments likewise left and went home. Commodore Barney posted his artillery so as to command the lower bridge
at the Navy Yard.

About ten o'clock next day, the 24th, General Winder
"received intelligence that the enemy had turned the head
of his column toward Bladensburg," leaving now no further
doubt of his intention to strike for Washington. General
Winder at once ordered General Smith with the whole of
the troops to move immediately to that point, while he himself, "leaving the President and some of the heads of departments at his quarters, where they had been for an hour
or more," hastened forward and arrived at the Bladensburg
bridge about twelve o'clock, where he found Colonel Beall
had that moment passed his command, having just arrived
from Annapolis. Upon inquiry, he learned that General
Stansbury was on rising ground on the left of his line,
where he soon found him and Colonel Monroe, who had
been aiding General Stansbury to post his command.
Meantime, General Smith with his troops had arrived on
the ground, and "Commodore Barney's men and marines
were halted on the turnpike about a mile" nearer the city,
in the rear of the main force.

Of this final struggle, all the accounts seem to agree as to
the main facts. About one o'clock of the 24th, a column
of the enemy appeared in sight, moving up the Eastern
Branch parallel to the position of our troops. A galling
fire from the advanced artillery and Major Pinkney's battalion of Baltimore riflemen was immediately opened upon
them with terrible effect as they were descending the street
toward the bridge. Mr. Gleig, referring to this encounter,
says: "While we [the British troops] were moving along

the street, a continued fire was kept up, with some execution, from those guns which stood at the left of the road, but it was not till the bridge was covered with our people that the two-gun battery on the road itself began to play. Then, indeed, it also opened, and with tremendous effect; for at the first discharge almost an entire company was swept down." This caused the enemy to leave the street, and they crept down under cover of houses and trees, in loose order, so as not to expose themselves to risk from the shot; it was therefore only occasionally that an object presented at which the artillery could fire. In this sort of suspension the enemy began to throw rockets, and his light troops to accumulate down in the lower parts of the town, near the bridge, but principally covered from view by the houses, and soon began to press across the creek, everywhere fordable, and in most places lined with bushes and trees, which sufficiently concealed their movements. The advanced American riflemen fired half a dozen rounds, when they retreated twenty or thirty yards while the enemy's rockets, being at first aimed too high, were flying over their heads. The President and Attorney-General Richard Rush were briskly riding toward Bladensburg, just before the battle begun, without perceiving that the British were so near as to be almost within musket range, and they were in great danger of being captured. They turned into the orchard among our troops, where they met the Secretaries of State and War, and where the greatest consternation was manifest. Soon the rockets "received a more horizontal direction, and passed very close above the heads of Shultz's and Ragan's regiments, composing the entire left of Stansbury's line. A universal flight of these regiments was the consequence;" nor could they be rallied, with the exception of about forty men of Colonel Ragan's and a part of Captain Showers' command, who, although thus deserted, made a gallant but ineffectual stand. Colonel Ragan, in his great efforts to rally his men, was wounded and taken prisoner. Major William Pinkney, the eloquent lawyer and distinguished statesman, was also seriously wounded. The Fifth Baltimore regiment, under Lieutenant-Colonel Sterrett, being the left of General Stansbury's brigade, still stood its ground, and except for a moment, when part of them recoiled a few steps, remained firm until ordered to retreat. The reserve under General Smith, with the militia of Washington and Georgetown, the regulars, and some detachments of Maryland militia, flanked on their right by Commodore Barney and his men, and Colonel Beall, maintained the contest with great effect until overpowered by numbers.

Commodore Barney had taken position, with three 18-pounders, between General Stansbury's and General Smith's commands, not far from the noted duelling-ground, and, feebly supported by Colonel Beall's militia on a neighboring eminence, by a well-directed fire the enemy was held in suspense and suffered severely more than an hour, until the British General, Ross, advanced with fresh troops to the rescue. All accounts agree that the most stubborn resistance was made under Commodore Barney, whose brave marines fought "until the enemy reached nearly to the muzzles of the guns; nor did they retire until ordered to do so, after every hope of victory vanished." The British narrator, Gleig, says the sailors not only "served their guns with a quickness and precision which astonished their assailants, but they stood till some of them were actually bayoneted, with fuses in their hands; nor was it till their leader was wounded and taken, and they saw themselves deserted on all sides by the soldiers, that they quitted the field." The gallant commander, as he was preparing to withdraw from an untenable position, received a ball in the upper part of his thigh, which was never extracted, and of which wound he died several years afterward. Thirteen of his men were killed in action before the order for retreat was given.

This ended the battle. Although General Winder hoped to be able to rally his troops and make another stand near the Capitol, his forces were so disorganized and scattered that he found it impossible; and both the Secretary of War and Secretary of State concurred with him that "it was wise and proper to retire through Georgetown and take post in the rear of it, on the height, to collect his force." He "accordingly pursued this course, and halted at Tennallytown, two miles from Georgetown, on the Frederick road." General Armstrong suggested throwing our troops into the Capitol building, but this plan was at once dismissed as impracticable, "since it would have taken nearly the whole of them to have sufficiently filled the two wings, which would have left the enemy masters of every other part of the city."

Meantime the President and heads of departments had made their escape in advance of the retreating troops, and the utmost terror reigned in the cities of Washington and Georgetown. A letter in the Baltimore *Patriot* of August 26, from an eye-witness, says: "The President, who had been on horseback with the army the whole day, retired from the mortifying scene and left the city on horseback accompanied by General Mason and Mr. Carroll. At Georgetown, the President met his lady, she having left the city only half an hour before, having remained with great composure at the President's house until a message brought her the tidings that the British were within a few miles of the city, and that our army was retreating without any chance of being rallied so as to check their march. The President and Secretary of State went to Virginia with their families, the other officers of the government to Fredericktown, where the President intends to meet his secretaries next week." I may add that our soldiers did not tarry long at Tennallytown, but kept on to Montgomery Court House.

I am inclined to believe that the President met his carriage on reaching the city, as I found in the Richmond *Enquirer*, of August 27, a statement to the effect that two gentlemen, who passed through Washington on the day of the battle, when about to start from Pennsylvania Avenue for the Long Bridge, heard the cry "There goes the President!" and looking, they saw him driving in his carriage towards the President's house. They had come in a stage from Baltimore, and the first intimation they had of danger was on the road near Bladensburg, where they were met by shrieking women who reported that the enemy were approaching, and the stage came into the city in a roundabout way. Mr. Charles J. Ingersoll says: "After Barney's and Miller's defeat and retreat [Miller was captain of the marines], Ross attempted nothing further. One-fifth of his army was killed, wounded, or missing, for they deserted whenever they could, and the rest were so entirely overcome by their labors and exertions from early in the morning until four o'clock [when the contest, begun at one o'clock, ended] that they were incapable of further effort. Rest was indispensable to them, and as they lay on the ground it was Barney's opinion, freely expressed, that five hundred well-disciplined cavalry could have rode through and taken them all, almost without waking them from their heavy slumbers. Cockburn's jocular and contemptuous official reason for not pursuing was, that the victors were too weary and the vanquished too swift."

There is no doubt as to the exhausted condition of a large part of the forces of both armies. The weather was very hot; many of our troops had been without proper food and rest for three or four days; and a writer in the Baltimore *Patriot* states that the British soldiers "were so overpowered by their rapid march that many of them fell dead on the road. As they passed through Bladensburg their mouths were open, gasping for breath, and their officers were ordering them forward with their swords and spontoons. Twelve were buried in one field that had not a wound." The *Na-*

tional Intelligencer, of September 1, says: " The loss of the enemy before he regained his ships [on the 29th of August] probably exceeded a thousand men. He lost at least two hundred killed in the battle and by explosion, and three or four hundred wounded. Many died of fatigue, numbers were taken prisoners by the cavalry hanging on his rear, and not a few deserted." Our loss was twenty-six killed and fifty-one wounded.

On August 20, in a sharp encounter near the coast, the British lost one of their distinguished officers, Sir Peter Parker, commander of the ship *Menelaus*, besides thirteen soldiers killed and twenty-seven wounded. According to *Niles's Register*, he had said he " must have a frolic with the Yankees before he left them," and, in order to gratify this desire, he went out with a detachment to surprise Colonel Read, a veteran of the Revolutionary war, who, with one hundred and seventy men, was watching the enemy at Belair. They met in the night, and in the " frolic" which ensued Sir Peter received a mortal wound and expired in a few minutes. It is worthy of note, singular as it may seem, that, for this military exploit, he has a monument in Westminster Abbey.

Accounts vary slightly as regards the entry and reception of the enemy into the city. A correspondent wrote from Baltimore, September 1: " The British army was halted on the plain near the capital. General Ross, Admiral Cockburn, and some other officers, with about one hundred and fifty men, entered the city. On passing a house near the Capitol, in which Mr. Gallatin formerly resided, a shot from a window, said to be fired by a French barber, killed the horse on which General Ross rode. This imprudent act caused the destruction of the house and adjoining buildings." Mr. Chester Bailey, a United States mail contractor, purporting to be an eye-witness, wrote to *Poulson's Advertiser*, Philadelphia, " After the battle, a small party of the British entered the city about 9 P.M.; on passing the first

house (this was at the corner of Second Street East and the
old Baltimore turnpike, which had been occupied by Mr.
Gallatin when Secretary of the Treasury) a volley was fired
from the windows, which killed General Ross's horse under
him, one soldier, and wounded three others; the house was
immediately surrounded and some prisoners taken (a part
of them were negroes) and the house set on fire." Ingersoll says: "Having given his exhausted soldiers some indispensable repose, Ross, with Cockburn, attended by a
body guard of two hundred bayonets, and saluted by the
fulminations from the Navy Yard, rode slowly into the
wilderness city, whose population was a little over eight
thousand, scattered over large spaces, and of whom almost
every male was then absent, either in arms, some distant
hiding-place, or a few keeping close in their dwellings.
Many passed the night in huts and corn fields around the
town. The first considerable dwelling the enemy was to
pass had been Mr. Gallatin's residence, the house of. Mrs.
Sewell, some hundred yards from the Capitol. From behind the side wall of that house, as is supposed, at all events
from or near to it, a solitary musket, fired by some excited,
and perhaps intoxicated person, believed to be a well-known
Irish barber, but never ascertained who was the perpetrator, no doubt aimed at General Ross, killed the bay mare he
rode."

Mr. Gleig said it was General Ross's intention only "to
lay the city under contribution, and return quietly to the
shipping," and that therefore "he did not march the troops
immediately to the city, but halted them upon a plain in its
immediate vicinity, whilst a flag of truce was sent in with
terms. But whatever his proposal might have been, it was
not so much as heard, for scarcely had the party bearing
the flag entered the street than they were fired upon from
the windows of one of the houses, and the horse of the
General himself, who accompanied them, killed. You will
easily believe that conduct so unjustifiable, so direct a

breach of the law of nations, roused the indignation of every individual, from the General himself down to the private soldier. All thoughts of accommodation were instantly laid aside; the troops advanced forthwith into the town, and having put to the sword all who were found in the house from which the shots were fired, and reduced it to ashes, they proceeded, without a moment's delay, to burn and destroy everything in the most distant degree connected with the Government."

It is proper to state here that this British account of an intention to spare the city is not credited, as Admiral Cockburn, Commander-in-chief of the British fleet, had, under date of August 18, addressed a letter to Secretary Monroe, informing him that he had received instructions from his government "to destroy and lay waste such towns and districts on the coast as may be found assailable," in retaliation for alleged depredations of our troops in Upper Canada. The Admiral, however, knew, or should have known, that full reparation had been made to the satisfaction of the Governor of that province in the preceding February, and he took the precaution to retain his threatening letter until ten days after the date before sending it off, so that it did not reach its destination until August 31, a week after the burning of the Capitol and other Government buildings. While the enemy were entering the city, the Navy Yard was being destroyed by order of the Secretary of the Navy, and the bridge over the Eastern Branch there was also blown up,—most unnecessarily, as it was considered, by United States engineers.

The first public building set on fire by the British was the Capitol. The British column continued its march to the eastern front of that edifice, then deployed into line, and directing a volley of musketry at it, took formal possession in the name of their king. It is a singular and interesting historical fact, that the British lieutenant who forced the Capitol, by breaking down one or more of its doors, was afterwards for many years a member of Parliament. He won great distinction in the army, serving in India, Portugal, and Spain, before he was sent to America, where he took part in the attacks on Washington and Baltimore, and was wounded before New Orleans. He served under Wellington, both in the Peninsular war and at Waterloo. He was noted for volunteering for storming parties. In 1835, he commanded a British auxiliary legion of ten thousand men in aid of the Queen of Spain against Don Carlos; was a lieutenant-general in the Crimean war, "and for his services at the Alma and Inkerman he received the thanks of Parliament, and the grand cross of the Bath, and was made a grand officer of the Legion of Honor." This was Sir De Lacy Evans, who was born in 1787 and died in 1870.

Finding that the Capitol was partially fire-proof, it was at first decided to blow it up with gunpowder, but, this determination being announced to the citizens nearest the building, their "expostulations, together with the entreaties of the ladies, induced the general to order it to be set fire to in every vulnerable point, and it was soon enveloped in flames." Mr. Ingersoll states that it was among the stories told when Congress met three weeks afterwards, "that the Admiral (Cockburn), in a strain of coarse levity, mounting the Speaker's chair, put the question, 'Shall this harbor of Yankee democracy be burned? All for it will say, Aye;' to which loud cries of assent being vociferated, he reversed the question, pronounced it carried unanimously, and the mock resolution was executed by rockets and other combustibles applied to the chairs and furniture (as well as library books and papers) heaped up in the centre and fired wherever there was a fit place. The temporary wooden structure connecting the two wings readily kindled. Doors, chairs, the consumable parts, the library and its contents in an upper room of the Senate wing, everything that would take fire, soon disappeared in sheets of flame, illuminating and consternating the environs for thirty miles around, whence the conflagration was visible. In a room adjoining the Senate chamber portraits of the King and Queen of France, Louis the XVI. and his wife, were cut from the frames, by whom has never appeared. The frames were scorched, but not burned." Some parts of the building, being fire-proof, escaped the flames, notably the vestibule of the Supreme Court Law Library, where some of the columns are ornamented with a unique and beautiful American order of architecture, representing Indian corn in the ear.

The Capitol, with its library and most of its public records, being thus destroyed, the troops, headed by Ross and Cockburn, and conducted by a former resident (who was soon after arrested as a traitor), marched along Pennsylvania Avenue, "without beat of drum or other martial sound than their ponderous tramp," and set fire to the President's house and Treasury building. Mr. Gleig states that "when this detachment, sent out to destroy Mr. Madison's house, entered his dining parlor, they found a dinner-table spread and covers laid for forty guests. Several kinds of wine in handsome cut-glass decanters were cooling on the sideboard; plate-holders stood by the fire-place filled with dishes and plates; knives, forks, and spoons were arranged for immediate use; in short, everything was ready for the entertainment of a ceremonious party." They sat down to this dinner, he says, "not indeed in the most orderly manner, but with countenances which would not have disgraced a party of aldermen at a civic feast; and having satisfied their appetites and partaken pretty freely of the wines, they finished by setting fire to the house which had so liberally entertained them." This grand dinner was no doubt a myth. The story is improbable for various reasons. In the first place, the President had been with the army in the field much of the time, for the two or three days the greatest alarm and confusion prevailed among the inhabitants

remaining in the city, and we have the testimony of the
President's porter, not only that there was no preparation
for dinner or eating beyond a small quantity of meat in the
kitchen, but if there had been food, that the British would
not have eaten it, such was their fear of poison. Mr.
Bailey, before cited, however, in his account, says the
troops entered and took some powder and collected some
papers, and soon an explosion was heard and the house
was seen on fire. The Treasury Office, he adds, was also
soon on fire; the President's house being first despoiled of
a few objects of curiosity—some pictures and books from
Mr. Madison's library, and a parcel of the pencil notes
received by Mrs. Madison from her husband while he was
with the troops. Before leaving the house she had seen to
the removal of many valuable articles, including the full-
length portrait of Washington, still preserved in the White
House. It has been often said that, in order to save this
portrait, she cut it from the frame, which it appears she
was ready, knife in hand, to do, but fortunately those
assisting succeeded in detaching it from the gilt frame and
preserving it intact on the inner wooden frame. She is
likewise credited with having saved the original Declaration of Independence.

The Hon. J. H. B. Latrobe, President of the Maryland
Historical Society, kindly placed in my hands an interesting
letter written to his mother by Mrs. Madison, December 3,
1814, giving a graphic account of her escape from the
White House. As an excuse for delay, she says that she
wrote a long letter, then in her drawer unfinished and out
of date, her husband having been taken sick before she had
described all her adventures, and continued indisposed so
long that she lost the thread of her story and became
ashamed of her egotism. She continues:

" Two hours before the enemy entered the city, I left the house where
Mr. Latrobe's elegant taste had been so justly admired, and where you
and I had so often wandered together, and on that *very day* I sent out the

silver (nearly all)—the velvet curtains and General Washington's picture, the cabinet papers, a few books, and the small clock—left everything else belonging to the publick, our own valuable stores of every description, a part of my clothes, and all my servants' clothes, &c., &c., in short, it would fatigue you to read the list of *my* losses, or an account of the general *dismay*, or *particular* distresses of your acquaintance. Mrs. Hunter and Mrs. Thompson were the only ladies who stood their ground. I confess that I was so unfeminine as to be free from fear, and willing to remain in the *Castle*. If I could have had a cannon through every window, but, alas! those who should have placed them there, fled before me, and my whole heart mourned for my country! I remained nearly three days out of town, but I cannot tell you what I felt on re-entering it—such destruction—such confusion! The fleet full in view and in the act of robbing Alexandria! The citizens expecting *another visit*—and at night the rockets were seen flying near us !"

In a letter to his wife, October 14, 1814, William Wirt wrote :

"I went to look at the ruins of the President's house. The rooms which you saw so richly furnished, exhibited nothing but unroofed naked walls, cracked, defaced, and blackened with fire. I cannot tell you what I felt as I walked amongst them. . . . From this mournful monument of American imbecility and improvidence, and of British atrocity, I went to the lobby of the House of Representatives, a miserable little narrow box, in which I was crowded and suffocated for about three hours, in order to see and hear the wise men of the nation. They are no great things. . . . I called on the President. He looks miserably shattered and woe-begone. In short, he looked heart-broken. His mind is full of the New England sedition."

Besides his excellent library, Mr. Madison lost a large amount of other private property, estimated at twelve thousand dollars. Whilst these buildings were blazing, eleven of the British officers, including Ross and Cockburn, were taking a supper at Mrs. Suter's boarding-house near by, which General Ross had ordered before applying the torch, insisting against the good woman's protest that he preferred her house to McLeod's tavern across the way "because [he said] he had some acquaintance with her, mentioning several familiar circumstances," showing that he had been there, no doubt as a spy, before the battle. The woman who waited at the table recognized two of the party, one of them, wretchedly dressed, pretending to be a deserter from the British army, having a few days before called at the house and begged for something to eat. Another had also been there previously, and was acquainted with the localities. Mr. Ingersoll, who received his information from the landlady herself, asserts that when the party came for supper, one of them, dressed in blue and mounted on a mule, rode partly through the low front door into the house, introducing himself as the much-abused Admiral Cockburn. At table he blew out the candles, saying he preferred the light of the burning palace and Treasury, whose conflagration hard by illuminated the room. The following appeared in the *Intelligencer* a few days afterwards:

" *Look out for spies!* It is an impression now very general that the fall of this city may be ascribed to the facility with which spies and traitors carried on their operations even within a week preceding the capture by the enemy. With a view to warn our neighbors against the evil into which it appears our citizens fell, we shall state a singular fact, which is susceptible of legal proof. The lady of a house where the British officers supped on the evening they entered the city, recognized among them a person who had been at her house, and even called on Mrs. Madison in the President's house (as the person declared) in the disguise of a distressed woman, *on the Saturday preceding the capture!* This is a fact which may be relied on. The number and names of all the landlady's family, then absent, were also known to this officer, with whom were General Ross and Cockburn, the incendiary."

After destroying the Capitol, President's house, and Treasury building, the British retired for the night to their main army in camp on Capitol Hill. The edifice of the State and War Departments and the building occupied by the Patent and General Post Office, on the present site of the latter department, being still unharmed, they sallied out again on the morning of the 25th, with orders to commit them also to the flames, together with the printing office of the *Intelligencer*. On their way up the avenue they

were confronted by a young man on horseback, whose name
was Lewis, "claiming relationship to General Washington," who discharged a pistol at them, when he was instantly shot down. It was said he thought thus to avenge
himself for having been impressed on a British ship and
compelled to fight against his own country. The column
kept on and the State and War Department building was
soon in ashes, but the Patent Office was spared through the
earnest intercession of its chief, Dr. William Thornton,
Rev. O. B. Brown, and other citizens, who urged that it
would be a shame and disgrace to burn the valuable models
and drawings deposited there, which would be useful to all
mankind. Thus the Post Office, too, was saved. Coming
to the office of the *Intelligencer*, which was obnoxious to
British vengeance on account of its bold denunciation of
British barbarities in the destruction and pillage of private
property on the coast and elsewhere, the incendiary torch
was about to be applied to that building, when, seeing that
its conflagration would involve the destruction of several
other private buildings adjacent thereto, the officer in
charge was prevailed on to spare it, taking care, however,
to destroy the editor's library and the presses and other
printing materials of the establishment. "Be sure," said
Cockburn, "that all the C's are destroyed, so that the ras-
cals can have no further means of abusing my name as they
have done. I'll punish Madison's man Joe (Gales) as I have
his master Jim."

While this devastation was going on, another detachment
of troops, both soldiers and sailors, was sent to complete
the destruction at the Navy Yard and Arsenal, which had
been partially destroyed by order of the Secretary of the
Navy, with one or more war ships lying in the river.
Having, as they thought, accomplished their vandal work,
among other things mutilating the Naval Monument, afterwards removed to the basin at the west front of the Capitol,
and thence, a few years ago, to Annapolis, Mr. Ingersoll

22

states that one of the men, as they were about leaving
Greenleaf's Point, where the Arsenal was located, "pitched
his torch, as a safe place for extinguishment," into a dry
well where large quantities of gunpowder, shells, and other
munitions of war had been concealed, when, "with a terrible
crash, the mine instantly exploded, flinging missiles of death
and mutilation wide around, killing and cruelly wounding
near a hundred of the surrounding destroyers." Mr. Edward Simms, of Washington, a well-preserved gentleman
of ninety years, who was officially mentioned for his
bravery at the battle of Bladensburg, told me, a few weeks
before his death, which occurred on the 14th of February,
1884, that this explosion was caused, not by the throwing
of a torch into the well, but from the ignition of a train
of powder which had fallen from the kegs in their removal
to the well. This seems more probable, since the incendi-
aries were sent to burn and not to extinguish. An officer
of the British ship *Regulus*, writing home at the time, and
giving an account of this disaster, states the number killed
as "about twelve, and wounded about thirty more, most
of them in a dreadful manner." He says he had the good
fortune to escape with whole skin and bones, but somewhat
bruised, adding, "the groans of the people, almost buried
in the earth, or with legs and arms broke, and the sight of
pieces of bodies lying about, was a thousand times more
distressing than the loss we met with in the field the day
before." Major Williams thinks the British loss was un-
derstated by this officer.

On the night of the 24th, or following day, the Long
Bridge over the Potomac was rendered impassable by the
burning or blowing up of both ends—the Washington end
by the British, and that on the Virginia side by a corporal
in charge of it, perceiving, as he thought, a body of the
enemy about to cross from the city; whilst, on the other
hand, the British were equally panic-stricken under the
apprehension that our troops, to the number, as they sup-

posed, of twelve thousand or more, were on their way from the other side to recapture the city. That night a complete Bull-Run panic reigned on both sides. "Early in the evening," says a British officer who was present, "the different British corps had been directed, in a whisper, to make ready for falling back as soon as darkness should set in. From the men, however, the thing was kept profoundly secret," although they were given to understand that an important movement was about to take place, and hints were thrown out to induce the expectation of a further advance instead of a retreat, which was carried out with all the secrecy and silence possible before morning. While the ruthless invaders were thus stealing away in alarm on account of the non-arrival of their fleet at Alexandria, as expected, and what they had erroneously supposed was a greatly augmented force of American troops ready to swoop down upon them from Georgetown Heights, the President and heads of departments, with Mrs. Madison, having crossed over into Virginia the evening before, had made their way to the point of rendezvous—a tavern sixteen miles from Georgetown, where they were to spend the night. At midnight they were startled by a report that the British were coming; and it had been given out that it was their purpose, if possible, to capture the President and take him to London. Telling his wife to disguise herself, use another carriage than her own, and fly still further, the President left "his hiding-place in the inn to pass the rest of that moist and wretched night in a hovel in the woods." Early next day tidings reached them that the British had withdrawn, and all now turned their steps towards the city.

When Mrs. Madison, still in her disguise, with only one attendant, arrived at Long Bridge, burned at both ends, Colonel Fenwick, in command there, and "busy in transporting munitions of war over the Potomac in the only boat left at his disposal, peremptorily refused to let any unknown woman cross in the boat with her carriage." She sent for him, and, on making herself known confidentially, she "was driven in her carriage into the frail boat, which bore her homewards," and she stopped at her sister's, Mrs. Cutts's house, which was owned and occupied many years, and to the time of his death, by ex-President John Quincy Adams, on F Street, one square from the Treasury Department. The President and his secretaries returned by way of Georgetown, and the government was soon again set on foot. After boarding at Mrs. Cutts's a few weeks, the President and family resumed housekeeping in the Ogle Tayloe mansion, still standing at the corner of Eighteenth Street and New York Avenue, where they passed the winter. The special session of Congress, called for the 19th of September, was held in the Patent Office.

The enemy did not stop to bury their dead, and they left many of their wounded behind. Philip Frenau thus describes their arrival and exit:

> " A veteran host by veterans led,
> With Ross and Cockburn at their head,
> They came—they saw—they burned—and fled !"

A part of their fleet pushed up the river to Alexandria, August 28, when that city at once capitulated on humiliating terms. Captain Gordon, the British officer in command, states that Fort Washington was abandoned and the magazine blown up by the United States garrison without firing a gun, leaving the way clear for his ships to reach Alexandria, and that he took from there seventy-one vessels loaded with flour, tobacco, cotton, wine, sugar, and other merchandise of value. With comparatively little damage, in spite of all that could be done to oppose them by shore batteries, fire-ships, and sharp-shooters, the enemy escaped with their booty. Their next move was against Baltimore, where, at the battle of North Point, September 12, Admiral Cockburn officially reported, " General Ross, in the first desultory skirmish, received a musket-ball through his

arm into his breast, which proved fatal to him on his way
to the water-side for re-embarkation." Thus fell the British
general who led the attack on Washington, and who, at a
dinner there, August 25, gave as a toast, "Peace with
America—war with Madison."

As will have been observed, I have introduced several
extracts from the British narrative of Mr. George R. Gleig;
and it may be interesting to state that some time after I had
prepared this sketch, I learned incidentally that he was still
alive, and, at the age of ninety-one years, the Chaplain-
General of the British army. Thinking he might favor me
with some reminiscences of the British invasion and occu-
pancy of Washington, I addressed him on the subject, and
have received two letters from him in reply, one dated
April 24 and the other June 4, 1884.

In the first he writes:

"You ask me for anecdotes connected with the battle of Bladensburg
and the capture of Washington. I could give you many were we face
to face. On paper I must confine myself to such as are least likely to
overtax your patience.

"1. Nothing could exceed the kindness of the inhabitants of Bladensburg to our wounded, both when thrust upon them and after we had
returned to our ships. In the same room with Colonel Thornton lay
your gallant Commodore Barney, both grievously hurt. A friendship
was at once struck up between them, which lasted through their lives.
The commodore told Thornton the following story: 'I commanded a
battery of artillery and saw one of your men deliberately pile up some
stones, then lie down behind them and take aim. "Oh," said I, to myself, "you are a crack shot, I suppose, but I'll balk you," which I did,
for I pointed one of our guns at him myself, and when the smoke cleared
away his parapet was in ruins, and himself nowhere. I hope he ran
away.'

"2. When your people gave way, one brave fellow tried to stop them
by waving the flag he carried and taking a few steps to the front. But it
is not easy to rally raw troops as yours were, and only a few men answered
to his call. One I well remember, for he fired thrice at me, and wore a
black coat. We were in loose skirmishing order, and, being very anxious
to capture the color, I ran directly towards the bearer. Before I could
reach him, he dropped the color, evidently having received a wound, and

my friend with the black coat moved off also, though not till with his third shot he gave me a scratch in the thigh. I got the color, which now hangs in the chapel of Chelsea Hospital. My wound, though slight, made me stiff, and I was glad to enter Washington on horseback.

"3. Two adventures befell me there. I was limping past a house in a street near the Capitol, when a window was opened and a negro woman invited me to enter. The family had quitted the town, and the servants offered me all manner of good things. I was amused, and told them I wanted nothing except a clean shirt, having only one which I had worn since the 19th. The clean shirt was immediately produced, which I put on, leaving mine to replace it.

"4. On the 25th a hurricane fell on the city, which unroofed houses and upset our three-pounder guns. It upset me also. It fairly lifted me out of the saddle, and the horse which I had been riding I never saw again. This is surely gossip enough."

In my letter of grateful acknowledgment, I inquired of Mr. Gleig respecting the conflicting accounts of the fatal explosion at the arsenal and of the alleged flag of truce. This is his reply:

"I really do not know what was the cause of the explosion to which you refer. The explosion itself I perfectly recollect; but, not being near the spot where it occurred, I have nothing more to revert to respecting its cause than the rumors of the camp. Both the accounts which you give to me were circulated among us. Which is the correct one, if either, I cannot tell. I have no doubt you are right as regards the shots fired after General Ross and Admiral Cockburn entered Washington. It was dark when they entered the town, and as the American army had, I believe, evacuated the place, the men [who] fired on the general would not understand either the nature of the roll of the drum, which demands a parley, or a white flag, if it were shown. With respect to the other point, bearing on Ross's instructions, the facts are these: Twenty-three American soldiers engaged in the invasion of Canada were recognized, when taken prisoners, as deserters from the British army. They were imprisoned preparatory to trial; whereupon General Dearborn immediately imprisoned as many British prisoners, and warned the English authorities that life would go for life. Forthwith forty-six more Americans, officers and non-commissioned officers, were put in arrest as guarantees for the lives of the British prisoners. On neither side were lives taken, but the incident embittered the feeling of hostility which, on the American side, vented itself in the burning of some Canadian villages during the winter, and, on the side of England, called forth the stern order to destroy American towns on the coast. Ross's despatch was not a happy one. He seems to have been hurried by indignation into sanctioning proceedings which met with no approval in London; indeed, so little was our vandalism approved that the government withheld from him the honors which he would have otherwise received after a brilliant though short campaign."

The enemy succeeded not only in destroying property valued at two million dollars, but by unparalleled barbarity in inflicting upon their country a stigma, the record of which there is not an Englishman of to-day who would not rejoice to see erased from the pages of history. Our own countrymen, too, I am inclined to believe, would be willing to see this done, provided the record and recollection of the not over-creditable defence of the capital could also at the same time be forever blotted out.

CHAPTER XI.

THE BLADENSBURG RACES.

EDITOR OF MAGAZINE OF AMERICAN HISTORY:

I wish I had known of an amusing production, which has unexpectedly come into my hands, touching "The Bladensburg Races," since your contributor, Colonel Norton, wrote me asking for some appropriate accompaniment to the burlesque British engraving of the "Burning of Washington," in your December issue. This is a ballad of sixty-eight stanzas, somewhat after the style of "John Gilpin's Ride." It opens in this wise:

> "James Madison a soldier was,
>   Of courage and renown,
> And *Generalissimo* was he
>   Of famous Washington.

> "Quoth Madison unto his spouse,
>   'Though frighted we have been
> These two last tedious weeks, yet we
>   No enemy have seen.

> " ' To-morrow is the twenty-fourth,
>   And much indeed I fear
>   That then, or on the following day,
>   That Cockburn will be here.'

> " ' To-morrow, then,' quoth she, ' we'll fly
>   As fast as we can pour
>   Northward unto Montgomery,
>   All in our coach and four.

> " ' My sister Cutts, and Cutts and I,
>   And Cutts's children three,
>   Will fill the coach; so you must ride
>   On horseback after we.'

> " He soon replied, ' I do admire
>   Of humankind but one,
>   And you are she, my *Dolly* dear;
>   Therefore it shall be done.' "

The " Generalissimo" thereupon prepares for the trip—
saying his " trusty steed the Griffin bold" would " safely
bear him through"—that he, with the members of his Cabinet, " would start as though for Bladensburg," but when
they had cleared the town they would put " for Montgomery, and o'ertake the coach at early noon." This seemed
greatly to please " Mistress Dolly," on whose ruddy cheek
he pressed a kiss.

> " O'erjoyed was he to find,
>   Though bent on running off, she'd still
>   His *honor* in her mind."

Fearing the " mob should grumble loud," the coach was
not allowed to start from the White House; but " six
precious souls, and all agog," entered it " at brother
Cutts's."

> " Smack went the whip, 'round went the wheels;
>   Were never folks so glad:
>   The dust did rise beneath the coach,
>   As though the dust were mad."

The "General" mounted to follow, when, "looking back," he "saw his Cabinet behind."

> "'Monroe, you're late!' quoth Madison,
> ''Tis late indeed, I fear,
> For us to steer for Bladensburg;
> The British are so near.'"

And now, as

> "The Cabinet on horseback sat,"

they "reasoned high," as to whether they should set out for the camp,

> "Or northward straight should fly."

Before the council ended "Cuffee screamed, 'De Shappohat and sword'" of the General "'be leave behind,'" when he was directed to bring them at once. This caused a little delay, but the "gallant Four"—Madison, Monroe, Armstrong, and Rush (the "Boatswain," Secretary of the Navy, was detained)—soon reached the "country road," when they moved on rapidly, not a little accelerated by the "loud blast of a bugle-horn," which disturbed "our hero," the General, "it scared his horse so."

> "Away went he, and after him
> Our heroes rode apace;
> They little dreamt, when they set out,
> Of running such a race."

With some mishaps and much trepidation, they at length all "came unto the spot where Winder's forces lay," when they anxiously inquired:

> "'Where are the British? Winder, where?
> And Cockburn, where is he?—
> D'ye think your men will fight, or run,
> When they the British see?'"

Now, telling Armstrong and Rush to "stay here in camp," the "General," with Monroe as his "aid," said he would return—adding:

> " ' And, Winder, do not fire your guns,
>   Nor let your trumpets play,
>   Till we are out of sight—forsooth,
>   My horse will run away.' "

They flew toward Montgomery, the " General:"

> " Then, speaking to his horse, he said,
>   ' I am in haste to dine:
>   'Twas for *your* pleasure I came here;
>   You shall go back for mine.'

> " Now, at Montgomery, his wife
>   Out of the window spied
>   Her gallant husband, wond'ring much
>   To see how he did ride.

> " ' Stop, stop! your Highness, here's the house!'
>   They all at once did roar;
> " ' Here, at Montgom'ry, you're as safe
>   As ten miles off, or more.'

> " ' Stop him, Monroe! here's sister Cutts,
>   The girls, and Cutts, and I;
>   The dinner's cold, and we are tir'd!'
>   Monroe says, ' So am I.' "

But the distant cannonade so frightened the steeds that " neither horse nor James a whit inclined to tarry there," and, with Monroe, the " General" kept on until they finally brought up at Frederick, much to the astonishment of everybody on the road—the women thinking " our General rode express:"

> " And so he did; for he first bore
>   The news to Frederick-town;
>   Nor stopt from where he first got up,
>   Till he again got down.

> " Now, long live Madison, the brave!
>   And Armstrong, long live he!
>   And Rush. and Cutts, Monroe and Jones!
>   And Dolly, long live she!

"And when, their country's cause at stake,
    Our General and Monroe
Next take the field, to lead our troops
    Against th' invading foe;

"But fly their posts—ere the first gun
    Has echo'd o'er the wave,
Stop! stop! Potomac! stop thy course!
    Nor pass MOUNT VERNON'S GRAVE!"

The whole production reveals an undercurrent of disrespect and bitterness—especially towards Madison—which leads to the supposition that the verses were written very soon after the battle. They were printed in 1816, but the author of them, so far as I am aware, is unknown.

WASHINGTON, December 2, 1885.

CHAPTER XII.

LETTER FROM MR. GEORGE R. GLEIG, CHAPLAIN-GENERAL OF THE BRITISH ARMY, CONCERNING THE BATTLE OF BLADENSBURG, IN WHICH MR. GLEIG WAS A PARTICIPANT—NOTE OF ANSWER TO HIM.

BYLANDS, WINCHFIELD, 11th Nov., 1885.

THE HON. HORATIO KING:

MY DEAR SIR,—I am very much obliged to you for sending me a copy of the *Magazine of American History,* which contains your interesting paper on the "Battle of Bladensburg and the Capture of Washington." You describe well the state of feeling among the inhabitants of the city, and are doubtless more correct than one of the invading force could be as to the strength of the defending troops brought into the field. But your authorities do us some injustice when they speak of large desertions from our ranks and acts of pillage by our men. We did not lose a single man by desertion. And never, perhaps, was so little damage done to the persons and property of the peaceable inhabitants by any hostile army on its march to or from the capital. You know what my opinions are of the wanton destruction to public buildings in Washington itself. They were those of the home Government at the time, and are entertained now by all classes. But in the details related by you there are many ludicrous mistakes. I was one of the battalion which first took up a position on the high ground overlooking the capital, and I can vouch for it that not a mortal shot was fired either before or after the conflagration took place. Of the dinner in the President's House, I certainly did not partake; but I was told by more than one of the officers who professed to have been present at it, that it was a reality and not a myth. So, likewise, in regard to our numbers, there can be no mistake. We landed four battalions of the line and one of marines, 3600 bayonets, which the sailors who dragged our 3-pounder guns, and the fifty artillerymen who worked them, raised to about 4000 in all. Writing as I did without reference to official documents, I much overrated our loss in battle, which, including several deaths by sunstroke, amounted to a little over 300, not 500. So difficult is it to be quite exact in writing history when historians of different nationalities undertake to describe events, each as it had represented itself to his own idiosyncrasy.

Born in 1796, I shall complete my ninetieth year on the 20th of April next, if I live so long.

Let me add that, while it lasted, the musketry fire of your people at Bladensburg was as sharp as any which I ever encountered from the French.

Once more thanking you for giving me the pleasure of reading your account of our operations, in which I took part upwards of seventy years ago, believe me,

Very sincerely yours,
G. R. GLEIG.

[NOTE.—Mr. Charles J. Ingersoll, author of an "Historical Sketch" of the war, is the authority for stating that the British troops fired at the Capitol before entering and taking possession of it. He says, "Drawing up their column on the east of the building, after a short consideration whether it should be exploded by gunpowder or consumed by fire, the latter was resolved upon by the enemy, as was believed, lest the blowing up should injure adjacent dwellings. The troops were ordered to fire a volley into the windows, after which the commanders let their followers into the interior." This statement is reiterated by a gentleman from Bladensburg, vouched for as reliable by Mr. Ingersoll, and "confirmed by the important testimony of a highly respectable English officer." This Bladensburg gentleman, "with all the recollections [Ingersoll says] of the very spot," gives the following account of the firing on General Ross. He says that after Commodore Barney was wounded and captured, "his sailors and marines, retreating reluctantly, were burning with anxiety to have another brush with the enemy, but were marched off by the officers, their rear being closely followed by the British troops until they entered the suburbs of Washington, when a party of the sailors entered a three-story brick dwelling-house belonging to Robert Sewell, and awaited the near approach of the enemy's column, led by General Ross in person, when they fired a volley which killed or disabled the horse upon which the general was mounted. The sailors then retreated by the rear of the building, and the British set fire to and destroyed the house." With respect to the elaborate dinner said to have been set out for the President and invited guests at the White House, Ingersoll says, "Mr. John Sousa, Mr. Madison's porter, a respectable Frenchman, who still (in 1849) survives, pronounces all this account of food a fable."

The private houses and the stores pillaged, according to Ingersoll, were those of Messrs. Spriggs, Boon, Burch,

Long, Rapine, Watterson, McCormick, Caldwell, Elliott, B. and C. Burns, Ricks, Crampton, and General Washington; and the dwellings burnt were those of Messrs. Sewell, Ball, Frost, Phillips, Tomlinson, and Mrs. Hamilton, including the large hotel belonging to David Carroll, of Duddington & Co. In his official report, Admiral Cockburn boastingly said, "In short, sir, I do not believe a vestige of public property or store of any kind which could be converted to the use of the Government, escaped destruction."

H. K.]

CHAPTER XIII.

THE PENALTY ENVELOPES: A LITTLE INSIDE HISTORY REGARDING THEIR INTRODUCTION.

It would require several pages to present a detailed account of my years of vexatious, gratuitous labor in obtaining the introduction of the official "penalty envelope;" but the following article which I furnished to the Boston *Herald* of July 12, 1894, must suffice for the present occasion:

In the *Herald* of the 9th inst., there is what appears to be a valuable historical account of United States postage-stamps, but it doubtless contains some errors, one of which I respectfully ask sufficient space to point out, since something of my own action ten years and over after I left the post-office department is connected with it. The writer states:

"In order to put a stop to abuses of the franking privilege, official stamps were provided in 1873 for each of the executive departments of the government for use on official matter sent through the mails. They were of about the same denominations as the ordinary stamps for the use of the public. After a few years' trial they were gradually abandoned, and in their place the post-office department issued official penalty envelopes for official business. The last of the official stamps, which turned out to be a still greater source of abuse than the old franking practice, came to pass in 1879."

The first act authorizing the use of the penalty envelope bears date March 4, 1877, when it went into effect at once. Its use would have been universal in the executive departments but for a decision of the Attorney-General that, Congress having made an appropriation for departmental postage-stamps at the same time, it was its intention that both the penalty envelopes and stamps might be used. It was natural for the third assistant postmaster-general, the financial officer of the department, to ask an appropriation for the stamps then in use, as it was not known whether the penalty envelope would be authorized or not; but, when the question arose, Senator Hamlin, chairman of the committee on post-offices and post-roads, who had requested me to submit my device to the committee (for I may be allowed, as I have the right in justice to myself, to say it was my device), wrote to me from his home in Bangor, saying: "You and I know it was the purpose of the law that the penalty envelope should take the place of the departmental stamps." However, he advised that I should seek for remedy by an amended bill, which I prepared, with various improvements, taking care to add a clause, as I did in the first bill, repealing the stamp act, and this was presented at the next session of Congress. When it came finally to pass, on March 4, 1879, as bad luck would have it, it was tacked on to the general post-office appropriation bill, as the first had been, leaving out the repealing clause. Meantime the third assistant continued to ask for the stamp appropriation, in defiance of the purpose and desire to get rid of the stamps, which the adjutant-general and commissioner of internal revenue both, I remember, denounced as an intolerable nuisance; and so both systems were kept up, to the annoyance of all the departments, except the post-office, where the penalty envelope was universally used from the passage of the first act.

To make a long story short, I drew a third bill and "lobbied" for it, *pro bono publico*, both through the press and in Congress, until at length, in spite of the persistent opposition of the third assistant postmaster-general, who, strange to say, was allowed to have his own way in the matter, the amended act became a law, broader in its scope than originally intended, and forbidding the further use of the departmental stamps on July 5, 1884. Thereupon the stamps in enormous quantities, mostly in the hands of the contractors, were ordered to be destroyed.

Now, I do not hesitate to say that, had the first penalty envelope act been allowed, as it was intended, entirely to supplant the official stamps, the government, in the seven years or more I literally fought for this reform, might have saved in clerk hire, the prevention of fraud, etc., thousands upon thousands of dollars.

CHAPTER XIV.

AN HOUR WITH DANIEL WEBSTER.

EVERYTHING relating to Daniel Webster is of interest, from his boyhood to the close of his life, October 24, 1852, at the age of threescore years and ten. The autobiography of his early life plainly shows "the stuff he was made of," exhibiting, as it does, the essential features of the best New England character. In the first school he attended, only reading and writing were taught, and as to these, he says, "the first I generally could perform better than the teacher, and the last a good master could hardly instruct me in; writing was so laborious, irksome, and repulsive an occupation to me always. My masters used to tell me that they feared, after all, my fingers were destined for the ploughtail."

In May, 1796, young Webster was placed in Phillips Academy, at Exeter, New Hampshire, where his instructors were Mr. Thacher, afterward judge of the municipal court of Boston, and Nicholas Emery, subsequently a distinguished counsellor and judge of the supreme court, well known to the writer, at Portland. Says Mr. Webster: "I am proud to call them both masters. I believe I made tolerable progress in most branches which I attended to, while in school; but there was one thing I could not do. I could not make a declamation; I could not speak before the school. The kind and excellent Buckminster [his Latin teacher] sought, especially, to persuade me to perform the exercises of declamation, like other boys, but I could not do it. Many a piece did I commit to memory and recite, and rehearse, in my own room, over and over again; yet when the day came, when the school collected to hear declamations, when my name was called, and I saw all eyes turned to my seat, I could not raise myself from it. Sometimes the instructors frowned, sometimes they smiled. Mr. Buckminster always pressed and entreated, most winningly, that I would venture; but I could never command sufficient resolution. When the occasion was over, I went home and wept bitter tears of mortification."

His instructors well knew how greatly success in life often depends on the ability to give free utterance to one's sentiments, without embarrassment, before a public assembly; and hence their urgency. What but that invaluable talent, or acquisition, assures the preference to many over their associates, who, in point of general information, are in all respects their equals if not superiors, but whose speeches, when called for, lie hidden, as it were, and only come to the mind with facility and triumphant effect when they are safe from observation,—oftener than otherwise, in bed.

In 1802, at twenty years of age, Mr. Webster went to Fryeburg, Maine, " to keep school," at the rate of three hundred and fifty dollars per annum. This (he says) was no small thing, for "I compared it not with what might be before me, but what was actually behind me. It was better, certainly, than following the plough." At an earlier date, he says: "I was fond of poetry. By far the greater part of Watts's psalms and hymns I could repeat at ten or twelve years of age. I am sure no other sacred poetry will ever appear to me so affecting and devout." About the same time, when his father brought home a copy of Pope's "Essay on Man," he says, "I took it and very soon could repeat it from beginning to end."

Webster was not only fond of poetry, as evinced by his poetic quotations in correspondence and speeches, but he sometimes courted the muses, his poetical inspirations not infrequently appearing in rhyme as well as in his prose productions. One of his earlier poems was addressed to George Herbert, supposed to be one of his college companions, on leaving Dartmouth College, December 20, 1798. He deplores their separation in twenty-two lines of heroic measure, and closes with this stanza:

> " Let love and friendship reign,
>   Let virtue join the train
>   And all their sweets retain,
>   Till Phœbus' blaze expire;
>   Till God who rules on high
>   Shall rend the tottering sky,
>   All nature gasping die
>   And earth be wrapped in fire."

In a letter from Salisbury, February, 1809, to an associate whom he addressed familiarly as "Brother Bingham," there is a hint that a Mr. Clark, another friend, had heard that he "was just about to (try to) be married;" and he introduces these original lines, presumably to describe the maiden in the case:

> " Bright Phœbus long all rival suns outshone,
>   And rode triumphant on his splendid throne;

When first he waked the blushes of the morn,
And spread his beauties o'er the flowery lawn,
The yielding stars quick hastened from the sky,
Nor moon dare longer with his glories vie ;
He reigned supreme and, decked in roseate light,
Beamed his full splendors on the astonished night.
At length on earth behold a damsel rise,
Whose growing beauties charmed the wondering skies !
As forth she walked to breathe the balmy air,
And view the beauties of the gay parterre,
Her radiant glories drowned the blaze of day,
And through all nature shot a brighter ray.
Old Phœbus saw—and blushed—now forced to own,
That with superior worth the damsel shone.
Graced with his name, he bade her ever shine,
And in his rival owned a form divine !"

It was about this time, 1801, writing to "Brother Harvey" Bingham, he got off the following distich. He says : "I expect to meet many disappointments in the prosecution of the law. I find I have calculated too largely on the profession. For this reason I have engaged a new auxiliary to support me under mortification; it is tobacco.

"Come then, tobacco, new-found friend,
Come, and thy suppliant attend
In each dull, lonely hour.
Then, while the coxcomb pert and proud,
The politician learned and loud,
Keep one eternal clack,
I'll tread where silent nature smiles,
Where solitude my woe beguiles,
And chew thee, dear tobac."

He now addresses his friend Fuller again—this time "all in rhyme"—an epistle so good I should like to quote it entire :

"Since, friend Habijah, you are thus distrest,
Since Love's fierce tortures thus inflame your breast,
Since . . . 's charms forever haunt your dreams,
And her fair form before you always seems,
A little poetry, perhaps, might roll
Love's boiling torrent from your troubled soul.

I, too, with Muses straying through the grove,
May soothe my pains, though not the pains of love.
For those blessed fields, where Love's gay Graces reign,
I once have tried, and tried, alas! in vain.
No longer on those verdant banks I tread,
No longer wander o'er the flowery mead;
Those fragrant lawns of Love, which you explore,
I once, perhaps, have known, but know no more.

"Come, then, together let us beat the field
Where Arts and Science their best laurels yield,
Together let us climb the ethereal height,
Where Freedom's flambeaux shed a living light!
To sing Columbia, then, shall be our care,
Her arts, her arms, her heroes, and her fair.
Columbia hail! thy glories fire my song,
Thy worth deserves, to thee the bays belong!
See Science glow within thy peaceful realm,
See her bright blaze old ignorance o'erwhelm!
See yon proud dome now register her name!
See Dartmouth blazon the bright rolls of fame!
Columbia's arms, too, soon shall awe the world,
And kings and tyrants from their thrones be hurled,
Her every hero shall a Eugene prove,
And bow to no one but the thundering Jove.
Her fair now rival Argos' nymphs divine,
Though all her daughters not like . . . shine,
For when she gently rolls that sparkling eye,
When her soft bosom heaves the tender sigh,
Not Venus' self to Paris did appear
Half so divine, so lovely, or so fair!!"

From a poem of ninety-two lines on the "Course of Life,"
addressed to Mr. John Porter, June 4, 1802, the following
is a characteristic quotation:

"'Tis true, let Locke deny it to the last,
Man has three beings, Present, Future, Past.
We are, we were, we shall be; this contains
The field of all our pleasures and our pains.
Enjoyment makes the present hour its own,
And hope looks forward into works unknown:
While backward turn'd our thoughts incessant stray
And 'mid the fairy forms of memory play."

The postscript of a letter of April 30, 1805, addressed to his brother Ezekiel, ends thus:

> " Fol de dol, dol de dol di dol,
> I'll never make money my idol ;
> For away our dollars will fly all.
> With my friend and my pitcher
> I'm twenty times richer
> Than if I made money my idol ;
> Fol de dol, dol de dol di dol !"

There are many of Mr. Webster's poems extant, but no one more remarkable, perhaps, than the lines on the death of his son Charles, in the winter of 1825, after a short illness, at the age of three years. In a touching notice of his death, Mr. E. Buckminster Lee observes that he was " a lovely child of singular attractiveness of mind and character. Shortly after his death, when the round contour of the cheeks had a little fallen away, his face and head were like a perfect miniature cast of his father. No marble bust can ever present a more perfect likeness of his noble father."

LINES ADDRESSED BY MR. WEBSTER TO HIS ANGEL CHILD.

> " My son, thou wast my heart's delight,
> Thy morn of life was gay and cheery ;
> That morn has rushed to sudden night,
> Thy father's house is sad and dreary.
>
> " I held thee on my knee, my son !
> And kissed thee laughing, kissed thee weeping,
> But, oh ! thy little day is done,
> Thou'rt with thy angel sister sleeping.
>
> " The staff on which my years should lean
> Is broken ere those years come o'er me ;
> My funeral rites thou shouldst have seen,
> But thou art in the tomb before me.
>
> " Thou rear'st to me no filial stone,
> No parent's grave with tears beholdest ;
> Thou art my ancestor, my son !
> And stand'st in Heaven's account the oldest.

" On earth thy lot was soonest cast,
　　Thy generation after mine,
　Thou hast thy predecessor past ;
　　Earlier eternity is thine.

" I should have set before thine eyes
　　The road to heaven, and shown it clear;
　But thou, untaught, spring'st to the skies,
　　And leav'st thy teacher lingering here.

"Sweet seraph, I would learn of thee,
　　And hasten to partake thy bliss !
　And oh ! to thy world welcome me,
　　As first I welcomed thee to this.

" Dear angel, thou art safe in heaven ;
　　No prayers for thee need more be made ;
　Oh, let thy prayers for those be given
　　Who oft have blest thy infant head.

" My father ! I beheld thee born,
　　And led thy tottering steps with care,
　Before me risen to heaven's bright morn,
　　My son ! my father ! guide me there."

Could anything be more touching?　This tenderness of feeling and dependence on an overruling power are manifest throughout Webster's life.　By nature he was devotional ; and while in seasons of gayety it was his wont " to lend himself gracefully and with infinite humor to the amusement of the hour," there was never any attempt to conceal the religious bent of his mind.　He was a member of the Congregational Church at Salisbury, which mode of worship, he said, he believed, " on the whole, to be preferable to any other," although, as he declared, he had " great respect for some other forms of service ;" and we have his creed in fourteen brief articles of faith as communicated by him in a letter to Rev. Thomas Worcester, former pastor of that church.　Of these, the two following are the eighth and the last :

" I believe in the universal providence of God, and leave to Epicurus, and more unreasonable followers in modern times, the inconsistency in believing that God made a world which He does not take the trouble of governing.

"Finally, I believe that Christ has imposed on all his disciples a life of active benevolence; that he who only refrains from what he thinks to be sinful has performed but a part, and a small part, of his duty; that he is bound to do good and communicate, to love his neighbor, to give food and drink to his enemy, and to endeavor, as far as in him lies, to promote peace, truth, piety, and happiness in a wicked and forlorn world, believing that in the great day which is to come, there will be no other standard of merit, no other criterion of character than that which is already established, 'By their fruits ye shall know them.'"

In a letter to his nephew, C. B. Haddock, March 21, 1828, he writes:

"It does not appear to me unreasonable to believe that the friendships of this life are perpetuated in heaven. Flesh and blood, indeed, cannot inherit the kingdom of God; but I know not why that which constitutes a pure source of happiness on earth, individual affection and love, may not survive the tomb."

Again, in his discourse on the life and character of his brother counsellor and bosom friend, the late Jeremiah Mason, delivered about 1849, he observed that "nothing of character is really permanent but virtue and personal worth. They remain. Whatever of excellence is wrought into the soul itself, belongs to both worlds. Real goodness does not attach itself merely to this life, it points to another world. Political or professional fame cannot last forever, but a conscience void of offence before God and man is an inheritance for eternity. Religion, therefore, is a necessity, an indispensable element in any human character. There is no living without it."

It would be instructive to make other extracts from his orations and addresses, which found their way into my scrap-book at the times of their delivery, but limited space forbids. Often we see that this man did not hold himself above recognizing a higher power whose blessings he humbly craved for his country and humanity. Not the least interesting features, alike of his private letters and his

speeches, are apt poetical quotations,—thus proving his love
of poetry, which some writers, in their superior wisdom,
nowadays presume to disparage,—and these are not infrequently from " Paradise Lost" and Pope's " Essay on Man,"
the latter of which, as already remarked, and much of the
former also, it might seem, he committed to memory in
youth, when, as he states in his autobiography, " We had
so few books that to read them once or twice was nothing.
We thought that they were all to be got by heart." He
was accustomed, also, as stated to the writer by a justice
of the United States Supreme Court, to keep a stock of
good things, as well in prose as in poetry, constantly in
memory, to be used whenever occasion offered. Some of
the best of these, as is well known, are gems from his own
rich mine.

In April, 1891, an article of mine was published in the
Magazine of American History, in which I mentioned having
long had in my possession an original pamphlet copy of
an oration which I supposed the only one of the kind extant, delivered by Mr. Webster, at Concord, New Hampshire, on July 4, 1806. I soon received a letter from Mr.
C. W. Lewis, of Boston, informing me that a copy of the
same is in the Boston Athenæum, and he sent me a pamphlet, copyrighted by him in 1882, containing a Fourth of
July oration by Webster, made at Fryeburg, Maine, in 1802.
The preface to this pamphlet states that this oration had slept
for eighty years, when it found its way, with a large mass
of Webster's private papers, to an old junk-shop in Boston,
and " was there secured from destruction by the proprietor,
whose keen eye happened to catch the name of Webster on
one of the papers." Mr. Lewis also called attention to the
fact that some portions of both orations are much alike,
and, what is more remarkable, that the last speech made
by Mr. Webster in the Senate of the United States, July
17, 1850, concludes with almost the same peroration with
which he closed those two early orations.

In his autobiography Webster observes: "Like other young men, I made Fourth of July orations,—at Fryeburg, 1802; at Salisbury, 1805; at Concord, 1806, which was published; and at Portsmouth, 1812, published, also." It is quite evident that he did not intend the one of 1802, and probably that of 1805, either, should ever see the light. The following extract is taken from the oration of 1802. After extolling in glowing terms the privileges vouchsafed to the American people in point of climate, soil, rivers, hills, etc., with a Constitution above all price, he exclaims:

"Amidst these profuse blessings of nature and of Providence, beware!. Standing in this place, sacred to truth, I dare not undertake to assure you that your liberties and your happiness may not be lost. Men are subject to men's misfortunes. If an angel should be winged from heaven, on an errand of mercy, to our country, the first accents that would glow on his lips would be, 'Beware! be cautious! you have everything to lose; you have nothing to gain.' We live under the only government that ever existed which was framed by the unrestrained and deliberate consultations of the people. Miracles do not cluster. That which has happened but once in six thousand years cannot be expected to happen often. Such a government, once gone, might leave a void to be filled, for ages, with revolution and turmoil, riot and despotism."

In the oration of 1806 the same expressions appear, and there is a similarity of expression all the way through it. He says, "A correct and energetic tone of public morals is the prop on which free constitutions rest. After all that can be said, the truth is, that LIBERTY consists more in the morals and habits of the people than in anything else. When the public mind becomes thoroughly vitiated and depraved, every attempt to preserve public Liberty must be in vain. Laws are then a nullity, and constitutions waste paper."

The closing sentences of the oration of 1802 are as follows: "A true patriot, with his eye and his heart on the honor and-happiness of his country, hath an elevation of soul that lifts him above the rank of ordinary men. To common occurrences he is indifferent. Personal considera-

tions dwindle into nothing, in comparison with his high
sense of public duty. In all the vicissitudes of fortune he
leans with pleasure on the protection of Providence and on
the dignity and composure of his own mind. While his
country enjoys peace, he rejoices and is thankful; and if it
be in the counsel of Heaven to send the storm and the
tempest, his bosom proudly swells against the rage that
assaults it. Above fear, above danger, he feels that *the last
end which can happen to any man never comes too soon if he falls
in defence of the laws and liberties of his country.*"

Mr. Webster's last speech in the Senate, July 17, 1850,
was on the "Compromise Measures," and its peroration is in
the following words: "I mean to stand on the Constitution.
I need no other platform. I shall know but one country.
The ends I aim at shall be my country's, my God's, and
truth's. I was born an American, and I intend to perform
the duties incumbent upon me in that character to the end
of my career. I mean to do this, with absolute disregard
of personal consequences. What are personal consequences?
What is the individual man, with all the good or evil which
may befall a great country in a crisis like this, and in the
midst of great transactions which concern that country's
fate? Let the consequences be what they will, I am careless. No man can suffer too much and no man can fall too
soon, if he suffer, or if he fall, in defence of the liberties
and constitution of his country." There is no need of
apology for these quotations, since one could hardly be
better employed than in committing to memory such noble
sentiments.

I think I never heard Mr. Webster speak in the Senate
more than two or three times. I listened to his oration on
the occasion of laying the corner-stone of the extension of
the Capitol, July 4, 1851, and his form and features, as he
then appeared, are indelibly impressed on my memory, as
they are, likewise, as I saw him at the President's reception,
when Washington Irving and "Boz" were among the dis-

tinguished guests. The crowd was so great that it was difficult to get a good sight of either Irving or Dickens. Webster was evidently in a happy mood,—he may have just come from a social dinner,—for, when the people were passing through the parlors, he took position close against the wall by the door of the East Room, and, with a roguish look, straightened himself back at full length, as if to have his height measured. I thought he was one of the noblest looking men I had ever seen, and he was certainly not less remarkable physically than mentally. He speaks of his father, who died in 1806, as "the handsomest man he ever saw, except his brother Ezekiel, who appeared to him the finest human form he ever laid eyes on."

There is a little historical story connected with Webster as Secretary of State under President Fillmore, about 1850 or 1851. Postmaster-General Nathan K. Hall one day took me with him to meet an engagement he had made at the White House. The business in hand related to the foreign mail service, of which I had charge at the time, and I was to make a statement with a view to obtaining the consent of the President, as required by law, to a retaliatory order that the Postmaster-General desired to make to counteract the practice of the British Government in charging the same postage on letters between the two countries—the single rate was then twenty-four cents—whether the sea conveyance was by the United States or British steamers. As soon as the facts of the case had been presented by the Postmaster-General, together with such explanations as were required from me, Mr. Webster raised himself up, and, with a jovial manner, said, in his deep tone of voice, "Mr. President,—as we boys used to say in our debating society,—'*I motion*' that you give your consent to the proposed measure of retaliation." Whereupon the order was at once made, receiving the President's approval, and it soon put a stop to the unjust practice, by enabling Brother Jonathan to give John Bull "tit for tat."

"Mr. Webster," observes one whose relations with him were intimate, "was never seen to more advantage than within his own household, at the family board, or in strolling with him over his farm at Marshfield, or standing with him upon the sea beach and looking out upon the ocean before us, which, like the scope of his intellectual vision, appeared boundless. To hear him converse upon the past, the present, the future, in a familar, colloquial manner—to listen to his great thoughts, expressed in purest words of our language, and wonder how he could thus speak and think, are joys which we can find no words to express."

Mr. Webster's kindness of heart was proverbial. A touching instance of this is shown by his letter of October 17, 1852, to President Fillmore—the last but one he wrote to him—asking that Mr. Conrad, Secretary of War, who had given attention to Mr. Webster's department in his absence, be allowed to sign a treaty, saying he "should be glad to show him some mark of grateful respect," and that "it is a feather in the life of a public man to sign a treaty." His letter to President Fillmore, on the morning of the following day, was the last letter he wrote with his own hand. He had not then given up all hope of recovery; but after a comparatively comfortable night, he wrote: "At this hour (ten o'clock) I feel easy and strong, and as if I could go into the Senate and make a speech!" Yet he sadly adds: "At one I shall sink all away, be obliged to go to bed at three, and go through the evening spasms. What all this is to come to, God only knows. My Dear Sir—I should love to pass the last moments of your administration with you, and around your council board. But let not this embarrass you. Consider my resignation as always before you, to be accepted any moment you please."

But the end was fast approaching; and when, late on the afternoon before his death, this announcement was made to him by his physician, Mr. Webster "received the announcement calmly, and directed all the members of his family to be called in, the female members first, and then his male relatives and personal friends, addressing each of them individually, and bade each an affectionate farewell." Between ten and eleven o'clock at night he uttered, somewhat indistinctly, the words, "Poet, poetry, Gray, Gray," whereupon Mr. Fletcher Webster repeated the first line of Gray's "Elegy,"—"The curfew tolls the knell of parting day." "That's it, that's it," said Mr. Webster; and the book was brought and several stanzas read to him, which seemed to give him pleasure; thus, to the last, showing his love of poetry. Having no fear of dissolution, he spoke of the difficulty of the process of dying, when Dr. Jeffries repeated the verse: "Though I walk through the valley of the shadow of death, I will fear no evil, for Thou art with me: Thy rod and Thy staff, they comfort me."

Mr. Webster said immediately: "The fact, the fact. That is what I want, Thy rod, Thy rod, Thy staff, Thy staff." Shortly after, at twenty-two minutes before three o'clock, he passed tranquilly, and with perfect trust, to the regions of the blest. In Edward Everett's speech of October 27, describing this closing scene, he said: "In the long and honored career of our lamented friend, there are efforts and triumphs which will hereafter fill one of the brightest pages of our history. But I greatly err if the closing scene —the height of the religious sublime—does not far transcend in interest the brightest exploits of his public life."

Who will doubt that, after a life devoted to the defence of "the Constitution, the laws, and the liberties of his country," this grand old patriot and statesman, "above fear, above danger, above reproach," reached his "last end," not, as in the providence of God, "too soon," but ripe for the transition, and that upon his entry into eternal life he was, as he had prayed to be, welcomed by his angel son, who "stand'st in Heaven's account the oldest"?

CHAPTER XV.

SIR ROWLAND HILL.

A Pleasant Announcement—Origin of Penny Postage—Handsome Reward—Postage-Stamps—Their Origin—A Personal Interview.

THE following item is going the rounds of the newspapers: "Sir Rowland Hill, the veteran ex-Postmaster-General of England, and Lady Hill, celebrated their golden wedding a short time since."

This is a pleasant announcement; and it may be interesting to the generality of readers to know something more of the life and character of this philanthropist. Sir Rowland Hill (he must not be confounded with Rev. Rowland Hill, born 1774, died 1833) has never been the actual Postmaster-General of Great Britain; but as first secretary of the British Post-Office Department for several years, and as post-office reformer previously, he undoubtedly exercised a greater influence in postal matters than any Postmaster-General of that kingdom ever did. Born at Kidderminster, December 3, 1795, "he early showed a great fondness for figures, which was subsequently developed in the study of mathematics. His first occupation was that of mathematical tutor in a school kept by his father, and for a number of years he devoted himself to improving school instruction and organization." As secretary, in 1833, of the South Australian Commission, he aided in founding that colony. Four years afterward he began to press for postal reform, and in 1838 succeeded "in having the matter referred to a special committee of the House of Commons." This committee, after due consideration of the subject, reported in favor of Mr. Hill's plan of penny postage, notwithstanding the post-office authorities, who were given a full hearing before them, were "hostile to the change." "In July,

1839, a bill to enable the treasury to carry Mr. Hill's plan into effect, introduced by the Chancellor of the Exchequer, passed by a majority of 102; and on August 17 the project became a law. A temporary office under the treasury was at the same time created to enable Mr. Hill to inaugurate his plan, and on January 10, 1840, the uniform penny rate came into operation." Notwithstanding it gave good promise of success, the post-office authorities continued unfriendly; he was left without adequate support, and "soon after the accession of the Peel ministry," about 1843, he was dismissed, and received the appointment of one of the directors of the Brighton Railway. The people, however, were on his side, and £13,000 was raised by subscription for a testimonial to him. If I am not mistaken this was used in the erection of his statue at Birmingham. At any rate, I am quite sure that my old friend, Elihu Burritt, told me there was, or was to be, such a monument erected there in honor of Sir Rowland. "Upon the return of the Whigs to power in 1846, he was appointed secretary to the Postmaster-General, holding divided authority with Colonel Maberly," and in 1854 he became sole secretary, which office he held until he was retired several years afterward. "In 1860 he was knighted in acknowledgment of his services at the post-office, and received a Parliamentary grant of £20,000, the first Albert gold medal of the Society of Arts, and the degree of D.C.L. from Oxford."

The above facts, long familiar to experienced post-office men, I have taken from the *American Cyclopædia.* Here is a newspaper account of the origin of postage-stamps:

"The origin of the stamp has a tinge of romance in it. It was thirty-seven years ago that Rowland Hill, while crossing a district in the north of England, arrived at the door of an inn where a postman had stopped to deliver a letter. A young girl came out to receive it; she turned it over and over in her hand and asked the price of postage. This was a large sum, and evidently the girl was poor, for the postman demanded a shilling. She sighed sadly, and said the letter was from her brother, but that she had no money; and so she returned the letter to the postman.

Touched with pity, Mr. Hill paid the postage and gave the letter to the girl, who seemed very much embarrassed. Scarcely had the postman turned his back, when the young innkeeper's daughter confessed that it was a trick between her and her brother. Some signs on the envelope told her all she wanted to know, but the letter contained no writing. 'We are both so poor,' she added, 'that we invented this mode of correspondence without paying for our letters.' The traveller, continuing his road, asked himself if a system giving place to such frauds was not a vicious one. Before sunset Rowland had planned to organize the postal service on a new basis—with what success is known to the world." [1]

I have no reason to question the correctness of this account.

In 1867, being in London with my youngest son, Henry Franklin, we called at the General Post-Office on the brother of Sir Rowland, Frederick Hill, Esq., who then, as at present, held the office of secretary. Having expressed a desire to see Sir Rowland, with whom I had formerly had extensive official correspondence, soon after reaching our boarding-house I received a note, dated June 15, from Mr. Frederick Hill, in which he said: "I saw my brother, Mr. Rowland Hill, this morning, and was glad to find that he was at present tolerably well. I mentioned your being just now in London, your having called here, and your desire to see him; and he said he should be happy to see both yourself and your son any morning you may be at liberty to ride over to Hampstead. He lives at Bertram House, half a mile on the London side of Hampstead."

Thus invited, on the 17th we presented ourselves at Bertram House, and sent in our cards. We were first conducted into the parlor, where Sir Rowland soon made his appearance, giving us a cordial welcome, and then asked

---

[1] In a letter to me, dated London, December 22, 1877, Sir Rowland wrote: "The story you have quoted belongs to Coleridge. I only quoted it as an argument in favor of prepayment. As regards the statue at Birmingham, this was paid for by a subscription raised by the townsfolk themselves for the purpose, and no part of the national testimonial was used to defray expenses."

us to accompany him to his library up-stairs. From our recollection of him we should judge that he was a man just about the height and size of President Hayes; and this is perhaps the most satisfactory description of his person I could give. He had not the look of an old man, but stood erect and was active in all his movements. He appeared to be in perfect health; but said if he undertook to walk any considerable distance—for instance, to the further end of his spacious garden, to which he pointed from the library window—he was troubled with vertigo. He treated us like old acquaintances, showing us many of the tokens of approbation he had received from various distinguished persons, including his commission of knighthood from the Queen. As a choice memento of our visit I have now before me a proof-sheet which he presented me of one of the first letter envelopes ever made. Upon the upper face, side, and ends are various devices, one of which represents a person writing, surrounded by a crowd eagerly looking on, with elephants in the background,—evidently an Eastern scene; on the opposite corner is a commercial picture, in which the civilized and savage world are brought together, of course through the means of cheap postage and other facilities for easy communication; below these, on either end, are female figures in the attitude of reading letters to listening children; and at the top, in the centre, is a kind of coat-of-arms, representing, also by a female figure, the spirit of universal communication despatching flying angels with messages in all directions.

After an hour's most agreeable interview, during which we were treated to cake and wine, Sir Rowland came downstairs with and presented us to Lady Hill, who greeted us in the pleasantest manner, and on the following day sent us, " With Lady Hill's compliments," tickets to the Zoological Gardens.

CHAPTER XVI.

INCIDENTS IN SIR WALTER RALEIGH'S LIFE.

He burns Materials he had prepared for his History of the World—His Confession, etc.

IN the third volume of his "Addresses and Speeches," Robert C. Winthrop has given us a valuable contribution to history that must be regarded as conclusive evidence that Sir Walter Raleigh made quite a long speech on the scaffold immediately before his execution. This speech—that has usually been called his "Confession"—has been discredited by some historians, but Mr. Winthrop found in the "Common Place Book of Adam Winthrop, the father of the first Governor of Massachusetts," among several accounts of historical events, carefully copied from seemingly authentic sources, "The Confession and Execution of Sir Walter Raleigh." This copy, with unimportant variations only, agrees with the general version of the "Confession." Says Mr. Winthrop, "Sir Walter was executed in October, 1618, when Adam Winthrop was living at Groton, England, at seventy years of age, a magistrate of the old county of Suffolk, who, a few years before, had resigned the auditorship of Trinity College, Cambridge, which he had held sixteen or seventeen years. His son, who, twelve years afterwards, came over to New England as Governor of Massachusetts, was then about thirty years old. Both of these men took an intelligent interest in public affairs, and might have personally witnessed the execution of Raleigh, had they chanced to be in London at the time." Mr. Winthrop, after considering it very fully, observes, "In conclusion, we can hardly doubt that this speech was made substantially as it has been reported."

Another incident in Sir Walter's life, hardly less im-

portant, and about which much more serious doubt has
been thrown, is the statement that he destroyed material
he had collected for a continuation of·his "History of the
World." This appears in a book entitled "Celebrated
Trials, Selected by a Member of the Philadelphia Bar"
(John Jay Smith, born 1798), and published by L. A.
Godey, in 1836. In this book it is stated that Sir Walter,
"some few days before he suffered, sent for Mr. Walter
Burr, who formerly printed his first volume of the 'History
of the World,' whom, taking by the hand, after some other
discourse, he asked how it had sold? Mr. Burr returned
this answer: 'It has sold so slowly that it has undone me.'
At these words Sir Walter, stepping to his desk, took
the other, unprinted part of his history, which he had
brought down to the times he lived in, and, clapping his
hand upon his breast, said, with a sigh, 'Ah! my friend,
hath the first part undone thee? the second part shall undo
no more: this ungrateful world is unworthy of it!' and
immediately going to the fireside, threw it in, and set his
foot upon it till it was consumed. As great a loss to learning as Christendom could have sustained; the greater
because it could be repaired by no hand but his."

Edward Edwards, author of a "Life of Sir Walter Raleigh,"
published in 1868, said to be the best ever written of him,
attributes this story of the bookseller to one Winstanley,
who, it would appear from the context, was, says Edwards,
"the author of a very worthless book, published in 1660,"
forty-two years only after Sir Walter's execution, when,
if not true, its falsity must have been known to thousands
of his contemporaries then living. Was it denied at the
time? Edwards says, "It has neither authority nor cor-
roboration," and, thereupon, enters into what seems to me
a weak argument to convince his readers that, "at any
period, the destruction, irrevocably, of the result of long
toil on the faith of a statement like that given in the story
of Walter Burr, smacks rather of fable than of history.

Strictly true [he continues] Winstanley's statement cannot be, since a second edition of the 'History of the World' had actually appeared before the date assigned, with so much precision, to this conversation in the Tower between the author and bookseller." What, I venture to ask, does this prove? Mind, it was not a " *second volume,*" which " had actually appeared," but a " second *edition* of the *first* and *only* volume ever issued,—the large octavo volume of 1614, a copy of which I have examined in the Congressional Library. Who knows that the bookseller's misfortune did not arise from undertaking a second edition, after the first, probably a small one, had been disposed of? Look at these additional facts. This old volume, as already remarked, bears date 1614, two years before Sir Walter was released from the Tower to take charge of his last and fatal Guiana expedition. It comprises the whole of his " History of the World." It is divided into five books, the fifth bearing this heading: "From the settled rule of Alexander's Successors in the East untill the Romans (prevailing over all) made conquest of Asia and Macedon." Of course, this fifth and last book is plainly not " brought down to the times he lived in." Now mark: In the closing paragraph of his history he wrote, "Lastly, whereas this Booke, by the title it hath, calls itselfe ' *The first part of the Generall Historie of the World,*' implying a Second and Third Volume, which I also intended and have hewne out; besides many other discouragements perswading my silence, it hath pleased God to take that glorious *Prince* out of the world, to whom they were directed; whose unspeakable and never enough lamented losse hath taught me to say with *Job,* '*Versa, est in Luctum Cithara mea & organum meum in vocem flentium.*' "[1]

What has become of the materials for these second and third volumes, thus " hewne out?" Evidently, whatever

---

[1] Chapter **xxx.** 31.

the bookseller might reasonably have supposed was a complete "second part" was, in fact, only what had been "hewne out" for such volume; and, now that Sir Walter knew he was about to suffer death, what more natural, independently of any irritation from seeing his great work was ill appreciated, than that he should wish to destroy his undigested notes, in order to prevent their possible use in a manner to detract from his well-earned "fame to come, which [Edwards declares] he loved with a passion hardly second in intensity to the love of wife and children." Moreover, we have seen that his "Confession," as related, presumably, by the same writer who gives us the story of the bookseller, agrees in all essential particulars with the best authenticated version thereof. Why, then, should that story, which Edwards says had been current "now for more than two centuries," be discarded as fabulous, since it forms a consecutive part of the author's account of the trial, conviction, and execution of Raleigh?

Finally, let it be remembered, that Sir Walter was confined in the Tower for at least two months immediately preceding his death. Is it not reasonable, therefore, to suppose that he occupied more or less of this time in collecting materials for the continuation of his history? However this may be, we have his positive and undoubted assertion that he had "hewne out" a second and third volume, and, unless these materials can be accounted for in some other way, there is the strongest presumptive evidence that he committed them to the flames in the presence of his publisher.

CHAPTER XVII.

THE STAR-SPANGLED BANNER.

Circumstances under which it was written—Two Accounts—Capture of Dr. Beans and other Americans—F. S. Key goes for their Release and is detained on a British Ship.

GENERALLY well known as are the main circumstances under which our stirring national song of the "Star-Spangled Banner" was written, the particulars thereof are not so familiar to all as not to be worthy of record in this place. Recently, in examining a file of the old *National Intelligencer*, I came across this song as first published in that paper on the 27th of September, 1814, a fortnight only after the battle of North Point, Baltimore. It appears there with the following heading and preface:

"DEFENCE OF FORT M'HENRY.

"(*From a Baltimore paper.*)

" The annexed song was composed under the following circumstances : A gentleman had left Baltimore, with a flag of truce, for the purpose of getting released from the British fleet a friend of his, who had been captured at Marlborough. He went as far as the mouth of the Patuxent, and was not permitted to return, lest the intended attack on Baltimore should be disclosed. He was therefore brought up the bay to the mouth of the Patapsco, where the flag vessel was kept under the guns of a frigate, and he was compelled to witness the bombardment of Fort M'Henry, which the Admiral (Cockburn) had boasted that he would carry in a few hours, and that the city must fall. He watched the flag at the fort through the whole day with an anxiety that can be better felt than described, until the night prevented him from seeing it. In the night he watched the bomb-shells, and at early dawn his eye was again greeted by the proudly waving flag of his country.

" *Tune*—Anacreon in Heaven."

Here follows the song, at the bottom of which is this note in brackets : "(Whoever is the author of those lines, they do equal honor to his principles and his talents.—*Nat-Int.*)"

It would appear that this famous song had not yet received its characteristic name, by which it has long been so well known throughout the civilized world. With the name of its author, Francis S. Key, it is destined to live as long as American independence shall hold a record in the history of mankind.

In Mr. Charles J. Ingersoll's "Sketch of the Second War between the United States and Great Britain," published in 1849, the following not less interesting account is given as having been furnished to him by "a gentleman of Bladensburg," writing of the remarkable battle fought there on the 24th of August, 1814.

"The [British] army having passed the village of Upper Marlborough *en route* for their shipping (the second day after the battle), leaving several stragglers to follow, several gentlemen of that village formed the determination to cut some of them off and make them prisoners of war. The principal of these gentlemen were Dr. William Beans, as prime mover, and General Robert Bowie and John Rodgers, who succeeded in making several prisoners, who were confined. The British officers, hearing of this occurrence, however, that night sent back a strong party to the village, who liberated the prisoners, and, taking these gentlemen out of their beds, hurried them off without allowing them a moment to clothe themselves, and, thus placing them on old horses, carried them, no doubt amid the jeers of the soldiery, to the shipping. After many entreaties and expostulations, two of the gentlemen were let off and permitted to return to Upper Marlborough, but they considered Dr. Beans a fair prize, and determined to take him to Halifax or England. Having the doctor on board, the fleet left the Patuxent River, and, ascending the Chesapeake Bay, appeared off Fort M'Henry. The numerous and influential friends of Dr. Beans immediately set to work to devise some plan by which an effort might be made to obtain his release from the fleet. Accordingly a petition was signed by some of the most respectable citizens of Prince George's County, among whom were individuals who had acted very kindly towards Colonel Wood and other British officers and soldiers who had been left [wounded] in Bladensburg, on the return of the British army, of which the commander of the army or fleet was no doubt aware. These preparations being made, the eloquent and talented Francis S.

Key, the friend of Dr. Beans, was appointed as the messenger and champion to go to the rescue. He accordingly proceeded to Annapolis, and, by means of a small craft and the white flag, he boarded the Admiral's ship, to make known his mission. The fleet being about to make an attack on Fort M'Henry, while the army effected a landing at North Point, Mr. Key was detained on board, and compelled, from his position, to witness the furious bombardment of Fort M'Henry. The novelty of his situation, a near view of the powerful means then operating for the reduction of Baltimore to the power of the enemy, and the further desecration of the American flag, his solicitude for the successful resistance of his countrymen, and noble emotions of a patriot heart thus excited and warmed, produced, amid the storm and strife by which he was surrounded, a memento worthy of the man and honorable to his country; and long will the 'Star-Spangled Banner' be sung, to light up in every American bosom the sacred fire of patriotic devotion to the flag of his country."

Francis S. Key was born in 1779, and died (I think) in Washington, in 1843. I remember him about that time as a mild, agreeable, entertaining gentleman; and I also recall the fact of having, on a Sunday afternoon, heard him eloquently address the Sunday-school scholars of the city in the East-Capitol park.

PART IV.

CHAPTER I.

EMPLOYMENT NECESSARY TO HAPPINESS

In every age and clime since Time began,
In town and city, hence to far Japan,
The world has aye been furnished, ready made,
With hosts of doctors, often poorly paid,
Whose mission, whether singly or combined,
Has been to tinker and improve mankind.
Some set themselves our bodies to amend,
And they are dubbed " M.D.," but for what end?
Then others take the title "LL.D.,"
And others " D.D.," as their high degree,
While those are common who these honors lack,
On whom the world confers the title " quack."
Some deal in doses gentle, some severe,
Some for effects hereafter, others here—
Prescriptions, whether from their heads or shelves,
Which they are seldom known to take themselves,
Thus demonstrating clearly what the fact is,
How much more easy 'tis to preach than practise.

Well, so it is, among this class you find
Your poet here to-day, with heart inclined
To proffer in this way a wholesome pill,
One made to ease and cure, and not to kill,—
Lest, when you come his title to proclaim,
The letter " Q" be added to his name!
It matters not; 'tis now, alas! too late,
Do what he may, for him to shun his fate;

Your kind forbearance, therefore, he would ask,
To bear him safely through his pleasant task.

At once, then, let us offer, if we can,
The best prescriptions for the ills of man.
What may these be?   Foremost among them all
Is what we ever have been taught to call
LABOR; a tonic, potent, free, and sure
A thousand ills to stop, if not to cure.
Yes, labor, labor, in His glorious plan,
God's noblest blessing to His creature, man.
Where seek we first the ruddy bloom of health,
A boon without which none can boast of wealth?
Where but among the happy, free and gay,
Where honest labor rules the livelong day?

Go, visit yonder farm-house on the green,
If it so happen you have never been,
And see what favors fortune doth allow
To him whose pride it is to hold the plough.
Go, in a summer eve, near set of sun,
And when the well-planned, hard day's work is done,
See how the farmer and his rugged boys,
The wife and daughters, cherish life's rich joys,
Free from the cares that hinder or destroy
The calm delight of those who shun employ.
Behold his fields of richly-waving grain,
Moved by the breeze that sweeps along the plain;
See how they smile, kiss'd by the rosy lips
Of mellow sunbeams ere the night's eclipse;
In shade just changing to a golden hue—
In every aspect beautiful to view.

Next turn we to those forests, deeply green,
That in their mimic grandeur may be seen
Spread out in rows well suited to adorn
Broad acres covered thick with Indian corn.

Look with what care all weeds have been removed,
How every means of thrift has been improved,
To aid the willing stalk for well-formed ear,
And bring a bounteous crop for winter's cheer.
Then see those other "patches" in between,
More modest, since their treasures are unseen.
Oh, come, immortal muses! show the way to
Immortalize that unpoetic plant, potato—
That glorious fruit, the French call *pommes de terre,*
Which meets a ready welcome everywhere,
Alike in palace, cabin, and in tent;
Would I could all its virtues here present!
What, let me ask, was General Marion's roast,
He set before his haughty British host,
When, without other courses, fruit or wine,
He asked him one day at his tent to dine ?
What but potatoes, mealy, sweet, and good?
"Behold," he said, "our wholesome daily food."
Well might the British general quick discern,
And well the British lion truly learn
The folly of contending with a foe
Thus ready every comfort to forego.
Not every comfort, either, since we see
They had potatoes plenty, duty free.

But we have rambled, and are passing by
Those splendid sights that all around us lie.
See there the garden, crowded with all kinds
Of fruits and flowers, while near its border winds
The mountain stream, whose crystal waters flow,
In merry glee, to greet the lake below.

What recollections scenes like these awake—
The mountain stream, the field, the placid lake—
Of boyhood's pleasant hours, when full of life
We dwelt contented, free from worldly strife ;

Content to labor till our work was done,
Ne'er seeking any useful task to shun!
Nor were we always made to dig and toil,
Lest work incessant might our tempers spoil.
One rule, I well remember, used to be—
A rule most wise, how plain it is to see!—
That when it rained too hard to work without,
We might employ the time in—catching trout.

Dressed in a suit the best for such a use,
A *hole-y* suit, exempt from all abuse;
Our boots of cowhide, coarsely made and stout,
With holes in toes to let the water out;
Thus well equipped, with hooks, and line, and bait,
We hastened to the brook at rapid rate.
Then cutting here a rod of proper length,
Elastic, slender, yet of ample strength
To bear the speckled swimmer safe to port,
We were prepared to enter on our sport.
And now, with cautious step, we near the place,
Some well-known haven of the finny race,
And throwing in our hook, with tempting bait,
In breathless silence we their motions wait.
The invitation to this treach'rous meal
Is quick accepted, and the hidden steel,
Its work performing, holds its victim tight,
Till safely landed, much to our delight.
Thus we proceed, exploring well the brook,
Through meadow, pasture, wood, in every nook,
Until well paid, and heedless of the rain,
We take our fish and saunter home again.
Here let us pause, a moral to discover:
Barbed baits are common, mark it, the world over.

Next, see the orchard, with its generous store
Of fruit delicious, near the farmer's door.

Here shall we find the " good sort" and the pear,
The "summer sweeting" and the "greening" fair;
Here the sound " russet" and the "blue pearmain,"
All adding to his comfort, health, and gain.
Some serve for autumn, some for winter use,
Some yield to pressure their enlivening juice,
A liquid once called cider, pure and plain,
But which, when " doctored," now they call champagne!
What sight more fair in all the world to see,
Go where we may, than fruitful apple-tree?
Its boughs low-bending with their precious freight;
From such, no doubt, Eve slyly plucked and ate.
How much they seem to speak our Maker's praise,
How much remind us of our childhood days
When apple-*parings* were so well *prepared*
That they who went to *pare* were often *paired!*

Behind the orchard, see the pasture green,
And herds reclining blissful and serene.
To-morrow's cares to them bring no dismay;
They chew their cud in peace, and seem to say
To us, who claim by right their lords to be,
" Go seek our trust, and evermore be free."

And now the milkmaid comes with honest heart,
Well trained from childhood to perform her part
In all the useful duties that pertain
To household work, ne'er thinking to complain.
With pail in hand she hastens o'er the lawn,
As well at eve as in the early dawn;
And in her daily task is sure to find
The food for health—a well-contented mind.
Nor is she left alone this work to do,
The farmer's boys assist, and nimbly, too,
Till soon the shining dairy swells in pride,
With pans of milk in line on either side.

But ere we pass from this delightful scene,
Turn we to view—'twill well repay, I ween—
The farmer's barn, where snugly packed away
For winter's use lie tons of well-made hay.
Of life industrious here behold the proof,
The mows, hard pressed, extend quite to the roof.
The swallow, twittering, forced to quit her nest,
Retires to seek afar some place of rest,
Where, undisturbed, the frigid winter through,
She sleeps till springtime calls to life anew.
Beneath the scaffolds here are stables fine,
With stalls arranged for oxen, horse, and kine,
And here, secure from winter's piercing snows,
The gentle herd may rest in calm repose.

Nor should we fail, in passing, to survey
The farmer's cottage, and our homage pay
To real worth; ourselves we honor most
By honoring thus our country's solid boast—
The hardy yeoman, whose athletic arm
Protects from want in peace, in war from harm.
What air of comfort, what convenience here
For household work, to every housewife dear!
In kitchen, pantry, cellar, and in hall,
See how complete for service, and how all,
With parlor, chamber, stairs above, below,
Is planned for comfort, not for empty show;
Yet while the leading purpose, it is true,
Is use and comfort ever kept in view,
Still equal care is used the eye to please,
In structure pure, in ornamental trees,
And all the various ways contrived by art
T' insure convenience and a grace impart.

These, then, and more than these, the happy fruits
Of honest labor in the world's pursuits—

Of life industrious, not on gain intent
For sake of gain; but to be wisely spent
In meeting all life's various wants, and save
From pains of poverty and the poor man's grave.

Next let us pass to the mechanic art,
Wherein so many well perform their part.
Here, in the busy workshop we shall find
Rare genius with ripe scholarship combined,—
Ripe in the knowledge of transactions past—
Ripe, too, in what concerns their trade, and—last,
Not least, I own—in knowledge true and plain,
That labor brings contentment, health, and gain.

How sweet the task, did I possess the skill,
This picture rough in all its parts to fill,
By sketching each profession, art, and trade,
And showing how employment e'er is made
If useful, not too constant nor severe,
To cater to our health and pleasure here.
Nor time nor skill will now allow of this;
Yet, ere the subject we for aye dismiss,
A word of caution may not be amiss.
I would not, sure, that man should be a slave
To labor constant, but that he should have
Time for repose and pastime when inclined,
And time, of course, to cultivate the mind.
Time for amusement never fail to take;
Who would exclude it makes a grave mistake.

What saith a real poet who once wrote
On this same point? Allow me here to quote:
" How often have I blest the coming day,
When toil, remitting, lent its turn to play;
And all the village train, from labor free,
Led up their sports beneath the spreading tree,

While many a pastime circled in the shade,
The young contending as the old surveyed;
And many a gambol frolicked o'er the ground,
And sleights of art and feats of strength went round.
And still, as each repeated pleasure tired,
Succeeding sports the mirthful band inspired;
The dancing pair that simply sought renown
By holding out to tire each other down,—
The swain mistrustless of his smutted face,
Whilst secret laughter titter'd round the place,—
The bashful virgin's sidelong looks of love,
The matron's glance that would those looks reprove:
These were thy charms, sweet village ! Sports like these,
With sweet succession, taught e'en toil to please."

One word for any ready with a sneer
(Full sure am I, none such are gathered here)
To speak contempt'ous of the lab'ring mass,
Because of labor—let their insults pass.
Look when you may, and you will surely find
They're wanting all in character refined,—
Their coat of arms 'tis easy to describe,
'Twill show whence sprang this self-inflated tribe:
Here, on one side, are lapstone, awl, and last—
A codfish, shears, and tailor's goose, well cast—
A butcher's knife, a wash-tub, and a mop;
On the reverse, a scaffold with—a drop.
All symbols, truly, save the one last named,
Of which they have no cause to be ashamed,
Howe'er it might disturb their pride to see
That we so well have traced their pedigree.
No, no, my friends, in pity turn away
From such poor creatures of the passing day,
And in the higher walks of life aspire
To win renown, nor ever think to tire;—

Press on! press on! proud of your high estate,—
Leave drones and upstarts to their sorry fate.

But ere we bring this rustic sketch to end,
The scholar's task our muse may well attend ;
For he who delves for knowledge, digs for gold,
And all gold-diggers bear the lab'rer's mould.
The student, then, deny it he who can,
Is well and truly styled a lab'ring man ;—
A worker of the soil—why is he not,
Since daily cultivation is his lot?
Wrought not by muscle, like the toiling swain,
But that far nobler labor—of the brain,
Without whose aid the muscles toil in vain.
His fields are boundless, he must needs explore,
So be he reaps, or delves for precious ore,
In all the various regions that present
Fair promise to the eye on gain intent;
Nor will he fail a harvest to enjoy,
Who thus his time and talents doth employ.
But this plain fact e'er let him bear in mind,
The seeds he sows will yield their fruit in kind,
And happy he who thus himself prepares
To gather naught but grain, unmixed with tares.
The student, too, may justly claim to be
A good mechanic, all will sure agree.
Is't not his wont, by true ambition fired,
To fashion well the implements required
In life's fierce battles, when, his school-days past,
He enters boldly on life's stage at last?
And then, again, as doubtless you're aware,
He's famed for—building castles in the air!
An undertaking which he would not start
Were he not trained in the mechanic art.
Thus have we shown how it doth come to pass
That students form an active working class.

25

Now, of the ladies may I say a word?
Of those, I mean, of whom we've sometimes heard,
Who vainly boast, would you believe? oh, fie!
They never made a bed nor baked a pie!
Nor boiled a pot, nor made a batch of bread,
Nor swept a room, nor combed a baby's head!
My goodness! Can it be that such there are?
Are any such in market? Oh, beware!
Young men love playthings, but not such as these
To keep; be sure of this, they're hard to please,
When in good earnest to select a wife—
A partner, helpmeet, counsellor for life.

Thus may we see, through all life's varied scenes,
That work brings wealth and wealth supplies the means
To make life easy and secure content
In what alone concerns a life well spent.

CHAPTER II.

LIFE.

O LIFE! what mystery thy birth enshrouds!
For ages past hath man in vain essayed
This mystery to solve—thy origin to learn.
O Soul! my Soul! speak out and tell me clear,
Whence came thou here? whence thy deep yearning for
Immortal life? Methinks I hear thee say,
"Be still and trust. In God we live, and move,
And have our being; more we cannot know."
Ah, true! but this great truth, full well I know,
Thy restless spirit ne'er will satisfy.
In One all-ruling Power we must, we do
Believe. No revelation, save what all

May read in Nature's open book, need we
To prove that this is so.   When we recall
The countless wonders of the Universe,
From merest atom to the glorious sun,
And stars, and planets, in their order, all
In perfect harmony upborne,—and earth,
So fraught with beauty, grandeur, light, and life,—
All, all proclaim One over-ruling Hand.
But this, does this assurance give that we,
The vale of death once passed, shall live again?
That in a higher, purer sphere, our souls
Shall mingle in communion sweet, and know,
As we, in this life present, one another know?
Momentous questions these, that ever rise
And constant audience seek.   'T is true, the words
Of revelation come belief to claim—
All doubt dispel; yet few, methinks, are there
Who do not crave more light.   Whence shall this come?
Whither to end all doubt, seek we for proof?
Not, surely, in the grovelling passions of
The carnal heart, that drag to lowest depths
And darkness dire; but upward, upward, where
The mental vision scope may take afar,
Without obstruction from the earth below.
We can ascend.   United by the bonds
Of love, and taking for our guide the rule—
The Golden Rule that never leads astray—
Our souls may rise to regions clear, so full
Of heavenly light that 'twixt eternal life
And this, no barrier appears.

CHAPTER III.

POETRY AN INSPIRATION: MR. STODDARD'S RATHER STARTLING
ASSERTION TO THE CONTRARY.

WHOEVER has read Sir Edwin Arnold's "Light of the World" will doubtless have observed that, in his introduction to it, Richard Henry Stoddard makes the rather startling assertion that what has heretofore been generally received as an admitted fact, that real poetry is an inspiration, is, after all, in his estimation, only "a delusion which was fostered by immature rhymesters to palliate their shortcomings and impart dignity to their trivialities." This would appear to be taking direct issue with the author of the oft-repeated epigram that "poets are born, not made," and he adds that poetry "is now as universally recognized to be an art as painting, sculpture, or music, and the rules to which it conforms have been gathered from the practice of the masters and formulated into a system of critical laws, which not to know is to know nothing of poetry." Undoubtedly, what passes for good poetry, so far as sense and rhythm are concerned, may be composed without any special inspiration, but I am inclined to believe that in order to the production of the most perfect *spirituelle* character of poetry, the author himself must be inspired above any help from art or "system of critical laws," just, for instance, as a mere mechanical performer on a musical instrument, with little or no ear for harmony of sound, may touch every note correctly without the ability to thrill the listener like an Ole Bull or a Bischoff. Says Cicero, "*Nascimur poetæ, fimus oratores.*" We are born poets; by education we may become orators.

Let us hear also what the "Autocrat of the Breakfast Table" says of his experience:

"A lyric conception hits like a bullet in the forehead. I have often had the blood drop from my cheeks when it struck, and felt that I turned as white as death. Then comes a creeping as of centipedes running down the spine; then a gasp and a great jump of the heart; then a sudden flush, and a beating of the vessels of the head; then a long sigh, and the poem is written. . . . I said written, but did not say copied. Every such poem has a soul and a body, and it is the body of it, or the copy, that men read and publishers pay for. The soul of it is born in an instant in the poet's soul. It comes to him a thought tangled in the meshes of a few sweet words—words that have loved each other from the cradle of the language, but have never been wedded until now. . . . No wonder the ancients made the poetical impulse wholly external—goddess, muse, divine afflatus, something outside always. I never wrote any verses worth reading. I can't. I am too stupid. If ever I copied any that were worth reading, I was only a medium."

Undoubtedly the art of poetry may be acquired, but without that inspiration which comes to the aid of every true poet, what is produced is little, if any, better than rhymed prose. Emerson calls it "that dream power which every night shows thee is thy own; a power transcending all limit and privacy, and by virtue of which a man is the conductor of the whole river of electricity."

As an appropriate conclusion to these hasty comments let us turn to Sir Edwin Arnold's proem preceding his beautiful poem:

> "The Sovereign Voice spoke once more in my ear:
> 'Write, now, a song unstained by any tear!'
> 'What shall I write?' I said. The Voice replied,
> 'Write what We tell thee of the Crucified!'
> 'How shall I write,' I said, 'who am not meet
> One word of that sweet speaking to repeat?'
> 'It shall be given unto thee! Do this thing!'
> Answered the Voice: 'Wash thy lips clean and sing!'"

WASHINGTON, D. C., May 10, 1891.

CHAPTER IV.

CROSSING THE OCEAN.

New Sensations—Singular Coincidence—Ocean Hymns.

FOR one who has never been out of sight of land, it is no slight undertaking to come to a fixed determination to cross the Atlantic. Speaking for myself, I am free to acknowledge that, when, in the year 1867, I began to think seriously of it—propelled by no imperative order or business, but moved mainly by a desire for rest and to see something of the Old World—it required all the resolution at my command to make up my mind actually to engage my passage and prepare for the voyage. In fact, even after I had reached this determination, and had selected my state-room on the good steamship *Fulton*, Captain Charles H. Townsend, to sail from New York to Havre on the 11th of May, it was not until we were fairly set out upon the great deep—no land in sight—that I came gradually to realize the actual truth that surely, beyond doubt, I was leaving my own country to set foot on another and far distant continent. . . . I was now keenly sensible to the truth of the remarks of Madame de Staël, that "It becomes a much more serious matter to quit one's country when in going away it is necessary to cross the sea. Everything," she adds, "is solemn in a voyage of which the ocean marks the first steps: it seems that an abyss opens behind you, and that the return may be forever impossible. Moreover, the sight of the sea always makes a profound impression; it is the image of the Infinite which attracts the soul incessantly, and in which, without cessation, the soul appears to lose itself."

Out to sea!. Only they who have bidden adieu to home and dear friends, and thus, as it were in a dream, found themselves on the bosom of the great deep, with no land nor a living thing outside their vessel in sight, save a flock of gulls—our constant companions much of the way over and back—can realize the feeling which I now experienced. It was a new sensation, one of the remarkable characteristics of which is a feeling, I may say, of utter helplessness as regards all human support. I am happy, however, to observe that this experience was to me a source of joy on account of the realization—more vivid, if possible, than ever before—of the Omnipotent Presence. . . .

On both Sabbaths going over—we had a long passage—there were religious services in the saloon, and, if I may judge from the interest and solemnity apparent on every countenance, there was on the part of all present—and there were few or no absent passengers on that occasion—a deep and increased feeling of dependence on the Almighty arm, a sincere and hearty thankfulness for His merciful care of us, which can never be effaced from our memories. It is, indeed, a fact, not a little singular, perhaps, that this feeling found utterance in two hymns composed by two of the passengers—Henry F. King and his father—without either knowing the intention of the other, which hymns were sung at those meetings, all who could sing joining in them, having supplied themselves with copies thereof. The first (the son's composition), to the tune of "America," was sung as follows :

Our Father, hear our prayer,
As we are gathered here,
   To worship Thee.
Keep us, a little band,
Well in Thy guiding hand,
And bring us safe to land
   Beyond the sea.

We give our thanks to Thee,
Gratefully, willingly,
   For all Thy care

Since we have left our home,
O'er foreign lands to roam;
And may we ever come
    To Thee in prayer.

O Thou who rul'st the wave,
And hast the power to save,
    Thy praise we sing.
Praised be Thy holy name,
Throughout the world the same,
Above all earthly fame,
    Great God, our King.

The other, to the tune of " Old Hundred," as follows :

Great God, we come with grateful hearts
    To offer up our thanks to Thee
For all Thy mercies, all Thy care
    Of us, Thy children on the sea.

Oh, bear us safely to the shore,
    With one united voice we pray ;
To Thee we look—Thee we adore—
    To Thee our heartfelt homage pay.

Watch o'er us evermore, and guide
    Our footsteps wheresoe'er we be ;
In storm or sunshine, oh, abide
    With us, Thy children on the sea.

Then shall we feel no dread alarm ;
    Our souls will rest in peace on Thee ;
Our trust sincere, safe from all harm,
    Behold Thy children on the sea.

Here is another ocean hymn and some impromptu stanzas, composed by the present writer on board the Cunard steamship *Scotia*, Captain Leiteh, on her outward trip, May 12, 1875, himself and wife being passengers. Our sailing day was Wednesday, and the hymn was sung to the tune of " God Save the Queen," as a part of the religious services on Sunday. It was also included in the religious services, one Sunday, on the Cunarder *Bothnia*, when we were returning home in the following May—arriving on the 16th of that month.

Father of Light and Love,
High on Thy throne above,
  Give us thine ear.
All weak and powerless, we,
Thy children on the sea,
Would turn our thoughts to Thee,
  And nothing fear.

O God, in Thee we trust;
On Jesus' bosom must
  Our safety be;
Then would we ever rest
Our heads upon His breast—
The haven e'er the best,
  On land or sea.

Oh, take us safe to shore,
Thy guidance we implore
  From day to day;
To Thee our thanks we bring,
Give us all hearts to sing
The praises of our King,
  His will obey.

"ALL'S WELL."

List to the sound of bells,
As on the air it swells
And in the darkness tells
  The hour of night;
Then hear the watchman's cry—
On lookout to espy
All danger far and nigh—
  That all is right.

The cheering words, "All's well,"
All nervous fears dispel
And to our senses tell
  That safety reigns.
Then sink we into rest,
Lulled by the foamy crest
Upon the ocean's breast,
  In solemn strains.

Now, when life's end is near,
And all seems dark and drear,
We breathless list to hear
  The last hour bell;
Oh, may the joyful word
In silver tones be heard—
"ALL'S WELL."

CHAPTER V.

SAVED BY FRIED CHICKEN—HOW COLONEL TARLETON FAILED TO CAPTURE THOMAS JEFFERSON.

IN 1781 Lord Cornwallis sought to capture the Governor (Thomas Jefferson) and the legislature of Virginia, sitting at Richmond, and afterwards at Charlottesville, to which town they hastily adjourned to avoid arrest. Failing at Richmond, Colonel Tarleton, in command of the expedition, with a force of cavalry and infantry, pursued, but succeeded, as history states, in capturing only "some members of the assembly," evidently not more than two or three.

There is a tradition that Tarleton's failure arose from his fondness for fried chicken. The scouting party stopped at Dr. Joseph Walker's plantation, some twenty miles from Charlottesville, for breakfast, when a messenger was sent in hot haste to warn the Virginians of their advance. Rations were distributed to the men, and the family cook made haste to get up a real Virginia meal for the colonel and his staff. Twice she prepared a delicious dish of fried chicken, and both times, when her back was turned, some of the hungry soldiers dashed into the kitchen and carried it off.

Tarleton was angry at the delay, but was told that what there was of the meal could be served at once if he desired, but that if he wished to have chicken he must set a cor-

poral's guard to protect the cook. This he ordered done.
The guard was set, the chickens were cooked and eaten,
but the delay enabled the messenger to reach Charlottesville and give the alarm in time.

TARLETON'S RAID.

In seventeen hundred eighty-one,—
  In revolution time,—
The march of Tarleton was begun
  In grandeur all sublime.

In Richmond town his forces lay,
  Whence government had fled
To Charlottesville, long miles away,
  By common prudence led.

Tom Jefferson, the chief, was there,
  The legislature, too ;
And Tarleton, balked, did then declare,
  " I'll capture the whole crew."

So off he started with his force,
  Made up with great display,
Of infantry, as well as horse,
  Full sure to win the day.

When he had reached the Walker place,
  Some twenty miles from town,
He called a halt and slackened pace ;
  The troopers all got down.

To breakfast, now, the order passed,
  For hunger called aloud,
And rations for the men flew fast
  Among the waiting crowd.

The colonel and his body-guard
  On Dinah did depend—
As kitchen maid, she thought it hard,
  But dared not to offend.

The colonel gave an order stern
  To get a meal right then
Of chicken fried and rolls the best,
  And keep it from his men.

Now, Dinah had received a hint
  To be in no great haste,
And never in the least to stint
  In catering to their taste.

Their breakfast being well set out
  As any one could wish,
Some soldiers, lurking thereabout,
  Broke in and seized the dish.

Again our Dinah turned a hand
  To get another meal ;
No sooner done than came a band
  And every crumb did steal.

Meantime a messenger had flown,
  As fast as horse could go,
To Charlottesville, to make there known
  What then they did not know,—

That Tarleton, by Cornwallis sent,
  Had started on the run
To capture all the government,
  Including Jefferson.

Black Dinah, feigning sore distress,
  To Tarleton made her way,
Her wounded feelings to express,
  And this to him did say :

" Dem deuced sogers, over dar,
  Did broke into my kitchen,
And, 'pon my honor, I declar',
  Dey stol'd dat mess of chicken.

" But, colonel, ef you is in haste,
  Dere's odder vittles cooked,
Dat can be fixt to suit you taste,
  Dem sogers is not hooked."

The colonel now began to rave,
  And swore right up and down,
That chicken fried he sure would have,
  Before he left the town.

"Den you must send de corp'l's guard,"
　　Said Dinah, with a look
Impatient, sharp, and very hard,
　　"For to protect de cook."

"Here, adjutant," the colonel cried,
　　"Go set a guard to see
That, when again the fowls are fried,
　　The rogues do not cheat me."

Then Dinah went to work again,
　　And in good time prepared
A breakfast luscious, though but plain,
　　In which no pains were spared.

With gusto, Tarleton and his staff
　　Now ate the food well done—
It was a scene to make one laugh—
　　And then they travelled on.

But when they came to Charlottesville,
　　The legislative hall
Was vacant, closed, and very still—
　　No members there at all.

All had escaped, save one or two,
　　Too weak to leave the place,
And knew no better way to do
　　Than knuckle in the race.

In haste the colonel pushes on
　　To Monticello's shade,
Full sure of seizing Jefferson—
　　Main object of his raid.

But, well forewarned, the able chief
　　Slipped off without delay,
While Tarleton, smothering his grief,
　　Turned round—and rode away.

Thus, 'twill be seen, the colonel had
　　Of chicken fried partaken;
And Jefferson was very glad,
　　For it had "*saved his bacon.*"

CHAPTER VI.

PATRIOTIC POEM.

RECITED AT THE REUNION OF THE ARMY OF THE POTOMAC, JULY
3, 1890, AT PORTLAND, ME.

Who shall tell in rhythmic measure
    All the story of the war?
What became of untold treasure?
    Who shall tell what it was for?

How the conflict, like no other,
    Spread affliction far and wide;
Brother madly fighting brother,
    Fiercely ranged on either side.

Oh, the wicked, fatal error
    Of the rash resort to arms!
Filling every heart with terror—
    Every day with war's alarms!

Now I mind me, when I started
    On life's mission, long ago—
Only just from boyhood parted—
    I beheld the signs of woe.

North and south I saw arising,
    Plain before my anxious eyes,
Little clouds, not yet surprising,
    On the face of tranquil skies.

True, to some they foretold danger,
    Meagre as their forms appeared;
Not so to the passing stranger:
    He saw nothing to be feared.

Nor was any early meeting
  Thought at that time to impend,
Of these clouds portentous—fleeting
  Whereso'er their motion tend.

Peace and Plenty held their places,
  Smiling on a happy land;
All serene their air, like Graces
  Crowned with beauty, hand-in-hand.

Strange that at a time so cheering
  I should see in vivid dream
Armies in the skies appearing,
  Hostile in degree supreme.

What, I asked myself in wonder,
  Does this startling vision show?
Is it this—in doubt I ponder—
  Must we meet a foreign foe?

Seemed no cause for such collision,
  All was quiet over sea;
What should aid to a decision
  In the matter, puzzled me.

But at length the clouds, expanding,
  Move in angry aspect near,
Dark before each other standing,
  Touching patriots' hearts with fear.

Look! what means this strange communion?
  See! emblazoned on each cloud,
In letters bold, the word DISUNION!
  All alarming, fierce, and loud!

Hark! what sound is that conspiring,
   Rumbling, trembling, from afar?
'Tis from guns on Sumter firing!
   Tocsin dread of civil war!

Oh! what act of direful madness!
   Oh! the folly of the strife!
Oh! what cause of deepest sadness!
   Who shall save the nation's life?

Such was my first exclamation,
   Standing near the helm of state;
Whence should come the declaration
   That should my distress abate!

"To arms! to arms!" the cry went forth
   From LINCOLN's proud and lofty post.
"Wake! East and West and South and North!
   Spring, spring to arms, a mighty host!

"Our flag insulted bids you come;
   It calls for patriots strongly nerved;
March quickly, cheered by fife and drum,
   The UNION it must be preserved!"

As when the mighty river's banks
   Are swollen by the sudden flood,
The people rushed to fill the ranks,
   And in a solid phalanx stood.

The nation's capital their aim,
   They moved at once in grand array,
As line on serried line they came
   Their noble chieftain to obey.

A brief suspense, and then they start
    To meet their bold and threat'ning foe;
Each man inflamed to do his part,
    Nor any hardship to forego.

Now, soon is heard the clash of arms,
    Afar the cannon's angry roar,
O'erwhelming all with war's alarms,
    That spread, like fire, from door to door.

Too late! the fatal shot was fired
    When aimed in hate at Sumter's shield;
Almost, alas! all hope expired
    When patriots fell on battle-field.

Too late! too late! the war goes on
    In blood and carnage—oh, how long!
Until, at last, the RIGHT has won—
    Until defeat o'erwhelms the WRONG.

Peace now resumed her rightful sway;
    Those hateful clouds have disappeared;
DISUNION sank with them away,
    And UNION her proud ensign reared.

Flag of our free, united land,
Float on! float on! o'er sea and strand!
We greet thee, seen away from home,
In foreign climes, where'er we roam,
With pride and satisfaction pure,
A shield and safeguard strong and sure.
Float on! float on! no longer fear!
All hearts are with thee, far and near.
Float on! float on! from shore to shore!
Float on! float on! forevermore!

PART V.

CHAPTER I.

At sunrise on a beautiful morning, the 24th of May, 1819, in an old palace looking out upon Kensington Park, Alexandrina Victoria was born. The privy councillors and great officers of state, near by, were immediately called in as certifying witnesses, and "the Duke of Kent, with his own hand, signified the joyful news to all his relatives both at home and abroad before he retired to rest." It was regarded as "an omen of goodly import that the day and hour which ushered the future sovereign into the world was the same which had eighty-one years before given birth to her revered grandfather." The event was the more joyful from the fact that the British nation had but recently been called to mourn the sudden death of the beautiful Princess Charlotte, wife of Leopold I., of Belgium, and heir to the throne. The British people will never cease to cherish with the warmest affection the memory of this lamented Princess, who so suddenly, with her new-born infant, fell asleep to awake no more on earth. A touchingly beautiful white marble monument in St. George's Chapel at Windsor, representing her reclining figure, is gazed upon with melancholy interest by all beholders.

The Duchess of Kent was a true mother to her infant princess, whose baptism and initiation into the church in the names I have given were performed "with all the *pomp of circumstance*" when she was four weeks old. Instead of taking what was said to be the usual course of the nobility

402

and turning her royal babe over to a third person for daily sustenance, with maternal tenderness she nursed the child herself, greatly to the satisfaction of the English people. Never, probably, were parents happier in the possession or prouder of a promising and lovely child than were the good Duke and Duchess of Kent with their little treasure. It is said of the Duke, who in a few short months was snatched by death from the amiable Duchess and her infant offspring, that he used with exulting joy to present his "smiling cherub to each succeeding guest, and listen with unwearied delight to their perpetually repeated praises of its activity, intelligence, and beauty."

It was unfortunate, not to say cruel, for so kind and devoted a parent to be wounded in feeling as he was on the occasion of a grand review which took place on Hounslow Heath not long after the christening. At this review "The Prince Regent was present, attended by a splendid train of military officers, among whom was the Duke of Kent. The Royal Duchess was on the heath in her carriage, accompanied by the Princess Victoria and her attendants. The Regent is said to have objected to this early display of parental pride, and, turning to the Duke of Kent, asked, with some displeasure, "Why was not that infant left at home? She is too young to be brought into public." The unkind rebuke evidently cut to the quick, since we are assured that "into the public the royal babe was brought no more during the short period of her father's life ; and it is believed that to this expression of the Regent's opinion may in some measure be attributed the extreme retirement in which the first ten years of the young Princess's life were passed."

Except this unpleasant episode, nothing appears to have occurred to disturb the current of happiness, during the following summer, at Kensington Palace. The Duke and Duchess were often to be "seen walking arm and arm in the beautiful grounds which surrounded the palace, mingling with pleasure among their delighted countrymen. The interest of the scene was much increased by the presence of the royal infant, who, in the arms of her nurse, would answer with her innocent smiles to the occasional caresses of her fond parents, and the more respectful notice of the spectators," no strangers, however, being permitted to approach her too closely.

During the ensuing winter months "their Royal Highnesses had removed into Devonshire for the benefit of its milder climate, but had scarcely domesticated themselves in their beautiful retreat, Woolbrook Cottage, Sidmouth, before the illustrious Duke was seized with severe indisposition, the effects of a neglected cold, which, defying all the efforts of medicine, terminated fatally within a fortnight from the first attack. The Duchess was immediately withdrawn from the scene of her bereavement," and returned to Kensington Palace, where she received the kindest attention of friends, including Prince Leopold, the Duchess of Clarence, then the amiable Queen Dowager, and other members of the royal family.

This touching incident is related of the Duke of York's first visit to his afflicted sister-in-law. Having inquired for his infant niece, she was no sooner, in compliance with his desire, brought into the room, than, recognizing, it is supposed, his great resemblance to her deceased father, she stretched out her little arms towards him and called him "Papa." The Duke was greatly affected, and, clasping her to his bosom, promised to be indeed a father to her. "This promise, as far as circumstances would admit, he always faithfully observed;" and his fatherly care and kindness were " repaid by her infantile love and gratitude, particularly exemplified in his last illness, when she visited him daily, always carrying in her hand a beautiful bouquet of choice flowers, with which the Duke delighted to decorate his private sitting-room, until it was replaced on the following day by a fresh supply from her store of sweets."

From all accounts the young Princess must have been an uncommonly interesting child, and she was frequently spoken of as beautiful, with her bright blue eyes and ruddy, round face. Like all smart children, her cunning childish actions were a constant subject of remark as well as source of pleasure to her friends. During these years of early childhood she "was daily to be seen riding or running about in Kensington Gardens, and her intercourse with the visitors" is represented as "of a very endearing description."

Her father, as is well known, was the fourth son of George III., and her mother was a sister of Leopold I., being at the time of the marriage, in the month of July, 1818, a young widow, the Princess Leiningen, with two children—a son whose name was Charles Emrich, and a daughter named Feodora—a prince and princess, of course. In all her early years Victoria had for a constant attendant or companion her half-sister, the young Princess Feodora, by whom she was frequently drawn in her little carriage, other attendants also being along. I may remark here that Prince Charles Emrich died in 1850, and the Princess Feodora (afterwards by marriage the Princess Hohenlohe-Langenburg) on the 23d of September, 1872. To the last the sisters were devotedly attached to each other. In her diary the Queen, referring to the time, in 1824, when she herself was only five years of age, and when she resided in company with Feodora at Claremont, says: "Those days at Claremont were the happiest of my childhood." Her German kinsfolk called Victoria "the little May Flower."

Very shortly after her fourth year the King issued cards for a state dinner-party, "signifying to the Duchess of Kent his wish that her infant daughter should accompany her and be presented to the assembled guests." Some time before this her uncle, the Duke of York, had made a present to her of a donkey, which she prized as "the greatest treasure she possessed in the world;" and, full of joyful anticipation on the morning of this memorable visit, " I am going," said she, " to see the King!" and, turning to her mother, she naïvely asked, "Oh, mamma! shall I go upon my donkey?"

From her cradle to her accession to the throne Victoria was never separated from her mother, who taught her her first lessons and superintended her education, assisted by Rev. George Davys, afterwards Dean of Chester, who was appointed her preceptor at an early period, and held the position until she was proclaimed Queen. At five years of age she could speak three languages,—English, French, and German,—and when she was eleven she not only spoke these with fluency, but also was acquainted with Italian, had made such progress in Latin as to be able to read " Virgil" and " Horace" with ease, and had commenced Greek and mathematics. Her moral training kept pace with her intellectual instruction. Says a late English writer, " The cultivation of the heart of her child" was what the mother first strove to accomplish; and, " above everything, any approach to pride or hauteur was discouraged." She was " trained to be courteous, affable, lively, and to put social inferiors perfectly at their ease." Mr. Davys was not alone with the Duchess as guide and teacher of the young Princess. She likewise had special instructions in the different branches, including music, drawing, etc., and always showed herself an apt student. The Duchess of Northumberland, at the suggestion of the King, was appointed her governess.

I could fill pages with many other things relative to the infancy and childhood of our illustrious heroine, but I must skip five or six years of this happy domestic life and come to her accession, at the death of William IV., on the 20th of June, 1837. In these intervening years she journeyed with her mother throughout the larger part of the United Kingdom, being everywhere received with pride and acclamation by the people as their future sovereign. To show something of the manner of this tour of inspection, information, and pleasure, I will mention one incident. It was on the occasion of her visit at Portsmouth to the *Victory*, a man-of-war. "Their Royal Highnesses, having completed their interesting inspection of the ship, seated themselves at one of the mess tables, and desired the dinner intended for the seamen of that mess to be laid before them. This being done, the Princess, with her mother and all the ladies of her suite, drank of the grog and partook of the beef and potatoes, served on wooden platters, and using the knives and forks belonging to the mess. The Princess declared that the dinner was much to her liking; and the delight of the sailors at this act of condescension exceeded all bounds."

I should also remark, before proceeding further, that the Princess was about eleven years of age when she first became aware of her exalted destiny; and this fact, which had been carefully kept from her, she herself discovered one day when reading English history with her governess. Both her governess and her mother were startled by the questions she put, and were obliged to admit the correctness of her conclusion. This was in 1830, the year William IV. was called to the throne. Seven years swiftly passed, and the young Princess, at the age of less than one month over eighteen years, was suddenly summoned, on the 20th of June, 1837, to take his place. The next day she "was publicly proclaimed, under the title of Alexandrina Victoria I.; but since that day she has disused the Russian name bestowed upon her by her Muscovite godfather, preferring to retain simply VICTORIA."

That I may be as brief as possible, I need not describe the accession and coronation ceremonies. Suffice it to say they were appropriate, as they were solemn and gorgeous. Says Miss Martineau, "If the millions who longed to know how the young sovereign looked and felt could have heard her first address, it would have gone far to satisfy them. The address was of course prepared for her; but the manner and voice were her own, and they told much. Her manner was composed, modest, and dignified; her voice firm and sweet; her reading, as usual, beautiful."

The next great event in the Queen's life was her betrothal and marriage to her cousin, Prince Albert, of Saxe-Coburg-Gotha, on the 10th of February, 1840. In her own journal we find it stated that, " when he was a child of three years old, his nurse always told him that he should marry the Queen, and that, when he first thought of marrying at all, he always thought of her." In her own memoirs of her lamented husband, we have also a full and touching account of their courtship and marriage. Their first meeting was in May, 1836, on the occasion of a six weeks' visit of the Duke of Coburg with his two sons, Ernest and Albert, to the Duchess of Kent. Albert was the younger of the two brothers, and three months the junior of Victoria. This visit is represented as having afforded great pleasure, particularly to the royal cousins, Victoria and Albert, who were then seventeen years of age; nor were they ignorant of what was undoubtedly its leading purpose. Albert's mother, the Dowager Duchess of Gotha, had often spoken to him, years before, of her earnest wishes on the subject; and although we have the Queen's authority for the statement that " nothing was settled" at the time of this visit, a letter from her, dated June 7, 1836, to King Leopold, who took a lively interest in bringing about this happy match, shows plainly what she designed and expected. That letter, referring to Prince Albert, concludes: " I have only now to beg you, my dear uncle, to take care of the health of one now so dear to me, and to take him under your special protection. I hope and trust that all will now go on prosperously and well on this subject, now of so much importance to me." The Prince, however, did not feel so sure of his position, " being kept in the dark;" and after waiting in suspense nearly two years, and knowing that any offer of marriage must now be made by the Queen, and not by himself, if they were ever to become husband and wife, he intimated to King Leopold that, while he was willing to wait provided only that he could have " some certain assurance to go upon," without such assurance he might in justice to himself feel obliged to take himself out of the way. Fortunately it was not so to be; and the Queen has since reproached herself that " she had not, after accession, kept up the correspondence with her cousin as she had done before it, instead" (she says) " of keeping him waiting for probably three or four years, at the risk of ruining all his prospects for life, until she might feel inclined to marry."

On the 10th of October, 1839, the two Princes, Ernest and Albert, arrived at Windsor Castle, bearing a letter from the King of the Belgians, commending them to the Queen, " who received them herself at the top of the staircase and conducted them at once to the Duchess of Kent." In less than one week thereafter, on the 15th, the Queen sent for Prince Albert to come to her room, where he found her alone. The next day the Prince wrote to " the old friend of the family, Baron Stockmar, who was naturally one of the first to be informed of his engagement. ' I write to you,' he says, ' on one of the happiest days of my life, to give you the most welcome news possible.' " He then describes what took place, " and ends by saying, ' More or more seriously I cannot write to you, for that, at this moment, I am too bewildered.' " The Queen herself says, " The Prince received her offer without any hesitation and with the warmest demonstration of kindness and affection," adding, in the words of her journal, " How I will strive to make him feel as little as possible the sacrifice he has made. I told him it *was* a great sacrifice on his part, but he would not allow it."

It was the commonly received report at the time, that at one of the palace balls, just before this final engagement, Victoria " took occasion to present her *bouquet* to the Prince at the conclusion of a dance, and that the hint was not lost upon the polite and gallant German. His close uniform, buttoned up to the throat, did not admit of placing the Persian-like gift where it would be most honored; so he drew his penknife and cut a slit in his dress in the neighborhood of his heart, where he gracefully deposited the happy omen."

Now, again, from the necessity of brevity, I am reluctantly constrained to dismiss this delightful subject with only a few more words. The young Princes returned to Germany on the 14th of November, but on the following 28th of January Albert came back to England in state, and on the 10th of February, 1840, his marriage with Victoria took place and "was magnificently celebrated in the Chapel Royal of St. James Palace."

Nothing now occurred seriously to disturb the happiness of the young couple until the 10th of June following, when, as they were driving in a phaeton up Constitution Hill in London, a young man named Oxford, seventeen or eighteen years of age, fired two pistol-shots at the Queen, but happily without effect. The fellow was at once arrested, and, as one writer states, "it being impossible to assign any conceivable cause for the act, he was declared insane and doomed to incarceration for life." Theodore Martin, author of the "Life of the Prince Consort," however, says, "There was no doubt that the wretched creature knew what he was about, and acted, so far as intentions can be judged by acts, with a murderous intent. It would have been well, as events proved [he continues], if he had been dealt with on this footing." The best comment on the lenity shown in allowing him to escape by "the insanity dodge," Mr. Martin further remarks, "was pronounced by Oxford himself on being told of similar attempts of Francis and Bean in 1842, when he declared that if he had been hanged, there would have been no more shooting at the Queen."

The next attempt on the life of the Queen, that of John

Francis, represented by Prince Albert as " a little swarthy, ill-looking rascal," occurred in 1842, close to the spot of the former shooting, and when the Queen and her husband were returing home from a drive. The scoundrel was only five paces from them when he fired, without effect, and was immediately seized by a policeman. He was tried, found guilty of high treason, and sentenced to death, which sentence, at the instance of the merciful Queen, was afterwards commuted into a sentence of transportation for life. We have Prince Albert's statement that, during the trial, the fellow was not out of his mind, but that he was " a thorough scamp," and that the populace were in a state of extreme indignation " against him. His answers," the Prince says, " are evasive and witty. He tries to make fun of his judges." " Yet," observes Mr. Martin, " after the sentence of death was pronounced upon him, the wretched vanity which, more than any murderous intent, had prompted his dastardly outrage, could no longer maintain the semblance of indifference which he had hitherto affected, and he fell swooning into a turnkey's arms, and was carried insensible from the court."

This merciful act of commutation had hardly become public before still another attempt was made on Victoria's life, the culprit this time being what Prince Albert, in writing to his father, under date of July 4, 1842, called " a hunchback wretch," whose name was Bean. He had tried to shoot at the carriage in which the Queen, Prince Albert, and their uncle Leopold were sitting; but his pistol missed fire. On being examined, it " was found to contain some powder, paper lightly rammed down, and some pieces of clay pipe."

Bean appeared to have been more fool than knave, and he was tried and sentenced, on the 25th of August, to eighteen months' imprisonment, under an act passed the preceding month, which act not only made all such attempts punishable by imprisonment or transportation, but also directed that the culprit should "be publicly or privately whipped as often and in such manner and form as the court shall direct, not exceeding thrice."

On the 19th of May, 1849, on Constitution Hill, an Irish bricklayer, named Hamilton, fired a pistol, charged only with powder, at the Queen, and he was sentenced to seven years' transportation. On the 27th of May, 1850, as she was leaving the Duke of Cumberland's residence in her carriage, she was struck in the face by Robert Pale, an ex-lieutenant of hussars, but not seriously hurt. He was likewise sentenced to seven years' transportation.

The latest attempt on the life of the Queen was in April, 1852, when "a worthless vagabond, by the name of Roderick McLane, fired a pistol-shot at her at the London Railway Station, but without effect. He was at once arrested, tried, and acquitted on the ground of insanity clearly proven."

On the 29th of February, 1872, Arthur O'Connor, a boy of seventeen, pointed an empty pistol at the Queen as she was entering Buckingham Palace after a ride. The plea was insanity, but he was sentenced to a whipping and twelve months' transportation.

It not being the purpose of this sketch to recount, as it might, the many wise public acts of administration in which the hand of the good Queen is often plainly visible, I will hasten to a close by the mention of a few incidents in which she has been brought lovingly into intimate relations with the people of the United States. One of the most noted of these occurred at the completion of the Atlantic cable in August, 1858, a wonderful feat, which astonished the whole world. On the 16th of that month Victoria addressed to President Buchanan this cablegram,—about the first, if not the very first, which passed over the wires: "Her Majesty desires to congratulate the President upon the successful completion of the great international work in which the Queen has taken the deepest interest.".

This despatch reached the President at the Soldiers' Home, when he immediately came to the White House and responded in a longer cablegram, cordially reciprocating the Queen's congratulations, and expressing the hope that, "under the blessing of Heaven," the telegraph might "prove to be a bond of perpetual peace and friendship between the kindred nations, and an instrument destined by Divine Providence to diffuse religion, civilization, liberty, and law throughout the world."

The next pleasant incident of the kind was in 1860, when President Buchanan, learning that the Prince of Wales was about to visit Canada, wrote Her Majesty, saying: "Should it be the intention of His Royal Highness to extend his visit to the United States, I need not say how happy I should be to give him a cordial welcome to Washington. You may be well assured that everywhere in this country he will be greeted by the American people in such a manner as cannot fail to prove gratifying to your Majesty. In this they will manifest their deep sense of your domestic virtues as well as their convictions of your merits as a wise, patriotic, and constitutional sovereign."

I copy the Queen's answer entire, as follows:

"BUCKINGHAM PALACE, June 22, 1860.

"MY GOOD FRIEND,—I have been much gratified at the feelings which prompted you to write to me, inviting the Prince of Wales to come to Washington. He intends to return from Canada through the United States, and it will afford him great pleasure to have an opportunity of testifying to you in person that these feeling are fully reciprocated by him. He will thus be able, at the same time, to mark the respect which he entertains for the Chief Magistrate of a great and friendly state and kindred nation.

"The Prince of Wales will drop all royal state on leaving my dominions, and travel under the name of Lord Renfrew, as he has done when travelling on the continent of Europe.

"The Prince Consort wishes to be kindly remembered to you.

"I remain ever your Good Friend,

"VICTORIA R."

How beautiful and how gratifying was all this !

We all know that the Prince of Wales did extend his visit to the United States, and that the President gave a special reception at the White House in his honor, where the young Prince and suite, with an immense crowd of the élite of Washington, citizens, and transient visitors were entertained in becoming style. I may add that it was my good fortune to be present and to have a pleasant chat with His Royal Highness.

And now we come to another, and, in its results, a vastly more important event,—the affair of the *Trent*. On the 7th of November, 1861, and near the beginning of our terrible war, that British steamer left Havana for England with the mails and passengers, and on the next day was met by the *San Jacinto*, a United States ship-of-war, commanded by Captain (afterwards Rear-Admiral) Wilkes. Brought to by a round shot, soon afterwards followed by a shell, fired by the *San Jacinto* across her bow, the *Trent*, by order of Captain Wilkes, was at once boarded by Lieutenant (afterwards Rear-Admiral) Fairfax, accompanied by a guard of marines, and Messrs. Mason and Slidell, accredited envoys of the Confederate States to England and France, respectively, with their secretaries, Messrs. McFarland and Eustis, were forcibly removed, and brought by the *San Jacinto* to the United States as prisoners of war.. As soon as this bold, but no doubt very imprudent, act became known in England, it produced the greatest excitement, and the British Lion instantly prepared for war ! Instructions of a threatening character were drawn up and submitted by Lord John Russell to the Cabinet, and then sent to the Queen for her approval, before being forwarded to Lord Lyons, British Minister at Washington. They embodied a demand for the release and restoration of the prisoners to British protection, as well as a disavowal of the act of Captain Wilkes, with instructions to Lord Lyons to retire from the United States should this demand be refused. I think

I am justified in expressing the opinion that, had these instructions gone out without material modification, either the United States would have been disgracefully humbled by yielding, or war with Great Britain would have been the fearful alternative, the result of which at that crisis in our affairs I shudder to think could have been nothing short of a fatal disruption of our glorious Union!

Prince Albert drafted a memorandum to accompany the Cabinet paper on its return. This was slightly changed in the Queen's own hand, as appears from a *fac-simile* of it which I have seen, and it contains their suggestions for a softening modification of the original despatch submitted by the Cabinet. It is most gratifying to know that it was couched in friendly terms, and the Cabinet paper being modelled upon the line thus indicated, it was divested of its harsh features, and led, as is well known, to an amicable settlement of the unpleasant affair. All honor and a thousand heartfelt thanks to the Queen and her noble husband.

Who will say that this happy settlement of a most dangerous complication was not in great measure due to the good offices, already cited, of Mr. Buchanan, and his remarkably agreeable relations with the Queen and Prince Consort while he was United States Minister to the Court of St. James? It is well known that he was a great favorite with both, especially with the Queen, and that he held them in highest esteem.

But I must turn for a moment from these pleasant reflections to sombre and sadder scenes. The Queen had, only a few months before, on the 16th of May, 1861, been deprived, by death, of one of the dearest and best of mothers, the estimable Duchess of Kent, and now, at the very time of greatest need of his counsel and assistance, her beloved husband was soon to be cruelly snatched from her by the all-destroying angel of death! The paper just described was the last political memorandum he ever wrote, and when he handed it to the Queen, being seriously ill, "he told her that he could scarcely hold the pen while writing it." This was on the 1st of December. At a quarter past ten o'clock on the night of the 14th of that month his great soul took its flight " to seek a nobler scope for its aspirations in the world within the veil," and the Queen was overwhelmed by a grief indescribable, and from which she can never entirely recover on this side of the grave. Intense, however, as her grief has been, impelling her to comparative seclusion, she has never failed to perform her sovereign administrative duties. For the first time after her bereavement, she opened Parliament in person not until February, 1876, and she never once appeared at the theatre, after the death of the Prince, until after the 4th of October, 1881, when she was persuaded by the Prince of Wales to attend a private dramatic entertainment gotten up by him at Abergeldie Castle, Scotland, expressly for her diversion.

In April, 1886, by act of Parliament proposed by Mr. Disraeli, she was authorized, in addition to her title of Queen, to assume that of Empress of India.

The Queen's own appalling bereavement has, no doubt, so wrought upon her finer sensibilities that whenever she hears of those similarly stricken, her heart at once goes out toward them in warmest sympathy. Thus, when President Lincoln was assassinated, she "sent to his widow a long letter, which her son, Robert Lincoln, described as the out-gushing of a woman's heartfelt sympathy,"—a letter which he informs me has never been published.

Not so with her touching appeals for exact information regarding the condition, from time to time, of our lamented President Garfield, and her repeated messages of earnest sympathy and condolence through the period of his fatal illness and death. I present these in their order of date, with the remark that she was also, no doubt, kept constantly informed on the subject through Mr. Lowell, our Minister in London. The first was sent through Lord Granville at five o'clock on the afternoon of July 2, 1881, the day the President was shot.

"*To Sir Edward Thornton, the British Embassy, Washington:* The Queen desires that you will at once express the sorrow with which she has learned of the attempt upon the President's life and her earnest hope of his recovery. Her Majesty wishes for full and immediate reports of his condition."

July 3, from Mr. Lowell to Mr. Blaine, Secretary of State : "Just received the following from the Queen: 'I am most anxious to hear latest accounts of the President, and wish my horror and deep sympathy to be conveyed to him and Mrs. Garfield.'"

Same date, from Sir H. Ponsonby, Windsor Castle, to British Minister: "The Queen is most anxious to learn as to the state of the President. Please wire latest news."

July 14, from Mr. Lowell, London, to Mr. Blaine: "I have received the following from the Queen: 'I wish to express my great satisfaction at the very favorable accounts of the President, and hope that he will soon be considered out of danger.'"

August 17, the Queen to Mrs. Garfield: "I am most anxious to know how the President is to-day, and to express my sympathy with you both." To this Mrs. Garfield sent an encouraging reply and grateful acknowledgment.

August 27, from Mr. Lowell to Mr. Blaine : " I have just received from Her Majesty, the Queen, at Balmoral, a telegram in these words: 'I am most deeply grieved at the sad news of the last few days, and would wish my deep sympathy to be conveyed to Mr. Garfield.'"

The next and last despatch was received on the morning of September 20, and discloses the long-dreaded and heart-rending end of this frightful tragedy:

27

"*Mrs. Garfield, Long Branch:* Words cannot express the deep sympathy I feel with you at this terrible moment. May·God support and comfort you as He alone can.

"THE QUEEN.

"Balmoral Court."

On the following day word came that the Queen had ordered the Court to go into mourning for the late President Garfield for a week from the 21st of September,—"a tribute of respect," the London *Times* remarked, "which will be all the more valued by the Americans, as it is unprecedented, no similar notice having been taken previously by the English Court of the death of an American President in office."

And, now, as her last beautiful offering, on the 22d of September the good Queen telegraphed the British Minister to have a floral tribute prepared and presented in her name with a mourning card bearing the following inscription:

"Queen Victoria, to the memory of the late President Garfield: an expression of her sorrow and sympathy with Mrs. Garfield and the American nation.

"September 22, 1881."

Under date of London, July 21, 1884, President Arthur received and gracefully acknowledged the following cable message:

"*To the President of the United States, Washington:* The Queen heartily congratulates the President and people of the United States on the rescue of Lieutenant Greeley and the gallant survivors of the Arctic expedition. She trusts that favorable reports have been received of the sufferers.

"THE QUEEN.

"Windsor Castle."

Yet once more, when the whole country was

"Robed in the sable garb of woe,"

at the death of the great soldier of the war, the Queen manifested the same considerate womanly feeling as on previous mournful occasions, through the despatch, July 21, 1885, to Mrs. Grant, saying: "Her Majesty, the Queen, requests me to convey to yourself and family her sincere condolence on the death of General Grant."

Finally, on the 2d of June, 1886, Her Gracious Majesty sent the following despatch to President Cleveland: "Pray accept my sincere congratulations on your marriage, and my best wishes for your happiness."

"Come, now, ye kings of the earth and all people, princes and all judges of the world, young men and maidens, old men and children," come and behold one of the kindest and most devoted of daughters; one of the most loving and considerate of mothers; one of the happiest and most irreproachable of wives; one of the sincerest and most sympathetic of friends; one of the wisest, the best, the most universally respected of sovereigns that ever sat on any throne. At her feet I lay this humble tribute with the devout and soul-inspired aspiration—"GOD SAVE THE QUEEN!"

(PERSONAL.)

[COPY.]

BRITISH EMBASSY, 9th May, 1894.

DEAR MR. KING,—I owe you many apologies for keeping so long the MS. you kindly lent me of your admirable biographical sketch of Queen Victoria. I finished its perusal a few days ago, and was about to write to you to say how much pleasure it gave me, when I received your note. I hasten to return the MS. and to express my high appreciation of its literary merit as well as of the kind sentiments toward England and her sovereign with which it is inspired.

Yrs. sincerely,
JULIAN PAUNCEFOTE.

www.ingramcontent.com/pod-product-compliance
Lightning Source LLC
Chambersburg PA
CBHW030812110726
47900CB00006B/1595